✦ A SAINT OF OUR OWN ✦

A SAINT
of OUR
OWN

HOW THE QUEST FOR A HOLY HERO

HELPED CATHOLICS BECOME

AMERICAN

✦

Kathleen Sprows Cummings

THE UNIVERSITY OF NORTH CAROLINA PRESS ✦ CHAPEL HILL

This book was made possible in part by support from
the Institute for Scholarship in the Liberal Arts,
College of Arts and Letters, University of Notre Dame.

Designed by April Leidig
Set in Garamond Premier Pro by Copperline Book Services
Manufactured in the United States of America

The University of North Carolina Press has been a
member of the Green Press Initiative since 2003.

Front cover: detail of Elizabeth Ann Seton canonization banner hung
from balcony at St. Peter's Basilica, September 14, 1975, courtesy of Sisters of
Charity Federation; watercolor painting of U.S.A. flag © iStockphoto.com/Elen11.
Back cover: complete Seton canonization banner, courtesy of
Sisters of Charity Federation.

Library of Congress Cataloging-in-Publication Data
Names: Cummings, Kathleen Sprows, author.
Title: A saint of our own : how the quest for a holy hero helped
Catholics become American / Kathleen Sprows Cummings.
Description: Chapel Hill : University of North Carolina Press, [2019] |
Includes bibliographical references and index.
Identifiers: LCCN 2018040234|
ISBN 9781469649474 (cloth : alk. paper) |
ISBN 9781469649481 (ebook)
Subjects: LCSH: Catholic Church—United States—History. |
Canonization. | Catholics—Religious identity—United States.
Classification: LCC BX1406.3 .C84 2019 | DDC 235/.240973—dc23
LC record available at https://lccn.loc.gov/2018040234

TO

Margaret Grace Cummings

✦

CONTENTS

FIGURES

✦ A SAINT OF OUR OWN ✦

American Saints Are Rare Birds

"Everyone loves a hero," wrote the American poet Phyllis McGinley in 1954, "and the saints are the best heroes of all." Saints, like most heroes, have extraordinary abilities. Summoned by the faithful, they can inspire repentance in the most recalcitrant sinners, heal the most acute suffering, and reverse the most ravaging disease. These miracles, Catholics believe, are made possible only by saints' eternal union with God. The faithful recall this during the most sacred part of their liturgy, the consecration of the Eucharist, when they join their prayers with those of the saints "on whose constant intercession in your presence we rely for unfailing help."[1] Yet the appeal of saints in the Catholic imagination derives not only from their closeness to God but also from their proximity to believers. As envoys from heaven to earth, saints make the divine manifest in the everyday lives of the faithful. Through what McGinley called "the miracles they made of their own lives," these holy men and women embody God's grace, as it flows through humans in particular times and places.[2]

Catholics have devised an elaborate method for acknowledging their holy heroes, a series of intricate steps collectively known as the canonization process. Although this lengthy and tedious process often frustrates the promoters of a prospective saint, successes at its various stages also prompt exuberant celebrations, in which devotees marvel anew at the saints' capacity to bridge the human and the divine. "Heaven touched earth!" exclaimed a participant in a ritual marking one such milestone.[3] Canonizations and their precursors, beatifications, have special meaning for those who feel particular affinity with the new saint by virtue of a shared profession, state of life, or geographical location. Through a separate canonical process, the Holy See at times officially designates canonized saints as "patrons" of a distinctive occupation, avocation, or place.

In terms of the latter category, Phyllis McGinley, like many other U.S. Catholics before her, felt decidedly overlooked. Aggrieved by what she saw as Rome's "odd myopia" regarding the United States, McGinley chided the Vatican for failing to take notice of the "very American brand of holiness."[4] The absence of American names in the canon of the saints left many U.S. Catholics feeling not only spiritually unmoored but also periodically subject to the condescension of their transatlantic counterparts. In 1953, for instance, Englishman Donald Attwater published *Saints Westward*, ostensibly to encourage his "American friends" to promote native saints. Whereas Catholics "in Europe and the nearer parts of Asia" encountered saints "every day in the places where they lived," Attwater sympathized, U.S. Catholics had to content themselves with cities and towns named for holy heroes who had lived an ocean away. "Saint Louis the saint had nothing to do with St. Louis the city," he pointed out. "To be able to look upon actual buildings or scenes that the saint actually saw makes them wonderfully real and 'living.' The time will come when Americans will have this joy and privilege."[5]

A Saint of Our Own is about U.S. Catholics' quest for that joy and privilege. It traces saint-seeking in the United States from the 1880s, the decade in which U.S. Catholics nominated their first candidates for canonization, to 2015, the year Pope Francis named the twelfth American saint in the first such ceremony held on U.S. soil.[6] As the book will show, U.S. Catholics' search for a saint of their own did indeed spring from a desire to persuade the Vatican to recognize their country's holy heroes. But U.S. Catholic believers had another reason for touting homegrown holiness. To them, saints served as mediators not only between heaven and earth but also between the faith they professed and the American culture in which they lived. Canonization may be fundamentally about holiness, but it is never *only* about holiness. In the United States, it has often been about the ways in which Catholics defined, defended, and celebrated their identities as Americans. Saint-seekers nominated candidates for canonization based not only on the virtues they were said to have practiced but also on the national values they were understood to have epitomized. If the Catholic criteria held constant, American ideals fluctuated dramatically between the 1880s and 2015—a factor that helps to explain both why the search for a U.S. patron saint is so revealing and why it ended in a way that would have surprised those who had launched it in the first place.

A Saint of Our Own focuses on multiple U.S. causes for canonization, including all the successful ones, as well as a few that are failed, forgotten, or still in process. The most illuminating causes receive more attention, and foremost among these is the one attached to Elizabeth Ann Bayley Seton. Born in 1774 into an Episcopal family in New York, Seton converted to Catholicism as a widowed mother of five and later founded the Sisters of Charity, the first Catholic women's religious community established in the United States without formal ties to a European congregation. Now a canonized saint, Seton is arguably the best known among the tiny subset of Americans who have received the church's highest honor. Catholic schools and parishes throughout the country are named after Seton—far more institutions are dedicated to her, in fact, than to any of the other eleven U.S. canonized saints.[7] Seton's prominence on the contemporary American landscape notwithstanding, her path to canonization was beset with so many complications that at times its success had seemed unlikely. At one critical juncture in the mid-twentieth century, Seton's cause attracted the support of New York's Cardinal Francis Spellman. When making a case for Seton's worthiness as a candidate for canonization, Spellman praised her above all for being "wholly American." Seton, he observed, had been a "charter American citizen" who had "breathed American air," "battled against odds in the trials of life with American stamina and cheerfulness," and "worked and succeeded with American efficiency." Her life, therefore, served as "a glorious tribute, by God's grace, to the health, zeal, and spirituality" of Catholicism in the United States.[8]

Seton and other U.S. saints were canonized not simply because they were holy people. They were canonized because a dedicated group in and subsequently beyond their inner circles wanted them to be *remembered* as holy people—and were willing to expend a considerable amount of time, effort, and resources to ensure that they would be. The primary and professed motive for these efforts may have been spiritual, rooted in a desire to inspire imitation and veneration at home and to deepen their connection to Rome and to God. As Spellman's paean to Seton suggests, however, U.S. Catholics also relied on saints to advertise a particular "American brand" of holiness to Vatican leaders and to their fellow citizens.

The story of Seton's labyrinthine journey to canonization is one of several threaded throughout *A Saint of Our Own*. The same twists and turns that exasperated generations of Seton's supporters provide a particularly revealing example of how the vagaries of personality, the complexities of historical memory, and the intricacies of the canonization process can combine to make it difficult for even the holiest of people to enter the ranks of the canonized saints. But Seton's saintly story can be fully understood only in tandem with those of the other potential patrons with whom she vied for paradigmatic American status, including ones who temporarily eclipsed her as well as those she ultimately overshadowed.

Because holy men and women gain popular support in specific contexts, studies of canonization can reveal as much about the priorities and interests of the people promoting the candidates as they do about the lives of the prospective saints themselves. Scholars of medieval and early modern Europe have long harnessed saints' interpretive potential, demonstrating that new models of holiness emerged in response to shifting papal prerogatives and developments in the larger culture.[9] By contrast, scholars of the Americas have only recently begun, in historian Peter Burke's words, to analyze saints as "cultural indicators, a sort of historical litmus paper sensitive to connections between religion and society."[10] *A Saint of Our Own* is the first study of multiple causes for canonization in a U.S. context.[11] By examining the many historical figures U.S. Catholics have offered as powerful expressions of Catholic virtue and American ideals, this book brings into focus U.S. Catholics' understanding of themselves both as members of the church and as citizens of the nation—and reveals how those identities converged, diverged, and changed over time.

Canonization, by definition, institutionalizes a private devotion. *A Saint of Our Own* thus considers both popular piety and structures of power, subjects not often well integrated in scholarship on American religion. This has been especially true since the 1960s, when, in what Thomas A. Tweed has characterized as the field's "quotidian turn," scholars increasingly adopted as subjects ordinary people engaging in everyday religious practices.[12] Influenced by social history and, in the case of Catholics, the Second Vatican Council, these historians offered a strikingly different perspective on the American religious past from that provided by their predecessors, who, in focusing on the men (and very few women) who exercised power within the church's institutional structures, had overlooked "the people in the pews" almost entirely.[13] In providing this much-needed revision, however, many scholars of popular or lived religion overcorrected and ignored church structures in a way that also distorts the experience of the U.S. Catholic faithful, who engaged with those structures repeatedly and in a variety of ways. The search for an American saint offers a fascinating case in point. All causes for canonization begin when a group of ordinary people lift up the holy heroes who populate their everyday lives; successful ones end when the holiness of the candidate is validated, first by local church authorities and finally by the Vatican. Canonization accordingly offers one model for developing creative approaches that integrate ecclesiastical and lived religious history and merge the perspectives of institutional elites and ordinary people.[14]

Because canonization entails multiple back-and-forth exchanges between the Holy See and the country from which causes are proposed, it also lends itself extraordinarily well to a transnational approach. In particular, this study of canonization joins an emerging body of scholarship that encourages historians to "return to Rome" by acknowledging, as the first historians of the U.S. church did reflexively, the centrality of the Holy See to the American Catholic story.[15] While U.S. Catholics' allegiance to the pope did not, as many of their fellow citizens alleged, compromise their ability to become full-fledged Americans, their ties to Rome did distinguish them from non-Catholic Americans in important ways. Here again, acknowledging this in scholarship runs counter to an approach adopted since the 1960s and 1970s by church historians who were not only disinclined to feature institutional structures but also, in contrast to scholars of earlier generations, more likely to limit their subjects to what transpired within U.S. boundaries.[16] As a matter of course, the story of canonization in America toggles between the United States and the Holy See; moreover, because most U.S. causes were conducted on behalf of candidates who belonged to religious congregations based in Italy or France, a third national entity was often involved. Examining U.S. Catholics' search for a saint of their own helps us interpret their history in local, national, and transnational registers.

Canonization is much more complex than any shorthand description can suggest, and it would be helpful to summarize its broader meaning and history before continuing with our American story. In the eyes of Catholic believers, canonization reflects a truth about an individual's afterlife in its literal sense. In raising a candidate to the "honors of the altar," the church affirms that the saint, having practiced certain virtues to a heroic degree, passed immediately upon death into the company of God and all the saints, where he or she is an advocate for and inspiration to the faithful on earth. To understand why the church elevates certain holy people and not others to the ranks of the canonized, as Peter Burke points out, we must look at both the periphery or local level, where devotion to the individual developed, and the center, where sainthood was made official.[17]

In the early church, there had been no distinction between periphery and center on the question of who was a saint; men and women were recognized as such either by tradition or popular acclamation. Between the tenth and seventeenth centuries, however, the Holy See increasingly reserved to itself the right of canonization, and eventually beatification. In 1588, Pope Sixtus V created the Sacred Congregation of Rites (from which emerged the present-day Congregation for the Causes of Saints) to oversee regulations on divine worship and the canonization of saints, and by 1634 Pope Urban VIII established the formal procedures that compose the "modern" canonization process.[18] The centralization of saint-making in Rome reflected broader Catholic reforms in the post-Reformation period and brought into sharp relief a key difference in dogma between Protestants and Roman Catholics. While Protestants insisted that, because the faithful have unmediated access to God, there was no need for saints, Catholics believed that these holy heroes could facilitate a relationship with the divine through channels unavailable to humans alone. As emissaries between heaven and earth, Catholics held, saints helped devotees grow closer to God both by interceding on their behalf and by providing models of holiness that the faithful could emulate.

Whereas canonization changes nothing about the people so honored, merely certifying their heavenly status, it does transform the relationship between the faithful and the saint. While Catholics may privately invoke the intercession of any person they believe to be in God's eternal presence, acts of public veneration—novenas, celebrations of feast days, recitation of prayers, or building of shrines—are reserved for the canonized or, in a limited capacity, to those who have reached the penultimate stage of the process, beatification.[19] Indeed, part of the motivation for formalizing the saint-making process was a desire to curb the public honoring of those whose sanctity—or in some cases, whose very existence—church authorities deemed questionable.[20] A common geography was the decisive factor in U.S. Catholics' attraction to Seton and other prospective saints whose causes were introduced from the United States. Securing a national patron, in fact, was U.S. Catholics' intention in nominating their first candidates for canonization.

Yet a contradiction implicit in the canonization process made finding a U.S. patron more difficult than the early saint-seekers imagined. Viewed from the perspective of the center, the criteria for holiness are presumed to exist apart from time and place. "No popular acclaim, no national rivalry can make Saints," insisted one U.S. authority in 1925. "The process is slow, deliberate, and strictly judicial."[21] Refracted through the lens of the periphery, however, sanctity appears much more fluid and historically contingent. Whether candidates would ultimately be canonized depended not just on how well their sanctity passed muster at the center but on how easily their lives could be framed to support U.S. Catholics' vision of themselves as Americans—a vision that would change, as we will see, between the late nineteenth century and the present. *A Saint of Our Own* thus also highlights a perennial dissonance in the experience of U.S. Catholics, who belong to a church that moves slowly—in this case through an often painstakingly sluggish process—but live in a culture that changes easily and rapidly. Even in the exceptional cases where a cause for canonization moved quickly in Rome, the interval between its beginning and its successful conclusion could seem an eternity when measured by American standards. For most of their nation's history, U.S. Catholics' attachment to a newly canonized saint rarely matched the enthusiasm shown by the generation that had originally proposed the candidate. This dynamic helps to explain why the United States still does not have a national patron saint.

The two U.S. saints who came closest to being designated for this honor were Seton and Frances Cabrini, an Italian-born missionary who arrived in New York in 1889 and died in Chicago in 1917. Seton and Cabrini both have shrines in Manhattan, a coincidence that highlights the tendency of U.S. saint-seekers to foreground candidates with ties to the northeastern part of the country. (Of the twelve canonized U.S. saints, Seton, Cabrini, and four others had roots in New York, while an additional two had come from Philadelphia.) Seton and Cabrini shared similar saintly stories, but one critical difference between them is particularly instructive. From start to finish, Cabrini's cause for canonization spanned less than twenty years, while Seton's took almost a century to complete. The differential mostly derived from the fact that Cabrini's advocates had close ties to the Vatican while Seton's did not. Also contributing to the gap, however, was an unexamined provision in church law that lends itself to an exploration of how women in patriarchal religious traditions seek to become actors in history.

It is widely acknowledged that church leaders have long used models of female sanctity to control and contain women—and that Catholic women have, conversely, cited the example of female saints as justifications for expanding gender roles. While *A Saint of Our Own* considers the ways in which expectations about female behavior shaped models of holiness, its more innovative approach to the study of gender and sanctity lies in its examination of the role of women as petitioners, the group of people who initiate and sponsor causes for canonization. Until 1983, canon law stipulated that women could petition the Holy See only through male proxies. In charting U.S. Catholic women's struggle to maneuver around this requirement and uncovering the surprises that followed success, *A Saint of Our Own* provides a fascinating glimpse into both the history of women in the Catholic Church and the complicated relationship between gender and power in the church in the early twenty-first century.

The above reference to canon law invites an important reminder about the daunting complexities of the modern canonization process. Peter Gumpel, SJ, an erudite Jesuit who worked at the Vatican's Congregation for the Causes of Saints for over four decades, captured them well: "I am not considered to be stupid," Gumpel observed, "and it took me six or seven years before I could begin to understand the whole business."[22] Gumpel enters our story in our final chapter, but for now, his words are intended to remind readers that this book will not provide a detailed analysis of the convoluted procedures through which the church confirms the citizens of heaven. While *A Saint of Our Own* describes elements of the process as it tracks U.S. candidates through its major steps, it primarily considers saints' "afterlives" in a figurative sense, exploring how citizenship status in the United States affected both their journeys to the honors of the altar and their place in American historical memory.

This panoramic view of American sanctity broadens the scope of canonization to encompass not only "official" narratives but also the multivalent turning points along any saintly trajectory. An instructive case in point is the "beginning" of Seton's cause. Records of Seton's congregation, as well as documentation submitted to the Holy See, pinpoint 22 August 1882 as its definitive start date. On that day Archbishop (later Cardinal) James Gibbons of Baltimore visited Seton's community at its headquarters in Emmitsburg, Maryland, and, while saying Mass at Seton's tomb, was inspired to nominate her as a saint. After Mass the archbishop shared his idea with the sisters and asked them to consider opening Seton's cause for canonization, allowing that doing so might countermand their natural instincts. "I know," he told them, "that the Sisters of Charity do not love nor seek to be known" but "love instead the silences, the shade, the obscurity." Yet, he went on, "I wondered whether there would not be a day in which the Church would bring [Seton] to the Altar, and whether it might indeed be our task to initiate the necessary steps toward her canonization." While volunteering to "gladly take the initiative, if I had any encouragement," he acknowledged that "the first movement must naturally begin here."[23] Here Gibbons was referring to two customary practices in opening causes for canonization: that they be launched from the diocese in which the candidate had died, and that nominations were to come from the laity rather than the clerical hierarchy.[24] Because Catholic sisters are not ordained and thus are members of the laity, Gibbons urged them to overcome their natural reticence and to contemplate opening Seton's cause, assuring them that its success would ultimately produce "the best results" for the women who carried on Seton's legacy. Multiple sources attest that the sisters agreed to follow his suggestion.

Upon closer examination, however, Gibbons's graveside vision appears less an inspired and decisive catalyst than the moment when national interests intersected with a long-cherished desire of Seton's spiritual daughters. It may well have been true that the sisters generally avoided publicity, but it most assuredly was not the case that they had never before considered proposing their founder for canonization. On the contrary, evidence suggests that Seton's closest companions had intended to pursue her cause for canonization long before 1882—and had in fact planned to do so from the very moment of her death in 1821. Seton's spiritual director, Simon Bruté, a French missionary priest who became the first bishop of Vincennes, Indiana, in 1834, enjoined the mourning sisters to be attentive at her deathbed: "Gather the fragments, lest they be lost." This was recognized as a sign that Bruté and others anticipated opening Seton's cause for canonization, as the founder's body, and anything it had ever touched, could serve as relics that her devotees could use to venerate and to invoke her intercession.[25]

An episode at Seton's graveside a quarter century after her death further signaled that her congregation had intended to initiate her canonization process well in advance of Gibbons's prompt. On 20 June 1846, when Seton's body was exhumed in preparation for a transfer to a new tomb, the sisters present prayed fervently to find an intact corpse. Sister Lucina Simms later remembered their "disappointment" and "emotion" at the scene: "For one moment we saw the blackened skull, eyeless sockets in the black skull—just for one moment, and then all sank to dust at the bottom of the coffin. Mother Xavier had expected to find the remains intact." Because incorruptibility is but one indicator of sanctity rather than an essential precondition of it, the discovery hardly spelled the end of Seton's chances for canonization. Still, one sister was so disheartened by their discovery that she "begged with irresistible earnestness" to be allowed a bone fragment for comfort. She received one of the small bones of the toes.[26]

Given Seton's credentials as the founder of a religious congregation, especially one that represented a historic American first, it was not surprising that she emerged as a candidate for canonization. The canon of the saints is dense with founders and firsts. Yet as we will see, even as the sister comforted herself with Seton's toe bone, a chain of events was unfolding that would transform what is usually an advantage in canonization—membership in a religious congregation—into a dangerous encumbrance and jeopardize Seton's chances to a far greater extent than would her bodily decomposition. A rupture within her congregation would later generate competing narratives about Seton's founding vision and cast a long shadow over her life and legacy. The extent of this problem, though, was not yet apparent in 1882, when Gibbons spoke to Seton's Emmitsburg congregation—or, more precisely, to what was by then one of six separate religious communities that looked to Seton as a founder.

Just as those earlier events indicate that the sisters' annals were not entirely accurate in attributing the idea of canonizing Seton solely to the archbishop, the momentum building for a number of other U.S. causes also belied the apparent spontaneity of Gibbons's inspiration. His words to Seton's spiritual daughters that August afternoon made clear that they would not be the only ones to benefit should her cause succeed. Canonizing Seton, Gibbons maintained, would validate the entire U.S. church in adding one of their number to the roster of the saints for the very first time. "American saints," he reminded them, "are rare birds," and thus "it would be great to see the name of Mother Seton on a list, alas, too short!"[27]

Gibbons's lament was only one sign of a saintly inferiority complex that had developed in the U.S. Catholic Church. In the decades to come, Gibbons would often remind U.S. Catholics that holy men and women had lived not only across the ocean but among them on this side of the water. In 1891, for example, he admonished the citizens of Vincennes, Indiana, that they "need not go on pilgrimages to visit the tombs of saints. There is one reposing here in your midst, namely, the saintly founder of this diocese, the Right Reverend Simon Bruté." Gibbons's effort to promote America's holy heroes was part of U.S. Catholics' larger attempt to secure, in the words of John Gilmary Shea, the era's leading American Catholic intellectual, patron saints who "lived and labored and sanctified themselves in *our* land, among circumstances familiar."[28]

The search for homegrown holiness—nurtured in the United States, validated by the Vatican—knit together a number of impulses that shaped the church in the late nineteenth century. It reflected in part U.S. Catholics' desire to strengthen the bonds of attachment between themselves and the Holy See. Even as the church in Italy lost its sovereign power in the wake of Italian unification—thereby consigning the pope to "prisoner" status behind the walls of the tiny Vatican state, the remnant of the church's once-vast territory—it had increased its spiritual hold over Catholics in Europe and across the Atlantic. In the late nineteenth century, as one churchman put it, U.S. Catholics "turned Romeward, as naturally as the needle seeks the North." Historian James O'Toole has described a number of phenomena that signaled this turn toward Rome. First, U.S. Catholics contributed more and more to Peter's Pence, a global collection taken up to support the pope's specific initiatives. Second, they looked approvingly at the rising number of U.S. priests awarded the title "Monsignor," an honorary title conferred by the pope for service to the church. Finally, U.S. Catholics increasingly recited special prayers intended to help the pontiff in his political distress.[29] Nominating prospective patron saints offered U.S. Catholics another opportunity to bind themselves spiritually to the Holy See.

U.S. Catholics launched their quest for a saint in the midst of a structural as well as a spiritual transformation in the American church. When Gibbons had visited Emmitsburg, the United States was still classified as a "mission territory" by the Vatican and operated under the jurisdiction of the Sacred Congregation for the Propagation of the Faith or, as it was often called, Propaganda Fide. Throughout the 1880s and beyond, correspondence between U.S. bishops and Propaganda Fide increased in frequency and treated more and more complex matters, prompting the Vatican to recognize the growing vigor and import of the American church and to increase its awareness of the singular challenges the church faced in a religiously pluralistic society. U.S. Catholics, meanwhile, were beginning to conceive of themselves as an organized, self-sustaining church on par with Catholicism in European countries rather than as a precarious mission territory. Pursuing a saint of their own helped reinforce this identity. Practically, the quest proved that the church had the necessary financial and institutional wherewithal to sponsor a cause; symbolically, the effort implied that uniquely American expressions of holiness were tantamount to those manifest in European countries where nationalism and sanctity had long been intertwined.[30] Even as U.S. Catholics proposed their first potential saints, for instance, their counterparts in France were looking to fifteenth-century Joan of Arc as both a national hero and a holy one. Using Joan's story to buttress their cause, French nationalists helped her advance to beatification in 1909. During World War I, Joan became even more potent as a French national symbol, and she was canonized in its aftermath.[31]

The relationship between saint-seeking and nation-building was less straightforward in the United States, where Catholicism had long been a controversial minority religion, than it was in France or other Catholic nations of Europe. Anti-Catholicism's most violent eruptions in the United States, such as the 1834 convent burning in Charlestown, Massachusetts, and the 1844 "Bible riots" in Philadelphia, had taken place in the antebellum period. Although regional loyalties were more pronounced than religious divides in the Civil War era, prejudice against Catholics resurfaced as a national force in the late nineteenth century, in part as a response to Catholics' growing influence and power in multiple realms. Members of the American Protective Association, for example, an anti-Catholic organization founded in 1887, vowed to never vote for a Catholic, go on strike with a Catholic, or hire a Catholic if a Protestant was available. In the minds of many Protestants, an alarming increase in migration from southern and eastern Europe magnified the Catholic menace. These newcomers were suspect not only because of their supposed allegiance to Rome but also because of their concentration in urban areas and industrial occupations. A number of U.S. Catholics looked to canonization as a remedy for this tense situation, believing that securing a national patron would help diminish anti-Catholicism, however dubious the proposition that one of the most provocative and exotic markers of Catholic difference could function as an agent of Catholic assimilation might seem.

Cementing a connection to the Holy See, presenting the American church as well beyond its infancy, and affirming U.S. Catholicism's place in the nation: a great deal rested on a prospective patron, and for almost fifty years it would be more than Elizabeth Ann Seton's afterlife could sustain. The first U.S. saint-seekers, in fact, did not look primarily to Seton to fulfill their high expectations. As well known as Seton's name was throughout the United States, her life story could not be easily crafted into the particular messages U.S. Catholics of that era wanted to send to the Holy See and to their fellow citizens. Indeed, two years after his visit to Emmitsburg, Archbishop Gibbons, acting on behalf of all U.S. bishops, would take an important step in launching the first cause for canonization from the United States but for a different candidate:

Tekakwitha, an indigenous convert to Catholicism born in 1656 in what became Auriesville, New York. Together with the Jesuit missionaries with whom her story was entwined, the "Lily of the Mohawks" would outshine Seton both as a holy exemplar and as an American icon, albeit for a limited time. This was part of the reason why the Holy See did not even officially introduce Seton's cause for canonization until 1940, almost sixty years after Gibbons's visit to Emmitsburg. At that point, Rome would permanently register Seton as the "second flower" of American sanctity recognizing that she had first blossomed in the holy shadow of a "Lily."[32]

New American moments generated new models of holiness. *A Saint of Our Own* reveals the "abundant" presence of holy heroes in U.S. Catholics' American story: during a landmark gathering of U.S. bishops in 1884, an exuberant public celebration in Chicago in 1926, a papal conclave in 1939, the Second Vatican Council in the early 1960s, and a charismatic pope's visit to Philadelphia in 1979.[33] Saints were also present during another momentous occasion for Catholics and their fellow citizens in September 2015—the event that provides a capstone to the book. Welcoming Pope Francis to the White House, President Barack Obama gave the pontiff a gift intended to evoke a meaningful connection between the Catholic Church and the United States. The exchange marked a significant departure within the long sweep of the nation's history. For most of that history, the prospect of a pope visiting the White House would have been cause for alarm rather than celebration, and the notion that a U.S. president would extend to a pope the courtesies reserved for a head of state would have been considered anathema. The gift itself, however, signaled continuity, in that it relied on a canonized saint to express Catholicism's resonance in American culture. The carefully chosen artifact—a key that unlocked Elizabeth Ann Seton's home in Emmitsburg—affirmed Seton's status as a woman perched at the nexus of holiness and American history.[34]

A Saint of Our Own takes readers inside the stories of Seton and other U.S. Catholic historical figures who have occupied this privileged position, including some who did so only fleetingly. The afterlives of these saints are interspersed with those of other candidates who, despite their supporters' aspirations, never quite attained iconic American status. The book ends with a brief examination of a few pending saints who might qualify as quintessential Americans, were their sponsors inclined to advance such an argument. That they are not so inclined points to a decisive shift in the U.S. Catholic story. Saint-seekers would spend almost a century proposing candidates whom they envisioned as embodiments of their uniquely American brand of holiness. The components of that American brand, however, changed far more rapidly than causes for canonization proceeded. Consequently it was not until 1975 that U.S. Catholics welcomed a saint who plausibly matched the moment in which they found themselves—and by then, a desire to prove and explain Catholics' Americanness had lost most of its force for U.S. saint-seekers. Once polarization within the church supplanted marginalization in America as the defining ethos of U.S. Catholicism, favorite saints would convey far less than they once did about U.S. Catholics' understandings of American identity. Instead, since the 1970s, candidates for canonization have increasingly emerged from debates over what it means to be Catholic and signify where their supporters position themselves on some of the most divisive issues in church and American society.

This situation highlights the deep irony at the core of this book's main argument. U.S. Catholics had originally sought a saint of their own in the hope that finding one would prove that they belonged in the United States. Ultimately, it would be the search itself, rather than its outcome, that proclaimed Catholics' Americanness most loudly. In each new moment, U.S. Catholics spoke about holy heroes in language that reflected not simply their sacred beliefs but the same secular developments—nation-building, urbanization, industrialization, depression, war, global politics, or social and cultural change—that were shaping the lives of all Americans. Officially, U.S. Catholics had to make the case that prospective saints had practiced the theological and cardinal virtues: faith, hope, charity, prudence, fortitude, temperance, and justice. Unofficially, it mattered a great deal to them that these men and women could also be said to have embraced American virtues and participated in American projects. Expressed as a Catholic initiative, the search for a wholly American saint unfolded as a history of the United States in the long twentieth century.

What follows is a complicated yet captivating tale that, while requiring occasional forays into esoteric regulations, demonstrates saints' potential to exacerbate and reconcile tensions between Catholics and Protestants and between Rome and America. *A Saint of Our Own* offers insight into the ways causes for canonization expose divisions within U.S. Catholicism, including those between men and women, between the clergy and the laity, and among religious congregations, ideological camps, racial and ethnic groups, and regional constituencies. This story takes us on multiple Atlantic crossings, as we shadow American holy heroes and interpret the lives of the Catholics who loved, invoked, and promoted them.

✦ NORTH AMERICAN SAINTS ✦

"Where does America stand," asked attorney Robert H. Clarke, in the "vast spiritual empire of the communion of saints?" The answer—that America was not represented at all among Catholic canonized saints—irritated Clarke. While U.S. Catholics could obviously share "the great saints of the universal church," it was inconceivable to him that a nation long past its "nascent period of colonial life" had yet to produce a saint of its very own. What is a nation, Clarke wondered, "without patrons or shrines?" For American Catholics, he predicted, this would be one of the most important "questions of the hour."[1]

Clarke's questions were not uncommon in the 1880s and 1890s, as rapid changes at home and rising aspirations abroad prompted Americans to struggle to define their nation and assess where it stood in relation to the rest of the world. How, many wondered, did increases in urbanization, industrialization, and new sources of immigration affect what it meant to be American? How should the United States educate its children to prepare them for citizenship in a new century? How should the United States position itself in relation to global empires, and how should it assert itself on a world stage? These and other "questions of the hour" were very much on the minds of Archbishop James Gibbons and other leaders of the U.S. Catholic church when they gathered for the Third Plenary Council of Baltimore in 1884. Clarke's musings on sanctity and American identity, in fact, had emerged in direct response to an initiative launched at the council, the largest gathering of American church leaders to date.

The Holy See had convoked the council to address a host of issues facing the church in the United States: increasing numbers of Catholic immigrants, conflict among ethnic groups, disputes between priests and bishops, Catholic workers' gravitation toward labor unions, and Catholic children's attendance at public schools.[2] Underlying the Vatican's concern regarding these specific issues was a broader skepticism on the part of its Congregation for the Propagation of the Faith about the very nature of Catholics' participation in the unfolding American experiment. Could the church thrive, as Gibbons and others insisted, in a religiously pluralistic society, under a government that enshrined freedom of religion?

Like Clarke's query about American saints, the Third Plenary Council itself represented an attempt by U.S. Catholics to claim for their nation the respect they believed it deserved from the universal church. Propaganda Fide, the Vatican body that directed the church's affairs in its mission territories, had intended to use the Third Plenary Council to increase Roman supervision of the church in the United States. Accordingly, Pope Leo XIII had originally appointed an Italian bishop to preside over the council, but in response to objections from U.S. priests and bishops, he had relented and designated Gibbons as his presiding delegate. The Holy See's confidence in Gibbons would only grow in the aftermath of the council. In 1886, he was elevated to the rank of cardinal and would serve as the de facto leader of the U.S. Catholic hierarchy until his death in 1921. The Vatican consulted him on all matters American, and the Holy See channeled all of its correspondence to the United States through him.[3]

It was thus Gibbons's signature that appeared on a petition that council delegates addressed to Pope Leo XIII and sent on behalf of the entire U.S. hierarchy. This was the "first step ever taken by American bishops" to initiate a U.S. cause for canonization. The petition's subject was the life and virtues of the woman it called "Katharine Tekakwitha," a native convert to Catholicism who had been born in 1656 in what later became northern New York and died in a Mohawk village in New France twenty-four years later. The bishops praised Tekakwitha as "a splendid example of every virtue" who had left behind "a renown for sanctity which has been confirmed by wonderful events."[4]

The petition summarized the central elements of a hagiography first established in the early eighteenth century. Two Jesuit missionaries had published biographies of Tekakwitha soon after her death, testifying to and increasing her reputation for holiness.[5] They and subsequent hagiographers emphasized her conversion, refusal of marriage proposals, habits of fasting and self-flagellation, and public vow of virginity. The other well-known "wonderful events" cited in the petition included Tekakwitha's deathbed transfiguration, in which small-pox scars had disappeared from her face, and miraculous healings that her devotees credited to her intercession.[6] The council's petition also named two other candidates for canonization: Isaac Jogues and René Goupil, two French Jesuit missionaries to New France who had been executed by indigenous people in the 1640s. Tekakwitha had been born very close to the site of Jogues and Goupil's martyrdom, and hagiographers often attributed her conversion to the missionaries' grisly sacrifice. Characterized as the "first fruit of their blood," Tekakwitha represented a validation not simply of their deaths but of the Jesuit missions more generally.[7]

The novelty of the Baltimore petition rested in its purpose rather than its content. The petition was to Tekakwitha's cause what Gibbons's proposal to Elizabeth Ann Seton's spiritual daughters had been for hers: the beginning of an attempt to elevate Tekakwitha from the unofficial sanctity long recognized by her devotees to a formal sanctity that would be acknowledged by the en-tire church. The U.S. bishops hoped the petition would eventually supply the U.S. church with a native patron. "Humbly beg[ging]" Pope Leo to initiate the causes for canonization of Goupil, Jogues, and Tekakwitha, the petition celebrated the spiritual benefits that would follow once the Holy See agreed to consider their cause, emphasizing that having models of holiness "drawn from their very midst" would "inspire the devotion of the faithful in this country" and "afford it native patrons."[8] Echoing this language, many of Tekakwitha's devotees declared that the petition reflected the will of the people; the laity, not the hierarchy, had felt most acutely "the need of a special intercessor in Heaven" and "had risen up to call her blessed."[9]

Most of the U.S. Catholics who beseeched the Vatican for a "native patron" were well aware that the church had already placed them under the spiritual protection of St. Rose of Lima, Peru, and the patronage of the Blessed Mother under the title Our Lady of the Immaculate Conception.[10] At this point in their history, however, U.S. Catholics yearned for a saint whose feet had walked on the same soil and whose eyes had seen the same landscape. They wanted, in other words, a "special intercessor in Heaven" who could match the new mo-ment in which they found themselves.

This new moment was readily apparent at the Third Plenary Council, where bishops approved a number of initiatives that would shape the U.S. church in the decades to come. One of the council's best-known decrees related to

Catholic education. Although Catholic schools had certainly existed before 1884, only at this council did U.S. bishops commit to building a parish school system that would rival its public counterpart in scale and quality.[11] Similarly decisive was the council's report on the pastoral care of Italian immigrants, which noted their rising numbers and the problems they presented for a U.S. church dominated by Irish American and German American priests and bishops.[12]

Debates within the council also foreshadowed an internal division within the U.S. hierarchy over how the church should respond to the social, cultural, and intellectual challenges of a rapidly changing world. While the battle lines between the dissenting camps were often blurred, two discernible mindsets emerged. On one side were bishops who, while recognizing the dangers that the modern world posed to the faith, believed that the Catholic Church could flourish in the American environment to an extent that would not be possible in European countries in which the democratic revolutions had caused the church to lose much of its power and relevance. These so-called liberal or Americanist bishops championed a rapid integration of Catholics into American culture, English-language worship, more decision-making power for U.S. bishops, and greater collaboration between Catholic and government-sponsored institutions. Those who came to be called "conservatives" adopted a less optimistic stance, focusing on the threats the modern world posed to the faith. They advocated a tightening of ecclesiastical discipline, careful maintenance of immigrants' native language and worship styles, and more insular parishes and schools. Intertwined with these issues was a disagreement over how much control the Holy See should have over U.S. Catholic affairs, especially as the church's organizational structure edged toward a reclassification from "mission territory" into a national church. In 1892, the Holy See's creation of a new ecclesiastical office in the United States, an apostolic delegation, exacerbated tensions between liberals and conservatives as they competed for the support of the new papal representative to the U.S.—even as the appointment sent off warning bells among anti-Catholics who worried his arrival signaled papal encroachment onto American sovereignty.[13]

The "school question," the "ethnic question," the "Americanist question," and the "Roman question" are subjects that have long engaged historians of U.S. Catholicism, and rightly so, as the debates over these collectively capture what it has meant to be both Catholic and American. Equally revelatory, this book argues, can be an exploration of the "saint question." To understand which historical figures U.S. Catholics nominated as prospective patron saints—and their hopes for what these nominations would achieve—is to understand how they defined themselves as Catholics and as Americans at this aspirational moment in their history.

A Saint from *Our* Land, among Circumstances Familiar

News of the "first step ever" in initiating a U.S. cause for canonization delighted many U.S. Catholics. Attorney Robert H. Clarke, for example, welcomed the "bold" answer to the question "Where are our national saints and shrines?" Pleading their causes "in the court of Rome," Clarke contended that the eventual canonization of Jogues, Goupil, and Tekakwitha would give North American Catholics the equivalent of Ireland's Patrick or Bridget or of France's Louis or Genevieve. "Yes, America has her saints," he declared, "and now we ask that they, too, may receive the homage paid to the servants of God."[14]

John Gilmary Shea, a prolific and prominent church historian, was equally elated, maintaining that the eventual beatification of Tekakwitha and the martyrs would satisfy U.S. Catholics' deep longing for national patrons who had "lived and labored and sanctified themselves in *our* land, among circumstances familiar."[15] Though Shea had been urging church leaders to pursue the causes of Tekakwitha and the martyrs since the early 1850s, his request had acquired a much greater sense of immediacy by the 1880s. By then, like Gibbons and many other U.S. Catholics, Shea was growing increasingly dissatisfied that, although "personages noted for eminent sanctity have flourished in Canada and the United States from the time of the earliest settlement," there had been "no active steps to secure the canonization of any of them." Shea did not hold church leaders in either country responsible for this: "The condition of the [North American] Church of the last century," he realized, "had taxed the resources of Catholics in both countries to the utmost," and the exigencies of building a mission church had left American bishops with little energy or capital to devote to pursuing a cause.[16] Instead, he blamed the lack of a North American saint on the length and rigor of the "modern" process of canonization. The more discriminating post-Reformation approach to saint-seeking left Catholics on the church's periphery—far from its center of wealth and power—at a distinct disadvantage. "If it were as easy today to obtain the honor of the altars as it was a thousand years ago," one priest lamented, "the calendars of all the dioceses of the United States would show many feasts of local saints, martyrs, confessors and virgins."[17] Recognizing the hurdle that a lack of financial resources constituted for pursuing a saint's cause, Edward McSweeny, a U.S. Catholic priest, suggested that the Vatican appoint a special group of cardinals to glorify the "hidden saints" of countries "whose people are too poor to stand all the necessary expense."[18]

Looking south only compounded U.S. Catholics' frustration. Seventeen men and women from Central and South America had been successfully elevated to the ranks of sainthood since the institution of the modern process.[19] "Without monarchs or wealthy communities to undertake the long and often expensive investigations demanded at Rome," one American Catholic grumbled, it was no wonder that "no servant of God who lived or labored . . . in any part of our continent lying north of the Rio Grande" had ever even been proposed for canonization.[20]

This perception that the Rio Grande marked a great divide between acknowledged and unacknowledged exemplars of Catholic holiness fostered a spirit of cooperation between saint-seekers in Canada and the United States. This manifested itself most clearly in causes that obviously straddled the border between the two countries. Tekakwitha had been born in what became the United States and died in what was later Canada. Accordingly, members of the Canadian hierarchy also drafted a petition to the Holy See on Tekakwitha's behalf at their own national meeting. The collaborative spirit between Canada and the United States was rooted not only in their shared position vis-à-vis the center of the church's power but also in the conviction that effecting the canonization of a person from either the United States or Canada would be a "rare accomplishment" considering that neither country "belong[ed] to the Latin races." In the eyes of many U.S. and Canadian Catholics, in other words, their joint quest for a national patron pitted a saint-deprived culture of North America against a saint-saturated one to the south.[21] Though this argument admittedly underscores the distinctly European American cast to the quest for a U.S. saint—it is difficult to imagine, for example, that a Catholic living in San Francisco, San Antonio, or anywhere in the western and southwestern United States would have perceived saints to be absent from their landscape—the imbalance was nonetheless dramatic. When it came to saints who had walked on American soil, the Rio Grande did mark a sharp divide.

One canonized South American emerged as a particular flash point for U.S. saint-seekers' discontent. In 1671, the church had canonized Rose of Lima, a Dominican mystic who had died in Peru in 1617. One of the first saints to pass through the modern canonization process, Rose was also the first successful cause to emerge from the "New" World. As such the Holy See proclaimed her "patron of all the Americas," encouraging Catholics from "Cape Horn to Alaska" to embrace Rose as their particular advocate, to build churches and shrines in her honor, and to commemorate her feast day.[22] Some late nineteenth-century U.S. Catholics did follow this advice and express fervent devotion to Rose. In one of the better-known examples, Rose Hawthorne Lathrop, daughter of author Nathaniel Hawthorne and literary figure in her own right, claimed a spiritual kinship with the Peruvian saint soon after her conversion to Catholicism in 1891 when she dedicated her newly founded community of Dominican sisters to Rose of Lima.[23]

The devotion of Lathrop and others notwithstanding, it had become increasingly evident by the late nineteenth century that many Catholics in the United States and Canada did not view Rose of Lima as an acceptable representative for their collective spiritual interests. One priest, convinced that most U.S. Catholics were not even aware of Rose's patronage, urged church leaders to make a greater effort to generate enthusiasm for Rose among their flock.[24] In fact, most North American Catholics were less inclined to embrace Rose than they were to replace her—perhaps literally, with a Rose of their own.

The desire for a North American analogue to Rose of Lima was strong enough to prompt the rechristening of Philippine Duchesne, a French-born member of the Society of the Sacred Heart who had worked as a missionary in Missouri from 1818 until her death in 1852. Duchesne had been baptized Rose Philippine, and although no one had called Duchesne "Rose" during her life, after her death the name became a particularly convenient way to highlight North Americans' absence from the canon of the saints. One American saint-seeker entreated church authorities to recognize Duchesne's extraordinary holiness by proclaiming her "a St. Rose of Missouri for these United States." The tag provides a strikingly clear example of how hagiography can illuminate the priorities of a saint's supporters, even to the point of obfuscating details about the saint herself. If it could be argued that the Rose of Missouri had met "the European standards of sanctity" in the same way that Rose of Lima had done, it would become increasingly difficult to justify the fact that the former was languishing as an "uncanonized saint."[25]

The search for a northern equivalent to Rose of Lima had also contributed to the popularity of a sobriquet attached to Tekakwitha, the "Lily of the Mohawks." The nickname had originally been used to evoke Tekakwitha's baptism, as the lily was the emblem of St. Catherine of Siena and was also used to con-note sexual and racial purity. In her 1891 biography of Tekakwitha, Ellen Wal-worth played on this floral imagery to associate the uncanonized "Lily" with the South American Rose, arguing that "the fairest flower of the American forest" deserved the same honors given to the Peruvian saint over two centu-ries earlier. Echoing her metaphor, one of the reviewers of Walworth's book declared, "Fair Lily of the Mohawks! Who does not wish to see her placed on our American altars in sweet companionship with the lovely Rose of Peru?"[26]

Duchesne and Tekakwitha shared other qualities that led to their becom-ing the two leading female candidates for canonization from North America. For one, their stories lent themselves to a nineteenth-century spirituality in which themes of suffering and conversion prevailed. A smallpox epidemic had orphaned Tekakwitha, and colonial upheaval and her own habits of self-mortification had led to more suffering. Duchesne, who had first become a nun in her native Grenoble, had witnessed the seizure of her convent and the disbanding of her congregation during the French Revolution. Devotees char-acterized her life in North America as one of great hardship, describing her as a "pioneer on a cold and desolate frontier" who had lived a life of "toil, disap-pointment, endurance and self-annihilation."[27]

Both women were also intimately connected to the French Catholic mis-sionary enterprise: Tekakwitha as its validation in the seventeenth century, Du-chesne as its extension into the nineteenth.[28] While the theme of conversion had long been central to Tekakwitha's hagiography, it required some embel-lishment in Duchesne's case. Though Duchesne had often expressed a desire to follow in the footsteps of the seventeenth-century French missionary martyrs, she had lived among indigenous people for only one of her thirty-four years spent in North America before she died, and, unlike many of the seventeenth-century missionaries she revered, Duchesne had never faced the prospect of martyrdom. Yet her hagiography nonetheless foregrounded her love for and devotion to indigenous people, and her supporters insisted that she *would* have died a martyr—and done so gladly—if given the chance. Although Duchesne may not have died at the hands of heathens, by living "in the midst of privations and sorrows, that Christ might be known and glorified," she "fell little short of the martyrdom of blood itself."[29]

Of course, many other men and women had suffered for the sake of saving souls, only to be forgotten. So what set Duchesne and Tekakwitha apart from other Catholics perceived as holy? As is the case with most canonized saints, part of the answer lies in supernatural phenomena. The first signs of these women's divine favor appeared as they died: the aforementioned facial transfiguration in Tekakwitha's case and, less dramatically in Duchesne's case, reports that she had passed away "in the odor of sanctity." (In Catholic parlance, the odor of sanctity was sometimes a literal and often sweet fragrance but more often manifested as an "aura" of holiness.) Another hallmark of Duchesne's potential sainthood emerged three years later, when her buried remains were unearthed and—unlike Seton's—were found largely intact, the evidence of the bodily incorruptibility often hoped for by saint-seekers. Even more promising for both women's causes were the reports of miracles: for Duchesne, the claim that the application of her relic had effected a local woman's cure from cancer, and for Tekakwitha, the "wonderful events" chronicled by her Jesuit hagiographers.[30]

But while uncanny events often set a cause in motion, more conventional factors usually propel it forward. One of these is a core group of devotees willing to sponsor a prospective saint's cause. For Duchesne, the Society of the Sacred Heart (or RSCJ, which stands for Religieuses du Sacré-Cœur de Jésus) served this function. The canon of the saints boasts an abundance of vowed men and women for good reason: religious congregations can supply the personnel, the funding, and the institutional memory to sustain a cause for the decades or even centuries it takes to shepherd a candidate to the honors of the altar. Duchesne's status as the first member of the Society of the Sacred Heart in the United States gave the order added incentive to pursue her cause, as the canonization of a founder both magnifies a congregation's fame and validates its projects. In 1872, twenty years after Duchesne's death, the Society signaled its intention to launch her cause by recording testimony from the people who could attest to her holiness and others who believed she had granted favors through heavenly intercession. The sisters also commissioned a biography, a crucial first step in providing the kind of documentary evidence that helps to move a cause forward.[31]

Until the 1980s, members of the Society of the Sacred Heart, like all Catholic women, could petition the Sacred Congregation of Rites only through a male proxy. Typically, a women's congregation would select a vice-postulator (the person who oversees a cause on the local level) and a postulator (the person who presents the cause in Rome) from the clergy of its home diocese or from the male congregation with which it had the closest ties. In cases where a congregation had both male and female branches, this often—though by no means always—simplified matters. While the RSCJs had no direct male counterparts, they did work closely with the Jesuits, and the sisters approached them first in their search for a postulator. It was an obvious choice. Certainly no congregation was more renowned for its prowess in canonization procedures; as one U.S. saint-seeker noted (not without a whiff of resentment), the Jesuits had "a general historian, as well as a chronicler, for each province, whose business it is to collect and preserve data of every single member. . . . They preserve the likenesses and publish the lives of almost every one of their order who acquires distinction for sanctity or for general usefulness. . . . The society . . . places in a sepulcher apart the remains of any individual member who is believed to have died in the odor of holiness."[32]

The Jesuits appeared more hesitant to use their vaunted saint-seeking skills to support women who had not been members of the Society, and they initially turned the RSCJs down in their request to provide a postulator for Duchesne; the Franciscans also refused them. The archbishop of St. Louis eventually assigned a diocesan priest to the task, but he suffered from ill health and did not communicate readily with the sisters. Frustrated by the lack of progress, an enterprising sister from the order named Ellen McGloin predicted that "the history of Mother Duchesne's process is to resemble that of her life in its delays, and ever-recurring obstacles."[33] Her words would prove prophetic, but McGloin herself did what she could to move the cause along. In fact she appeared to have acted as Duchesne's postulator, at least unofficially, during the two years she spent in Rome gathering and copying all of Duchesne's writings. When she was called back to the United States in September 1901, McGloin wrote that "the poor Postulator accepts her deposition, as she did her election, from the hand of God, thanking her Mother for the confidence reposed in her thus far."[34] McGloin's unsuccessful effort to assume responsibility for shepherding Duchesne's cause foreshadowed other attempts U.S. Catholic sisters would make to wrest control over their causes for canonization from male clergy.

If the Jesuits' initial refusal to act as her postulator stalled the progress of "the Rose of Missouri," the congregation's decision on the Lily of the Mohawks led to an even longer postponement. By 1900, the Jesuits had separated Tekakwitha's cause from those of Jogues and Goupil and resolved not to take any further action on hers until after the missionaries were canonized. While this decision highlights the difficulties facing female candidates for canonization, gender was likely less of a factor in that decision than Jogues and Goupil's martyrdom. For all of her suffering, Tekakwitha had not died as a martyr, a status inextricably linked to sainthood since the days of the early church, when the two were essentially interchangeable. The church interpreted a willingness to die for the faith as the ultimate proof of holiness and thus sufficient evidence of sanctity, and it was not until the fifth century that it began to recognize non-martyrs as saints.[35] Even the modern process of canonization awarded a logistical advantage to martyred candidates, who required one fewer miracle than confessors (as non-martyrs were designated) for beatification.[36]

Separated from Tekakwitha, Jogues and Goupil were bundled instead with six of their confreres who had also perished at the hands of indigenous people in New France in the 1640s. Here they were following the precedent set in 1652 by the archbishop of Rouen, whose diocese was home to the eight men and who had initiated their cause by directing the Jesuits in Québec to collect testimony on their virtues and martyrdoms. The creation of the Diocese of Québec in 1674 arrested that effort, however. As authority for pursuing the case shifted to the new bishop, he was too focused on the establishment of missions and local infrastructure to undertake something as comparatively frivolous as a canonization process, lending credence to Shea's explanation for the paucity of North American saints. England's victory over France in 1763, followed by the 1773 suppression of the Jesuits, delayed the cause even further.[37]

The Jesuits' restoration in Canada in 1841 helped revive interest in the cause, which was also supported by a concurrent effort to publish their historical records (collectively, the *Relations des Jésuites de la Nouvelle-France*, or simply the *Relations*). Felix Martin, a French-born historian who became Jesuit superior in Montreal in 1844, spearheaded the latter effort, combing Huron missions and Roman archives for materials pertaining to New France, writing a biography of the martyrs, and persuading the Canadian government to publish a three-volume translation of the *Relations* in 1858. John Gilmary Shea, who had spent two years at St. Mary's College in Montreal, translated Martin's biography and parts of the *Relations* into English. Thanks in large part to these efforts, prominent American historians such as George Bancroft and Francis Parkman included the martyred Jesuits in their histories of New France.[38]

In categorizing the French missionaries as martyrs, however, the church stretched the classical definition of the term, which required not only that the Christian had been executed by hostile forces but also that the murderer had been acting *in odium fidei* (in hatred of the faith). Certainly Jogues, Goupil, and their confreres understood themselves as martyrs. They expected and welcomed death, viewing it as a small price to pay to secure not only their individual salvation but also the transplantation of Christianity on a new continent. But as

Emma Anderson has pointed out, modern Catholic proclamations of martyr-dom tend "to assume or impose rather than to truly investigate the motives" of the murderers. In the case of the slain Jesuits, indigenous people viewed them as hostile invaders determined to eradicate their culture. It is also possible to view their deaths as casualties of what Anderson describes as "a decade of carnage and confusion" against a backdrop of "debilitating epidemics, war, and the so-cial, cultural, and religious changes that accompanied European contact" with aboriginal nations.[39] In this case, Anderson points out, "centuries of hagiogra-phers have simply imputed the necessary anti-Christian animus onto the native slayers of the North American martyrs."[40] In the late nineteenth century, when a growing Catholic publishing industry disseminated detailed accounts of the martyrs' gruesome deaths, their stories were viewed as the ultimate proof of Catholic holiness on the American periphery. Rev. Clarence A. Walworth, a diocesan priest from Albany (and the uncle of Ellen Walworth, Tekakwitha's modern biographer), expressed this conviction in dramatic verse:

> Say not America's saints are all foreign
> That martyrs have left no rich blood on our sod
> On the atlas of souls Lake George is the high road
> Of heroes that hastened to die for God.[41]

Saint-seeking necessarily involves marketing. Even with substantial congre-gational backing and attention, causes rarely succeed unless they are able to generate attention beyond their petitioners. In the case of Tekakwitha and the martyrs, a discovery in the early 1880s helped supporters make the critical leap to garnering national attention. Thanks to the collective effort of historians, archeologists, and Jesuits, the Mohawk village of Ossernon—by then known as Auriesville, New York—was identified as the precise site of Jogues and Goupil's martyrdom and Tekakwitha's birth. This discovery energized Joseph Loyzance, SJ, the martyrs' American vice-postulator, who built a shrine on the site dedi-cated to the Blessed Mother under her title "Our Lady of the Martyrs."[42] This nomenclature was necessary according to a provision in canon law that reserved public veneration only for the canonized. As is the case today, before Vatican of-ficials could formally investigate a cause for canonization, diocesan courts had to certify that no public veneration of the candidate had taken place. In the first issue of *Pilgrim of Our Lady of Martyrs*, the devotional published monthly at the shrine, the Jesuits emphasized that while the site was intended to keep fresh the memory of Jogues and Goupil, "it will in no religious sense be dedicated to their honor. It is entirely under the invocation of her whose rosary was in the hands—and the name of whose Son, Jesus, was on the lips—of René Goupil, when he was struck dead at the village gate."[43]

Loyzance's efforts demonstrated the possibility, indeed the necessity, of promoting the cause as far as possible without cultivating "public" veneration. The inaugural Mass at the shrine, which took place on 15 August 1885, struck this careful balance. The feast being observed was that of the Assumption of Mary, and accordingly the Mass was in her honor; however, the Jesuits also designed the celebration to call attention to the lives and deaths of the prospective saints, especially by organizing a pilgrimage to the shrine that its sponsors proclaimed to be "the first of its kind in the United States." John Gilmary Shea, who attended the inaugural Mass along with thousands of others from Troy and nearby villages, praised it as a "truly pious and edifying" spectacle such as "the Church in this country had never before witnessed." Other participants welcomed the shrine as a "guarantee of what God will do in this place as He has done in Lourdes in our own day and as He will continue to do abundantly for the sanctification of our beautiful America."[44] The reference, of course, was to Lourdes, France, where in 1858 a peasant girl had reported apparitions of the Blessed Virgin. Devotion to our Lady of Lourdes quickly spread throughout world with the help of Catholic missionaries.[45]

The comparisons between Auriesville and Lourdes, like the search for an American saint itself, captured U.S. Catholics' spiritual longing for official validation of their nation's homegrown holiness. Supporters of the shrine would continue to characterize the site as an American Lourdes, occasionally with qualifications, but invariably with great optimism that Auriesville would eventually rival Lourdes in terms of pilgrims, miracles, and renown. If it seemed presumptuous to compare an internationally known shrine in the heart of Catholic Europe to a humble temporary chapel in a missionary outpost of the church, Auriesville's sponsors pointed out that people had once asked, "What good can come out of Nazareth?"[46] Like their broader quest for an American saint, U.S. Catholics' grandiose aspirations for an American Lourdes stemmed from their desire for holy people and places they could claim as their own.[47]

While the comparison with Lourdes pleased many American Catholics, it troubled some of their Protestant fellow citizens. "A *shrine* is to be found in the heart of our most populous State," warned one horrified writer, "and we shall soon, doubtless, see deluded pilgrims flocking to it by the hundred, just as now they crowd the roads to Knock and Lourdes and La Salette."[48] The writer's disdain points to a second reason why U.S. saint-seekers felt closely allied to their Canadian counterparts: both groups agreed that the long-standing suspicion of saints in Protestant Anglophone cultures would make pursuing a saint's cause even more difficult. Shea identified the challenge explicitly: to elevate either an American or a Canadian to the altars of sainthood, he claimed, North American Catholics would have to contend with "a Protestant supremacy" in the first instance and "a Protestant government" in the second.[49] Even so, Shea and others had their reasons to believe that the pursuit of a North American saint might not only persuade the larger Catholic church of American holiness but also actually help diminish Protestants' suspicions of all things Catholic, a proposition that, implausible at first glance, nonetheless galvanized U.S. Catholic saint-seekers.

Patron Saints of U.S. Patriotism

While the U.S. bishops' 1884 petition on behalf of Tekakwitha, Jogues, and Goupil prompted celebrations among many U.S. Catholics, it generated concern in some non-Catholic circles. Protestants who paid attention to such matters also recognized the petition as a major step on the road to naming a national patron, alarming many of them who had long hoped that the United States would remain untainted by canonization and all it implied. Viewing an "American saint" as a travesty if not an outright contradiction in terms, Robert Breckinridge had "beseech[ed] God" in 1841 that "no American papist may ever be corrupt, debased, and infamous enough during his life, to be esteemed by Rome worthy of being a saint in her calendar after his death."[50] Writing in direct response to the 1884 petition, the editors of the *Methodist Review* urged all "thoughtful Protestants" to beware of what it portended and to remember that the movement to canonize so-called Americans reached "beyond the pale of the Romish Church."[51]

The editors apparently did not find it necessary to elaborate on the reasons why thoughtful Protestants should object to a prospective U.S. saint, assuming the potential dangers would have been obvious enough to their Methodist readers. The Reformation-era accusation that veneration of saints amounted to idolatry routinely surfaced in Protestant America. According to a mid-nineteenth-century writer in the *Princeton Review*, "The Pagan prays to dead men," while "the Papist prays to dead men and women." Other critics objected to the elaborate ceremonies that accompanied both canonization and beatification. On a visit to Rome in 1888, Jane Addams attended the beatification of a Capuchin monk and found it "absurd . . . to connect all this pageant pride with the religion which Christ himself taught." Still others doubted the scientific accuracy of the process. One U.S. historian insisted that "Protestants and other rationalistically minded persons" would investigate reported miracles far more thoroughly than the members of the Sacred Congregation of Rites did.[52]

Some U.S. Catholics, aware of the manifest contempt with which many of their fellow citizens viewed saints and saint-seeking, despaired of ever securing a patron to call their own. Canonization "smacks too much of Rome," one woman observed, making it impossible for U.S. Catholics to venerate even the "old saints" properly, let alone voice public support for the elevation of new ones.[53] Yet by the late nineteenth century, an increasing number of Catholics began to argue precisely the opposite: that, by seeking and finding a saint of their own, they could weave their religion more seamlessly into the American fabric. Given the contentious history of sainthood, the reasoning behind this proposition was not immediately apparent. Canonization, after all, connoted miracles, relics, and Vatican investigations, all of which accentuated Catholics' Roman identity over their American one.

Viewed more broadly, however, it made sense that saint-seeking emerged as an instrument of Americanization during this period. Since the early nineteenth century, ethnic parishes named for St. Bridget, St. Hedwig, or other European national patrons had helped Catholics forge cohesive communities and ease newcomers' transition to the United States. Long conditioned to view saints as intermediaries not only between heaven and earth but also between a minority church and a hostile host culture, U.S. Catholics moved logically from a reliance on transplanted saints to the embrace of homegrown ones.

Although a lengthy and rigorous process awaited any would-be American saint, some U.S. Catholics realized that the extensive documentation and publicity could advance the cause of Americanizing Catholics. No one grasped this potential benefit better than John Gilmary Shea, whose desire for a North American saint sprang from a scholarly as well as a spiritual impulse. If Shea felt slighted by the Vatican's sluggishness in formally acknowledging the holiness of the early missionaries to New France, he was positively outraged by what he viewed as his fellow scholars' tendency to minimize the missionaries' role in the history of North America. Shea believed that the "religious predilections" or "incomplete reading" of most U.S. historians had caused them to misrepresent the American past, and he became the leading spokesman for a group of Catholic scholars determined to reorient the nation's founding narrative away from the Puritans and Plymouth Rock and toward the Catholic origins of America.[54] Shea and other Catholic historians were gratified that Protestant historians such as George Bancroft and Francis Parkman had included the Jesuit missionaries in their respective histories of New France. Parkman had described Jogues as "one of the purest examples of Roman Catholic virtue which this Western continent has seen," and Catholic authors often quoted this line, citing it as evidence that even Protestants connected Catholicism with the origins of American virtue and civilization.[55]

Yet Shea and other Catholic writers also criticized what they perceived as the anti-Catholic biases embedded in Parkman's and Bancroft's accounts. Seeking to correct errors based on "false, unjust, even calumnious ideas," they crafted an alternative version of the nation's history that stressed Catholics' long presence in North America and their role in "civilizing" and exploring the continent. In these narratives, French missionaries emerged as the pioneering Christian proselytizers who had arrived "long before Pilgrim Fathers landed at Plymouth Rock" and had "become American to win Americans for Christ."[56] In this sense, Shea and other Catholic scholars saw the documentation marshaled to promote American saints not only as evidence for individuals' virtue but as chapters in "the Catholic pages of American history."[57]

While professional church historians looked to the canonization *process* to accelerate Catholics' Americanization, some other church leaders believed that the very *purpose* of canonization—the creation of new models—would be a boon to that cause. An American saint could potentially provide a double model that could both convince Vatican officials that holiness could indeed thrive in a religiously diverse culture and persuade a skeptical Protestant public that Catholics could be loyal American citizens. Archbishop John Ireland of St. Paul, Minnesota, a leading figure among the "Americanist" bishops, never missed a chance to highlight Catholicism's compatibility with American citizenship, and canonization presented a particularly enticing opportunity to do so. Speaking in 1897 at an event honoring Joan of Arc in her native France, Archbishop Ireland proclaimed her "the patron saint of patriotism," arguing that her life proved it was both possible and necessary for Catholics to "love [both] country and Church with undying affection." By increasing their own devotion to Joan, he insisted, U.S. Catholics could "consecrate" the love they had for their country and broadcast that patriotism to their non-Catholic fellow citizens.[58]

If Ireland believed that recasting a European saint in the image of an American patriot would help convince Protestants of Catholics' nationalism, he looked toward the canonization of an actual American as an even more effective strategy for doing so. Ireland anticipated the day when U.S. Catholics could celebrate "a Saint, enthroned on our altars . . . whose name at once commands respect and admiration" from American Protestants.[59] Even bishops who disagreed with Ireland on other fronts shared his view that prospective saints offered effective vehicles to integrate Catholics into American life. Archbishop Michael Corrigan of New York, a prominent opponent of the Americanists, arranged for statues of Isaac Jogues and Tekakwitha to be placed at Dunwoodie, his new diocesan seminary in Yonkers, as a sign that "this great training school for the priesthood [would be] a thoroughly American institution in every way."[60]

Even as the men and women who emerged as early favorites in the quest for the first North American saint met certain criteria for holiness, they also presented a model of Catholicism that their supporters believed would appeal to American Protestants. This points to a distinction between the saints of the Old World and the earliest contenders for the patrons of the New: while U.S. Catholics had embraced the former to retain bonds with the world many of them had left behind, they chose the latter to disassociate themselves from it. As Allan Greer has argued, church leaders may have seen the early choice of Tekakwitha as a prospective patron as a preemptive strike against Protestant perceptions of European Catholic immigrants as alien invaders. Charting her "post-mortem naturalization" as an American citizen, Greer attributed her popularity in the 1880s to her emergence as the "perfect antidote" to nativist perceptions of the church as foreign, industrial, and urban. In proposing Tekakwitha as a saint, he writes, U.S. Catholics were trying to "solidify the church's position in a predominantly Protestant society with pronounced anti-Papist traditions" by proposing an "American saint who could symbolically root the Church in American soil."[61] The perspective of the editors of the *Methodist Review* suggests that church leaders had indeed chosen their first candidates wisely. Though the petition on behalf of Tekakwitha and the North American martyrs had disturbed the editors, they were more concerned the next batch of prospective American saints might be "more closely allied in race to the present superstitious masses of our country—genuine Catholics, of Irish or Italian extraction, perhaps."[62]

The nineteenth- and early twentieth-century arguments in favor of particular candidates for sainthood were clearly shaped by a long-standing Catholic belief that early missionaries were engaged in a salvific and civilizing venture, rather than operating as extensions of colonizing powers.[63] The preponderance of French missionaries among the early U.S. favorites rested in large part on perceptions of the French as educated and cultured—which in the context of the period also made them ideal counterpoints to the new arrivals from Italy, Poland, and elsewhere who were linked in most Americans' minds to urbanization and industrialization. Catholics routinely characterized Jogues and Goupil as "men of exquisite culture and refinement."[64] The Jesuit missionaries of the seventeenth century were, in other words, cast as men of culture who bore little resemblance to the "superstitious masses" criticized by the editors of the *Methodist Review*.

U.S. saint-seekers also claimed credit for French missionaries' civilization-building in what later became Canada. They supported the causes of two French-born women who had ministered in seventeenth-century Québec: Ursuline Mary of the Incarnation and Marguerite Bourgeoys, founder of the Sisters of the Congregation of Notre Dame. U.S. Catholic publications celebrated both women, arguing that their stories both testified to American sanctity and documented Catholics' role in establishing civilization in North America.[65]

The links between Catholic sanctity and American civilization also figured prominently in the hagiographies of nineteenth-century French missionaries, many of whom had been inspired by the martyrs' stories. Advocates for Philippine Duchesne, for example, praised her for bringing the civilizing impulse she had cultivated in Grenoble to the wild Missouri frontier.[66] Supporters made similar arguments about Duchesne's counterpart in Indiana, Mother Théodore Guérin, a native of Étables who arrived in the Indiana wilderness in 1840 and built dozens of hospitals and schools under the auspices of her congregation, the Sisters of Providence.[67] By the 1890s, Guérin was being praised as "a woman of magnificent education" who, in the best American tradition, had transformed a rustic log cabin church into "a handsome structure of brick and stone, the most beautiful church in Indiana ... valued at somewhere in the neighborhood of a million dollars."[68]

Guérin's story was distinguished from Duchesne's in one remarkable aspect, the details of which were included in a biography that Sister of Providence Mary Theodosia Mug published in 1904. Mug recounted the serious troubles Guérin had had with the bishop of the Diocese of Vincennes, Indiana, Célestine de la Hailandière. He had controverted Guérin's authority in a number of ways: replacing her as superior during her return to France, ordering the sisters to staff a new school, and forcing them to admit postulants they found unacceptable. Hailandière grew increasingly erratic between 1845 and 1847 and accused Guérin of conspiring against him and stealing money. Finally, in April 1847, during her courtesy visit to his residence in Vincennes, Hailandière removed Guérin as superior, forbade her to return to St. Mary of the Woods, dispensed her from her vows, threatened her with excommunication, and locked her in his room until members from her convent obtained her release. Exhausted by the conflict and gravely ill, Guérin resolved to leave Vincennes and start over in another diocese. Meanwhile, news came from Rome that Propaganda Fide had accepted Hailandière's letter of resignation a few months before. The bishop left Vincennes; Guérin and the Sisters of Providence stayed and flourished. Mug's inclusion of this conflict in Guérin's biography was unprecedented. Though adversarial relationships between sisters and their local ordinaries have since become a staple of Catholic historiography, in 1904 "the Catholic public was not accustomed to learning about behind-the-scenes conflicts reflecting badly on a bishop's behavior."[69]

It was even more remarkable, then, that Baltimore's James Gibbons, by this point elevated to the rank of cardinal, provided an introduction to Mug's book. While he obliquely referenced all that Guérin had suffered in her attempt to establish the Sisters of Providence in Indiana, he emphasized that her story affirmed how Catholic female missionaries had educated and civilized the American nation. He urged readers to capitalize on "the growing tendency of late to acknowledge woman's work in the domain of education" by calling attention to the role of Catholic sisters. "We American Catholics are proud of our country's rapid progress. Let us not forget the power that initiated and developed some of its grandest institutions."[70]

Another French missionary to the Midwest was Mathias Loras, a native of Lyon and the first bishop of Dubuque, Iowa. Loras was a favorite of Archbishop Ireland; in Loras's day, the Diocese of Dubuque had encompassed Minnesota, so Ireland was in fact supporting the canonization of a person he viewed as his predecessor, a pattern hardly unusual in saint-seeking. But Ireland also emphasized the national import of Loras's contribution and argued that promoting Loras's cause would inspire all Americans, Catholic and non-Catholic, to revere him for civilizing the "prairies and forests of the American west." Loras, like Duchesne and Guérin, was praised as an "uncanonized saint" who had not only embodied heroic virtues but used them to transform the American frontier.[71]

Americans had long believed that the frontier played a central role in the development of their national character, and thus casting Duchesne, Guérin, and Loras as civilizers of the West helped U.S. Catholics integrate their holy heroes into the foundations of American history. The same publications that promoted U.S. candidates for canonization referenced the work of historian Frederick Jackson Turner, whose "frontier thesis" argued that American democracy was born of the experience of westward movement across the continent. Near the turn of the century the *Catholic Journal* of Rochester, New York, published an excerpt from one of Turner's articles in the *Atlantic Monthly*, which laid out the "gifts of the West," including Jefferson, Jackson, Lincoln, and industrial power unmatched in the world. Could an American saint be one more "gift of the West"? Catholic leaders often made that case.[72]

Archbishop Ireland's Americanist inclinations also led him to promote the cause of another "pioneer priest" who had once worked within Loras's diocesan administration in Dubuque, Samuel Charles Mazzuchelli. Born in Milan in 1806, Mazzuchelli had given up a promising future in banking to enter the Dominican order in 1824.[73] Hearing his fellow Dominican Edward Fenwick, bishop of Cincinnati, speak of the need for missionaries in the expanding United States, Mazzuchelli left Italy and set out across the Atlantic later that year.[74] The Italian was ordained a priest in Cincinnati in 1830 and sent immediately to Mackinac, in the Michigan Territory, one of the most remote places in the diocese.[75] From his first posting, Mazzuchelli began a career of building churches, converting Native Americans, and shepherding flocks of European Americans on the frontier. In 1847, he founded the Congregation of the Most Holy Rosary of the Order of Preachers, more commonly known as the Sinsinawa Dominican sisters.[76] Mazzuchelli left his personal papers to the Sinsinawa Dominicans, and he urged them to preserve the records of their community "in an almost scrupulous manner." Their founder's wish, combined with the sisters' desire to promote his cause for canonization, prompted them to gather testimony about his virtues and to scour archives in Wisconsin and Italy for biographical information about him. The sisters' meticulousness in compiling these sources led subsequent advocates for Mazzuchelli's cause for canonization to praise their thoroughness and their "sense of history"—a compliment not often bestowed on U.S. petitioners.[77]

While the efforts of Sinsinawa Dominicans kept Mazzuchelli's memory alive at the local level, the critical leap to a more national following came early in the twentieth century, with the publication of an English translation of his *Memorie istoriche ed edificanti d'un missionário apostolico*, a memoir written during a trip to Italy to recruit missionaries and to raise funds. Translator Sister Mary Benedicta Kennedy, a Sinsinawa Dominican, declared that while the original edition had appeared in Italy in 1844, it concerned itself in "every line . . . with the people, the customs, and institutions of these United States." Mazzuchelli was not only a devoted and zealous missionary, she wrote, but also "an ardent admirer of this great Republic" who had "a prophetic vision of the place it was to occupy among the nations." Ireland expanded on this theme in an introduction to the volume, describing Mazzuchelli as a "saint, immaculate of life, scrupulous of duty, exquisite in tenderness of piety," whose passionate zeal for the church and for the salvation of souls had been limitless. According to Ireland, Mazzuchelli may have been a foreigner by birth and education, but "he was American to the core of his heart, to the tip of his finger. He understood America; he loved America." This "Builder of the West," he argued, had served not only God but the nation; it was his loyalty to and understanding of "the principles of American law and life that earned him the admiration of all of his fellow-citizens."[78]

If the causes Archbishop Ireland promoted illuminate his ideal "patron saint of patriotism," equally telling is a potential saint he refused to endorse. John Nepomucene Neumann was born in Prachatitz, Bohemia, in 1811 and studied for the priesthood at diocesan seminaries in Budweis and Prague. In 1836, the bishop of Budweis suspended ordinations temporarily because of a surfeit of candidates. Neumann left abruptly for New York, where Bishop John DuBois, in desperate need of priests for his sprawling diocese, ordained Neumann shortly after his arrival and sent him to Buffalo. In 1840, Neumann entered the Congregation of the Most Holy Redeemer, an Italian order more commonly known as Redemptorists. Following an untraditional novitiate (during the course of which he moved eight times and traveled three thousand miles), Neumann made his religious profession in Baltimore on 16 January 1842—the first Redemptorist to do so in the United States. He was assigned to parishes in Baltimore and Pittsburgh and served as superior of Redemptorists in the United States before his appointment as the fourth bishop of Philadelphia in 1852. Neumann was a fierce supporter of language preservation among European American Catholic immigrants. Already a polyglot upon his arrival in the

United States, he reportedly learned new languages to permit more immigrants to confess in their native tongues. As bishop, he championed national parishes and parochial schools and invited other European missionaries to staff them. He had planned to import a German congregation of Dominicans to Philadelphia, but while in Rome in 1854 for the proclamation of the Immaculate Conception, he learned that a Bavarian-born widow in Philadelphia wished to establish a new congregation of women religious. On the advice of Pius IX, he worked with her to start a Franciscan community within his own diocese.[79] Neumann died suddenly in 1860.

Seeking to open Neumann's cause in the 1880s, Redemptorists in Philadelphia solicited letters of endorsement from bishops throughout the United States, and while most complied, John Ireland pointedly refused. A firm supporter of English-speaking worship and cooperative efforts between public and private schools, Ireland was unlikely to champion a prospective American saint who had been so committed to national parishes and the preservation of native languages. Ireland acknowledged that Neumann had been "a holy man" but stipulated that he was "not one whom I would wish to see held up as an example to the country of what the priest and bishop should be."[80]

Ireland's objections were not enough to overcome Redemptorists' determination to see their first American member raised to the honors of the altar, and they situated his story in the context of nineteenth-century Catholic spirituality. Having died a natural, if premature, death, Neumann had not been martyred, but his devotees nonetheless praised his cheerful acceptance of suffering and his proclivity toward self-abnegation. One witness from Buffalo, New York, provided a particularly compelling insight into the high premium placed on self-denial. Asked whether Neumann had exhibited the virtue of temperance, he testified that although Neumann had lived in "the immediate neighborhood of the world-renowned Niagara Falls, [he] never looked at them."[81]

Several other early U.S. candidates for sainthood were also associated with the European Catholic missionary undertaking on the frontier. Of these, Slovenian missionary Frederic Baraga had assumed "a thirty-seven-year apostolate among the red-skinned inhabitants of Michigan and Northern Wisconsin," and his memoirs had helped awaken a missionary vocation among other European Catholics, including John Neumann.[82] Neumann was personally acquainted with Bavarian-born Francis Xavier Seelos, another Redemptorist missionary to the United States. Ordained in Baltimore in 1844, Seelos spent his first nine years as a priest in Pittsburgh, where he lived with John Neumann for several years. In the last five years of his life, Seelos traveled around the United States preaching missions, a specialty of the Redemptorists.[83] Seelos died of yellow fever in New Orleans in 1867, and the Redemptorists opened his cause for canonization soon after initiating Neumann's.[84]

Rounding out the list of prospective missionary saints were Felix de Andreis and Joseph Rosati, two Italian-born members of the Congregation of the Mission, more commonly known as the Vincentians, which had been founded by St. Vincent de Paul in France in 1625. In common with their French-born counterparts, Mazzuchelli, Neumann, Seelos, Baraga, de Andreis, and Rosati cut a striking contrast to the immigrants so disdained by many Protestants. All of these men, though born in eastern and southern Europe, had arrived in the United States long before the vast majority of migrants from those nations, and their hagiographies had foregrounded their experience in the rural Midwest rather than in the teeming tenements of the Northeast.[85]

Among the leading candidates for the first U.S. patron saint in the late nineteenth century, only one was unconnected to the European missionary enterprise: Elizabeth Ann Bayley Seton. Born in 1774, Bayley married merchant William Seton twenty years later. In 1803, financial troubles and William's tuberculosis led them and one of their five children to travel to Livorno, Italy, in the vain hope of restoring William's health. After William's death in that port city, brothers Filippo and Antonio Filicchi took his widow and child into their care. Seton had been forewarned by Rev. John Henry Hobart, her Episcopalian minister at New York's Trinity Church, not to let the "sumptuous and splendid worship" of Catholic Italy "withdraw her affections from the simple but affecting worship at Trinity."[86] Seton nevertheless found herself increasingly drawn to the Catholic pageantry and artwork she was exposed to during her Italian sojourn, and after her return to New York she engaged in an extended period of spiritual discernment. In conversation with Hobart and with the Filicchi brothers, she considered weighty theological questions that divided Episcopalians and Catholics, such as debates over apostolic succession and the real presence of Christ in the Eucharist. In the end, persuaded that the Catholic answers were the true ones, Seton made her profession of faith in the church of St. Peter's on Barclay Street in Lower Manhattan on 14 March 1805.

Seton's conversion distanced her from family and friends and compromised her efforts to earn a living by teaching children of the local Protestant elite.

Searching for a means to support her own sons and daughters, as well as for a climate more amenable to her new faith, Seton opened a school for girls in Baltimore, then the epicenter of the U.S. Catholic church. Under the guidance of William DuBourg, a member of the Society of Saint Sulpice and rector of St. Mary's Seminary, and Baltimore's John Carroll, the first U.S. Catholic bishop, Seton had welcomed other pious women into her home and began to consider forming a new religious congregation, or community of sisters in service to the church. "It is expected," she wrote to her sister-in-law in New York, that "I shall be the mother of many daughters."[87]

In the summer of 1809, Seton moved the fledgling community sixty miles north to Emmitsburg and became the first superior of the Sisters of Charity of St. Joseph. Though Seton used the rule of the French Daughters of Charity as a model, hers was the first women's religious community established in the United States without formal ties to a European congregation. By the time she died in 1821, the congregation had also established communities of sisters in Philadelphia and New York. Seton's renown continued to grow after her death as the Sisters of Charity expanded in numbers and geographical reach. Her fame even followed her grandson Robert to Rome, where he was studying in 1858 when he wrote to his older brother, William Jr.: "Without wishing to make you proud yet I can tell you that no name is better known among Catholics in America than that of Mrs. Seton, even just today an American bishop said before all my [classmates] that it was a name much loved in America."[88] This grandson later became a priest in the diocese of Newark, New Jersey, and eventually merited consecration as a titular archbishop.[89] Newark's first bishop, James Roosevelt Bayley, was another Seton relation.[90]

The publicity provided by Seton's biological descendants and her spiritual daughters in the Sisters of Charity helped to spread her reputation for holiness and therefore compensate for her anomalous status as a non-missionary among the first U.S. prospective saints. Having been a convert to Catholicism also explained why she became a popular candidate despite her failure to conform to the era's prevailing model of holiness. U.S. saint-seekers were candid about their expectation that Seton would appeal to U.S. Protestants, the second of their imagined audiences, because she had "started out as one of them."[91] Seton's supporters also routinely touted her connections to the "the great American families of Bayley, Seton, and Roosevelt," looking toward her future elevation to sainthood as the ultimate triumph over U.S. Protestant elites. Once the church canonized Seton, they predicted, Americans who had scorned Catholics and their saints would change their minds and rejoice in having "a saint of their blood."[92]

While they may have overestimated U.S. Protestants' investment in the quest for an American Catholic saint, Seton's supporters were correct that her lineage had already insulated her from the most virulent anti-Catholic prejudice of the nineteenth century. For one, the nursing services provided by Seton's Sisters of Charity and other Catholic women religious during the Civil War had helped diminish Protestant antipathy. In his otherwise unflattering appraisal of Roman Catholics in the *Atlantic Monthly*, published soon after the hostilities ended, James Parton reserved a few kind words for the Sisters of Charity, noting that "all the world approves and will ever approve" of them.[93] Other anti-Catholic screeds also presented Seton and her sisters as aberrations among Roman Catholics. As the *Ladies Repository* observed, "The term— Sister of Charity—is not synonymous with Papist, or the thick, impassable walls of a convent, and the utter annihilation of the human affections."[94]

Catholics made their own gender-based comparisons regarding Seton. In 1890, Paulist priest Walter Elliott contrasted Seton with the emerging "New Woman," arguing that while contemporary endeavors to improve women's condition were often misguided, Seton was anchored firmly to a long Catholic tradition and was therefore far more worthy of imitation than imprudent modern reformers.[95] In characterizing Seton this way, Elliott implemented a strategy commonly employed by church leaders in the nineteenth century, in which Catholic women were urged to model themselves on saints rather than on suffragists or other female reformers. One writer described St. Clare of Assisi as a trailblazer who was happier, more peaceful, and more worthy of imitation than were modern women influenced by the "feministic movement," while others suggested that St. Elizabeth of Hungary had developed a vision for social service six centuries before Jane Addams opened Hull House.[96]

Seton completes the list of early exemplars of American homegrown holiness, all of whom, to some extent, had embodied a model of U.S. Catholicism designed to appeal to American Protestants. Although it is difficult to gauge whether the search for a "patron saint of U.S. patriotism" improved U.S. Protestants' views of their Catholic fellow citizens, there were some tentative signs of non-Catholics' acceptance of and interest in American saints. John Gilmary Shea would have been heartened by J. Franklin Jameson's 1907 annual presidential address to the American Historical Association, in which he called for the "American *Acta Sanctorum*" and observed that a saint was at once "a member and a champion of the universal church" and "a man of his own country and age." The "chief saints of a nation," Jameson observed, "have come to that position through a congeniality with the nation's traits that has brought them its steady and natural veneration." Jameson reminded his fellow scholars of American history that their medieval and European counterparts had benefited a great deal from the work of hagiographers, and he urged them to look attentively to "the analogous body of material" at their disposal. To be sure, Jameson was using "saints" mostly in the Protestant sense of people who had lived true Christian lives close to God, but he mentioned a number of Catholic saints as well, citing Reuben Thwaites's recently published seventy-three-volume English edition of the *Jesuit Relations and Allied Documents* as a potentially valuable source. Jameson, in a sentence that could have been crafted by a U.S. Catholic saint-seeker, suggested that "the lives of the American saints may enlarge our knowledge of the social background, the substantial warp of our American fabric." Jameson cited "dexterity, versatility and practical efficiency" and "a cheerful and hopeful spirit" as the defining characteristics of an American saint.[97]

Saint-seekers were quick to cite examples of individual Protestants who helped advance U.S. causes. Jesuits in charge of promoting Jogues and Goupil, for example, often pointed to the support they had received from General John D. Clark, an expert in Indian remains who had collaborated with Shea and Walworth in determining the location of Jogues's martyrdom. They viewed Clark's willingness "to aid in any manner possible in the Beatification of Jogues and his companions" as affirmation of the widely held belief that Protestants who learned about the Catholic saints could not help but adopt them as their own heroes and heroines.[98]

That non-Catholic newspapers frequently reported favorably or without comment on the progress of American causes also suggests that many Protestants' fascination with the canonization process may have caused them to suspend their reservations about Catholic saints in general. Catholics often responded to these reports with the same mixture of pride and frustration that they showed toward Bancroft's and Parkman's histories: they were glad their compatriots were paying attention but complained that they had gotten the details wrong. Secular newspapers sometimes prematurely announced the "canonization" of an American saint, mistaking the transition to a new stage in the complicated canonization process for the actual completion of a cause. This happened repeatedly with John Neumann, prompting the editors of the *Baltimore Catholic Mirror* to caution American Catholics to "not look for Catholic news from secular papers, which for the most part strive after sensation rather than truth."[99] To be fair, non-Catholic reporters could hardly be blamed for misunderstanding the various stages in the complex canonization process. Its intricacies eluded most Catholics, including some of those charged with shepherding candidates through it.

To the Center

U.S. Catholics initiated their first causes of canonization just as the Holy See was attempting to codify its unwieldy and often poorly understood procedures. Though the 1917 Code of Canon Law, which included no fewer than forty-two canons on the saint-making process, spelled out the norms rather than simplified them, the path to canonization could be understood as having five major milestones.[100] The first of these was the opening of the "informative" or "ordinary" process in the diocese in which the candidate—called in this stage a "Servant of God"—had died. This initial phase had three separate components. In the first, the local bishop would convene an ecclesiastical fact-finding court under his own authority. In the presence of diocesan-appointed judges, each witness would take an oath of secrecy and give testimony about the candidate's virtues and any miracles attributed to his or her intercession. The information gathered would be transcribed, bound, sealed, and hand-delivered to the Sacred Congregation of Rites.

The second component of this stage, the *non-cultus*, investigated whether devotees of the Servant of God had ever crossed the aforementioned line between private and public veneration. An affirmative decision—that there had been no public cult—allowed the cause to move forward, while a discovery of evidence of public veneration put an immediate halt to it. This was the only step in a cause for canonization in which judgment was rendered by a diocesan court. The third part of the informative phase entailed collecting the writings of the Servant of God. One mid-twentieth-century account explained what this exhaustive search process required: "Sermons, letters, diaries, autobiographical writings, books—printed, hand-written or dictated—all must be investigated. Suppose you have a letter or a holy picture with a little message written by the holy person to you. You treasure it privately as a relic and are unwilling to part with it. What then? Too bad! The Promoter of the Faith may not come around with a gun, but he may 'search out' all pertinent documents and if he wants them, you will just have to make the sacrifice."[101]

Upon receipt of the required information, the Sacred Congregation would translate all relevant documents into Italian and certify that the three components of the ordinary process were in place. If the Sacred Congregation determined that a cause had at least a reasonable chance of succeeding, it was "introduced"—the second major milestone.

After a cause's official introduction, the Sacred Congregation would essentially repeat the ordinary process, this time under its own authority, in what was called the apostolic process. The Promoter of the Faith—a member of the Sacred Congregation more commonly known by his fearsome nickname, the "devil's advocate"—scrutinized that material and raised objections, each of which the postulator would attempt to rebut. These back-and-forth exchanges could go on for years. Only after the Promoter of the Faith was satisfied would the Holy See promulgate a "Decree of Heroic Virtue." At that point the Servant of God would be called "venerable."

It was at this stage that the search for miracles—unexplainable events, almost always a medical cure—would begin. The vice-postulator, who worked at the local level, would solicit reports of miracles and send promising ones on to the postulator in Rome, who would determine whether they were worthwhile to pursue. If so, the local bishop would convene another diocesan court, which interviewed the recipient of the miracle, witnesses, and medical experts. Supporting documentation was sent to Rome, where it would be scrutinized first by doctors. If the doctors judged the cure medically inexplicable, theologians would then consider the evidence to determine whether the cure could be accredited to the intercession of the saint in question. Affirmative decisions would be confirmed first by the Sacred Congregation and subsequently by the pope. The number of required miracles for beatification varied: one for a martyr, two for most causes based on eyewitness testimony, and up to four if no such testimony was available. Once the requisite number was reached, the venerable was beatified and called "blessed." Two more authenticated miracles, which must have occurred after the beatification, were required for canonization.

How long it takes to complete this process varied widely, as it continues to do under the present guidelines, which have been in force since 1983. In 2012, Cardinal Angelo Amato, then the prefect of the Congregation for the Causes of Saints, observed that "it depends on the adequacy of the preparation, elaboration, and maturation. There is no fixed time." According to Amato, canonization "is a divine project" and the "time and ways of [a cause's] maturation are often beyond our grasp."[102] Amato's caution notwithstanding, canonization is also a human project. As two case studies from the United States show, error and sin often intrude upon it in ways that can affect its progress.

The first ordinary process that was opened in the United States was undertaken on behalf of John Neumann in Philadelphia in 1886. Three judges, a secretary, and a "Promoter of the Faith" heard testimony from forty-seven witnesses about his virtues and miracles, resulting in 1,223 pages of documentation bound into four volumes. Along with material gathered in separate ordinary processes in Neumann's native Budweis and in Rome, which he had visited in 1854, the material was hand-delivered to the Holy See, thus marking the first transferal of an ordinary process from the United States to the Sacred Congregation. The Catholic press presented this landmark deposit and the official "introduction" of Neumann's cause in 1895 as events of such consequence that they should gratify "all true lovers of our country." That Rome had agreed to consider "a citizen of this our Republic" for its highest honor proved that "America is not ungenerous soil for the cultivation of true Christian virtue and for the production of heroes of sanctity."[103]

U.S. outlets continued to report steady progress in Neumann's cause.[104] What those positive reports did not reveal, however, was that Roman reviewers had been distressed to find in the Philadelphia testimony abundant procedural errors, improperly formulated questions, and vague answers. More ominously, the substance of Neumann's case was also giving them pause. Canonization was meant to recognize those who had practiced virtues to an extraordinary degree, and the evidence suggested that Neumann had been, well, decidedly *ordinary*. He had clearly been a good person, but it was far from obvious to his Roman judges that he had done anything beyond what the church would expect of any bishop or member of a religious community. The Promoter of the Faith raised objection after objection, and the implications were plain: had U.S. Catholics been so desperate for a saint that they had nominated one who was so unremarkable that he stood little chance of success?[105]

It fell to Claudio and Arturo Benedetti, two Redemptorists who presented Neumann's cause in Rome, to respond to these critiques. For ten years, the brothers refuted every objection with a combination of fierce argumentation, rhetorical flourishes, circuitous reasoning, and prolonged appeals. The debate ended in high drama, when the brothers' most recalcitrant opponent literally dropped dead on the morning of the crucial vote.[106]

In the end Pope Benedict XV sided with the Benedetti brothers. In 1921, the pontiff proclaimed Neumann "venerable," certifying that he had practiced the virtues to a heroic degree. The pope explained that the key element of holiness was "the faithful, perpetual, and constant carrying out of the duties and obligations of one state of life," and by this measure, he believed that Neumann qualified. Against the allegation that Neumann's holiness was "simple" or "ordinary," the pope wrote that "the most simple of works, if carried out with constant perfection in the midst of inevitable difficulties, can bring every Servant of God to the attainment of a heroic degree of virtue." Quotidian holiness, in other words, was not necessarily a barrier to canonization.[107]

Having passed this hurdle, the Redemptorists promoting Neumann were optimistic that his cause would move along with alacrity. Neumann's vice-postulator in Philadelphia had accumulated a stockpile of reported miracles and predicted that two of them would be certified within four years.[108] Instead, largely because of American inexperience, it would take over four decades. An Italian Redemptorist would later refer to Neumann's cause as the most complicated in the entire history of the congregation.[109]

Even so, Neumann's path to official sainthood looked smooth compared to that of Elizabeth Ann Seton. Her story, in fact, turned an axiom of canonization—that membership in a religious order increases the likelihood of success—on its head. The problem arose not from an event during Seton's life but from a conflict that began a quarter century after her death, at approximately the same time of her first exhumation. The trouble started in New York City, where Seton had first sent the first Sisters of Charity from Emmitsburg in 1817. By the 1840s, the community's decision to enforce the rule that the sisters were not to care for boys over the age of seven in asylums or schools irritated New York's fiery archbishop, John Hughes. In Hughes's view, the sisters' stubbornness both undermined his attempt to open more parochial schools and challenged his episcopal authority. In 1846 Hughes forced each sister to make a choice: stay in New York, withdraw from the Emmitsburg-based Sisters of Charity of St. Joseph, and form a new diocesan community; or leave New York and remain with the Emmitsburg community.[110] Thirty-three of sixty-two women chose to stay in New York, and their splinter group became the Sisters of Charity of St. Vincent de Paul of New York, subject to the authority of Hughes and his successors. The separation was absolute, and the sisters who remained in New York were forbidden to have further contact with the community at Emmitsburg.[111]

Meanwhile, the Emmitsburg-based Sisters of Charity, at the behest of their clerical advisers, had begun to seek unification with the Daughters of Charity of St. Vincent de Paul in France—the very community that Seton had once looked to as a guide. In 1850, the Emmitsburg community formally joined the Paris-based international community and became the Daughters of Charity Province of the United States, thereby becoming official members of the Vincentian Family, which also included the all-male Congregation of the Mission.[112]

From that point on, the sisters at Emmitsburg were known as the Daughters of Charity. They also changed their manner of dress, adopting the attire worn by the French community, including their rather elaborate headgear, the "cornette." Originally adapted from the sunbonnet of peasant women in Brittany and starched heavily, resulting in "wings" swept upward, the cornette became a distinctive feature of the members of the Daughters of Charity. The community that had chosen to stay in New York retained the name "Sisters of Charity"—though with "of New York" appended to the title—and the original dress of the community, which included a small black cap commonly worn by widows during Seton's lifetime. This diocesan community was accordingly nicknamed the "Black Caps."

It was not long before Seton's spiritual family tree became even more intricate. The most complicated offshoot sprouted in Cincinnati, where the Sisters of Charity had been established since 1829. In 1852, the Cincinnati community separated from Emmitsburg, citing concerns that the union with France would force the sisters to change the work they did in their local missions. They also objected to the union on the grounds that affiliation with the French community contravened Seton's original wishes, maintaining that she had been a thoroughly American woman who fiercely opposed foreign control of the congregation.[113]

In 1856, the Sisters of Charity of New York sent members to form a new diocesan community in Halifax, Nova Scotia, and three years later representatives of the Cincinnati and New York Sisters of Charity formed a new diocesan community in Convent Station, New Jersey, in response to the invitation of Newark's first bishop and Seton's half-nephew James Roosevelt Bayley. In 1870, the foundation of the Sisters of Charity of Seton Hill in the diocese of Greensburg, Pennsylvania, brought to six the total of separate congregations that considered Seton their founder (figure 1).[114]

The original New York–Emmitsburg rupture and subsequent developments had launched Seton's spiritual daughters onto two separate paths. The Emmitsburg sisters were distinguished from members of the diocesan communities not

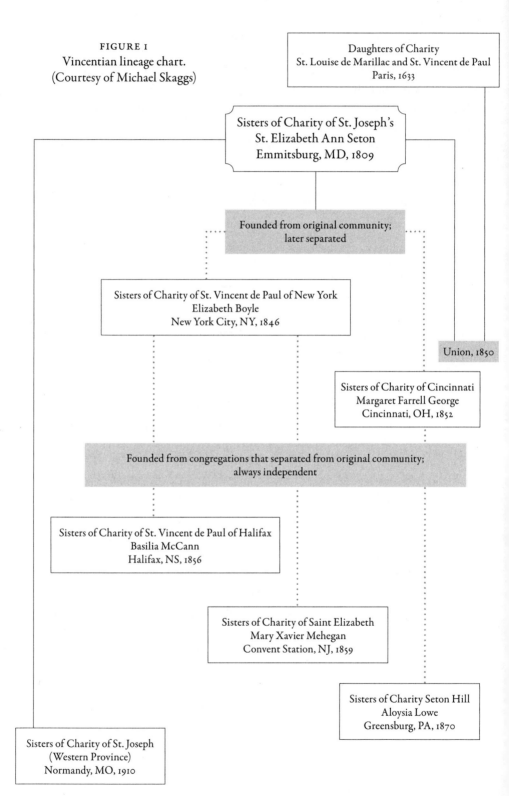

FIGURE I
Vincentian lineage chart.
(Courtesy of Michael Skaggs)

Daughters of Charity
St. Louise de Marillac and St. Vincent de Paul
Paris, 1633

Sisters of Charity of St. Joseph's
St. Elizabeth Ann Seton
Emmitsburg, MD, 1809

Founded from original community;
later separated

Sisters of Charity of St. Vincent de Paul of New York
Elizabeth Boyle
New York City, NY, 1846

Union, 1850

Sisters of Charity of Cincinnati
Margaret Farrell George
Cincinnati, OH, 1852

Founded from congregations that separated from original community;
always independent

Sisters of Charity of St. Vincent de Paul of Halifax
Basilia McCann
Halifax, NS, 1856

Sisters of Charity of Saint Elizabeth
Mary Xavier Mehegan
Convent Station, NJ, 1859

Sisters of Charity Seton Hill
Aloysia Lowe
Greensburg, PA, 1870

Sisters of Charity of St. Joseph
(Western Province)
Normandy, MO, 1910

only in name and dress but also in their respective institutional memories of their founder. The Emmitsburg-based Daughters of Charity understood Seton to have been a loyal daughter of St. Vincent who would have viewed formal affiliation with the French Daughters as the realization of her greatest dream. Rev. Charles White's 1853 biography, *The Life of Mrs. Eliza A. Seton*, proved critical in making this case. According to White's account, only political upheaval in France had prevented a more formal alliance: the government of Napoleon Bonaparte had refused to issue passports to several French Daughters, thereby preventing them from traveling to Emmitsburg to join and presumably to supervise Seton and her sisters. A French missionary priest had obtained a copy of the Daughters' rule, though, and carried it to Maryland, where Seton used it as a model for the Sisters of Charity of St. Joseph. According to White, the Emmitsburg community's incorporation into the Vincentian Family had long been "earnestly desired and fondly expected," and its fulfillment represented "the most important event connected with the recent history of the society in this country."[115]

The diocesan or "Black Cap" communities, on the other hand, subscribed to the Cincinnati sisters' argument that Seton would have opposed the union with France and believed themselves to be Seton's authentic spiritual heirs.[116] Throughout the nineteenth century there was no need to reconcile these competing narratives, as there was little contact between the various communities. Had Seton never emerged as a candidate for canonization, these opposing viewpoints might have continued to coexist in perpetuity. Canonization, however, requires a single story, and Seton's supporters would need to agree on one before her cause could succeed.

The first sign that this would be the case appeared during the preparations for the ordinary process, when it became necessary to stipulate who, exactly, would serve as Seton's petitioners. There was no question that Emmitsburg, the place where she died, would be the epicenter. What was up for discussion was the extent to which the multiple diocesan communities who considered Seton a founder would participate. Not only did these communities have a stake in Seton's cause, but their very existence lent the cause a tremendous practical advantage. Founders of religious communities are often granted an exemption from one of the required miracles—again, something that could accelerate a cause. Whereas Seton was clearly not a founder of the Daughters of Charity, which had originated in France in the seventeenth century, she was certainly the founder of the diocesan communities that grew from her initial foundation.

There appears to have been some debate over whether and how to enlist the support of the various diocesan communities in this early stage of the process. Infrequent contact and geographical distance would have made coordination very difficult, and ultimately the decision was left not to the sisters themselves but to their ecclesiastical superiors and the male proxies who would represent them as petitioners of Seton's cause—in this case, their brothers in the Vincentian Family, the members of the Congregation of the Mission. In 1897, after deliberating the matter, Vincentian superiors and the congregational postulator decided that the Daughters of Charity should become the sole sponsors: "The responsibility should rest on St. Joseph's, Emmitsburg, as the Institution founded by Mother Seton and her home during the closing years of her life."[117]

In normal circumstances, being under the oversight of a European-based congregation would have been a boon to the U.S.-based petitioners; as in Neumann's case, more experienced European counterparts could compensate for U.S. Catholics' missteps and apply steady pressure in Rome. Seton's situation, however, was far from normal, and when it came to pursuing her cause, her posthumous entrance into the Vincentian Family—in the sense that the Emmitsburg sisters' formal union with the French Daughters had occurred almost thirty years after Seton's death—created more problems than it solved. In sharp contrast to the Redemptorists, who were fiercely committed to Neumann's saintly success, the Vincentians had less incentive to make Seton's cause a priority. The congregation was simultaneously sponsoring Louise de Marillac, the cofounder of the Daughters of Charity, and Catherine Labouré, a French Daughter of Charity who had seen apparitions of the Blessed Virgin Mary and Christ and who had received the Miraculous Medal. Most of the congregation's saint-seeking energy was thus channeled toward the causes of two French women with impeccable Vincentian bona fides rather than that of an American daughter who had adapted and modified the Vincentian rule. Although this lackluster French interest would eventually turn out to be the least of the obstacles presented by Seton's ambiguous status within the Vincentian Family, early on it played a role in delaying the opening of her ordinary process.[118] Years passed without any significant movement.

Seton's ordinary process did not commence until 1907, a full quarter-century after Gibbons's exhortation at her grave. The only witness who had known Seton personally was a ninety-six-year-old widow named Esther Kearney Barry, who had come to the school at Emmitsburg at the age of nine. "Though I was but a child then," she claimed, "the impression is as fresh today on my mind as it was then."[119] The lack of detail in Barry's testimony suggested otherwise, and the Sacred Congregation would subsequently dismiss her contribution as worthless.[120] Equally unimpressive was Barry's response to the standard question of whether and why she supported Seton's cause canonization: "Yes," she said, "because she deserves it." The fundamental flaw of this response, from a theological point of view, is that the purpose of canonization is to use the saint's life to glorify God, not to glorify the saint herself.[121] By contrast, Daughters of Charity gave theologically impeccable responses to the same question: Sister Augustine Park, for example, desired Seton's beatification and canonization "because it will redound to the glory of God—and because we will have another intercessor in Heaven—and because her good example, as a woman of the world, will be better known." Sister Margaret O'Keefe echoed Park in insisting that while she, too, "was greatly desirous" of Seton's canonization, "the thought of any honor for our religious community has not entered my mind." Ernest Lagarde, professor of modern languages and English literature at Mount Saint Mary's in Emmitsburg, was perhaps more honest about having mixed motives, confessing that in "most ardently" desiring Seton's beatification and canonization his impulse was "very strongly patriotic," though he also believed that Seton's elevation would contribute to the "advancement of our holy religion in the United States of America."[122] Cardinal Gibbons's testimony seconded that of Lagarde. In a reformulation of the argument he had made at Emmitsburg in 1882, Gibbons explained that he "desired most earnestly" Seton's beatification not only because of his personal conviction of her sanctity but also because she was "an American Lady, of American ancestry and parentage." Persuaded that the canonization of the first American-born person would "contribute very much to the greater glory of God in this country," Gibbons further argued that it would "quicken the zeal not only of the Sisters of Charity" but also of "the immense army of teaching sisters now laboring in the United States."[123]

Cardinal Gibbons additionally testified that his knowledge of Seton had come from Father Charles White, who had baptized him and for whom he retained a lifelong affection.[124] Most of the other witnesses also referenced White's biography as their primary source of knowledge about Seton.[125] In this way, the ordinary process reproduced White's version of events regarding the relationship with the French Daughters of Charity: namely, that "the tyranny of the times and the then rulers of France" had prevented the French sisters from coming to Emmitsburg, thus thwarting a more formal alliance.[126] The Daughters of Charity interviewed for the investigation also confirmed that the original community at Emmitsburg had followed the French rule scrupulously from the time of its founding.[127]

Even as the official documentation for Seton's cause was being prepared, however, disagreement over what Seton would have thought of the union with France was becoming public, as were debates over whether the "Black Caps" or "Cornettes" had a greater claim as Seton's direct heirs. In 1917, Sister Mary Agnes McCann, a member of the Sisters of Charity of Cincinnati, published a history of the community in which she took exception to the insinuations that Seton had always longed for affiliation with the Daughters of Charity. On the contrary, McCann claimed, Seton had fiercely relished her independence and therefore would have been appalled by the union with the Daughters. "Every founder of a religious order has a distinctive badge and Rules peculiar to the country and the times," McCann wrote. It was very clear to her that Seton, intending the "community to be one suited to the needs of the new country," had resisted the clerical superiors when they raised the possibility of affiliating with France. Had the New York and Cincinnati sisters followed Emmitsburg's example and aligned themselves with France, McCann asked, "what would there be now to show the work of Mother Seton?" As a French import, she argued, the Daughters of Charity did not have a unique meaning for the United States. It was only in founding an indigenous, independent community that Seton had represented "a brilliant type of the truest American."[128]

Noting that "the Catholic World is at present interested in the Beatification of Elizabeth Ann Seton," McCann implied that the case for Seton as an American saint rested heavily on the history of the communities that had remained independent, rather than on the French-affiliated Daughters at Emmitsburg. Yet none of the diocesan sisters testified in Seton's ordinary process. This omission also undermined Seton's credibility as a "founder," which would have made her eligible for the miracle exemption. Eventually Seton's petitioners would need to reconcile this discrepancy, but for the time being the preparation of her ordinary process was proving challenging enough.[129]

All told, the diocesan court investigating Seton's virtues met in eighty-one sessions between 1907 and 1911. The testimony, along with supporting documentation, was transcribed and bound into four volumes that totaled 1,288 pages. The problem was that this covered only one-third of the requirements of the ordinary process. The sources of the lapse remain unclear, but once the Archdiocese of Baltimore learned about the missing *non-cultus*—the declaration that public veneration had not yet arisen around Seton—it authorized another diocesan court in August 1914. Six Daughters of Charity, including one who had been present when Seton's body was transferred to a new tomb in 1877 (to accommodate Archbishop Bayley's request that he be buried next to his beloved aunt), reported that there was "no large concourse of people at the exhumation." Another sister testified that she had never encountered a sign of public worship at her frequent visits to Seton's tomb. Relics had not been venerated, she insisted, and no votive offerings had been placed. The process of *non-cultus* was not officially closed until 1920; why it took six years to complete is also unclear, though some sources vaguely blamed "the war." Whatever had delayed the cause, Cardinal Gibbons signed the 229 pages that constituted this part of the process, and the volume was sent to Rome.[130]

Gibbons's death the following year meant that it would fall to his successor to receive the next installment of bad news from Rome: the informative process was still missing Seton's collected writings. The Archdiocese of Baltimore convened yet another session of the diocesan court and appointed Charles Souvay, a French-born Vincentian priest and seminary professor, to gather and catalog Seton's writings.[131] By this point Souvay had already established himself as an authority on Seton's life and a strong proponent of her canonization. He devoted a great deal of time to the technical question of her baptism. While it was assumed she had been baptized soon after her birth in Trinity Church, where her family worshipped, any record of that had apparently been lost in 1776, when a fire swept through southern Manhattan and destroyed Trinity's baptismal registers. This lack of documentary evidence presented a problem, as unbaptized persons cannot be canonized.[132]

Souvay had also emerged as the primary challenger of Sister Mary Agnes McCann, and he decried her counternarrative in print and in public. During an address to the Sisters of Charity at Convent Station, New Jersey, for example, the Vincentian urged them to disregard the version of history rendered by their Cincinnati sister. He lambasted McCann's study as "woefully incomplete in the documentation, lame in the interpretation of the documents cited, illogical in the argumentation. It is irretrievably biased, and lacking in poise, equanimity, and dispassionateness."[133] To Souvay the matter was clear. While he allowed that Seton had "never actually belonged to the Religious Family of St. Vincent de Paul," he claimed that, in this case, "intention ought to be regarded as the equivalent of action." Seton, he insisted, had never wished the American community to be independent. As proof of this, he reproduced White's original explanation—namely, that several Daughters of Charity had been "already *en route* for America" when they "were prevented from sailing by Napoleon," leaving the "young Community" to organize itself.[134]

For the moment, the debate over Seton's intentions was isolated to the American side of the Atlantic. Souvay scoured archives in Baltimore, Emmitsburg, and Cincinnati and traveled to Livorno, Italy, the site of the Filicchi home and the city near where her husband had died, in search of additional writings by Seton. His findings were compiled in thirteen volumes and sent to Rome in 1925, completing the ordinary process at last.[135] It was time to wait for the Sacred Congregation to review the material and decide whether it would be "introduced" in Rome.

If Neumann's and Seton's causes point to the elements that can go wrong in a cause for canonization, the North American martyrs' cause illustrates what happens when the process goes well. By the time Seton's ordinary process closed, the cause of the martyrs, including Jogues and Goupil, had advanced considerably. In part, the martyrs' swift progress was a natural consequence of the Jesuits' influence and experience in promoting their own. Certainly no other prospective American saints had anything comparable to the Shrine of Our Lady of the Martyrs to help buttress their cause. The shrine helped to advance the Jesuits' cause materially and spiritually by providing a place to send financial contributions and to pray for and report miracles and favors that devotees believed the martyrs had granted through their intercession with God. Five years after its inaugural issue, the *Pilgrim of Our Lady of Martyrs* reported that the shrine drew visitors from within a fifty-mile radius of Auriesville, and the monthly journal itself extended considerably the reach of the devotion.[136]

Having a brilliant and indefatigable person at the helm also helped. The Jesuit John Wynne, director of the martyrs' shrine and their vice-postulator, stands out among American saint-seekers for his firm grasp of the canonization process. At the close of the ordinary process in 1904, Wynne allowed that it had been "a long and tedious labor" but dared hope "that the end will bring the reward sought, namely, the canonization of Father Jogues and his companions. The evidence has been furnished. It remains for the cardinals to decide the merits of the facts presented. America has done its part."[137] In this case, at least, America had done its part rather well, and the cause proceeded smoothly.

A final advantage for the North American martyrs was the aforementioned martyrdom exemption. In 1925, the Sacred Congregation issued a decree of beatification for the eight men. Beatification is more than a simple precursor to canonization in that it permits limited public veneration to the new blessed among a specified segment of the local church, usually Catholics within a particular diocese or religious congregation. Canonization, the final step, then broadens the right of veneration by making it incumbent upon the universal church. One nineteenth-century Catholic expert explained the distinction this way: "Beatification is permissive; canonization is mandatory. The former is special and local, the latter general."[138]

In the case of the North American martyrs, the Sacred Congregation extended the right of public veneration to an unusually wide range of people. It permitted Catholics within all Canadian dioceses and dioceses in the state of New York to solemnly mark the martyrs' beatification and celebrate their feast days. According to Wynne, this gesture reflected the Vatican's awareness that the canonization of the Jesuit martyrs would have special meaning for Catholics in both Canada and the United States. Wynne urged U.S. Catholics to embrace the Jesuit martyrs as saints of their own. Considering the enthusiasm that U.S. Catholics had evinced for the cause at the outset, one might have expected them to do so.[139] But a great deal had changed on the American periphery since the U.S. bishops had sent the first petition on behalf of Tekakwitha, Jogues, and Goupil in 1884, and those changes affected how Catholics greeted the news of the martyrs' beatification.

And Back Again

The most significant change involved an increase of national identity among U.S. Catholics. In 1908, the Holy See's Apostolic Constitution *Sapienti consilio* had reclassified the American Catholic church from a "mission territory" into a national church, thus placing the church in the United States under the responsibility of the Vatican's secretary of state. Broader world events had also contributed to the sense of national identity. During World War I, for example, U.S. bishops had created the National Catholic War Council to coordinate the war efforts of diverse Catholic groups. After the armistice, in the face of opposition from Rome and from a number of U.S. bishops who feared that it would undermine their authority in individual dioceses, Cardinal Gibbons decided to make the organization permanent. Explaining his reasoning, Gibbons made clear that church leaders and laity had become convinced that they were a group whose voice should not be ignored: "The Catholic Church in America, partly through defective organization, is not exerting the influence which it ought to exert in proportion to our numbers and the individual prominence of our people." The National Catholic War Council, Gibbons argued, would provide a "unified force that might be directed to the furthering of those general policies which are vital to all."[140]

U.S. Catholics' growing confidence on the national stage manifested itself in journals such as the Jesuit weekly *America*, which Wynne had established in 1909. *America* sought to insert a distinctively Catholic perspective on the nation's political, social, and intellectual life, and throughout the 1910s and 1920s the magazine increasingly lived up to its ambitious name, touting the possibilities that Catholicism and its teaching presented for the transformation of American society.

U.S. Catholic leaders had also grown in stature in the eyes of the Holy See. In 1911, Pope Pius X elevated two more U.S. bishops, New York's John Farley and Boston's William Henry O'Connell, to the rank of cardinal. They were part of a coterie of U.S. bishops who, throughout their careers, cultivated *romanità*—a kind of Vatican ecclesiastical spirit, or doing things "the Roman way"—both by visiting the Eternal City often and by sending diocesan seminarians to study there. Dennis Dougherty, archbishop of Philadelphia between 1918 and 1951, represented a quintessentially "Romanized" bishop. Dougherty had studied in Rome and served as a bishop in the Philippines and in Buffalo, New York, before his appointment in Philadelphia. "It would be difficult to exaggerate," wrote one historian, "the effect that Rome had upon Cardinal Dougherty." He traveled frequently to the Eternal City, where he relished the pomp and the pasta in equal measure.[141] George Mundelein of Chicago and Patrick Hayes of New York, both elevated to the cardinalate in 1924, also exercised decisive influence during this era of Romanization.

It is important not to overstate the U.S. cardinals' influence in Rome in the first quarter of the twentieth century, during which they played only a minimal role in the task reserved exclusively for cardinals: electing new popes. In 1903, following the death of Leo XIII, Gibbons had become the first U.S. bishop to participate in a conclave. The next two popes, however, were chosen with little or no American input. When Leo's successor, Pius X, died in 1914, two out of three eligible U.S. cardinals missed the conclave that elected Benedict XV, because they were not able to get to Rome in time to vote.[142] The same thing happened after Benedict's death in 1922. Although a provision had been made for latecomers to enter a conclave-in-process, Philadelphia's Dougherty and Boston's O'Connell arrived in Rome just as the bells announced the election of Cardinal Achille Ratti, archbishop of Milan, who took the name Pius XI.[143]

Despite these missed opportunities, it was nonetheless clear that by the 1920s the U.S. church had gained what it had lacked in the late nineteenth century: powerful bishops who could lobby the Holy See in support of American priorities—the causes of U.S. candidates for canonization among them.[144] In the wake of the North American martyrs' beatification, in fact, John Wynne hoped to use Dougherty's influence and authoritarian style to the martyrs' advantage. Dougherty's response surely disappointed him.

The Sacred Congregation had decreed that U.S. Catholics outside of New York State would be permitted to solemnize the beatification provided their local ordinary submitted a petition to the Sacred Congregation asking to do so, and Wynne wrote to the Philadelphia archbishop several times beseeching him to make that request. Dougherty ignored Wynne for over a year, explaining later that he had not had the time. When he did respond, he referred to the cause as that of the "Canadian martyrs."[145]

Dougherty's word choice was merely one sign that the cooperative spirit between Canadian and U.S. saint-seekers that had been so decisive in the 1880s had eroded by the 1920s. The North American causes had become popular at a time when U.S. Catholics felt closely allied to their Canadian counterparts and relied on continental boundaries rather than national borders to define their American saint. By the time the martyrs were beatified in 1925, however, published material about the Jesuits increasingly presented them as belonging to Canada. One priest predicted—accurately, as it happened—that U.S. Catholics would be little interested in the martyrs because they had been "French" people whose exploits and adventures did "not touch Americans." Jesuit Michael Lyons admitted that his martyred confreres were "probably not sufficiently appreciated" by U.S. Catholics. Still Lyons appealed to his fellow citizens to "do all we can to promote the causes of those who have lived and died in *our* country." Others pointed out that none of the Jesuits had ever become "a naturalized citizen of the United States."[146]

Anachronisms are common in studies of canonization, but the observation that the French Jesuits had never become naturalized citizens of the United States, which was not founded until well over a century after their deaths, is particularly revealing. Rather than welcome the beatification of Jogues and Goupil as the fulfillment of the long search for their first saint, U.S. Catholics evidently interpreted it as reason to approach that quest with renewed vigor—and for an entirely different kind of saint. The quest for an American saint had been launched by narrowing the perspective from hemisphere to

Novena in Honor of
the only Saints of North America

✠

THIS novena is out of the ordinary. It is designed to honor the only Saints of North America, and through them obtain blessings.

There are eight Saints and each exemplifies one of the eight beatitudes: so for each a day is given with his sketch, medallion and beatitude.

The ninth day honors their saintly companions and heroic Indian converts not yet canonized, listing them with their ninth beatitude.

Each day records a blessing attributed to their intercession, two declared miracles by the Holy See.

Each day has its own prayer — of praise, thanksgiving, propitiation, petition — several from the Roman Missal.

FIGURE 2
Novena in Honor of the Only Saints of North America
pamphlet, 1930. (In possession of author)

continent; a half-century later, it narrowed again, from continent to nation. Saint-seekers now had a new target: a canonized saint who labored under the "Stars and Stripes."[147]

Wynne, undeterred by his fellow citizens' apathy and Dougherty's nonchalance, persisted in his quest. The martyrs' cause continued to move quickly, and in 1930, with two authenticated miracles to their credit (significantly, both involving Canadians), the North American Jesuits were canonized by Pope Pius XI. By elevating them to the roster of universal saints, the event meant that U.S. Catholics no longer required a special dispensation to venerate the martyrs publicly. Wynne urged them to celebrate their feast days, erect statues or altars in their honor, and invoke their intercession publicly. He published a new biography of the Jesuit martyrs and distributed pamphlets with a special novena in their honor but soon expressed frustration that U.S. Catholics' were not paying enough attention to the new saints. "It is a pity the Martyrs are not better known," he lamented in a letter to American pastors. "It took time and labor to bring about their canonization. It is well worth the time and labor to have our people know and invoke them." Wynne certainly did his part. In 1937, he sent reminders about Jogues's feast day to every U.S. bishop along with the nation's 13,500 pastors and 800 school leaders.[148]

Throughout the 1930s, Wynne would promote the martyred Jesuits as the "*only* saints of North America" (figure 2).[149] Yet it soon became clear that they would not lay claim to that distinction much longer. Thanks to developments both in Rome and in the United States, American causes for canonization would advance more rapidly during the 1930s than they had in any other decade since the quest for a U.S. patron saint had been launched half a century before. Which saints U.S. Catholics supported, however, would say more about their own priorities than they would about the lives of the saints they embraced.

2

✦ NATION SAINTS ✦

"More candidates for beatification than ever before!" So read a 1937 headline in *Queen's Work*, a Catholic monthly magazine based in St. Louis. The November issue featured an interview with Rev. Carlo Miccinelli, SJ, one of thirty full-time postulators at the Vatican's Sacred Congregation of Rites charged with guiding causes through the canonization process. A sharp increase in the number of new candidates had left Miccinelli and his colleagues overworked yet inspired: "Let those talk badly of the world who want to," he challenged. "The fact remains that more people are being introduced for canonization than ever before."[1]

There were certainly reasons enough to talk badly of the world in the 1930s, a decade unsettled by worldwide depression and the rise of fascism in Europe. As Miccinelli suggested, saints offered Catholics a unique source of solace and inspiration during troubling times. Another Jesuit, an American named John LaFarge, often used the lives of the saints as a point of reference throughout the Depression years. In articles he published in *America*, LaFarge reminded Catholics that saints not only could help them land "safely in eternity" but were available to assist them in establishing a just and equitable social order on earth. Because the lives of the saints were often "marvelously, providentially adapted to the problems of our times," it made sense to LaFarge and other Catholics that the church would be recognizing more of them during a period when the world seemed particularly bleak.[2]

Whatever the faithful may have believed, however, divine reassurance was not solely responsible for the uptick Miccinelli described. It could also be traced to temporal developments such as Pius XI's elevation to the papacy in 1922. The new pope would demonstrate far more interest in canonization than had his immediate predecessors. Soon after his election, Pius XI accelerated the path to sainthood for Thérèse of Lisieux, a French contemplative nun who had died in 1897 and whose devotees knew her as the Little Flower. Although canon law stipulated that the church could not begin an official investigation into a candidate's "heroic virtues" until fifty years after his or her death, popes were free to dispense with that requirement, and Pius, recognizing widespread devotion to Thérèse, beatified her in 1923.[3]

Pius XI also contributed to the increase in the number of causes for canonization by adding a new element to the process. On 6 February 1930, Pius issued *Già da qualche tempo*, an apostolic letter (known technically as a *motu proprio*, as it was issued "on his own will," with no need for justification whatsoever) that established a Historical Section within the Sacred Congregation to oversee causes for which no eyewitness testimony was available.[4] Developed in response to advancements in the discipline of historical criticism, this innovation signaled the beginning of a "change in mentality, in the sense of a growing historical consciousness at all levels," which would culminate in a major revision of the canonization process in 1983. More immediately, the creation of the Historical Section made it possible for petitioners to introduce causes for candidates who had died long ago or to revive causes that had stalled due to insufficient eyewitness testimony or the passage of time. This structural change helps to explain why Pius XI, who remained on the papal throne until 1939, named twenty-eight new saints, while his two immediate predecessors had canonized only seven between 1903 and 1922.[5]

Softening diplomatic relations between the Holy See and the Italian government during the 1920s may also help to account for the proliferation of new causes. Italy's 1870 takeover of the Papal States had created a diplomatic crisis that held popes "prisoner" in the Vatican and ensured that canonization would be overshadowed by more pressing priorities. As negotiations between Pius XI and Italian officials moved gradually toward resolution, however, observers saw a correlation between an independent Vatican and a greater openness to naming saints. When Pius XI canonized the Little Flower in 1925, some Catholics viewed the illumination of the dome of St. Peter's for the occasion, the first time since 1870 that the basilica was "visible for miles around the city of Rome," as an indication of "the possible resumption of political relations between the Vatican and the government of Italy."[6] Four years later, Pius XI and Benito

Mussolini signed the Lateran Pacts, establishing diplomatic relations between the Holy See and Italy and limiting the pope's temporal authority to Vatican City.[7] By permitting Vatican officials to focus more of their attention on the Holy See's ordinary business, this truce may have indirectly helped accelerate the pace of canonization in the 1930s.

This generally more favorable saint-making climate in Rome was part of the reason why Miccinelli had such good news to share with U.S. saint-seekers in 1937. The Sacred Congregation of Rites was at that moment considering a dozen American causes—more than three times the number under Roman review at the start of the twentieth century. Yet this vast increase could not be attributed to Miccinelli's hard work or even the pope's activism, which alone could not have done much to advance the quest for the first U.S. saint. According to a story then circulating in the United States, Pius XI had approached the prefect of the Sacred Congregation of Rites shortly after his election to ask, "Why can't you give me an American saint?" The prefect's simple answer was, "I can't give you one until they give me one." If the pope's query confirmed U.S. Catholics' conviction that Rome was "very happy, perhaps anxious," to name an American saint, the prefect's answer underscored a reality of canonization: no matter how receptive the center, the responsibility for initiating, supporting, and presenting a cause to the Vatican for consideration belongs with petitioners on the periphery.[8]

By the 1930s, American saint-seekers had gained a number of advantages over those who had first set this quest in motion. The U.S. hierarchy had become both better organized at home and more influential in Rome. Whereas only one man at the Third Plenary Council of Baltimore in 1884 had been designated a cardinal, Pius XI's 1924 elevation of Chicago's George Mundelein and New York's Patrick Hayes gave the United States, with Philadelphia's Dennis Dougherty and Boston's William Henry O'Connell, a total of four cardinals.[9] Each enjoyed an extensive network at the Vatican that they could tap to support canonization campaigns. Although Dougherty may have rebuffed John Wynne's request to promote the Jesuit martyrs, he did not hesitate to throw his formidable episcopal weight behind a number of other causes in which he had a vested interest.[10]

U.S. saint-seekers acquired an even more powerful ally with the 1933 appointment of Amleto Cicognani as apostolic delegate to the United States. Although Cicognani acknowledged that some Europeans looked askance at U.S. Catholics' quest for a native patron, believing it "rather presumptuous that a young nation should seek to have its own [causes] of beatification and canonization," he considered it his mandate to prove them wrong.[11] Cicognani readily placed his diplomatic skills at the service of U.S. Catholics' saint-seeking aspirations, corresponding regularly with sponsors of open U.S. causes and often supervising aspects of the process. Cicognani's advocacy, combined with the collective and individual influence exerted by U.S. cardinals, would help facilitate the necessary transatlantic connections required to deliver American causes to Rome, putting what in 1884 had seemed to U.S. Catholics like a distant dream—a canonized saint of their own—now well within their grasp.

Who would that saint be? For his part, John Wynne fully expected Kateri Tekakwitha to capture the honor. North American Jesuits, having deferred pursuit of her cause until the canonization of their own confreres, made it a priority after 1930. Wynne, who now served as Tekakwitha's vice-postulator, prepared her *positio* according to the guidelines of the new Historical Section of the Sacred Congregation. Its creation had proved a boon to Tekakwitha's cause, which had foundered due to a lack of supporting documentation. By 1932, Wynne reported that at least eighteen miracles ostensibly had been wrought through the intercession of the Mohawk virgin, including a promising one involving the cure of a Fordham football player.[12]

Dispatches from Rome convinced Wynne that his efforts would soon bear fruit. The "Huron Indian girl" was the lone American named by Miccinelli in his interview with *Queen's Work*. Identifying her as the most promising of American candidates, Miccinelli reported that her cause was "arousing considerable interest and hope" in Rome; the semi-official Vatican newspaper, for example, had devoted a front-page story to it. Amleto Cicognani confirmed Tekakwitha's popularity in Vatican circles, attributing it to the publication of an Italian-language biography and to his own efforts on behalf of her cause.[13] Wynne reported that Tekakwitha's piety had impressed Monsignor Carlo Salotti, a lawyer from the Sacred Congregation of Rites who would become its prefect in 1938. Salotti had described her cause as "one of the most beautiful that I have ever known" and boasted of his own success in "making her admired and appreciated by the entire Congregation."[14] All of this news, of course, heartened John Wynne, and throughout the 1930s his confidence in Tekakwitha's imminent canonization tempered his disappointment over U.S. Catholics' evident disinterest in the newly canonized Jesuits.

In retrospect, Wynne would have done well to pay less attention to bulletins from Rome and listen more carefully to what one of his Jesuit confreres was saying—or, more to the point, was not saying—when he made the era's most impassioned plea for the elevation of a U.S. saint. Although Leonard Feeney, SJ, is now best remembered for the unorthodox theological views that led to his excommunication in the 1950s, in the 1930s Feeney was solidly in the church's good graces and the American Catholic mainstream.[15] Through his essays in *America*, where he served as literary editor, and from the pulpit at New York's St. Patrick's Cathedral, where he frequently delivered riveting sermons, Feeney expounded on what he declared to be the essential harmony between Catholic beliefs and American ideals. In one widely publicized homily at St. Patrick's in 1936, he allowed that this compatibility often eluded outsiders: "In Europe they think we cannot be good Catholics because we are Americans. Here they think we cannot be good Americans because we are Catholics." Canonization, Feeney suggested, could help correct both misconceptions. "An American saint taken right out of our midst" would create a formidable symbol of harmony between church and state; "nothing," he insisted, "will do so much good for the Church in this country."[16]

Feeney's call for a "saint taken right out of our midst" echoed the bishops' 1884 petition on Tekakwitha's behalf and evoked John Gilmary Shea's 1890 plea for saints "who lived and labored and sanctified themselves in our land, among circumstances familiar." Similar language, however, belied considerable differences between Feeney's approach to saint-seeking and that of those who had first launched the quest. While they shared a belief that an American saint would affirm U.S. Catholics as believers and citizens, they disagreed about which candidates best embodied homegrown holiness. When Shea, for example, had written those words, he was deeply engaged in his crusade to promote the Jesuit martyrs and the Lily of the Mohawks. By the time Feeney delivered his homily, the Jesuits had been canonized for six years and, according to Vatican sources, Tekakwitha was well on her way. Considering Feeney mentioned neither in exhortation in St. Patrick's Cathedral, his lament appeared to signify what U.S. Catholics' lackluster response to the "Canadian" martyrs had already made clear: none of Shea's original favorites would capture the affection of a new generation of saint-seekers.[17]

Like John LaFarge, Feeney believed that saints were marvelously and providentially adapted to the times. As other parts of his homily made clear, the times had changed a great deal since the late nineteenth century. Shea, the architect of a hagiography that foregrounded colonial missionaries on a remote frontier, would have been startled by Feeney's prediction that a "St. Michael of

New York, St. John of the Bronx or St. Mary of Jersey City" would soon join Rose of Lima, Anthony of Padua, and others on the roster of the canonized saints.[18] Neither would the first U.S. saint-seekers have resonated with other traits of Feeney's ideal patron: a saint who would be "a subject of our nation . . . [who] spoke our idiom, was familiar with our occupations; someone whose house we can point out, whose photograph we can show." Feeney's homily thus signaled both continuity and change in the search for an American saint. While the passage of time may not have diminished U.S. Catholics' desire for a saint whom they recognized as familiar, it did transform what U.S. Catholics perceived as familiar.

Feeney's exhortation in St. Patrick's Cathedral was not an isolated example; other U.S. Catholics, too, clamored for saints better fashioned to the spirit of the age. Transformations in the church and the nation would prompt U.S. Catholics to tell a new American story about themselves that, even among the anxieties of the interwar period, testified to Catholics' optimism about America and their place in it. This new narrative, in turn, would affect which U.S. causes—ones long underway as well as those more recently introduced—moved forward during the mid-twentieth century. Neither Vatican insiders nor the American faithful alone would determine which U.S. cause for canonization would succeed next. As U.S. Catholics continued to search for a national patron saint, they would discover that the stories of some holy men and women could be easily rendered in the American idiom. The lives of others, by contrast, would be lost in translation.

Not a New Deal but a New Ideal of Sainthood

Soon after his appointment as apostolic delegate, Amleto Cicognani corresponded with both the Sacred Congregation of Rites and with religious congregations in the United States to ascertain the present status of causes already underway. In 1939, he published the results of his research in *Sanctity in America*, a compilation of biographical sketches of sixteen "Servants of God whose sanctity has enriched this nation," which Cicognani hoped would "blaze the way" for their canonization. Ordinary processes had already been undertaken on behalf of many of the candidates but had stalled by the 1930s. In the case of Elizabeth Ann Seton, the delay had been caused by omissions in the ordinary process. For Francis Xavier Seelos, the Bavarian-born Redemptorist missionary, the suspension seemed to reflect congregational priorities, as Seelos's postulator had taken no further steps since depositing the results of five separate ordinary processes at the Sacred Congregation in 1903. This was in contrast to the aggressiveness with which Redemptorists had promoted the cause of Seelos's Bohemian-born counterpart, John Neumann, who had been declared venerable in 1921.[19]

The preponderance of European missionaries among the early U.S. candidates was evident in Cicognani's research; fourteen of the sixteen entries in *Sanctity in America* belonged to them. Cicognani's cursory biographical sketches often elided the complicated history behind the subjects. Describing Mother Théodore Guérin's missionary work, for example, Cicognani reported only that the founder had endured "great trials" in Indiana and that the Diocese of Indianapolis had gathered testimony for an ordinary process in 1909. A notable witness had been her biographer Mother Mary Theodosia Mug, who had testified forthrightly that the bishop of Vincennes had been responsible for Guérin's greatest trials. When the bishop had ordered her to leave, Mug recounted, Guérin had calmly responded, "God sent me here, and until He makes known to me by my Superiors in France that His will calls me elsewhere, I shall stay at the place He has assigned me." Mug and other sisters offered Guérin's fortitude in the face of her suffering as evidence of her virtues. By the time she testified, Mug had received a special affirmation of Guérin's closeness to God: in 1908, Mug's debilitating stomach tumor had disappeared overnight after she invoked Guérin's intercession.[20]

In Guérin's case and others, Cicognani's inquiries appeared to breathe new life into causes that had not moved forward, often for reasons that had eluded the petitioners. The Sisters of Providence in Indiana, for instance, had mistakenly assumed that equivalent ordinary processes had been undertaken by the dioceses in France where Guérin had lived. Once Cicognani's probing revealed the omission, the Diocese of Indianapolis sent a priest to Rome to "ascertain what remained yet to be done." The diocese compiled additional testimony from France and submitted the completed ordinary process in 1937.[21]

Sanctity in America referenced the recently canonized North American Jesuits, but the apostolic delegate took pains to emphasize that other religious congregations had also supplied "heroes of sanctity among the pioneers of the Gospel in this land." In particular, he highlighted the contribution of the Franciscans, a congregation that proposed a number of its own members in the late 1920s and 1930s. Many Franciscan causes were spearheaded by Marion Habig, OFM, a Franciscan priest and historian. Like John Gilmary Shea in a previous generation, Habig was determined to write a version of U.S. history that foregrounded Catholics' contribution to the nation's past. Unlike Shea, Habig restricted his list of saints to those who had died only "within the present day confines of the United States," a move undoubtedly intended to privilege the North American presence of the Franciscans over the Jesuits. Inter-congregational competition, a perennial prompt and product of the saint-making process, clearly provided one impetus for Habig's quest. In contrast to the Jesuits, whose main foothold had been in New France, the Franciscans had established missions throughout what became the southern and southwestern United States, and Habig's campaign strongly asserted Franciscans' primacy in the American story. Although he acknowledged that "other religious orders have likewise labored valiantly" in North America, Habig maintained that "if we consider the pioneers in the field, the extent and duration of the missions, and the number of their personnel, the Franciscans undoubtedly hold the foremost position in the missionary annals of North America."[22]

Among the Franciscan causes Cicognani profiled, the one that would gain the most traction in the United States belonged to Junípero Serra, a Spanish missionary friar who established nine missions in California between 1769 and his death in 1784. Historians and at least one California bishop had expressed some interest in introducing Serra's cause in the early twentieth century, but real movement started in the late 1920s, ostensibly in advance of the sesquicentennial of Serra's death in 1934, although the attention garnered by the Jesuit martyrs may have also inspired Franciscans to act on behalf of one of their own. In 1931, the state of California commissioned a statue of Serra to stand in National Statuary Hall in the nation's Capitol Building, which also helped affirm the friar's historical significance.[23]

Another Franciscan featured in *Sanctity in America* was Leo Heinrichs, a German-born Franciscan missionary who had worked in Paterson, New Jersey, and Denver, where he had been shot in the chest by an Italian anarchist in January 1908. Local Catholics and his Franciscan confreres remembered Heinrichs as a martyr, and in the late 1920s the Diocese of Denver conducted an ordinary process on his virtues and reputation for sanctity, as well as a separate inquiry into his martyrdom.[24]

The Franciscan cause that revealed the most about the tenor of this period was perhaps that of "Martyrs of the United States of America," a group of 116 men who had died between 1542 and 1886.[25] The causes that are proposed during a particular era are often even more revelatory than those that are already underway, and that is the case in this instance. Though the vast majority of these men had been Franciscans, the primary unifying thread among them was the location of their deaths: all had occurred within the present boundaries of the United States. Bishop John Mark Gannon of Erie, Pennsylvania, the U.S. martyrs' champion among the U.S. hierarchy, admitted that his fervent support of the cause had been inspired by the attention paid to the North American Jesuits. The beatification of the U.S. martyrs, Gannon insisted, would bring a particular "honor to our beloved country." The idea of bundling together all the men, who had died in places scattered around the United States, appears to have originated with John Wynne, who throughout the 1930s and 1940s readily advised other U.S. petitioners seeking to initiate or advance causes for canonization. Wynne's success in shepherding the North American Jesuits placed his service in high demand, and his invariably generous responses to requests to share his expertise reflected his conviction that the canonization of one American would increase rather than diminish the likelihood of another. Saint-making, he understood, was not a zero-sum game.[26]

By 1939, Gannon had persuaded his fellow Pennsylvanian Cardinal Dougherty of Philadelphia to assist him in generating a petition on behalf of the martyrs at the annual meeting of the U.S. bishops.[27] As had been the case at the Third Plenary Council in 1884, the bishops' discussion resulted in a unanimous petition to the Holy See. Now much shrewder about the process, however, church leaders took the additional step of assembling a committee devoted to advancing the cause. With Gannon as chair, the Commission for the Cause for Canonization of the Martyrs of the United States also included Habig and Wynne. In 1941, the commission completed a detailed report that relied heavily on Habig's research and chronicled the lives and often gruesome deaths of the men. Gannon delivered the report to Dougherty, who signed it on behalf of all U.S. bishops and forwarded it to Rome along with his own letter of support. In a delay that canonization veterans would not have found surprising, two years elapsed before the Sacred Congregation even acknowledged receipt of the file. Though the delay was officially blamed on the outbreak of World War II, it was also prompted by various missteps and lapses of communication. American Catholics remained saint-seeking novices, after all.[28]

The false starts in Rome frustrated Gannon, but the martyrs' failure to capture the American imagination vexed him even more. Before long, Gannon began to sound much like John Wynne on the subject of colonial martyrs: he chided U.S. Catholics for not invoking their intercession frequently enough and for failing to make them more widely known. Gannon also blamed the U.S. martyrs' failure to progress on an incompatibility between Americans' characteristic restlessness and Vatican protocol: "The fault is with Americans themselves," he declared to a group of Catholic editors and publishers in 1939. "We are not sufficiently patient to persevere through the long, tedious processes established by the Church."[29]

Gannon was further discouraged when, as some supporters of the cause had feared, the Sacred Congregation judged the evidence too thin to warrant a joint pursuit of a single cause for the 116 men. Instead, officials recommended dividing them into subgroups, compiling separate supporting documents for each group. This would have created a herculean task, but, more to the point, if Habig, Gannon, and others had already experienced difficulty generating enthusiasm for the large group, it seemed unlikely they could stir up much interest in the martyrs in smaller batches. The U.S. martyrs effectively became a "cold cause" in the Sacred Congregation of Rites, though Gannon would continue to promote the cause until his death in 1968. The U.S. martyrs, it seemed, were doubly doomed: to grisly deaths in North America and to obscurity in their American afterlives.[30]

The aloofness of American audiences to the U.S. martyrs baffled Gannon and other supporters of the cause. Given that U.S. Catholics had appeared to dismiss the Jesuit martyrs largely on the grounds of their Canadian connection, their subsequent failure to embrace candidates who hailed exclusively from within the nation's "present confines" was on the surface a bit puzzling. Gannon himself unwittingly supplied part of the explanation for U.S. Catholics' lack of interest via a history lesson he delivered to the pope soon after World War II, when he was still optimistic that the pontiff's support would salvage the cause. In explaining to the pope how U.S. Catholics of the mid-twentieth century had changed, Gannon was hoping to inspire the pope to advance the cause of the U.S. martyrs. He was unaware that the very transformations he described had hagiographical implications and would explain why U.S. Catholics of the period never mustered much interest in the martyrs' cause.

"You realize, Your Holiness," Gannon said, "that millions of Catholic immigrants who moved from Europe to the United States during the past hundred years, reached the American shores without funds and were immediately compelled to seek work in order to subsist. . . . [They] were deprived of a college education, and the honors and privileges of the upper social classes." Presently, though, Gannon went on to say, "their descendants are in possession of colleges, universities, and a tremendous educational system, together with a brilliant core of scholars and a world renowned Hierarchy." With newfound leisure and resources, the American Catholic community was determined to "re-appraise the forces that fused to form the United States today."[31]

Whether the era's scholars and church leaders warranted Gannon's effusive praise is debatable. It was true, however, that the bishop had identified several key hallmarks of the U.S. Catholic community at midcentury: collective educational advancement, robust institutional expansion, rising wealth, and a steady decrease in the percentage of foreign-born Catholics in the United States. By the 1930s, the largest groups of nineteenth-century European immigrants were well into their second, third, or even fourth generation. The restrictive immigration legislation acts passed in 1921 and 1924 ensured that the 1930s was the first decade in over a century in which the U.S. Catholic Church could turn its attention to tasks other than absorbing thousands of new immigrants each year. Church resources flowed instead to massive building campaigns in cities and suburbs, prompting an institutional explosion that encompassed not only the colleges and universities mentioned by Gannon but also Catholic hospitals, parochial schools, and new church buildings.

Ambitious bishops often led aggressive building campaigns. Philadelphia's Dennis Dougherty earned his nickname of "God's Bricklayer" by opening ninety-two parishes, eighty-nine parish schools, three diocesan high schools, fourteen academies, a women's college, and a preparatory seminary in his first ten years as archbishop. In Philadelphia and elsewhere, collective increases in leisure, wealth, and ambition also facilitated a Catholic cultural expansion that matched the brick-and-mortar one in scope. As one historian of the 1920s and 1930s cannily observed, it was as if church leaders aspired to "make it possible for an American Catholic to carry out almost every activity of life—education, health care, marriage and social life, union membership, retirement and old age—within a distinctly Catholic environment."[32] The proliferation of groups such as the Catholic Educational Association, the American Catholic Historical Association, the Catholic Poetry Society, the Catholic Library Association, and the Catholic Book Club appeared to indicate that there was no occupation or endeavor that a Catholic perspective could not infuse or enhance. As Sister Madeleva Wolff, the poet-president of Saint Mary's College in Indiana, would observe, "There is a Catholic way to do every important thing in life."[33]

U.S. Catholics interpreted this institutional and organizational escalation both as evidence of their own vitality and as affirmation of the possibilities of the American enterprise. Indeed, scholar William Halsey has identified optimism as a singular attribute of Catholic Americans in the interwar period, arguing that their professional, social, intellectual, and religious subcultures insulated them from the discontent that gripped American culture more generally throughout this period. This attitude shaped the work of a number of U.S. Catholic reformers, who looked to Catholic teachings as the key to the transformation of modern society. Typical among them was *America*'s John LaFarge, who also founded the Catholic interracial movement. The solution to America's racial problems, he argued, could be found not in the principles of the U.S. Constitution but rather in the theology of the Catholic Church and the lives of its saints. In particular, LaFarge touted Martin de Porres, a Peruvian Dominican beatified in 1837, as an appropriate patron of social and interracial justice.[34]

Diminishing anti-Catholicism within U.S. society at large also buoyed U.S. Catholics' confidence during the interwar period. As the rhetoric surrounding Al Smith's 1928 presidential bid made clear, anti-Catholic bigotry had by no means disappeared from the American landscape. Still, there was no doubt that demographic transformations among U.S. Catholics, coupled with their distance from nineteenth-century immigrants, had diffused much of the fiercest religious prejudice. As one sign that antipathy to Catholics, and particularly to their saints, was less pronounced in American culture than it had been in earlier decades, U.S. Catholics cited the enthusiastic coverage of the 1925 canonization of the Little Flower in secular newspapers. Writing on the Fourth of July that year, the editors of *America* noted "with especial pleasure . . . the entrance of this most engaging Saint into the hearts of non-Catholics. It has been said that at least half the newspapers of the United States carried some part of the cabled account of her canonization and commented on it. Invariably the comment was respectful."[35]

A particularly public display of American Catholics' newly acquired confidence took place in June 1926, when the twenty-eighth International Eucharistic Congress convened in Chicago. This was the very first time the pilgrimage in honor of the Blessed Sacrament was held in the United States, and Chicago's archbishop, Cardinal George Mundelein, spared no expense or effort in making it as magnificent as possible. Ten Roman cardinals, including Giovanni Bonzano, Mundelein's friend and one of Cicognani's predecessors as apostolic delegate to the United States, sailed from Italy to New York, where they stayed with the city's Cardinal Patrick Hayes before embarking for Chicago on a special Pullman train, painted red and gold in their honor. As it sped toward its destination, the "Cardinals' Express" paused in several cities to greet cheering crowds in what Mundelein characterized as "unique demonstration[s] of Catholic faith, and, incidentally, Catholic strength."[36]

Mundelein greeted the train at a specially built station near Chicago's Holy Name Cathedral. A five-day celebration followed, including an open-air Mass at Soldier Field, candlelight vigils, and a final procession to the newly opened Mundelein Seminary on the city's outskirts. Hundreds of thousands of U.S. Catholics participated in the event, which both celebrated their connection with the Holy See and expressed their confidence in American culture and their place in it.[37] In so many of its aspects—visible Roman representation, exuberant public presence, and unabashed display of the Blessed Sacrament—the spectacle of the Eucharistic Congress would have been unimaginable even a few decades before, when papal representatives, displays of Catholic strength, and devotional practices provoked suspicion and anxiety in a largely Protestant public.

Bishop Gannon's ebullient postwar history lesson reflected U.S. Catholics' triumphalism. In order to reflect their new status within "the most powerful and leading nation on earth," he explained to the pontiff, U.S. Catholics were determined to "re-write the story of the origin and development of the United States of America." At the cornerstone of this revised narrative would be "the pioneer saints and martyrs who planted the seeds of our holy faith in what was once a pagan land." Therefore, Gannon explained, should Pius be inclined to extend to U.S. Catholics a "gesture of affection," they would find a papal nod to the U.S. martyrs a most welcome and appropriate salute.[38]

Gannon never wavered from his conviction that the U.S. martyrs were the logical national patrons. He assumed—wrongly, as it happened—that the saint-seekers of the mid-twentieth century would measure American holiness according to the same criteria their predecessors had adopted a half-century before. Obviously, Gannon realized that his contemporaries had tightened the focus of their ancestors' saintly lens, zooming in on country instead of continent—a geographic adjustment he believed could work only to the advantage of his favorite cause. In anticipating widespread support for the U.S. martyrs, however, Gannon had also been counting on thematic continuity. American sanctity, he believed, would remain the same in its essentials, embodied most perfectly by the men and women who had brought faith to heathens, forged civilization in the wilderness, and sacrificed their comfort and often their lives in the nation's colonial period. But Catholics' indifference to the U.S. martyrs was just one sign that the transformations Gannon described would lead them to support different saints. American holiness had not only narrowed geographically since 1884 but also shifted conceptually over the course of fifty years.

One U.S. priest, invoking the parlance of the day, echoed Leonard Feeney when he argued that what U.S. Catholics needed most in the Great Depression was not "a New Deal, but a New Ideal of Sainthood." Imagining a hagiography of the future that featured saints "using typewriters, adding machines, and automobiles," he joined Feeney and others in outlining a vision of American sanctity that differed markedly from the one that had emerged in the 1880s.[39]

Accounts of Feeney's "American Saint" homily appeared not only in Catholic newspapers but also in the *New York Times* and *Time* magazine. Editors of the latter even dared to propose their own candidates for canonization, naming Notre Dame football coach Knute Rockne, poet Joyce Kilmer, and military chaplain Rev. Francis P. Duffy as possible American patrons.[40] Although some Catholic leaders quickly dismissed such proposals as exhibits of "journalistic alacrity rather than theological sense," what had been true at the outset still applied: U.S. Catholics presumed that their national saints would speak to an audience beyond themselves.[41] What had changed was the message saint-seekers wanted to send to their fellow citizens. Whereas earlier generations of saint-seekers had seen in their quest an opportunity to prove their Americanness, Catholics in the 1930s viewed the canonization of one of their own as a chance to revel in the fact that they had done so. As U.S. Catholics' position in and perspective on American culture changed over the next half century, they would indeed create a "New Ideal of Sainthood"—one that privileged the saints who evoked transplantation of European Catholicism rather than the conversion of native people, who had braved Protestant scorn in urban centers rather than hostile heathens on a remote frontier, and who had, above all, embraced the nation rather than antedated it.

A Study in Contrasts

The contours of this interpretive shift can be seen more clearly in a comparison of the interwar trajectories of John Neumann and Philippine Duchesne. Unlike the U.S. martyrs, Neumann and Duchesne were not recent causes. They had emerged as candidates for American sainthood in the late nineteenth century, and, also unlike the U.S. martyrs, they had met with reasonable success at the Roman center. By the time Feeney delivered his homily, both Duchesne and Neumann had attained venerable status. Only one of their stories, however, would translate to the new American saint-seeking vernacular.

Exactly one century before Feeney called for an American saint from the pulpit at the "new" St. Patrick's on New York's Fifth Avenue, Bishop John Du-Bois had ordained Neumann on the site of the city's original cathedral on Mott Street.[42] The Bohemian native and future Philadelphia bishop had been a rough contemporary of Duchesne's, and their lives had paralleled each other's in striking ways. Both missionaries had been born in Europe during times of political upheaval. Both had found inspiration in the accounts produced by earlier generations of missionaries to North America, and both had encountered significant obstacles before finally following their heroes' examples. Both Neumann and Duchesne represented significant "firsts" for their respective congregations: Duchesne, as the first Sacred Heart sister in North America; Neumann, as the first Redemptorist ordained in the United States. Both adhered to a spirituality of deprivation and self-denial, and they died in their adopted land only eight years apart. Finally, both Neumann and Duchesne emerged as candidates for canonization in the late nineteenth century, their lives tailored to a hagiography that privileged missionaries' efforts to convert a native population.

To be sure, linking Duchesne and Neumann to the default hagiographical model had initially required some rhetorical finesse. Duchesne had spent only one of her thirty-four American years among indigenous people. Neumann, for his part, was known not for attracting new converts to the faith but for preserving it among European migrants to the United States. Throughout the 1880s and 1890s, in fact, Neumann's attachment to European languages, as well as his efforts to import foreign clergy and religious, had led some church leaders to question his suitability as a national patron; recall that John Ireland's fierce commitment to Americanization had led to his outright refusal to support Neumann's cause.[43] Neumann's petitioners had nonetheless introduced his cause in Rome, and the hundreds of pages of documentation sent to Rome in 1886 had constituted the very first U.S. submission to the Sacred Congregation of Rites.

The Archdiocese of St. Louis completed Philippine Duchesne's ordinary process in 1900.[44] The same types of flaws that had dogged Neumann's progress surfaced in Duchesne's supporting documentation. The Sacred Congregation dismissed four of the witnesses, leading the sisters of the Society of the Sacred Heart to lament that officials in Rome "do not seem to have realized the situation" in St. Louis. By 1912, however, a Jesuit was serving as Duchesne's postulator, and by the 1930s Carlo Miccinelli was also actively involved at the Sacred Congregation. This support was likely a major factor in advancing Duchesne to venerable in 1935. At that point, her cause caught up to John Neumann. Both needed two authenticated miracles to proceed to beatification.[45]

Though Neumann's ordinary process had already been exceptionally complicated, it was primarily the search for authenticated miracles that would lead one of his advocates to characterize his cause as "the most difficult of all such" in Redemptorist history. The problem was not that reports of local healings attributed to Neumann were in short supply—they had flooded the shrine since his death—but the process of proving them was another matter. In the 1920s, shortly after Neumann had been declared venerable, Redemptorists submitted three cures—all of Philadelphia-area children—for consideration at the Sacred Congregation. Although canon law required that miracle cases be sent to the Holy See in pairs, Neumann's supporters had included an extra one to increase the odds of success. However, the cushion made no difference; all three failed the "initial cursory investigation" due to "a lack of scientific documentation of even the simplest sort." As had been the case with the ordinary process, Neumann's Italian promoters stepped up to compensate for U.S. Catholics' saint-seeking inexperience, supplying two "spectacular cures" attributed to Neumann's intercession from the Diocese of Reggio Emilia in Italy: a 1922 cure of a local peasant from purulent cystitis and the 1923 recovery of an eleven-year-old girl named Eva Benassi from acute peritonitis. Though both were promising, the weaknesses in each prompted the postulator to recommend waiting for a third miracle to materialize.[46]

As Neumann's supporters waited for another miracle to make its appearance, Duchesne's passage through this stage in the process was proving more smooth. By 1939, she had two authenticated miracles attributed to her intercession, and her beatification took place in May 1940 (figures 3 and 4).[47] Duchesne's promoters had good reason to expect that U.S. Catholics would be very enthusiastic about the new American blessed, as her thirty-four years in the central United States insulated her from the charge leveled against the "Canadian" Jesuits. Yet U.S. Catholics reacted to Duchesne's beatification with a detached nonchalance that called to mind their tepid response to the Jesuits martyrs a decade before. Public celebrations were largely contained to Missouri, and Sacred Heart sisters or alumnae supplied most of the publicity. One Jesuit, perhaps already resentful of the scant attention paid to his own confreres,

FIGURE 3
Philippine Duchesne with Map, beatification
commemorative portrait, 1940. (Courtesy of Archives of the
Society of the Sacred Heart—United States and Canada)

chastised U.S. Catholics for their lack of interest in "the splendid heroism of Philippine Duchesne." In a moment of wishful thinking, he urged them to put aside the best-selling *Gone with the Wind* and pick up a newly published history of the Society of the Sacred Heart in America. Duchesne's adventures, he insisted, were comparable to Scarlett O'Hara's in their "elements of romance and heroism."[48]

Duchesne's real competition, however, was not a fictional southern belle but other U.S. Catholic historical figures, like Neumann, whose stories matched newer models of American holiness. While Duchesne had overtaken Neumann at the Roman center, their positions on the periphery were reversed. As

FIGURE 4
Duchesne's beatification, St. Peter's Basilica, Vatican City, 1940.
(Courtesy of G. Felici, Fotografia Pontificia, Roma; Archives of the
Society of the Sacred Heart—United States and Canada)

the Rose of Missouri faded in the American Catholic imagination, the public image of the "little bishop" from Philadelphia steadily brightened. In August 1930, Redemptorists in Philadelphia founded an organization dedicated to promoting Neumann's cause through popular devotion. Although membership drives initially targeted locals, as joining required a promise to visit the bishop's tomb once a week, Redemptorists soon expanded their efforts. By 1932, the Neumann League reported that it had 73,000 members representing "every state in the Union."[49] Four years later, in an address commemorating the centenary of Neumann's ordination, Father Albert Waible reported that the league had further increased in size and geographical diversity. The Philadelphia shrine, too, was attracting more pilgrims from places as far away as Colorado and Toronto. Catholic newspapers throughout the nation published articles about Neumann and his cause, and many predicted that Neumann would be "the first individual to be canonized whose labors were confined largely to our own country."[50]

In part, Neumann's surging popularity had resulted from Cardinal Dougherty's energetic lobbying on his behalf. Because Neumann had been bishop of Philadelphia, his elevation to sainthood would reflect honor and glory on the seat Dougherty himself occupied—no small matter for a man who relished his status as a "prince of the Church" as much as Dougherty did.[51] Shortly after his elevation to the cardinalate, Dougherty wrote to the Redemptorists pledging his support. Reminding them that he was "most anxious to see my sainted predecessor be raised to the honors of the altar," Dougherty promised he would "do all in my power to accomplish this result."[52] While officials at the Sacred Congregation were considering the Eva Benassi cure in 1924, Dougherty also wrote to the pope asking that the investigation be accelerated.[53]

Dougherty's endorsement was not the only reason Neumann eclipsed Duchesne in popularity. She, too, had hailed from an archdiocese with the resources and leadership to propel her to a national stage, yet her devotees were largely confined to her particular geographical and congregational inner circles. Neumann's cause generated interest beyond both the Redemptorists and Philadelphia because his story resonated with the interwar American Catholic faithful in a way that Duchesne's did not. In this respect, the parallels in the lives of the two nineteenth-century missionaries were overshadowed by key distinctions in their afterlives. It is precisely these contrasting elements—the people they served, the places they labored, the enemies they faced, and above all the relationships they established with their adopted nation—that explain Neumann's rising credibility and Duchesne's diminishing appeal as prospective national patrons. These distinctions, in turn, reveal a great deal about how midcentury U.S. Catholics interpreted their own past and present in the United States.

A decline in numbers of immigrants was the first important factor that nudged U.S. Catholics toward Neumann and away from Duchesne during the 1930s. It was hardly coincidental that American Catholics' admiration for the progenitors of the "immigrant church" increased at the very moment that they themselves were less inclined to attend a national parish or to speak a foreign language. Only in retrospect were U.S. Catholics able to cultivate and express an admiration for migrants' role in sustaining and expanding the church in the United States. In his 1946 assessment of "the American contribution to universal holiness," Rev. Joseph Code characterized the church in the United States as "an extension of Old World Catholicism." Code distinguished the U.S. church from its counterparts in Africa and Asia, in which, he argued, the church had sprung from the conversion of native people. In the United States, by contrast, the indigenous population had been almost incidental to the church's progress. "Even if every Red Man had been converted and had remained faithful," Code observed, "the effect would have been meager in the face of the millions of Catholics who came from Europe."[54]

Few statements expressed more clearly the vicissitudes in U.S. Catholics' saintly expectations over the course of half a century. Duchesne and other European missionaries, as well as the indigenous convert Tekakwitha, had emerged as candidates for canonization during the 1880s, a time when many Americans dismissed U.S. Catholics as recent and unwelcome visitors. The earliest U.S. Catholic saint-seekers had looked to their holy heroes for help in establishing a Catholic presence in North America from the earliest days of European contact and in diminishing Protestants' antipathy toward recent Catholic arrivals. From the vantage point of the mid-twentieth century, however, with members of many Catholic ethnic groups more assimilated into American culture, participation in the colonial missionary enterprise carried far less weight in saintly circles. The passage of time had accomplished what the first U.S. saint-seekers had looked to their favorite saints to provide: distance from the "superstitious masses" so despised by Protestants.

This new perspective worked to Neumann's considerable advantage. His allegiance to European languages, parishes, and women and men religious, once partial liabilities, became unalloyed assets in his promoters' campaign to cast him as the ideal U.S. patron. Neumann's birth in Prachatitz, once a part of the Habsburg Empire, enabled Americans of Bohemian and Czech ancestry to claim a special kinship with him. In 1932, the National Alliance of Bohemian Catholics, based in Chicago, organized a pilgrimage that brought two hundred devotees to Neumann's birthplace. Before crossing the Atlantic, pilgrims made a stop at Neumann's tomb at his Philadelphia shrine, enabling his petitioners to tout the journey as "part of a vigorous movement to further the Cause of Beatification of an American Bishop."[55]

But Neumann's true strength as an immigrant saint derived not from his Slavic connections but from his appeal to a panoply of Euro-American Catholics. Neumann's devotees often reminded Italian American Catholics of their debt to the Philadelphia Redemptorist, who had founded "the first Italian parish in the United States"—a claim they attached to St. Mary Magdalen de Pazzi and one they strived mightily to confirm.[56] Irish American Catholics were similarly exhorted to consider Neumann one of their own. According to one often-repeated story, Neumann had resolved to acquire Irish upon learning that, unless he did so, Irish immigrants in rural Pennsylvania would be otherwise unable to participate in the sacrament of confession in their native tongue. "Praise be to God," one elderly Irishwoman had purportedly said upon meeting Neumann, "we have an Irish bishop!" Neumann's biographical sketches routinely touted his linguistic abilities. In the deft hands of his promoters, Neumann's language facility carried over into his afterlife. Because "husky Poles, vivacious Frenchmen, [and] Venetian gondoliers [had] all confess[ed] themselves to the Bishop in their native tongue," he belonged to their children and grandchildren as well.[57]

Closely related to U.S. Catholics' shifting perspective on their immigrant past was their new perspective on anti-Catholicism. Neumann had arrived in Philadelphia on the heels of the Bible riots of the 1840s, an infamous expression of anti-Catholicism that resulted in the torching of two Catholic churches and thirty homes. In the nineteenth century, Neumann's biographers had presented his religious "persecution" as evidence of his missionary zeal; like his deprivation on the frontier and his studious avoidance of pleasure, his suffering under the burden of anti-Catholicism resembled "a kind of martyrdom" for the sake of souls.[58] By the mid-twentieth century, U.S. Catholics interpreted Neumann's encounters with anti-Catholicism as evidence not of his personal suffering but as an occasion to celebrate their collective victory over religious prejudice. In a city that "had openly boasted of an anti-Catholic reputation," in which "the Know-Nothing crowd was on its way to taking over the machinery of city government," Neumann had forged ahead fearlessly, remaking the city in a Catholic image. Given that the building that housed St. Mary Magdalen de Pazzi parish had originally been owned by Protestants, one Redemptorist imagined how satisfying it must have been for Neumann to contemplate that transformation: "Bishop Neumann liked to think of that church ... [and] imagine all the flowers and incense and Madonnas, the little 'bambini' in what was once a Puritan 'meeting house!'"[59]

U.S. Catholics' sense of triumph over religious prejudice shaped accounts of Neumann's successful efforts to introduce the Eucharistic devotion of "Forty Hours" to the United States. Neumann's desire to implement the devotion, which involved continuous veneration of the Blessed Sacrament at a particular church, was endowed with symbolic meaning given his arrival in the United

States on the liturgical Feast of Corpus Christi, which honored the body of Christ. But Neumann's plan to begin that practice at St. Philip Neri parish alarmed Philadelphia Catholics; that had been one of the churches burned in the Bible riots of the previous decade. As his devotees recounted the story a century later, the fearful Catholics tried to dissuade the bishop: "We have had enough church burnings already," they said. Why subject the Eucharist to "threats of violence and desecration"? Neumann almost conceded that "maybe the Forty Hours wasn't meant for America." A late-night heavenly vision and miraculous escape from an overturned burning candle restored Neumann's faith and courage. He persisted in his plan, and the devotions people had once believed not "meant for America" took place without disturbance not only at St. Philip Neri Church but elsewhere in the diocese. By the time Neumann was declared venerable, Forty Hours devotions had become a common practice throughout the United States. Neumann's role in transplanting the devotions to American soil was widely hailed as "the brightest jewel in his saintly crown."[60]

Even as they used Neumann's life story to help consign massive immigration and fierce religious prejudice to their past, U.S. Catholics also looked to Neumann's legacy to affirm the urban-centered institutional and cultural expansion that shaped their present. Accordingly, Neumann's eight years in urban Philadelphia assumed ever-increasing importance in his story. Though he had spent much of his North American life in remote and isolated areas, and though the Philadelphia diocese itself had encompassed a sprawling 37,000 square miles during his episcopate, most of his midcentury biographers situated him at the epicenter of a thriving and rapidly expanding urban Catholic subculture—a setting that, not coincidentally, bore a much stronger resemblance to Dougherty's Philadelphia than it did to the one of Neumann's era. One historian, citing inflated increases in the both the number of Philadelphia priests and the size of the diocesan population, has accused Neumann's petitioners of "pious exaggeration."[61] Certainly one of Neumann's most cited accomplishments, his establishment of seventy-three new parishes, does not square with official diocesan records.[62] By allowing the bishop's boosters to claim that he had opened one every forty days, however, the statistic invoked biblical imagery to boast of Neumann's institutional record.[63] In the era when "God's Bricklayer" occupied Philadelphia's episcopal throne, routine exaggeration helped buttress Neumann's popularity.

Creative license worked especially to Neumann's advantage when it came to his involvement with parochial schools. Reports often credited him with founding a hundred of them, even though diocesan directories show only thirty-eight in place the year of his death.[64] To be sure, no one doubted that Neumann's insistence on language preservation and his resistance to anti-Catholicism during the 1850s had prompted him to champion parish schools. But given that nothing approaching a coherent educational "system" existed until much later in the nineteenth century, labeling him "the Father of the Parochial school system" bordered on anachronism. Still, the Redemptorists did their best to make their case, and while Neumann was never acknowledged as the undisputed parent of American Catholic parochial education—Elizabeth Ann Seton's petitioners also claimed that honor for her in the 1930s—the title raised his stock in a number of ways. In practical terms, it provided the justification for Dougherty, the Redemptorists, and others to enlist Catholic schoolchildren across the nation in "crusades of prayer" for the success of his cause. Aside from the obvious effect of expanding Neumann's constituency far beyond Philadelphia, this marketing strategy also boosted the number of reported healings attributed to his intercession, thereby increasing the chances of finding a credible miracle that could enhance his saintly reputation.[65] In symbolic terms, extolling Neumann as the founder of the school system also worked in his favor by transforming him into a prescient leader during a period when the number of Catholic schools was rapidly expanding. In Philadelphia alone, the number of Catholic schools increased from 175 to 305 and enrollment grew from 87,857 to 133,025 during Dougherty's tenure as archbishop.[66]

Neumann's vigorous effort to recruit men and women to religious life further enhanced his reputation for farsightedness. Indeed, if Neumann's search for "foreign" religious once led some critics to impugn his Americanness, it appeared to be a sound business plan at a time when the demand for religious teachers exceeded the supply. Supporting material for Neumann's canonization emphasized all he had done to inspire vocations among many native-born Americans as well. During his ordinary process, one elderly member of the Georgetown Visitation sisters testified that her own entrance into religious life had represented one of the bishop's earliest miracles. In 1860, she had confided to him that both her mother and "Protestant stepfather" had been staunchly opposed to her vocation. "Before the month had expired," she testified, Neumann "was in eternity and I was in the convent."[67] Neumann's promoters also cited as evidence of his sanctity his role in supporting Bavarian-born widow Maria Anna Boll Bachmann in establishing the Sisters of the Third Order of St. Francis in Philadelphia. Eventually, as he approached canonization, his advocates would make a case that Neumann had actually "founded" the congregation, though that argument was rooted less in fact than in a desire to claim for him the coveted exemption from a required miracle.[68]

Each of the factors that enlarged Neumann's midcentury appeal as a prospective national patron throughout the 1930s corresponds to a limitation to the allure of Philippine Duchesne, whose life proved far less adaptable than Neumann's to a hagiography that privileged the transplantation of an Old World church over one founded on indigenous converts. However tenuous it had been, her connection to the colonial missionary enterprise proved enduring. Enthusiasts continued to venerate the "frontierswoman" who had willingly gone "off to some far-off country to be a light bearer to savage races who dwelt in darkness."[69] Unlike Neumann's story, the narrative of Duchesne's American life lacked components around which an immigrant narrative could have been constructed; consequently, while it was conceivable that the grandchildren of "vivacious Frenchmen" may have considered her their heavenly ally, the descendants of "husky Poles" and "Venetian gondoliers" had no basis on which to do so.

Like her indelible missionary status, Duchesne's habitat on a remote frontier both distinguished her from Neumann and isolated her from the prevailing currents of American Catholic life in the mid-twentieth century. Although Duchesne's memorable characterization of her new home as a place "without a wall" had captivated a nineteenth-century audience intent on glorifying a pristine frontier, an increasingly urban Catholic population—actively building as many walls as they could—would find Duchesne's struggle in the "crude world" of the "raw, undisciplined, unshapen West" far less compelling. Nor could Duchesne's petitioners claim for her an institutional legacy on the scale of Neumann's. A few articles in the U.S. Catholic press did acknowledge Duchesne as a saint of special interest to U.S. Catholics by virtue of the fact that she had introduced the Society of the Sacred Heart to the country.[70] Still, stacked against Neumann's, Duchesne's institutional legacy amounted to little.

Duchesne's lack of connection to Catholics' perceived triumph over religious prejudice also distanced her from the Catholic ethos of the mid-twentieth century. Though Missouri had, in fact, been a hotbed of anti-Catholic sentiment during her lifetime, her story offered no threads that her promoters might have woven into a setting similar to their own milieu.[71] And no matter how ardently

U.S. Catholics admired Duchesne's cheerful willingness to risk her life at the hands of "savages," her courage did not strike the same chord with them as did Neumann's brave disregard for Protestant disdain in crowded Philadelphia. The irony in this latter instance was that Duchesne had suffered the consequences of anti-Catholicism to a much greater extent than had Neumann: her original congregation had been one of the many religious institutes forcibly disbanded in the wake of the French Revolution. The French connection was also significant, as, in the end, nationality would best explain Neumann's upward trajectory and Duchesne's downward spiral: Neumann had been a citizen of the United States, while Duchesne had not.

Citizenship was an important part of the national discourse in the 1930s, for non-Catholics as well as Catholics. When the issue of citizenship had surfaced early in the decade, in reference to the cause of the North American Jesuits, it was difficult to criticize the martyrs for not being U.S. citizens because, as one commentator pointed out, they had arrived in North America during the seventeenth century, when there had been "no question then of any naturalization, or any new nation to which one could attach oneself by personal choice."[72] It was a different matter altogether for Duchesne, who had been living in Missouri when it became a state in 1823. Foreign-born residents were not considered citizens, and those who wished to apply had to present themselves before a local, state, or federal court to declare their intention and promise to uphold the Constitution. There is no evidence that Duchesne ever did this.[73]

Yet technically speaking, the Redemptorists also lacked any tangible evidence of John Neumann's naturalization. Promotional and biographical material related to Neumann routinely referred to him as a U.S. citizen, and his confreres had "long suspected" it, though they lacked any corroborating documentation. In the late 1920s, recognizing that being a citizen could distinguish him from the Jesuit martyrs and cement his status as a patriot, the Redemptorist overseeing Neumann's cause initiated an extensive correspondence with clerks in Pittsburgh, western New York, Baltimore, and other places where Neumann had lived to see if he had applied to become a citizen. The search yielded some enticing leads but ended in disappointment. One prospect, a resident of western New York, had declared his intent to become a citizen—but he spelled his surname "Newman." In still another dead end, a different John Neumann had recorded Ireland, not Bohemia, as his birthplace. This hunt continued for several decades. It was not until April 1963 that Neumann biographer Rev. Michael Curley stumbled upon definitive proof in the National

Archives. On Neumann's 1854 application for a passport—necessary for a trip to Rome for the declaration of the Immaculate Conception—he had listed himself as a U.S. citizen.[74]

Long before they uncovered "proof positive" of Neumann's naturalization, his promoters capitalized on the oral tradition that supported it. Redemptorists also made the most of Neumann's image as an "American by choice" by linking him to national historical sites in Philadelphia and its environs.[75] They often coupled organized pilgrimages to his shrine with tours of Independence Hall or the revolutionary battlefield at Valley Forge.[76] An "Ardent Prayer," which circulated in pamphlet form in 1933, hinted that Neumann's canonization would match in magnitude some of Philadelphia's best-known historical events:

> Here, in its world-famous Independence Hall ... the Declaration of Independence was adopted and signed, giving birth to the world's mightiest nation; here, George Washington, the Father of Our Country, accepted his appointment by Congress, as General and Commander in chief of the Continental Army; here, too, our national flag and the immortal United States Constitution were adopted. And through the prayers of a mighty nation, may Philadelphia, the cradle of American liberty, add still another transcending glory to her colorful and magnificent past—the Solemn Beatification and Canonization of one of her illustrious bishops, the Rt. Rev. John N. Neumann, whose last resting-place is only about a mile or so away from her national shrines.[77]

Redemptorists were hardly the only ones who emphasized Neumann's connection to the City of Independence. Jesuit Francis Heiermann cited Neumann in rebutting the idea, put forward by an American sociologist, that "the traditional idea of a saint is strangely out of place" in a democratic era.[78] On the contrary, Heiermann argued, Neumann's impending beatification proved that the saint "is a reality in our modern age." Raising him or another holy American to the altars of sainthood, the Jesuit maintained, would benefit the United States "more than the invention of the steam engine and electric power and wireless ... combined." It followed, then, that U.S. Catholics should honor Neumann's images and relics in the same way all U.S. citizens showed respect for "the abode of George Washington or his sword, the pen of the signing of the Declaration of Independence, [or] the Liberty Bell in Philadelphia."[79]

Duchesne's petitioners and devotees had no similar recourse. Unable to point to her naturalization, they were left without much else to suggest that

Duchesne had ever embraced the American nation. Marjorie Erskine, RSCJ, a member of Duchesne's congregation, did her best to argue in a 1927 biography that "Philippine Duchesne was much more American than French, even before she crossed the Atlantic," but her case did not prove very convincing.[80] Even Archbishop (later Cardinal) John Glennon of St. Louis, arguably the bishop most invested in Duchesne's cause, touted her love of her country—France. In an introduction to Erskine's biography, Glennon praised Duchesne for responding to God's call to abandon her beloved "native land" for a death in exile.[81] The same dynamic was evident in the congregational celebrations of Duchesne's beatification. While a few made efforts to connect Duchesne to the "epic of America," most presumed a different national allegiance. At the order's San Francisco College for Women, for example, the students celebrated Duchesne's beatification by staging a play titled *A Daughter of Dauphiny*.[82]

Other saint-seekers used Duchesne's love of and loyalty to France to associate her with the Jesuit missionaries. "The seventeenth-century martyrs, put to death with hideous tortures by the Indians, were French missionaries, very French indeed," observed one Catholic writer, and "Blessed Philippine" resembled the Jesuit martyrs more closely than she did other nineteenth-century missionaries, in the sense that she had been "French, and remained so."[83] Though the link to the martyrs may have enhanced Duchesne's attractiveness in the eyes of the first U.S. saint-seekers, it did very little to endear her to U.S. Catholics in the 1930s. Chronologically, Duchesne may have belonged to the nineteenth century, but figuratively she was best understood as a peer of the seventeenth-century North American martyrs. Like them, she had "brought light to the savages." Like them, she evoked images of "the log cabin, the wooden shack with an improvised door . . . frozen water, the frozen fingers, the hunger and pain."[84] Like them, she died in exile, eternally French in both her life and afterlife.

Duchesne may have lived and died solidly within the nation's "present confines," and the sum total of her years in the United States may have exceeded Neumann's by roughly a decade. But by the time of her beatification neither measure seemed to matter. To the U.S. Catholics who regarded her as an exiled frontier missionary, Duchesne did not make a very convincing American. By contrast, John Neumann—ever the polyglot—mastered a final language from beyond the grave: the American Catholic idiom of the mid-twentieth century. As an immigrant, urban, empire-building bishop and patriotic citizen, Neumann would elicit the sense of familiarity that U.S. Catholics had longed for in a national patron.

Could U.S. Catholics find a saint who spoke their dialect even more fluently? As Neumann's promoters waited for the diminutive bishop to produce a miracle that would withstand Rome's rigorous investigation, the era's most prominent saint-seeker suggested Americans had just such a candidate in their history. Shortly after he issued his clarion call at St. Patrick's, Leonard Feeney published a biography of Elizabeth Ann Seton subtitled *An American Woman*, in which he predicted that "Elizabeth of New York" would soon rank "in equal brilliance with such spiritual heroes as Teresa of Avila, Thérèse of Lisieux, Catherine of Genoa, Rose of Lima, Joan of Arc, Jane Frances of Dijon, Bernadette of Lourdes." Once canonized, Feeney asserted, Seton would represent "the first American saint in the American manner."[85] His reasoning strongly suggested that the period's hagiographical shifts would also work in Seton's favor, slowly transforming her from an outlier in American holiness into its near-perfect instantiation.

Mother Seton Was an American!

Unlike Neumann, Seton had not been an immigrant. Yet neither had she been a missionary. If Seton's lack of connection to the European missionary enterprise had made her an anomaly among the first prospective American saints, it would work to the advantage of her cause by the mid-twentieth century. Having never been connected to the missionary model, her fortunes as a saintly hero were less dependent on its endurance. Moreover, by virtue of her 1803 sojourn in Italy and her continuing relationship with the Filicchi family, Seton could be plausibly connected to a narrative of transplantation.[86] Characterizing her conversion as Italy's "gift" to the church in the United States, Seton's devotees argued that U.S. Catholics could repay the debt by welcoming Italian and other immigrants to the United States.[87]

Seton's afterlife could accommodate the era's other hagiographical transformations even more easily. Many of these were highlighted at a May 1931 celebration at St. Peter's in Lower Manhattan, the church where Seton had made her profession as a Catholic in March 1805. The event, arranged by the Mother Seton Committee of the International Federation of Catholic Alumnae (IFCA), featured New York's Cardinal Patrick Hayes, who presided over the unveiling of a large bronze plaque that explained the significance of Seton's conversion to the church.[88] Notably, the tablet listed seven communities as the home of Seton's spiritual daughters: the Daughters of Charity in Emmitsburg and St. Louis (the Daughters of Charity had divided into two provinces in 1910, establishing a western provincial house in Normandy, Missouri, a suburb of St. Louis), and the Sisters of Charity of New York, Cincinnati, St. Elizabeth (New Jersey), Seton Hill (Greensburg), and St. Vincent de Paul (Halifax).

The ceremony at St. Peter's reflected the same impulse that had motivated the 1926 Eucharistic Congress. While that event had temporarily transformed Chicago into a sacred, Catholic—yet still public—space, other efforts sought to install permanent Catholic markers on the American landscape.[89] The Catholic triumphalism so evident in Chicago in 1926 was also vividly on display five years later at St. Peter's Church. Reporting on Seton's celebration there, the editors of *Commonweal* reminded readers that Seton's attempt to run a private school in New York had been thwarted by "public resentment and opposition" as evidence of how far U.S. Catholics had gone "from the atmosphere of such unhappy prejudice." Given that U.S. Catholics were now so firmly situated in the intellectual life of the nation, they observed, it was difficult "to imagine that such ostracism and opposition as Mother Seton encountered would be met by a Catholic educator opening a new school" in the 1930s.[90]

Similar observations peppered the spate of biographies about Seton that appeared in the 1930s and 1940s. Leonard Feeney, in particular, dramatized the consequences of Seton's conversion to Catholicism, marveling that "the leading vanguard of the Catholic Sisterhood in America is the result of the courage and sacrifices of a one-time Protestant girl." According to another sketch, Seton had "lived the life of a martyr. . . . From the day she was received into the Catholic Church . . . she was disowned by her whole family and that of her husband; they wished to see her no more." Seton's loss of support and income constituted a "new martyrdom, a new privation, a new sacrifice . . . a spiritual martyrdom no less meritorious than that of blood."[91] Catherine O'Donnell, Seton's most recent biographer, argues convincingly that it was not Seton's conversion per se but rather her relentless proselytizing that made her so unpopular among New York's Episcopalians.[92] For Catholics interpreting Seton in the 1930s, however, envisioning Seton's "spiritual martyrdom" helped them translate her heavenly triumph into their own temporal one: her courage and suffering at the hands of fierce religious prejudice, much like Neumann's, had helped to make the nation become more amenable to Catholicism. By exaggerating the extent to which anti-Catholicism had circumscribed Seton's life, in other words, her supporters were able to celebrate her triumph over it—and by extension, their own—even more exuberantly.

Also like Neumann, Seton was touted as the progenitor of a vast institutional legacy. Feeney's biography listed all the institutions that traced their origins to the "one little American girl": 8 colleges, 160 high schools and academies, 447 parochial schools, 91 hospitals, 69 nursing schools, 6 orphanages. Of particular importance in this litany was the high number of parochial schools linked to Seton. As the parochial school system expanded throughout the interwar period, brick-and-mortar bishops such as Philadelphia's Dougherty increasingly saluted Seton as the system's "mother," despite Neumann's competing claim. They also did so over and against the repeated objections of the period's leading church historian, Peter Guilday, who insisted that Seton had no right to the title "Foundress of the Parochial School System in the United States."[93] Guilday was correct, in a technical sense: the idea of a Catholic school system, in competition with state-sponsored schools, was not conceived until decades after Seton's death. Yet an argument against Seton is not necessarily an argument for Neumann, and it is not clear whether Guilday was willing to let the claim that Neumann was the founder stand. Certainly, Neumann's fervent commitment to parish schools, as well as his later advent on the American scene, gives him more of a right to the distinction than Seton. In any case Seton's devotees paid little heed to Guilday's admonitions. One biography, published in 1942, devoted its entire opening chapter to defending Seton's right to the title of foundress of the American parochial schools, and some Catholic leaders and educators repeat the anachronism to this day.[94]

The commemoration of Seton's conversion at St. Peter's was one of many ways her midcentury supporters highlighted her New York roots. As one devotee put it, "the saint from the sidewalks of New York" was "as American as the Declaration of Independence, which was signed a few weeks before her second birthday."[95] This link to the nation became ever more crucial for her cause, as it did for Neumann's, as citizenship loomed larger in the American lexicon. Just as Redemptorists had done on Neumann's behalf, Seton's advocates went to considerable lengths to erase any lingering doubts about her national status. In Seton's case, their quest involved an extended foray into the technicalities of marriage and naturalization laws rather than a hunt for a certificate of naturalization. Both Elizabeth and her husband, like all British subjects residing continually in the United States at the time, automatically became U.S. citizens after independence. On his final voyage to Italy in 1803, however, William carried with him a document that identified him as a British subject. It may have been a mistake, but it was theoretically possible that William's acceptance of this credential abrogated his U.S. citizenship, which would have also called into question Seton's citizenship status. Until the passage of the Cable Act in 1922, a woman married to an alien renounced her U.S. citizenship, though some court cases suggested that it would be restored once the marriage ended. After a detailed survey of all relevant case law, Seton's 1951 biographer concluded that Seton had probably never been a British subject after 1783. On the slim chance that she had been, however, "this alien status lasted only briefly from September 28, 1803 [when the aforementioned traveler's document was issued] to December 27, 1803, when [William] Seton died."[96]

Despite this small wrinkle, there was little question that Seton was firmly anchored to the nation—and to its most elite families. After the unveiling of the plaque at St. Peter's in 1931, the members of the IFCA proceeded to a nearby hotel for a Communion breakfast.[97] Over the course of the meal they were read a letter from New York governor Franklin Roosevelt in which he offered his homage to his distant relative: "In our family, we have many traditions of the saintly character of Mother Seton," Roosevelt wrote; "she was a very close connection of the Roosevelt family."[98] The governor's move to the White House two years later only increased the excitement of Seton's supporters. As one of them wrote in 1937, Seton's family connections to the U.S. president helped her seem especially "near to this generation."[99]

Franklin Roosevelt frequently invoked his distant relative in Catholic circles, and he may well have done so in October 1936 when he hosted Cardinal Eugenio Pacelli, the secretary of state of the Holy See and at the time the highest-ranking Vatican official to have visited the United States, at his family home in Hyde Park, New York. Apostolic delegate Amleto Cicognani broached the subject of Seton's cause for canonization with Pacelli, who was widely predicted to succeed Pius XI as pope, during his U.S. tour.[100] Cicognani assured the papal diplomat of U.S. Catholics' vibrant devotion to Seton and urged him to promote her cause at the Holy See.[101]

Gender added yet another dimension to Seton's appeal throughout this period. In the 1890s, Seton had served as a refreshing Catholic contrast to the New Woman; by the 1930s, she was marshaled against that period's gender models, which appeared even more disturbing to some American Catholics.[102] Feeney, for example, used Seton as a foil for a perceived weakening of gender differences, contrasting her peace and contentment in the roles of "sister, daughter, bride and mother" with the restlessness of the modern female "business executive, channel swimmer, or tennis champion," roles that made any woman "easy prey for a psychiatrist." Seton, Feeney explained, had been brought up in an age when a girl was given "a distinctly feminine education, one that coincided in practically nothing with the training given a boy." By contrast, "one of the greatest horrors of our day is the way in which a girl and a boy are treated indiscriminately in the matter of education and environment. . . . The liberation [of women] has gone altogether too far."[103]

A few years before Feeney published his biography, Bishop James Griffin of Springfield, Illinois, encouraged members of the National Council of Catholic Women to model themselves on both Seton and another woman to whom she was often compared, Rose Hawthorne Lathrop. There were indeed a number of parallels in their biographies.[104] Lathrop had also converted to Catholicism from one of America's elite Protestant families. Like Seton, Lathrop had observed Italian Catholicism firsthand: she lived in Europe for much of her childhood, including stints in Liverpool, where her father served as American consul between 1854 and 1857, and in Rome.[105] Like Seton, Lathrop had been a widow when she founded her religious community.[106] Again like Seton, Rose had been a bereaved mother: her only son died at the age of four. After Lathrop founded a Dominican congregation devoted to the care of indigent cancer patients, she was known as Mother Alphonsa until her death in 1926. Bishop Griffin, speaking at the national convention of the National Council of Catholic Women in 1936, emphasized another common thread between Seton and Lathrop: their cheerful willingness to sacrifice their own desires for the sake of Christianity. He urged Catholic women to follow their example, rather than those offered by modern American women, whom he described as so focused on achieving success that they had forgotten how to put the needs of others before their own.[107]

Writing about Seton also showed that, while clerics often relied on sanctity to contain gender roles, women could use it to expand them—provided they could cast innovations safely within the framework of Catholics' idealized vision of womanhood. The IFCA, the sponsors of the 1931 plaque dedication at St. Peter's Church, provides a case in point. Since its founding in 1914, the IFCA had sought to harness the organizational power of college-educated Catholic women for the benefit of American society. As its membership increased throughout the 1920s and 1930s, so, too, did its public presence. Brooklyn native Clara Sheeran led fund-raising campaigns for the Basilica of the National Shrine of the Immaculate Conception throughout the 1920s. The IFCA's Mother Seton Committee offered Sheeran a position of authority and a platform to amplify her own voice within the church. Writing to U.S. bishops, she evoked Seton's power as a symbol of ideal Catholic womanhood, presenting the nineteenth-century religious woman as a safe model for a modern age characterized by "laxity of morals, false philosophy, loss of courage, and consequent sapping of faith."[108]

Even as they gathered in Lower Manhattan in May 1931, Sheeran and the other members of the Mother Seton Committee had their eyes on a grander St. Peter's: the basilica in Rome. Later that summer a group of fifty Seton devotees replicated their heroine's 1803 journey from New York to Italy, carrying with them a twenty-eight-volume petition bearing 152,000 signatures in support of Seton's canonization. The signatories came "from the mighty and the lowly, the rich and the poor, the learned and the ignorant" and represented not only the IFCA but also many other organizations of Catholic women, all of whom wished "to see the church recognize the far-reaching results of the pioneer work of Elizabeth Seton."[109] Sheeran and her fellow pilgrims presented the petitions to Pope Pius XI in a private audience. In the account of the meeting she subsequently provided to U.S. bishops, Sheeran reported that the pope had been very receptive and that, she believed, the endeavor would help to accelerate Seton's canonization.[110]

At least one American observer had a decidedly different appraisal of the whole affair. A Vincentian priest named Salvator Burgio, recounting the IFCA's Roman adventure to a confrere, expressed his embarrassment over the spectacle his American compatriots had made of themselves. He remembered the "smiles on the faces of Romans" as they watched U.S. pilgrims "parade through the streets of Rome with placards supporting Seton's canonization." Locals, Burgio explained, dismissed such efforts as a "Cosa Americanata [sic]."[111] Burgio's characterization of the IFCA pilgrimage as "simply silly" may have been uncharitable, but it was accurate. The contrast between eye-rolling Romans and cheerleading Americans was a visual manifestation of a glaring disconnect: for all her popularity at home, Seton's canonization process had barely budged in Rome. Seton's cause had lain dormant since 1925, when the final part of the informative process had been sent.

As we have seen, Seton's posthumous entry into the Vincentian religious family had been a liability for her cause, not only because of the disagreement it generated about her relationship to them but also because of the lackluster French interest in their American daughter. The 1933 election of longtime Seton supporter Charles Souvay as superior general of the Vincentians solved the latter problem. Now in a position to make Seton's cause a congregational priority in a way it had not previously been, Souvay was confident that it would move forward quickly. Encouraged rather than embarrassed by the exuberance of the IFCA pilgrimage and other displays of devotion to Seton, Souvay was frustrated by his inability even to learn what the obstacles in Rome were, let alone to remove them. Like many others in his position, Souvay turned to John Wynne for advice. While America's foremost expert in canonization responded with characteristic generosity, he might have been less inclined to do so had he known what the Vincentian was saying privately about Tekakwitha. Reporting on the status of Seton's cause to the congregation, Souvay bristled at the attention Tekakwitha was garnering in Rome. "Another cause is being pressed forward, that of a young Indian girl, Tekakwitha," who "is not an American. . . . Mother Seton was an American. . . . All our Americans of to-day are descended from Europeans!"[112]

Souvay's personal stake in Seton's cause may have predisposed him to overstate her credentials as a national emblem and to dismiss those of Tekakwitha and other competitors. Nevertheless, enough other U.S. saint-seekers echoed his argument to suggest that further disappointment was in store for Wynne, this time in regard to the Indian maiden. Far from having arrived, it seemed, Tekakwitha's moment had passed. As an indigenous person—or what Rev. Joseph Code had described as a "Red 'Man,'" Tekakwitha may have been a powerful symbol of Catholic Americanness in 1884, when holiness had depended on the conversion of heathens, civilization of the wilderness, and bodily suffering. The same hagiographical shifts—from conversion to transplantation, from frontier to cityscape, from bodily suffering to cultural isolation, and from colony to nation—that had elevated John Neumann and Elizabeth Seton would also work against the Lily of the Mohawks, who would wilt as surely as the Rose of Missouri had done. Both Tekakwitha and Duchesne would blossom again on the American periphery, though each would do so in ways their first promoters could not have predicted.

For now, though, the story of American sanctity would center on two other women, one of whom was Elizabeth Ann Seton. It had taken Seton much longer than either Tekakwitha or Duchesne to emerge as a genuine "flower of American sanctity." Unlike them, however, Seton was well on her way to full bloom by the 1930s—at least from the vantage point of her U.S. boosters. Her cause remained at a virtual standstill in Rome. There it would stay until 1939, when, as many had predicted, Eugenio Pacelli was elevated to the papacy, taking the name Pope Pius XII. Cicognani's nudge of three years earlier would begin to pay dividends on Seton's behalf. Not only did the new pope's passing familiarity with Seton's story raise the hopes of her supporters, but the conclave that elected him placed a few of them in a position to engineer a breakthrough in her cause—moving it at last beyond the impasse in which it had been mired since 1925.

By the time of Pacelli's election, though, Seton had already been upstaged at the Roman center by a new *beata*, a candidate to whom neither the new pope nor any other Vatican official needed an introduction. As noted previously, when it comes to using canonization as an interpretive tool, the causes that are introduced during a particular era often reveal as much about that era as those that move forward or backward during it. In this case, the brand-new cause belonged to a woman whose life story could be easily rewritten in the interwar U.S. Catholic vernacular, largely because she not only seemed metaphorically "near to this generation" but had almost literally been a part of it. The next chapter of American saint-seeking centered almost exclusively on her.

3

W hile John LaFarge believed that the canonization of the Peruvian Martin de Porres would help Americans tackle modern social problems, he was even more confident about the contemporary relevance of a prospective saint closer to home—a woman he had known personally and whose achievements, he believed, had epitomized the distinctive American spirit. LaFarge had first met Frances Cabrini, the Italian-born founder of the Missionary Sisters of the Sacred Heart (MSC), in 1906, when, as a novice at the Jesuit house on the Hudson River, he had preached his first retreat at the MSC convent on the river's opposite bank. LaFarge returned to the convent on a frigid morning in early winter 1918, when, having walked across a frozen Hudson, he delivered the English homily at Cabrini's funeral Mass. LaFarge praised Cabrini's ability to get "stupendous things done" quickly and, as Cabrini's cause for canonization progressed, hailed her as "pre-eminently the organizing type of saint." Cabrini's rise to the honors of the altar would be especially meaningful for U.S. Catholics, he argued, who merited "an extra claim to a share in her saintly intercession."[1] LaFarge would be one of Cabrini's many acquaintances who would live to see her beatified and canonized, as her cause's rapid path was literally exceptional. Pope Pius XI, who had also crossed paths with Cabrini in his former role of prefect of the Ambrosiana Library in Milan, dispensed her from the same fifty-year rule that he had previously for Thérèse of Lisieux.[2]

Cabrini and the Little Flower had been linked during their lifetimes through another pontiff, Leo XIII, who had played a decisive role in shaping both of their futures as consecrated women. In November 1887, Thérèse, then a young teenager, had traveled to Rome from her native France. Cabrini, a native of Lombardy in northern Italy who had established a religious congregation there in 1880, also visited Rome for the first time that autumn, and at least one of Cabrini's hagiographers suggests that the two women had probably "passed each other on the street" during "those glorious autumn days."[3] The coincidence of their visits foreshadowed a number of points of intersection in their saintly stories. While in Rome, Thérèse secured Pope Leo XIII's blessing to enter the Carmelites, and she spent the rest of her short life in that enclosed community, remaining unknown to the wider world until the posthumous publication of her journal, *The Story of a Soul*.[4]

By contrast, Cabrini's audience with Pope Leo would lead her on a series of journeys across three continents that would take her a cumulative distance of over 55,000 miles by land and by sea.[5] That, at least, is the number calculated by Mother Antonietta Della Casa, her close friend and successor as the MSCs superior general, as she designed a splendid, gold-embossed map depicting those travels. In 1928, the Archdiocese of Chicago sent this remarkable document to the Sacred Congregation as part of the ordinary process it conducted on Cabrini's virtues.[6] According to all accounts of Cabrini's life, her meeting with Pope Leo had determined the pivotal points on that map, which were very different from the places she had originally envisioned for her life's work (figure 5).

During her childhood in northern Italy, Cabrini had learned from visiting Franciscan missionaries and reading the *Annals of the Propagation of the Faith* about the unevangelized peoples of Asia. Her biographers paint an evocative image of young "Cecchina" placing violets in little boats in a stream near her home, pretending they were missionaries on their way to save souls in China. According to those accounts, a year before her audience with Pope Leo XIII, Cabrini had knelt at the altar of St. Francis Xavier at Rome's Church of the Gesù and vowed that she would travel with her sisters to East Asia. But at the urging of Giovanni Battista Scalabrini, bishop of Piacenza in northern Italy, Cabrini began to consider going instead to the United States, to minister to the rapidly growing population of Italian immigrants there. New York's Archbishop Michael Corrigan, too, prevailed upon Cabrini to help solve the "Italian problem" that had troubled U.S. bishops at the Third Plenary Council of Baltimore, assuring Cabrini that local benefactors would support the sisters in establishing an orphanage and other institutions to help alleviate the suffering of the city's many Italian-born residents. These recent arrivals to the United

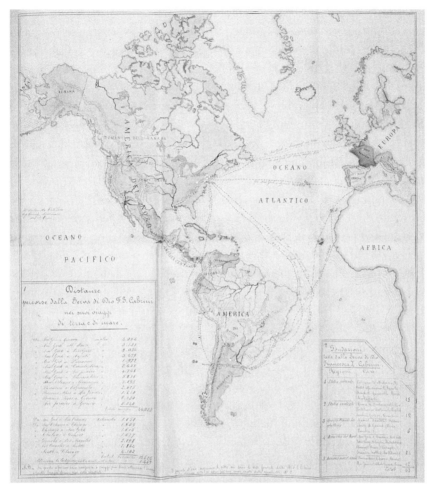

FIGURE 5

Map of distances traveled by Servant of God Frances Cabrini on her voyages
by land and by sea, designed by Mother Antonietta Della Casa, 1928.
(Vatican Secret Archives)

States were living and working in desperate conditions and were at risk of losing
their Catholic faith because of a shortage of Italian-speaking priests and nuns
to staff parishes and schools.

A standard account of what happened next was offered on the tenth anniversary of Cabrini's death by Monsignor Carlo Salotti, the lawyer at the Sacred
Congregation of Rites who had been so impressed with Tekakwitha's piety.

Cabrini, Salotti claimed, had found Scalabrini's and Corrigan's arguments compelling but was torn. Finding it difficult to abandon her plan to go to East Asia, "where millions of infidels awaited the light of redemption," Cabrini appealed to Pope Leo for guidance. The pope, who had been moved by "the sad picture of a vast multitude of abandoned Italians spread over the wide regions of America," spoke plainly: "Not to the East, but to the West!" According to Salotti, the moment Cabrini heard these words she "hesitated no more." The pope's command would later find its way into most biographical sketches of Cabrini, with authors imparting varying degrees of reluctance or resignation to Cabrini when it came to letting go of her China dreams.[7]

Ubiquitous as this vignette has become in accounts of Cabrini's life, it controverts considerable evidence that by the time Cabrini had met with Pope Leo she had already made a firm decision in favor of New York. She had begun instruction in English earlier that fall—and had even booked her passage.[8] She later recounted that her answer had come after a second moment of private prayer in the Church of the Gesù, kneeling before the relics of the missionary from whom she took her name in religious life. Cabrini, it appears, had sought Leo's blessing, not his instruction.

Nevertheless, the claim that Leo himself had sent her to the United States gave Cabrini a special source of authority. When, for instance, Archbishop Corrigan told her to return to Italy when the promised benefaction in New York did not materialize, Cabrini responded that the Holy Father had sent her to New York, and she therefore intended to stay there until he told her otherwise. Apparently unaccustomed to being defied, the archbishop, according to one witness of the exchange, "grew red in the face and then became very quiet," but he allowed her to stay.[9] Cabrini's interaction with Corrigan, which evoked Mother Théodore Guérin's calm refusal to give in to the demands of the bishop of Vincennes in the 1840s, points to a recurring pattern in the history of Catholic sisters, who often cited higher authorities in their efforts to work around the opposition of local leaders.

In Cabrini's case, the story of her papally mandated diversion from China to New York would prove as decisive in historical memory as it had in her lifetime. For U.S. Catholic saint-seekers in the era of the nation saint, it would affirm her special connection to them. As one Catholic newspaper put it in 1938, nothing short of papal intervention had ordained that Cabrini would "work out her destiny not among pagodas, but skyscrapers."[10]

Frances Cabrini's cause for canonization offers a rare instance in which the process proceeded with alacrity and without complications. In comparison, thirty-five years had elapsed between the opening of John Neumann's ordinary process in Philadelphia and the Holy See's declaration on his virtues; for Elizabeth Ann Seton, over half a century would pass between these milestones. In Cabrini's case, by contrast, the Archdiocese of Chicago opened an ordinary process in 1928, and the Holy See declared her venerable a mere nine years later. If Cabrini's extraordinarily smooth passage at the Roman center set her apart from Seton and Neumann, however, the perspective of her U.S. supporters highlights what she had in common with them. Because Cabrini's life story magnified the very attributes that explained Neumann's and Seton's surges in popularity during the 1930s, her cause for canonization offers an even more obvious instantiation of the operative dynamic at work in U.S. saint-seeking: the faithful often see in their holy heroes what they want to see about themselves.

"Go Yourself to Rome"

On 19 March 1889, Cabrini and six other Missionary Sisters of the Sacred Heart left the motherhouse in Codogno, Italy, traveling by train first to Milan and from there to Le Havre, France, where they boarded a steamship to New York. Cabrini was then thirty-eight years old, and her companions, all natives of northern Italy, ranged in age from twenty-one to thirty-six. The memoirs of one of them, Sister Gabriella Linati, who had only recently entered the congregation, describe the sisters "crying like babies" when they lost sight of the European coast. The sisters traveled in second class—a luxury that Cabrini's devil's advocate would later question in his vain attempt to identify weaknesses in the case for her extraordinary virtue—but they spent a great deal of time in steerage comforting less fortunate Italian passengers. "Finally, after twelve days of sickness and tribulation we saw the beautiful Statue of Liberty at about 4 o'clock," Linati recalled. "Oh how happy Mother [Cabrini] was. I could read the joy on her face. She called us together to sing the 'Ave Maris Stella.'"[11]

The elation did not last long. Upon landing, Cabrini and her sisters discovered that neither the archbishop nor the Scalabrinians had arranged lodging for them. The sisters spent their first night in New York in a dirty tenement, unable to rest in the filthy beds but consoling themselves in constant prayer. For the next three weeks, they lived at a convent of the Sisters of Charity of New York, who had established a vibrant presence in the city in the seventy-two years since Seton had sent the first members there. In 1869, for example, Sister Mary Irene Fitzgibbon had opened a foundling home with only five dollars, and by the time she met Cabrini, the institution sheltered six hundred women and eighteen hundred infants at a time, sponsored day care for working mothers, and operated a maternity and children's hospital.[12] Fitzgibbon offered Cabrini both material support and practical advice, as did other Sisters of Charity. Although Cabrini could not speak English and her hosts could not speak Italian, she learned a great deal about her new environment from them. Members of other local communities of women religious, including Duchesne's Society of the Sacred Heart, also lent support to Cabrini and her congregation.[13]

Cabrini soon proved to be as enterprising as Fitzgibbon and other U.S. sisters. Within three months of their arrival, the MSCs were staffing an orphanage and a parish school for Italian immigrants. Determined to do more to assist New York's Italian community, Cabrini sent to Italy for three more sisters to help with the work. Cabrini herself returned to Italy in midsummer, taking with her two American-born postulants to instruct other sisters in English. She was back in New York the following April, and over the course of her second three-and-a-half-month stay in the United States she purchased property from Jesuits in West Park, New York, where she transferred the orphanage and opened an American novitiate for her congregation. She left for Italy again in August 1890 and would not return to New York for over a year. She then stayed for only a month before traveling to Nicaragua, where she opened another new community of MSCs, and returned to New York by way of New Orleans, where she opened a second U.S. foundation. In 1892, Cabrini named her congregation's new hospital in New York in honor of Christopher Columbus, following the lead of many U.S. Catholics who adopted the Italian explorer as their hero in the late nineteenth century for the same reason they had begun to search for a national patron saint: to stake a claim for themselves in the national story of the United States.[14]

In between multiple trips back and forth to Italy, Cabrini continued to expand the congregation across the United States. She opened parish schools in Newark, Chicago, Denver, Seattle, Los Angeles, and Philadelphia, as well as orphanages in most of those cities, and established two more Columbus Hospitals in Chicago and Seattle. Priests from Italian neighborhoods across the country invited Cabrini to visit their cities, hoping that once she saw the needs of the parishioners she would open a new foundation there. In 1892, Cabrini spent nine days in Cincinnati, Pittsburgh, and Buffalo, where, unlike the abstemious John Neumann, who allegedly refused to look at the nearby Niagara Falls, Cabrini took the time to marvel at the beauty of the falls, interpreting it as evidence of God's omnipotence.[15]

Cabrini also traveled to Central and South America and across western Europe. She opened MSC foundations in Panama, Buenos Aires, Brazil, Paris, Madrid, and London, as well as additional ones in Italy. At the time of her death, she presided over sixty-seven foundations across nine countries. After her first Atlantic crossing to New York, Cabrini made twenty-three more ocean journeys between 1889 and 1912, after which a combination of ill health and war kept her in the United States until her death in Chicago five years later.

In making these multiple Atlantic crossings, Cabrini replicated broader patterns among Italian emigrants. Between 1880 and 1915, 13 million people left the Italian peninsula in what historian Mark Choate has called "the largest migration from any country in recorded history."[16] Many of these migrants thought of "America" not as the United States but as the two continents named for the Italian Amerigo Vespucci, and many also traveled to South America.[17] Cabrini's brother Giovanni was one of thousands of Italians who migrated to Argentina during this period, and at least part of her motivation for establishing a foundation in Buenos Aires derived from a desire to build a school his children could attend.[18]

Few Italian emigrants left with the intention of staying away permanently, however. As a group, they had higher rates of repeat and return migration than other European arrivals, pulled to the United States primarily by opportunities to work and save money to return to Italy.[19] As the superior of a multinational missionary congregation, however, Cabrini was hardly a typical Italian migrant. The reasons for Cabrini's frequent trips, over land and sea, stemmed from her need to supervise operations in her far-flung foundations, where her physical presence, she understood, was often required to "settle things with certainty."[20] Leading her sisters also required frequent trips to Rome, and in some cases extended stays there. In 1906 and 1907, for example, she spent over a year in Rome as she awaited the Holy See's formal approval of the MSC constitutions.

Philadelphia's Mother Katharine Drexel soon benefited from Cabrini's experience. A member of one of the city's wealthiest families, Drexel had established a religious congregation of sisters in 1891. A command from Pope Leo XIII, coincidentally, had also been decisive in Drexel's story. When she had met the pontiff during her grand tour of Europe in 1887, Drexel had implored him to consider how the church could do more to help Native Americans and African Americans, whose suffering and poverty she had witnessed on her own travels around the United States. "Why don't you become a missionary yourself?" he is said to have responded. Leo's prompt set Drexel on a path that would lead her to enter the novitiate of the Sisters of Mercy in Pittsburgh and eventually to found the Sisters of the Blessed Sacrament for Indians and Colored People (later shortened to the Sisters of the Blessed Sacrament). Drexel chose the name both to reflect her personal devotion to the Eucharist and to underscore her belief that all peoples, regardless of their ethnic or racial background, were united in the body of Christ. Until her death in 1955, Drexel used her family's wealth to establish schools for Native Americans and African Americans, staffed by her congregation.

When Drexel herself became a candidate for canonization, her hagiographers would later imagine her 1912 visit from Cabrini as a union of two "kindred spirits . . . on fire with zeal for souls."[21] At the time, though, the meeting must have seemed to Drexel less an ethereal encounter than a practical opportunity to learn from a seasoned superior. Frustrated by her failure to get her congregation's rule approved at the Holy See, Drexel received the following advice from Cabrini: "You see, it is like this. You get a lot of mail every day. Some of it you must take care of immediately. Other items are important but you put them on the shelf to take care of tomorrow. Then tomorrow, something else demanding attention comes in and you leave the other letter still on the shelf. Before you know it, there are a lot of other items before it. It is like that in Rome. Things get shelved even though they are important. If you want to get your Rule approved, you go yourself to Rome and take it with you."[22] Drexel soon followed Cabrini's advice and gained papal approbation the following year.

Beyond moving congregational matters off the metaphorical shelf, Cabrini also used extended stays in Rome to handle financial disputes or to prepare to expand the MSC missions to other nations. Other crises sometimes called Cabrini away from Rome to one of her far-flung foundations. While visiting Italy in March 1912, for example, what would turn out to be her final transatlantic journey was cut short when Cabrini learned of a crisis at New York's Columbus Hospital. She returned to the United States directly from Naples, forgoing a planned visit to France and England and a scheduled departure from Southampton the next month. Her changed itinerary may well have given her an extra five years of life. Had she adhered to her original schedule, she would have been a passenger on the *Titanic*'s ill-fated voyage.[23]

Over the course of her extended stays in Rome, Cabrini acquired influential allies at the Holy See. Many of these relationships developed over decades. The Bologna-born Monsignor Giacomo Della Chiesa, for example, had been working at the Holy See's Secretariat of State in 1889 when he supplied Cabrini with crucial letters of introduction to U.S. bishops. They would maintain sporadic contact until 1914, when Della Chiesa was chosen to succeed Pope Pius X. Cabrini was "most happy" to hear of her friend's election and certain that the "pure and saintly" man would benefit the church in general and her institute in particular. Indeed, Cabrini's congregation received "many benefits" from the man now called Pope Benedict XV.[24] The pontiff was merely the highest-ranking among the hundreds of church leaders who sent condolences when they learned of Cabrini's death in Chicago on 22 December 1917. At one of many memorial masses held throughout the country, Seattle's Archbishop Edward John O'Dea observed that the Italian nun had "counted among her friends [the] members of the highest hierarchy of the Church, the most eminent Cardinals, and the best known prelates." A year after Cabrini's death, her successor, Mother Antonietta Della Casa, arranged for the eulogies, condolences, and remembrances of the founder to be published in a remarkable 478-page multilingual volume. The ostensible purpose of the commemorative book was to comfort Cabrini's daughters and to testify to the legacy she had left around the world, but it was also likely that Della Casa was laying the foundation for a cause for canonization on Cabrini's behalf.[25]

Cabrini's admirers often cited her Roman connections and her ability to use them for the benefit of her congregation as testaments to her ingenuity. Only rarely did these friendships elicit resentment. One such instance was a grudge that Rev. Henry Malak developed while he was promoting the cause for canonization of Mother Theresa (née Josephine) Dudzik, one of Cabrini's contemporaries in Chicago. Unlike Dudzik, who, Malak pointed out, had arrived on American soil as "an unknown immigrant girl" and relied on God alone to build her congregation in the United States, Cabrini had come to the United States "wearing a religious habit, in company with a group of Sisters, armed with the personal recommendations from Pope Leo XIII" and "from Cardinals and Bishops" that had "opened doors and loosened diocesan purse strings for her."[26]

However helpful Cabrini's allies among the hierarchy had been to the success of her earthly endeavors, they had undoubtedly helped secure her distinctive postmortem accomplishment—even if her promoters often insisted otherwise.

One of these, Monsignor Aristeo V. Simoni, a diocesan priest from Rockford, Illinois, who served as the vice-postulator of Cabrini's cause, maintained that Cabrini's "casual acquaintance" with the sitting pope had absolutely no bearing on the speed at which her cause progressed. It does seem likely, however, that the pontiff's memories of his personal encounter with the woman he described as "a great missionary, yes—and a saint" made him sympathetic to her cause.[27]

Mother Antonietta Della Casa worked tirelessly behind the scenes to advance Cabrini's cause for canonization, although her name rarely surfaces in the official material submitted to the congregation. Even an Italian woman with close connections to the Vatican could petition the Sacred Congregation only through male proxies, a requirement that had previously been part of church tradition but was actually spelled out in the Code of Canon Law of 1917. Della Casa and the MSCs found a congenial and cooperative representative in Cardinal George Mundelein. Cabrini and Mundelein had first met when he was serving as auxiliary bishop of New York, and his 1915 appointment as archbishop of Chicago had brought him into regular contact with the MSCs there. Cabrini spent the last years of her life at the Chicago convent, where Mundelein visited her often. He also claimed to be the last person to visit Cabrini before her death and presided at her funeral Mass.

Bishop Giovanni Bonzano, apostolic delegate to the United States, was a frequent correspondent of Cabrini who had advised her in a few tricky situations and was a great admirer of her work.[28] Bonzano had ended his term as apostolic delegate and returned to Rome in 1924, but two years later, by then a cardinal, he joined the other Vatican dignitaries who rode the special Pullman train from New York to Chicago for the International Eucharistic Congress. The event, by reuniting him with Mundelein in the diocese in which Cabrini had died, served as a catalyst for Cabrini's cause for canonization. During their days together in Chicago, Mundelein asked Bonzano for advice about opening an ordinary process and for recommendations of lawyers at the Sacred Congregation. After his return to Rome, Bonzano facilitated an introduction between Mundelein and Carlo Salotti, the canon lawyer at the Sacred Congregation who spoke on the tenth anniversary of Cabrini's death. Salotti needed little prodding to become Cabrini's champion in Rome. He already anticipated the day when the church would pronounce "this strong and tireless woman" worthy of veneration of the world. Although Salotti could not handle the cause personally, as he was on the verge of leaving the Sacred Congregation of Rites for a new appointment as secretary for the Propagation of the Faith, he recommended another Italian canon lawyer who was conversant in English. After consulting with Mother Antonietta Della Casa, Mundelein agreed to work with him.[29]

Amleto Cicognani's 1933 appointment to the position formerly occupied by Bonzano gave Cabrini's cause another influential U.S.-based supporter. In one of his first acts as apostolic delegate, Cicognani witnessed the exhumation of Cabrini's body from its resting place in upstate New York, a regular part of the canonization process intended to verify the identity and condition of the body and to procure relics that the faithful could venerate once the cause succeeded. After this exhumation Cabrini's remains were reinterred at her congregation's convent in the Washington Heights neighborhood in Upper Manhattan— incidentally, a place at the island's opposite end from Seton's monument at St. Peter's Church—which was both more visible and more accessible to pilgrims than the upstate location.[30] Two years later, Cicognani made the official petition to the Holy See to grant Cabrini an exemption from canon 2101, the stipulation that fifty years must pass between a person's death and the Holy See's discussion of his or her virtues. Pope Pius XI was more than amenable. "The Holy Father was very much in favor of the cause," the apostolic delegate assured Mother Antonietta, "which he himself knew personally."[31]

Cabrini's personal friendship with influential church leaders, from the pope to the local bishop overseeing her cause, undoubtedly helped her cause for canonization advance so rapidly. Cabrini's connections at the center cannot account, however, for the enthusiasm her cause generated among ordinary U.S. Catholic citizens during this period. It may be ironic that these believers considered Cabrini, by so many measures a Vatican insider, to be the most fully "American" candidate. Yet the intensity with which they embraced her is hardly surprising, given the way her life story confirmed what many U.S. Catholics saw as the best aspects of their own American narrative.

A Saint "Who Overlaps Our Lives"

Rev. Henry Malak had made a valid point when he distinguished between Josephine Dudzik, who had arrived in the United States as "an unknown immigrant girl," and Cabrini, who had done so wearing a religious habit. Traveling as a missionary was arguably quite different from traveling as an immigrant, and Cabrini *had* been a missionary, according to canon law and her own self-understanding.[32] In fact, Cabrini had struggled mightily to get canonical approval to use the feminine form of "missionary" (*missionarie*) in her congregation's name, as only one female congregation, the Franciscan Sisters of Mary, had so incorporated it before. "This title of 'Missionarie' is entirely new," observed the director of the Foreign Missionary Society in 1890. "As far as I know in the history of the Church there is no trace of it before our time. It is not even in the dictionary."[33]

As Cabrini was breezing through the canonization process, however, any distinction between missionary and immigrant disappeared in accounts of Cabrini's life as U.S. Catholics placed her, along with John Neumann, squarely in the latter category. "Mother Cabrini, the immigrant," argued one admirer, "became an American very truly and in the best sense."[34] Cabrini's diversion from her original destination of China to the United States further enhanced her attractiveness as an American symbol. For a U.S. Catholic audience newly persuaded that American holiness had its genesis in the transplanting of a European church rather than in the conversion of a native population, Cabrini's divinely ordained transfer from "the more romantic fields of China and Asia" to the squalid ethnic enclaves of New York confirmed that she belonged especially to their own national story.[35]

Accounts of Cabrini's service in the United States often acknowledged her special affinity for Italian immigrants. Soon after her arrival, according to one story, Cabrini had been reading a letter to an illiterate Italian informing him of his mother's premature death and, at that moment, vowed to become both "the mother and the solace" to the immigrant in America.[36] As Italians themselves, Cabrini and her sisters also suffered because of ethnic prejudice. After the murder of the Franciscan Leo Heinrichs in 1908, for example, the Denver-based Missionary Sisters of the Sacred Heart reported that they had been victims of guilt by association, as his death at the hands of a Sicilian anarchist had led many local benefactors to withdraw monetary support from the Italian congregation.[37]

Yet Cabrini's appeal as an immigrant saint, again like Neumann's, extended well beyond her own ethnic group. As her first U.S. biographer insisted, Cabrini had "never thought of her work as being exclusively for Italians" and had "impressed herself upon the consciousness of America, not simply upon that of America's Little Italies."[38] Devotees also emphasized that the "Apostle to the Italians" had looked beyond her own ethnic group when recruiting new members for the MSCs. "Many an Irish girl," said one sketch, "after looking into Mother Cabrini's wonderful eyes, felt it her vocation to help this wonderful little woman in the work she had in hand."[39] This appears to have been exactly what happened when Winifred Sullivan, an Irish American from Avoca,

Pennsylvania, met Cabrini; though Sullivan had been familiar with the MSCs, she had not considered joining them until her personal encounter with their founder.[40] In the case of this claim and others, the issue is not veracity but purpose. It *was* true that, at the time of Cabrini's death, approximately one-fourth of the members of her congregation came from non-Italian backgrounds. Cabrini's openness to aspirants of other ethnic backgrounds was one piece of the evidence that helped her supporters depict her as the spiritual mother to all U.S. Catholics descended from Europeans.

John LaFarge also presented Cabrini as a bridge between racial and ethnic groups, recalling that she had been as comfortable with "Catholic Negro stevedores from Jamaica" as she was rescuing "bewildered Italians from angry mobs" and had served immigrants of all backgrounds during "hot summer months in the east-side New York tenements." Like her other admirers, LaFarge linked Cabrini to another pillar of U.S. Catholics' triumphal midcentury narrative, their defeat over religious and ethnic prejudice. Cabrini's faithfulness and resolve, he recalled, had enabled her to "drag thousands and millions into light and health and salvation with one terrific drag of the net."[41] Another devotee insisted that it was "largely through her personal toil" that "Americans of Italian descent have won a just integration into the American scene."[42] And others went so far as to assign Cabrini credit for single-handedly "solving the Italian immigration problem" in the United States. Various reports affirmed that Italians from the lowest laborer up to the Italian ambassador to the United States acknowledged her as the American savior of Italian migrants.[43]

Cabrini's most celebrated triumph over ethnic and religious prejudice had occurred in New Orleans, where she was remembered as having arrived "when Italians were most in need of a friend." Echoing Neumann's appearance among Philadelphia Catholics in the wake of the Bible riots, Cabrini established her first institution in New Orleans in 1892, one year after the lynching of eleven Italians who had been tried for the killing of the city's police chief, supposedly for cracking down on organized crime. Writing about the episode forty years later as part of the celebrations of Cabrini's beatification, one writer with the Louisiana Works Progress Administration described the precarious situation of the city's Italians at the time: "Every poor 'dago' was looked upon as a Black Hand and the cry of 'Who Killa Da Chief?' rang out whenever a son of Italy showed his face." Cabrini's intervention had saved the day. "The little nun set about almost immediately to establish a more peaceful relationship between her people and citizens of other nationalities. . . . And soon New Orleans was a better and safer place to live."[44] Catholics in New Orleans also celebrated their enduring connection to her through the institutions Cabrini had founded there.

Louisiana Catholics also evinced a proprietary interest in Philippine Duchesne, who had stayed in New Orleans before traveling up the Mississippi and whose Society of the Sacred Heart had established an institution in Grand Coteau. But Duchesne had left little tangible evidence of her sojourn in New Orleans, whereas Cabrini was remembered at the two institutions she opened there, both of which were still in operation in the 1930s. The fact that Duchesne's and Cabrini's causes were being evaluated in Rome at roughly the same time invited frequent comparisons between the two women. While typically acknowledging that Cabrini and Duchesne had shared both holiness and an American connection, these juxtapositions inevitably emphasized that the two women had undertaken "different kinds of work in the New World" and had labored against remarkably different backdrops. Whereas Duchesne had inhabited "a log cabin" in a "crude village," Cabrini's hagiographical keywords were *city* and *skyscraper*.[45] Like Duchesne, Cabrini had never mastered the English language. Unlike Duchesne, however, Cabrini had a story that translated easily to the U.S. vernacular. Perhaps nothing demonstrates that difference better than a memorial image of Cabrini produced to commemorate the twenty-fifth anniversary of her death.

Robert J. Smith, who had worked as a muralist for the Works Progress Administration, painted a particularly arresting depiction of her as an urban denizen (figure 6). *Saint among the Skyscrapers* inspired Archbishop Samuel Stritch, Mundelein's successor in Chicago, to emphasize Cabrini's proximity to Chicago's Catholics: "Here, in the heart of this great metropolis, lived Mother Cabrini . . . here, where the elevated trains with all their noise and the automobiles flying past and the victims of accidents being rushed into her hospital, in just the same conditions of life in which we live today."[46] A New York journalist echoed Stritch, marveling that America's first *beata* had lived "right in the middle of the twentieth century with its streetcars and automobiles. Slap in the middle of modern progress. She saw these trolley tracks and these buildings. . . . And now she's in heaven."[47]

Della Casa's map records that Cabrini had traveled "parte a cavallo" (on horseback), and at least one surviving image depicts her traversing the Andes on a mule.[48] Yet there was no question which image was more popular in Cabrini's hagiography. In U.S. Catholics' midcentury memory, Cabrini had traveled

FIGURE 6
Saint among the Skyscrapers,
by Robert Smith, 1942. (Cabrini University)

using modern methods of transportation. Through her urban, contemporary way of life, Americans connected with Cabrini in a way they did not with earlier saints. Notre Dame professor John Logan expressed it in verse: Cabrini was a saint "who overlaps / Our lives . . . [who] helped shape our city and the city in the sky."[49]

In terms of U.S. cities, Chicago and New York competed most actively over which one could lay claim to Cabrini—she had died in the former but rested in the latter. But no city was more important to Cabrini's American afterlife than Seattle, Washington, where she had applied for and received citizenship in

1909. Although Cabrini's naturalization, unlike Neumann's, had never been in dispute, her reasons for seeking American citizenship were another matter. She herself had never disclosed them and had most likely been following the advice of her lawyer, as U.S. citizenship not only helped Cabrini secure the MSC's property holdings but also facilitated her frequent border crossings.[50] In the 1930s, however, Cabrini's devotees in the United States ascribed her decision to naturalize to less pragmatic motives. One U.S. priest, for instance, insisted she sought citizenship because she had become "so enamored of America." The editor of Chicago's Catholic newspaper claimed that Cabrini had chosen to swear allegiance to the flag of the United States because "she fully realized how her work could identify itself with the great destinies of the new world," while another biographer declared that Cabrini "had from the outset intended to seek naturalization," attributing the delay to the practical demands of running her missionary network.[51] Mundelein also maintained that Cabrini had viewed her own naturalization as a way "to link her institutions more firmly to the country."[52] Amleto Cicognani, too, insisted that Cabrini's naturalization proved her "attachment to the United States" and understanding of "the American mentality," although he often stretched the truth in support of these assertions. To suggest that Cabrini had "reserved special love for the United States," for example, he pointed out that she had spent the last five years of her life within its boundaries, neglecting to mention the practical factors that had kept her from returning to Italy during that time.[53]

In molding Cabrini's story into a narrative that foregrounded her "Americanness," Cicognani's desire to sponsor a U.S. saint evidently overcame his instinct as a native Italian, as others among his compatriots in the Roman hierarchy regarded the United States as incidental to Cabrini's story. For Salotti, the United States was simply the place where she happened to have died: her body may be resting in America, he said, but "her heart beats in Italy, the land of her gentle affections and her fruitful inspiration." In Salotti's view Cabrini had been above all an "illustrious daughter of Italy" whose true measure of sanctity lay in her efforts to help her exiled compatriots retain their attachment to "the glorious land of Dante and Columbus."[54] Many others characterized Cabrini as "a good Italian"—a misleading term at best, considering that, over the course of Cabrini's lifetime, regional allegiances had superseded national ones throughout the only recently unified Italian peninsula.[55]

To cast Cabrini as either an Italian or an American patriot, however, is to misunderstand that her primary allegiance was to church over state. She criticized other congregations that seemed to embrace too fervently the cause of Italian nationalism; in 1889, for example, she chided the Scalabrinians for a spirit that seemed "more attached to the tri-color flag than the Pope."[56] Many of Cabrini's spiritual daughters in the Missionary Sisters of the Sacred Heart viewed the founder as a woman whose life and loyalties transcended national boundaries. It is telling, for example, that Mother Saverio de Maria, MSC, never mentioned her naturalization as a U.S. citizen in the biography she published of Cabrini in 1927, instead portraying Cabrini as a nomad whose worldly wanderings were punctuated by periodic return visits to Italy. Mother Antonietta's map of Cabrini's transatlantic travels also suggests that her U.S. destinations served as constellation points rather than as termini.

In the mental map of her U.S. devotees, however, Cabrini was firmly anchored to a U.S. center. Theodore Maynard, a British transplant and enthusiastic proponent of U.S. Catholicism who published a biography of Cabrini in 1945, found in her an ideal subject to make his case about the harmony of Catholic belief and "the American idea." In Maynard's interpretation, Cabrini's life testified to the possibilities that the United States presented to Catholics who chose to embrace it. Characterizing Cabrini as "the most typical of Americans," Maynard complimented her for accomplishing tasks with "the utmost dispatch."[57]

Others among Cabrini's hagiographers echoed Maynard, praising her as an American who had grasped the national formula for success: "The buildings she erected," one wrote, "still scrape American skies as do those of big business." Admirers reported that she had mingled regularly with "businessmen, politicians, philanthropists" and that she displayed "exceptional executive abilities" and developed "rare qualities of leadership."[58] Others emphasized Cabrini's quintessentially American traits of ingenuity and flexibility. According to La-Farge, she never hesitated to "scramble up a ladder" and was willing to work as "architect and contractor and stone mason and everything else when a twelve-month job of remodeling had to be completed in eight."[59] A *New York Times Magazine* profile praised Cabrini's "uncanny instinct" for knowing in what direction a city would expand, noting that it paid lasting dividends; her congregation's "real estate investments alone now run into millions."[60]

Cabrini's admirers looked no further for evidence of her spiritual and temporal prosperity than her multiple institutions. Like those who chronicled the life of Neumann, her biographers inevitably embellished her story with accounts of her rich and varied institutional legacy. "Schools, convents, orphanages, and hospitals seemed to spring up out of nothing," marveled one.[61] Cabrini's resourcefulness in finding the means for her institutions impressed even her Protestant lawyer. Testifying at the diocesan inquiry into her virtues, the attorney described the esteem he had developed for his client over the thirteen years she had retained him. "The spread of her Community in the United States is most remarkable," he declared, "and there are some elements in which it would be called miraculous."[62] At the same time, as one academic noted in 1946, Cabrini hardly resembled a typical American millionaire. As she was an "architect who built her life around the designs of God," he argued, Cabrini's story should serve as an enduring corrective to the United States, a "nation that bows before the streamlined gods of success."[63] Cabrini, in other words, had not simply attained success; she had sanctified it.

But no matter how firmly U.S. Catholics believed in a person's holiness, the process of proving it to officials at the Sacred Congregation almost always presented challenges. The results of investigations into Cabrini's virtues and reputation for sanctity were deposited at the Sacred Congregation by 1933, and the debate over Cabrini's virtues began quickly.[64] Witnesses had not all spoken positively about Cabrini, and the job of the "devil's advocate" was to ferret out people who might call her sanctity into question. In Cabrini's case, two former members of the Missionary Sisters of the Sacred Heart had seemed obvious candidates. Early in the twentieth century, Mothers Placida Massa and Diomira Bertelli had accused Cabrini of a lack of orthodoxy and other nefarious crimes and had attempted to discredit her at the Holy See. Massa and Bertelli eventually retracted their accusations and apologized to Cabrini and later left the MSCs to establish their own group. During the investigation of Cabrini's virtues, however, they made even more outlandish claims against her, suggesting that her tyrannical style would have made her a good wife for "Il Duce" (Benito Mussolini) and implying that Mother Antonietta Della Casa was her illegitimate daughter.[65]

None of the negative evidence appears to have given Cabrini's examiners any pause, though it did attract a flurry of American attention for a brief moment in the 1970s, when an American actor wrote a sensational—and largely unsubstantiated—account of Mother Cabrini's "trial" at the Vatican that captured the imagination of a young Italian American filmmaker named Martin Scorsese. Fresh from his success directing *Taxi Driver*, Scorsese purchased the production rights to "The Trial of Francesca Cabrini" and told a *New York Times* interviewer that he planned to make his next movie about Cabrini, "an unsaintly saint who hustled in the streets and clawed her way through society."[66] Back in the 1930s, though, officials at the Holy See did not see much credibility in any of the adverse testimony, particularly since Della Casa dispensed with the accusations handily.

The Holy See ruled that Cabrini had indeed practiced the virtues to a heroic degree and declared her venerable on 21 November 1937.[67] As a person for whom eyewitness testimony existed, Cabrini needed two miracles to proceed to beatification. Many petitioners looked upon this next stage with dread, and with good reason. One Redemptorist—frustrated by the long-standing failure to confirm a miracle for Neumann—described this process as "so involved, so bristling with legal formalities and medical cross examinations, requiring the cooperation of so many persons, and costing so much money, that it might be said to need a miracle of its own to see it through."[68] Here again, Cabrini would prove exceptional, as the cures attributed to her intercession proceeded relatively quickly through the process.

Heaven Touched Earth

To qualify to advance the cause to beatification, miracles could have occurred at any point after a candidate's death. While the Sacred Congregation could not review testimony until after the Servant of God had been declared venerable, testimony supporting that person could be gathered in advance. In 1933, the Archdiocese of Chicago gathered witnesses from New York and Seattle to testify to two extraordinary cures attributed to Cabrini's intercession. In 1921, Mae Redmond Cirillo, a nurse at New York's Cabrini Hospital (the former Columbus Hospital, renamed after Cabrini's death) made a horrific mistake. After assisting at the delivery of a baby boy, Cirillo administered what she thought was a 1 percent silver nitrate solution to his eyes, as mandated by state law. Two hours later, noticing inflammation of his eyes and burn marks on his cheeks, she discovered she had accidentally used a 50 percent solution. At the very least, the baby would be blinded for life, but it seemed that the consequences would be even more dire: having ingested the poison into his lungs, the baby, named Peter Smith, contracted pneumonia and developed a high fever. The prognosis was death. After a nursing sister attached a piece of Cabrini's veil to the baby's garments, however, his fever receded and his sight returned. He left the hospital completely healed. The baby's mother and attending doctors also testified in the case, first in a local court in New York, then a second time in the advance process in Chicago in 1933, and finally in the official process submitted to the Holy See in 1937.[69]

As noted earlier, miracle causes are typically sent in pairs, and Smith's cure was bundled with that of Sister Delphine Graziela, an MSC from Seattle who had mysteriously recovered from a near-fatal stomach ailment in 1925. The superior in Seattle broadcast the news to all the MSCs in the United States: just before her recovery, Sister Delphine had seen Cabrini standing by her bed. Mother Mary Josephine of the New York–based MSCs responded effusively that while all of Cabrini's spiritual daughters could "boast of graces and favors received through her intercession," other convents envied "the singular favor with which your fortunate community has been favored—such favors are rare and very precious."[70]

After offering preliminary testimony in Seattle, two Protestant doctors traveled to Chicago to appear before the official ecclesial court. Dr. Milton Sturgis, who had operated four times on Sister Delphine, testified that he could not "explain from a surgical point of view how this sudden change for the better took place." Dr. Carl S. Leede also gave his expert opinion that the cure was inexplicable from a medical standpoint. He admitted that he had known Cabrini personally and admired her but, as was customary for witnesses in such processes, swore that he had no selfish motive in testifying and that no one had instructed him in what to say: "I came out of a feeling of friendship for the sisters. I am willing to give the facts as I know them leaving to others their interpretations." As was the case with Smith's cure, pages of hospital charts related to Delphine's case were included in the official testimony.[71]

The Archdiocese of Chicago sent all this testimony to the Sacred Congregation for examination in late 1937. Once their discussion was scheduled—for between ten and twelve o'clock, Rome time, on 10 July 1938—Cabrini's postulator communicated the details to superiors at all the MSC convents and recommended that they encourage all the sisters to spend those hours in adoration before the Blessed Sacrament so "all goes well."[72] It did. The vote was positive on both necessary counts: the cures were deemed inexplicable, and they were attributed to Cabrini's intercession. The date for Cabrini's beatification was set for 13 November 1938.

One final ritual remained. Two months before the scheduled beatification, Monsignor Salvatore Natucci, Promoter General of the Faith at the Sacred Congregation of Rites, visited New York to procure a relic from Cabrini's body, which he would take back with him to Rome and present to Pope Pius XI.

Natucci's departure for Rome on the ocean liner *Conte di Savoia* on 24 September, which, according to one reporter, "was of the deepest interest to all the Roman Catholics of America," generated a dockside spectacle. Although Cardinal Patrick Hayes had died the previous summer, his auxiliary bishop and other "leading members of New York's papal aristocracy" had come to bid farewell to Natucci and his entourage. Mother Antonietta Della Casa and several other MSCs also joined the traveling party, another indication that they enjoyed a position of prominence rarely afforded to women religious in official canonization proceedings.[73]

A month after the *Conte di Savoia*'s departure, seventy-seven other Missionary Sisters of the Sacred Heart of Jesus from across the United States converged in New York Harbor to embark on another ocean liner bound for Italy, where they would attend Cabrini's beatification. The sisters from Seattle, Denver, and Los Angeles had first met in Chicago, where they spent time in the room in which "Blessed Cabrini took her flight to heaven" in 1917. From Chicago, they traveled in a reserved railroad car to New York with Cardinal Mundelein and, before boarding the SS *Rex*, had an opportunity to venerate Cabrini's remains at Mother Cabrini High School at Manhattan's northern tip. Fourteen seniors from that high school had been chosen to accompany the sisters on the pilgrimage, and Peter Smith, the now-seventeen-year-old miracle baby, was also an honored guest. A number of priests joined the group, including Salvator Burgio, the Vincentian priest who had scoffed at the International Federation of Catholic Alumnae's pilgrimage to Rome seven years before. No stranger to Rome, Burgio envisioned this trip to the Eternal City less a chance to celebrate Cabrini than an occasion to press forward the cause of Elizabeth Ann Seton, his own favorite candidate.[74]

Rumors circulated that Cardinal Mundelein, the most prominent Catholic passenger on the SS *Rex*, also had an ulterior motive in traveling to Rome. Critics alleged that the cardinal, having delivered on his promise to ensure "victories for President Roosevelt's candidates" in recent midterm elections, planned to discuss with Pius the establishment of diplomatic relations between the Holy See and the United States. This speculation forced Mundelein to release a public statement stipulating that Cabrini's beatification was the sole object of his visit.[75]

From New York, the pilgrims sailed to Naples, retracing a route that Frances Cabrini had followed on two of her transatlantic crossings.[76] For Sister Ursula Infante, a native of Brooklyn who had been received into the MSCs by

Mother Cabrini in 1915, the opportunity to attend Cabrini's beatification was the chance of a lifetime. She recounted that after an overnight stay in Naples, the pilgrims arrived in Rome, where the U.S. sisters "had the joy of meeting our sisters from various parts of the globe" at the congregation's motherhouse. On Saturday, 12 November, they had an audience with Pope Pius XI, who spoke warmly of their founder: "Her life," he said, "is a poem of activity, of intelligence, of charity, and of sanctity."[77]

Yet Pius XI did not attend Cabrini's beatification Mass at St. Peter's Basilica, as popes did not preside at such events, which were meant to highlight the local church. The honor usually went to a prelate from a diocese in which the new blessed had lived and died, and in this case the celebrant was Chicago's Cardinal Mundelein. The short interval between Cabrini's death and beatification afforded him an unprecedented honor: he became the first prelate ever to celebrate the Mass of beatification for a person at whose funeral Mass he also officiated.[78] Cabrini admirer Carlo Salotti also played a prominent role at Cabrini's beatification, as two months earlier, Salotti—now a cardinal—had returned to the Sacred Congregation as its prefect. In that capacity, the morning's most sacred task was entrusted to him: reading aloud the papal decree of beatification.

It was a dazzling moment. Silver trumpets heralded the new blessed as her image, previously veiled, was revealed to the congregation. One MSC who attended the ceremony insisted the moment was too sacred to describe but made a valiant attempt: "Heaven had touched earth, and we bathed in the glory of our mother."[79] At precisely five o'clock in the morning New York time—the very hour that Salotti read the decree in Rome—Cabrini's casket was transferred from an anteroom at Mother Cabrini High School in New York to an onyx-lined, glass-encased tomb beneath the white marble altar in the school chapel. Cabrini's more elaborate resting place connoted her new status as blessed and encouraged more pilgrims to visit the site.[80]

In Rome, more rituals followed the morning Mass. In the afternoon, as was customary, Pope Pius XI visited St. Peter's to venerate the relics of the new blessed—the artifacts Monsignor Natucci had traveled to New York to obtain. As the pope arrived at St. Peter's, pilgrims waved mauve-colored handkerchiefs imprinted with Cabrini's image, so designed to evoke the violets the former "Cecchina" had once pretended to be missionaries. The Swiss guards took one of them and handed it to Pius to examine. Recalling the color's symbolism, the pope smiled, pronounced it a "beautiful idea," and pocketed it. Three Masses of

Thanksgiving, held on consecutive days at different Roman churches, typically follow beatifications and canonizations. One of Cabrini's Masses took place at the Church of the Gesù, where Cabrini had so often invoked the help of St. Francis Xavier. The U.S. pilgrims then left Rome for northern Italy, traveling to Codogno and to Cabrini's birthplace in Sant'Angelo, where residents decorated the village entirely with violets to honor its newly beatified native daughter.[81]

More remarkable than the awe that Cabrini's beatification inspired among those who had a direct connection to her was the extent to which the momentousness of the occasion registered with U.S. Catholics who had no links to either the Italian nun or her congregation. The minute Cardinal Mundelein read Pope Pius XI's decree of beatification on that November morning, U.S. Catholics would be able to venerate publicly a saint who had once lived among them. Mundelein emphasized this milestone to his fellow citizens in a radio broadcast shortly after the beatification Mass—the first of its kind delivered by an American prelate from St. Peter's Basilica. Mundelein also suggested that the new medium amplified the theological message. Americans, he noted, had traditionally struggled to grasp what it meant to communicate with their heavenly intercessors. Now, for the first time, "the millions who are thousands of miles away across a vast expanse of land and water" could feel connected to a blessed who belonged especially to them and understand at last "how very possible, how very real, is the communion of the saints."[82] Citing Cabrini's naturalization as a U.S. citizen as the factor that differentiated her from previous saints, the cardinal pointed out to his listeners that "many of us are still immigrants or children of immigrants" and thus it was fitting "that a foreign-born citizen was the first to be raised to the honors of the altar, to become a national heroine."[83]

Back at home another Chicago priest echoed Mundelein. Though "the Jesuit martyrs who were canonized not so long ago [may] confer a distinct honor on the country," the fact that they "had offered their lives for the Indians long before the United States was conceived" limited their national significance.[84] Newspapers around the country, including those published in places that neither Cabrini nor her sisters had ever visited, emphasized her beatification as an unambiguous American triumph. Over and over, they noted that while Cabrini may not have been an American by birth, she was thoroughly American in "citizenship, sympathy, and service."[85] Patriotic celebrations in New York hailed Cabrini not only for her virtue but also for her "association with the American flag."[86] Some of Cabrini's advocates used sports metaphors to celebrate her triumph, noting that Cabrini had "broken all modern records," even those set by the Little Flower.[87] Cabrini's beatification, incidentally, had been Pius XI's last; as saintly bookends to his papacy, Cabrini and Thérèse of Lisieux were linked yet again.

While the Great War had curtailed Cabrini's travel for the last five years of her life, the outbreak of a second European conflict would not stall her progress toward canonization. Although petitioners of other U.S. causes underway at the time routinely lamented the delays in communications and other disruptions caused by World War II, Cabrini's vice-postulator used the war and his own status as an army chaplain to enhance her popularity. He assured readers of the *Mother Cabrini Messenger* that Cabrini, having lived through the First World War, was looking over her "beloved country" and praying that "the trial be shortened and this cross be lifted from the world." The Cabrini League regularly offered Masses for "our boys in service," among them the miracle baby, Peter Smith.[88]

While the miracles for beatification could have occurred at any point after a saint's death, the miracles for canonization had to have been effected after the beatification, as they were understood to be a divine sign that God wanted the saint to be venerated beyond the local population, however defined. Given the importance of this step, it may seem surprising that the *Mother Cabrini Messenger* devoted so little space to the news that two more cures had been attributed to Cabrini's intercession. That both of the reported miracles had taken place in her native province of Lodi may explain why U.S. audiences heard so little about them, in marked contrast to the widespread publicity given to the cures of Smith and Sister Delphine.[89] Discussions of these cases moved swiftly through the process. Pope Pius XII—the former Eugenio Pacelli—signed Cabrini's decree of canonization in 1944, but the exigencies of war required that the official elevation ceremony be postponed. It took place in July 1946—the first canonization after World War II. The scheduling of the canonization was another point at which Cabrini's Italian sisters seem to have been successful in applying pressure to the Holy See, as one U.S. priest who attended the canonization reported that the pope would have preferred to wait until Rome had recovered more fully from war, but "the Italian sisters insisted."[90]

From a technical standpoint, Cabrini now belonged not just to Catholics in the United States but also to the faithful throughout the world. In his homily at the canonization Mass, Pius XII emphasized that sanctity transcended national borders. In an exhortation made more poignant by the fact that the world had only just begun recovering from a horrific war, the pontiff looked to this new heavenly ally as an agent of peace. "Nations and peoples will learn from her," he predicted, "that they are called to constitute a single family, which must not be divided in ambiguous and stormy rivalry nor dissolve itself in eternal hostilities."[91]

The pope's plea to celebrate Cabrini as a universal saint largely fell upon deaf ears in the United States. Greeting Cabrini's canonization as a national triumph, U.S. Catholics celebrated the occasion through sacred rituals, such as an outdoor Mass that drew a hundred thousand faithful to Chicago's Soldier Field—surpassing in size even the crowd at the Eucharistic Congress Mass two decades before. U.S. Catholics' sense of ownership of Cabrini generated a flurry of new hagiographical material in multiple genres, ranging from a Hollywood movie titled *Citizen Saint* to a comic book that celebrated "Our Country's First Saint."[92] The editors of *America* magazine urged their readers to use the occasion of Cabrini's canonization to eradicate any lingering anti-Catholic prejudice, claiming that Cabrini's own triumph should inspire other U.S. Catholics "to dedicate themselves to wiping out what still remains to mock our pretensions to democracy."[93]

Others Catholics were more attentive to the pope's emphasis on Cabrini as an international unifier. One Irish priest, for instance, upbraided U.S. Catholics for trying to nationalize a woman who had just been affirmed as a citizen of heaven. "Chicago and New York boast that she was their citizen," he wrote, but Americans had forgotten that "she sought for a city that is to come."[94] Some U.S. Catholics did gesture to the primacy of Cabrini's heavenly citizenship. *Commonweal*'s editors, for example, reminded readers that dwelling on the glory that Cabrini's canonization bestowed on the American flag would be "a back-front approach": the achievement honored God, not the United States. Yet even they could not contain their jubilation; the same editorial described Cabrini's canonization as the "most honorable event in American history." Although other saints and blesseds of "what is now the United States may have sanctified our soil," Cabrini was "an American citizen and so an American saint of a new kind."[95] Shortly before her canonization, *Commonweal* had also published a review of a new biography of Cabrini that criticized it for, among other flaws, containing "no account—indeed no mention—of her naturalization, or of the reasons that prompted her to take this step."[96]

Cabrini's proximity as well as her citizenship rendered her a new kind of saint in the eyes of U.S. Catholics. Her vice-postulator, Aristeo Simoni, observed that most saints were "so distant from us that they are almost lost in the dim light of history.... Their voice reaches us from afar, muffled and indistinct." Not so for Cabrini, he argued, who "lived in our time and moved in our midst."[97] One New Yorker emphasized that Cabrini had walked "not on Roman streets, not Canterbury or Assisi hundreds of years ago, not the Holy Land," but in America. Chicago's Archbishop Stritch juxtaposed the Little Flower with Mother Cabrini: "Thérèse of Lisieux, in a poor little village in France ... [was] clothed with some sort of poetic haze very far away." Mother Cabrini, on the other hand, was "nothing far off, a saint coping with the same conditions and the same difficulties which surround us in our own lives."[98] As it happened, Cabrini had fallen almost a year short in terms of beating the Little Flower's canonization "record." On another level of competition, though, Cabrini emerged as the clear victor. To U.S. Catholics, Thérèse was eternally remote, while Mother Cabrini was "nothing far off," a saint who belonged especially to them.

In 1890, John Gilmary Shea had insisted that U.S. Catholics would find solace in the canonization of the Jesuit missionaries, saints who had "lived and labored and sanctified themselves in our land, amid circumstances familiar." Shea could not have predicted that, half a century later, those missionaries would appear almost as distant to U.S. Catholics as the medieval saints did. It would be Frances Cabrini—the immigrant, the saint among the skyscrapers, and, above all, the proud U.S. citizen—who would finally capture their imagination.

Patron of ... Emigrants?

For Mother Antonietta Della Casa and others of Cabrini's spiritual daughters, Cabrini's canonization was "one of the most beautiful days" of their lives. In an emotional interview with an American reporter, Della Casa's eyes filled with tears as she beseeched him and other Catholics to keep invoking Cabrini: "Today we have gained a great glory and a powerful help for the fulfilment of our mission. We must pray ... pray ... and pray."[99] The *Mother Cabrini Messenger*, which continued to be published from Chicago six times a year, testified that U.S. Catholics still sent their prayers in Cabrini's direction. Each issue reported favors and graces that devotees attributed to her.

Della Casa served as the MSCs' superior general until her death in 1955. Her obituary in the *Mother Cabrini Messenger* praised her accomplishments.

Notably, she had sent the Missionary Sisters to China in 1926, in what the editors portrayed as the realization of Cabrini's original dream. She had also opened Mother Cabrini High School in Washington Heights, arranged for Cabrini's reburial there, and spearheaded the construction of an even more elaborate national shrine to Cabrini in Chicago. According to the editors, Della Casa's most magnificent achievement involved her "tireless and relentless efforts" against "insurmountable difficulties" in raising her beloved predecessor to the honors of the altar.[100] Yet Cabrini's rapid path to canonization suggests those difficulties were minimal at best, and certainly they pale in comparison to the difficulties experienced by promoters of the next two U.S. saints—whose canonizations were still some thirty years in the future. What is clear is that Della Casa wielded what was, for women religious, an extraordinary amount of influence in pushing a saint's cause forward.

It does not diminish either Cabrini's holiness or the efforts of Della Casa and Cabrini's other champions to note that Cabrini's story was a remarkably easy sell to U.S. Catholics in the 1930s and 1940s. Even after Cabrini's canonization, U.S. Catholics' continued to mold her life and example to fit their own American stories. The *Mother Cabrini Messenger* encouraged readers to invoke Cabrini as a heavenly soldier in the unfolding Cold War, especially after China expelled the MSCs from their missions there in 1949. Cabrini also entered the postwar debate over separation of church and state when five Protestant clergy members sued a civil district court in New Orleans to remove a statue of her erected on city-owned property, claiming that a statue featuring a woman "in religious garb" violated state and federal constitutional regulations. The local appeals court ruled against them, judging that while the statue may have been erected by Catholics, it "was accepted by a grateful city" in memory of a woman who had given it so much.[101] Devotion to Cabrini also reflected changing gender roles. Presenting what he called "A United Nations of Holiness for the Woman of Today," Rev. Luke A. Farley suggested that Cabrini offered one of the best models of holiness for the Catholic woman "who finds herself in the steel jungle of IBM machines, mountains of filing cabinets, and the staccato drums of typewriters." Cabrini had known the value of a human soul, Farley wrote, but she had also known the value of a dollar.[102]

And yet Cabrini would not be named the patron saint of the United States. On 8 September 1950, Pope Pius XII designated her "Patrona degli Emigranti" (Patroness of the Emigrants), expressing his hope that Cabrini would console the "very many people" who "in our disturbed and evil days" had been forced by poverty or persecution to leave their homes. Pius XII's successors would continue to invoke Cabrini under the title of "Patron of Emigrants," and in that sense her relevance endures to this day.

Notably, U.S. English publications—but not those in British English—identify Cabrini as the Patroness of *Immigrants*, a word choice that associates border crossers with the countries in which they arrive rather than the countries from which they left.[103] This mistranslation of *emigranti* not only conformed to long-standing U.S. perceptions of Cabrini's mission but also reflected the American exceptionalism that intensified during the postwar years. This attitude, in fact, helped redirect U.S. Catholics' search for a national patron yet again. While Cabrini might be said to be the unofficial patron saint of American exceptionalism, there is no evidence to suggest that U.S. Catholics ever contemplated petitioning the Holy See to name Cabrini the patron of the United States. Their failure to take this additional step can certainly not be attributed, as had been the case with the North American martyrs, to any lack of identification with their citizen saint. Yet the same dynamic that had diminished enthusiasm for the martyrs was at work with Cabrini. Even in the exceptionally short interval between the opening of Cabrini's cause and its completion, U.S. Catholics had already moved on to another new moment, and they needed a saint to match it.

However fervent their public enthusiasm for Cabrini, U.S. Catholics familiar with the inner workings of the Vatican grasped that Cabrini's cause for canonization had been, at its core, an Italian project. If U.S. Catholics were able to succeed in shepherding a candidate without Cabrini's Roman connections through the process, however, they would be able to claim a singularly American achievement. Elizabeth Ann Seton—or, as she was increasingly called, "Elizabeth of New York"—would become that candidate. U.S. church leaders, including New York's Cardinal Francis Spellman, the one most closely associated with America's rise as a global superpower, now touted a woman "born and bred" in the United States as the saint who embodied the new temper of the times.

U.S. Catholics could not have chosen a more complex cause on which to flex American muscle. Though Seton's American story closely paralleled Cabrini's, their trajectories diverged dramatically at the Sacred Congregation of Rites. While the case of the Italian missionary had shown how center and periphery could align to make canonization almost a foregone conclusion, Seton's cause would make many detours along the way to the official declaration of her sainthood. In addition to the inherited problems caused by U.S. inexperience, Vincentian apathy, and Seton's ambiguous status vis-à-vis the French congregation—all of which had left her cause languishing in a protracted ordinary process—a host of new problems now arose that threatened to silence it forever.

✦ SUPERPOWER SAINTS ✦

In July 1947, Salvator Burgio, the Vincentian who had once dismissed the International Federation of Catholic Alumnae's pilgrimage to Rome as ineffective in advancing Elizabeth Ann Seton's cause, pursued what might have seemed an equally dubious—if more daring—course of action in support of the same purpose. In a private audience with the pope at his summer residence, Burgio declared in no uncertain terms that canonizing Seton would be an appropriate way for the pontiff to express his gratitude to the American people for all the support they had given Italy and Europe during and after World War II.[1] Burgio's imperiousness may have been exceptional, but the imperialist assumptions behind his demand reflected the American postwar mood. U.S. Catholics had ample reason to absorb the confidence of their national culture. With help from the GI Bill, for example, they were on the way to becoming one of the United States' wealthiest and most educated demographic groups. Having established themselves as fervent anti-communists, moreover, they reveled in their patriotic bona fides in the context of an escalating Cold War. Saint-seeking efforts would be colored both by U.S. Catholics' exuberance about their place in the nation and by their awareness of America's emergence as a global superpower. When Bishop John Mark Gannon of Erie made his own postwar appeal to Pius XII on behalf of the U.S. martyrs, he, too, had linked the martyrs' canonization to the emergence of the United States as "the most powerful and leading nation on earth."[2] Though Gannon had shown more deference than Burgio, and his candidates' stories were less tailored to the era than Seton's, his expectation was the same: Catholic citizens of a powerful nation should have saints of their own. The days in which U.S. Catholics would "humbly beg" the Holy See to accept a U.S. cause had long passed. Vatican recognition of the uniquely "American brand of holiness" had become less a privilege than an entitlement. [3]

Salvator Burgio was a native of New York and so, too, was his hero—a detail that became increasingly more important throughout this era of American saint-seeking. When Leonard Feeney had dubbed Seton "Elizabeth of New York," he departed from the hagiographical convention by which saints are typically associated with the place of their death rather than the place of their birth. And although Seton herself had professed an affection for her native New York, maintained ties with friends and family there, and sent three Sisters of Charity to open a convent in the city in 1817, she had never physically returned to New York after her departure for Maryland in 1808. But Frances Cabrini's abrupt arrival on the American saintly scene created a rhetorical opening for Seton's supporters. As the Italian nun's cause moved swiftly through the process, they would argue that only by canonizing "Elizabeth of New York" would the United States finally have "a saint that is *truly* its own, by birth, by residence, and by service."[4] Feeney and others were thus implementing a classic canonization strategy, in which supporters of a candidate suggest that he or she will fill an unmet spiritual need.

But apart from any symbolic edge it afforded Seton, the designation "Elizabeth of New York" was both apt and telling. New York threads were woven through the complicated tapestry of Seton's afterlife, especially during the middle decades of the twentieth century, when the center of gravity of Seton's cause for canonization would shift there from Emmitsburg. This transition was in part the result of a directive from the Sacred Congregation, issued to resolve a discrepancy long embedded in Seton's cause. It also reflected the priorities of the periphery, especially as defined by Francis Spellman, the man who occupied New York's episcopal throne throughout the most critical stages of Seton's canonization process. Spellman became a fervent supporter of the woman he celebrated as "a New Yorker born and bred," and it was no coincidence that Seton's ascent to the honors of the altar paralleled his own rise to great influence on both sides of the Atlantic. Indeed, without the interventions of the "American pope," it is unlikely Seton would have become the next successful U.S. cause—and quite possible she may never have been canonized at all.[5]

Spellman was never far from the center of the plot in a saga that had been set in motion in the late winter of 1939, when saint-seeking once again intersected with a momentous encounter between U.S. Catholics and the Holy See. Just as the Third Plenary Council of Baltimore in 1884 had generated the U.S. bishops' petition in support of Tekakwitha and the Jesuit martyrs, and the Eucharistic Congress of 1926 had provided the occasion for Cardinals Mundelein and Bonzano to discuss the logistics of opening a cause on Cabrini's behalf, so, too, did another prospective U.S. patron hover on the edges of the principal action at a landmark event in the life of the American church. At the papal conclave of 1939, it was finally Seton's turn.

With three cardinals, the U.S. delegation to the papal conclave that followed the death of Pius XI was substantially larger than any of its predecessors. A single U.S. cardinal had attended the secret assemblies of 1903 and 1914, while none had voted in 1922, when travel delays had caused the United States' only two cardinals to miss the voting that elevated Pius XI. The new pontiff soon extended the maximum period between a pope's death and the beginning of a conclave from ten to eighteen days to accommodate cardinals traveling from outside Europe—a decision that was itself apparently the result of rising American influence within the Holy See. Reporting on a meeting between Boston's Cardinal William O'Connell and the newly elected Pius XI, the *New York Times* had quoted the pontiff's declaration that "all the American Cardinals will be present at the next Conclave" because "the United States is too important to be ignored as she has been."[6] This time, the two cardinals who had missed the previous conclave, O'Connell and Philadelphia's Dennis Dougherty, were joined by Chicago's Cardinal George Mundelein. The outcome of the conclave came as no surprise. The electors chose Cardinal Eugenio Pacelli, who had served as Pius XI's secretary of state.

Pacelli, who took the name Pius XII, had first learned about Seton's cause when apostolic delegate Amleto Cicognani discussed it with him during his 1936 U.S. visit. Though the new pope recalled that exchange and expressed his "paternal and heartfelt" interest in Seton's progress after the election, the pontiff would play a very minor role in the drama that would unfold over the next quarter century.[7] Starring roles went to Spellman and Cicognani, as well as to Burgio, whose pomposity introduced a number of twists into the plot. The cast of characters also included several Italian priests from the Sacred Congregation, who continued to find U.S. Catholics falling short in their attempts to prepare causes for canonization. Three Philadelphia bishops played supporting roles—and in one case, a surprising one—in advancing the plot. Seton's spiritual daughters would feature increasingly prominently as protagonists in the drama's final acts, thanks to the efforts of one Daughter of Charity. By insisting that her religious family come to terms with their tangled history, this sister prefigured Catholic women's desire to move from the sidelines of their church to its center stage. The drama's unsung heroes, of course, were the countless U.S. Catholics who sent their prayers in Seton's direction, who ultimately cared far less about the national implications of her saintly triumph than they did about the miracles she might effect in their own personal lives.

The story of the people who championed, challenged, loved, and invoked "Elizabeth of New York" in the middle third of the twentieth century is, in the particular, a case study of the ways in which personality and power intersected to shape the afterlife of an American saint. Broadly speaking, it is also a narrative about how saints became stand-ins for U.S. Catholics' new role in the nation and in the world—and harbingers of more transformations on the way, in sanctity and beyond.

"The Hub of the Wheel"

Born in Brooklyn in 1895, Salvator Burgio had been dying of tuberculosis in a Vincentian seminary when he was ordained by special dispensation in 1927. After a miraculous recovery, Burgio became friends with Cardinal Dennis Dougherty over the course of an extended convalescence in Philadelphia. For the next two decades, "Sal" accompanied "His Eminence" on vacations and official voyages, to Manila, to Mexico, and, most frequently, to Rome, where Dougherty used his connections to place Burgio in prominent positions at official ceremonies. In 1939, Burgio joined Dougherty for his trip to the papal conclave.[8]

Being at the Vatican before and after the conclave allowed Dougherty and other voting cardinals to press their priorities through face-to-face conversations with Vatican leaders—opportunities to execute, in other words, the very strategy Frances Cabrini had once recommended to Katharine Drexel for advancing initiatives at the Holy See. Cabrini would surface in several conversations that Dougherty initiated with members of the Sacred Congregation of Rites, with a view toward advancing the cause of his personal favorite U.S. candidate for canonization. In his early years as Philadelphia's archbishop, Dougherty had taken a more activist approach on behalf of John Neumann. By the 1930s, however, Burgio's influence had helped to tilt Dougherty's interest toward Elizabeth Ann Seton. It was with her in mind that both men scheduled meetings with cardinals from the Sacred Congregation of Rites, including Carlo Salotti, its prefect since the previous September, in the week before the conclave opened.

Burgio had already laid the groundwork for these conversations several months before. When he had sailed with Mundelein on the SS *Rex*, the luxury liner bearing pilgrims for Cabrini's beatification, Burgio had pressed the Chicago cardinal to mention Seton to the newly appointed prefect during the course of the celebrations. At the time, Seton's cause was still languishing in a protracted ordinary process. Burgio and others of Seton's devotees hoped that by eliciting Salotti's support, they could at least identify, and ideally remove, the barriers preventing Seton from moving on to the official stage of "introduction" in Rome.

Speaking directly to the prefect in February 1939, Dougherty and Burgio opened with the same argument Leonard Feeney and others had employed: that Cabrini's beatification, while certainly meaningful to U.S. Catholics, had also left them longing even more desperately for a canonized saint who had been "born and raised in America." Salotti needed no convincing that Cabrini was an Italian saint, as he had never thought otherwise, and he readily conceded the American shortage: "We have so many brother and sister saints in Italy," he acknowledged, "that it is no more than right that we should advance the Cause of a servant of God in a country that has no saint of its own." Salotti did remember that Mundelein had spoken to him about Seton's cause during the celebrations of Cabrini's beatification. He also shared that he was vaguely familiar with Seton's story; during his earlier appointment at the Sacred Congregation, he had reviewed some of the material that had arrived in support of her cause in the mid-1920s.[9]

If Dougherty and Burgio were encouraged by this promising beginning, the conversation later took a downward turn. Salotti had a distinction of his own to make, between Seton and the only other "Servant of God" who had been born on American soil: Tekakwitha. The prefect confided to the Americans what to him was very good news: the Historical Section had completed its examination of documents in support of Tekakwitha, a favorite candidate of his own, and he would soon be announcing that her cause would move to the next official stage. By contrast, Salotti informed Dougherty and Burgio that the Historical Section had not yet begun to examine Seton's material.[10]

While Dougherty (who had entered the conclave with a biography of Seton that he planned to read during his "leisure moments") and other cardinals were locked away to conduct their solemn duty, Burgio met with Father Ferdinand Antonelli, who worked for the Sacred Congregation's Historical Section.[11] Antonelli informed Burgio that the main reason the cause had not yet been introduced in Rome was the Sacred Congregation's judgment that the lack of eyewitnesses in the original testimony, gathered during the informative process between 1907 and 1911, had rendered the cause hopelessly flawed. The good news was that the establishment of the Historical Section had thrown Seton a lifeline, as the new department eliminated the need for firsthand accounts; the bad news was that supporting documentation would have to be prepared all over again before it could be sent to the Historical Section. "Love's labor lost," Burgio lamented of the original 1,288 pages yielded in the original informative process.[12]

Some other gaps remained. Seton's birth certificate, for example, had yet to surface; Burgio promised to chase down a rumor that a Sister of Charity had stumbled upon it accidentally. But conversations with Rev. Giuseppe Scognamillo, the Vincentian postulator based in Rome, revealed to Burgio an even thornier problem, one that derived from the fateful 1897 decision to list the Daughters of Charity as the sole petitioners. No matter how much sense that simplification had made in those early days, it resulted in an inconsistency that would not meet the exacting standards of the Sacred Congregation when authority for the cause shifted there, as it would once the ordinary process was complete. The documentation gathered in Seton's ordinary process made clear that the members of the various diocesan Sisters of Charity also looked to Seton as their spiritual mother, and, moreover, the argument that she was a founder—and thus eligible for the miracle exemption often awarded on these grounds—depended upon this claim. Considering that Seton's cause did not rest on eyewitness testimony, she would need four authenticated miracles for beatification. The prospect of a reduction was therefore very appealing.[13] Essentially, the Sacred Congregation made clear that Seton's promoters could not have it both ways. If they were going to make the case that Seton truly had been "the mother of many daughters," the Daughters of Charity could not remain the sole petitioners but needed to share that role, not only with the New York branch that had separated from Emmitsburg in 1846 but also with the other independent Seton communities whose founding postdated the original breach.[14]

Yet the formal inclusion of the "Black Caps" into the cause would be far easier said than done. The logistical challenges that had originally prevented it still obtained, and any attempt to unite Seton's spiritual daughters would also necessarily involve reconciling the dueling narratives regarding Seton's original intentions with regard to a possible Vincentian alliance. The two versions—the insistence by the Daughters of Charity that Seton had always desired a union with the French sisters, and the counterclaim, advanced most prominently by Cincinnati's Sister Mary Agnes McCann, that she had been fiercely committed to independence—could no longer coexist.

Despite these challenges, Dougherty and Burgio left Italy heartened by the support they had garnered at the Sacred Congregation. Combining impassioned arguments with a dose of flattery, they had succeeded in capturing Salotti's attention and assuring him and other key players that the hopes of "the Cardinals and the whole of American hierarchy" were pinned on Seton, not Tekakwitha, being "raised to the altar as the first American saint." Cardinal Dougherty gloated that "more has been accomplished [for Seton's cause] in the last four days than has been for years," and Burgio reported that Salotti had "promised TO PUT MOTHER SETON'S CAUSE AMONG THE TOP OF THE LIST if not THE TOP."[15]

Salotti delivered. Within a year, he promulgated the "Decree in the Baltimore Case Concerning the Beatification and Canonization of the Servant of God, Elizabeth Ann Bayley Seton, Widow, Foundress of the Congregation of the Sisters of Charity of St. Joseph."[16] Among its standard elements— biographical details about Seton, testimony of her virtue, and assurances of her enduring "fame of sanctity"—Seton's decree of introduction contained several noteworthy features. One was that it was published in English, a distinction Seton's supporters claimed was a first for the Vatican and interpreted as a sign of increasing respect for the United States. Another was that it parenthetically mentioned Tekakwitha, acknowledging Seton as "the second flower of North America" but stipulating that "Catharine Tekakwitha was the first."[17] Indeed, as Salotti had indicated to Dougherty, Tekakwitha's decree of introduction had been issued the previous May. The reference may have reflected Tekakwitha's preferred status at the Holy See or it may have been a nod to John Wynne, who would continue to work assiduously on her cause until his death in 1949. The most noteworthy phrase in the decree of introduction of Seton's cause was the one that listed Seton's petitioners as "the Sisters of Charity, *founded by the Servant of God, whether they retain separate status, or are merged into one moral entity with St. Vincent's Sisters of Charity.*" With these words, the Sacred Congregation effectively overrode the 1897 decision to list the Daughters of Charity as Seton's sole petitioners.[18]

Mediating the transition from a project shepherded almost exclusively by the Daughters of Charity to one sponsored by all the communities who considered Seton their founder would require considerable sensitivity and tact. Neither were strong suits of the man who emerged from the winter 1939 conversations as the local overseer of Seton's cause: Burgio, who had secured an appointment as Seton's vice-postulator.

There is no question that Burgio was fiercely committed to seeing Seton raised to the honors of the altar. In the days that followed Pacelli's election, he traveled to the northern Italian city of Livorno to meet members of the Filicchi family, descendants of Seton's hosts during her Italian sojourn, and returned to Philadelphia only to pack his bags. He had accepted the appointment as Seton's vice-postulator on the condition that he be released from all other duties and ministries and be permitted to relocate to Emmitsburg and establish an office there. Burgio's superiors had undoubtedly agreed to these stipulations out of deference to Dougherty, but they and other members of the Vincentian Family would later have reason to regret the unusual amount of latitude they permitted him, especially when his tactics began to raise a serious question: Was Burgio more committed to Seton's glorification, or to his own?

Initially, though, Burgio received a "royal welcome" at Emmitsburg.[19] Sister Paula Dunn, visitatrix (superior) of the Daughters of Charity, supplied Burgio with an office and assigned two sisters to serve as his assistants. From this home base he established the Mother Seton Guild, an organization designed "to promote the canonization of Mother Seton in every way possible."[20] He traveled extensively to each of the "Black Cap" communities to scour their archives for additional documentation relevant to Seton's cause, as well as definitive evidence of her baptism. He had hoped to find the latter in Vincennes, Indiana, where Seton's spiritual director Father (later Bishop) Simon Bruté had died and was buried, but it was not there. He did find other treasures, however, including an extensive collection of material related to Seton, especially the correspondence of her grandson William Seton, at the archives of the University of Notre Dame.[21]

Burgio's second purpose in making his visits to the Black Cap communities was to extend to each a formal invitation to join the Daughters of Charity as Seton's petitioners. For an ostensible mission of reconciliation, however, Burgio's efforts engendered an uncommon amount of dissension. Misrepresenting the Vincentian superiors' original motivation for not including the Sisters of Charity in Seton's cause—which had been one of simple expediency—he informed each superior that the Sisters had been deliberately excluded because the Daughters had been determined to maintain exclusive control over Seton's cause. The only reasonable explanation for this false version of events is that it allowed Burgio to present himself as the champion of the Black Caps. Indeed, he often claimed to be the first Vincentian to reach out to them on behalf of Seton's cause, which was demonstrably untrue, since the congregation had asked the superior of the Sisters of Charity to send a petition to Rome in support of Seton's cause in 1924.[22] Whatever Burgio's intentions, thus emerged what would become a recurring pattern, in which Burgio would inflate his own importance and exacerbate long-standing tensions under the guise of reconciling them.

Over the course of these visits, Burgio also made clear that he expected material as well as moral support from each diocesan community. He levied what he called a "tax" of $100 per month per community to support the work of the cause, explaining that progress on the cause required steady injections of funds and reasoning that if each community bore an equal share in the expenses, each would feel equally invested.[23] The imposition startled many among the Sisters of Charity, who believed—correctly—that church regulations on canonization permitted petitioners to solicit donations but not require them. Mother Maria Concilio of the Sisters of Charity of Convent Station, New Jersey, for instance, refused to comply with the request, though she promised that the sisters would, "of course, try to do our part, for we are all anxious to see the Cause so dear to us proceed rapidly to its happy conclusion."[24] Nonetheless, several of the Sisters of Charity congregations believed that they were bound by the "tax," which was not officially removed until 1971.[25] In the name of mediating tensions between the Daughters and the Sisters, Burgio again overreached his own authority, stretched the boundaries of canon law, and, not incidentally, increased his own power, in this case by augmenting his budget.

Burgio's high-handedness ruffled feathers not only on the road but in Emmitsburg, where Sister Paula increasingly challenged his autocratic attitude toward his two sister assistants and his stubborn refusal to render a precise accounting of the Mother Seton Guild's expenditures. In a missive apparently intended to mollify her, Burgio conceded that the sister assistants were beholden to their religious superiors, but he nonetheless insisted that they were subject to his "immediate control" on all matters related to Seton's cause since that authority had been vested in him through the Sacred Congregation. In case Sister Paula should miss his point, he enumerated the arenas over which he had absolute authority: finances, publications, all branches of the Mother Seton Guild, and lay volunteers. By virtue of his position as vice-postulator, Burgio declared, he had unfettered access to all congregational archives and traveled at his own discretion. When it came to overseeing Seton's cause, Burgio invoked what was to become his favorite metaphor: as vice-postulator, he functioned as "the hub of the wheel," with the Daughters and the Sisters constituting its spokes.[26]

Burgio's response understandably did little to placate Dunn. With the support of her congregation's leadership and their clerical superior, she informed Burgio in June 1940 that he should begin to look for another site for the guild's office, as he was no longer welcome at the Emmitsburg motherhouse. Borrowing a page from Burgio's playbook, Dunn used the need for equity as a smokescreen to mask the real source of contention, explaining that "as there are many branch communities of Mother Seton's children in the United States and one in Canada, a location separated from any one Community House will be more satisfactory to all concerned." For the same reasons, Dunn told him, the two sister assistants would no longer serve as secretary and treasurer.[27] Outraged by his "eviction," Burgio appealed immediately to Dougherty, who "saved the day" by securing an official proclamation from Cardinal Salotti in Rome. Citing the need for "unity of action," the prefect affirmed that Burgio, by virtue of his appointment, was "the legitimate representative of the Cause before the Holy See" and had authority over the guild's finances and activities. From his continued base in Emmitsburg, Burgio immediately circulated copies of the declaration to the superiors of each community and in years to come would furnish it whenever anyone challenged his authority.[28]

Though the Daughters' refusal to pay the monthly "tax" irked Burgio, the relationship remained free of open conflict until 1944, when Sister Isabel Toohey became visitatrix. The Boston-bred Toohey was even less inclined than Dunn had been to cede authority to the haughty Vincentian and became Burgio's primary adversary in what he characterized as his "war" with Emmitsburg.[29] Burgio would level two main accusations against Toohey, the first of which was that she wished to retain for the Daughters of Charity the exclusive right for sponsorship over Seton's cause. Toohey, Burgio complained to the Vincentian superior in Paris, was reluctant "to have the Black Cap communities share in the honor of the sponsorship the Cause" because accepting this "UNION of ALL Communities" would require the Daughters to acknowledge what they denied, namely, "that the Black Cap Communities are REAL DAUGHTERS

OF MOTHER SETON."[30] There is little evidence to support this unfair claim. Sources do intimate that Toohey wished to retain a "first among equals" status for the Daughters of Charity, justified both by their longer investment in Seton's cause and considerable financial outlay, which by that point had far exceeded anything the Black Caps had contributed. Sister Isabel was both intelligent and pragmatic, however, and had no desire to flout the decree of the Sacred Congregation; shared sponsorship, she knew, was a necessity.[31]

On the other hand, Burgio's second accusation—that Sister Isabel did not respect his authority—was undoubtedly true. Toohey's real objection was the need to work through Burgio. In January 1945, she presented her case to Giuseppe Scognamillo, Seton's Roman postulator: "It is with hesitation that I write to you about some circumstances occurring between the members of our Council and Fr. Salvator Burgio, C.M. Nevertheless I feel that I ought to make you aware of the affair such as it is, or such as I see it. For some time there has been a difference of opinion . . . he has asked the Council to make a monthly contribution of $100. We have consistently refused to do so, for from the beginning our Province has accepted all financial responsibility and it claims the right to that responsibility from which it has never been relieved. We have no desire to change that relationship since we feel that we are, as a Province, a more responsible and permanent organization than the Mother Seton Guild founded by Fr. Burgio."[32]

In arguing that the province was "a more responsible and permanent organization than the Mother Seton Guild founded by Burgio," Sister Isabel was asking that the Daughters of Charity be permitted to replace Burgio as the arbiter of Seton's afterlife. Unfortunately for her, the Catholic Church prohibited such an arrangement.

When Ellen McGloin had attempted to act as postulator for Philippine Duchesne in the early years of the twentieth century, tradition had prevented women from participating officially in processes of canonization. Since then, the 1917 Code of Canon Law had made the prohibition explicit, stipulating that petitioners could "act personally or through a procurator legitimately constituted for this; women [cannot act] except through a procurator."[33] Any women's congregation proposing one of their own members for canonization, in other words, would need to have the case mediated by a man—and by a man selected by the Sacred Congregation, not by the sisters themselves. In his reply, Scognamillo directed Toohey to Cardinal Salotti's proclamation of May 1941, explaining that "the Emmitsburg Community should accept and obey the decisions rendered by the Sacred Congregation of Rites."[34] Privately Scognamillo sympathized with Sister Isabel and the Province of Emmitsburg, admitting in a letter to Cicognani that the establishment of the Mother Seton Guild had effectively taken away "that exclusive 'paternity,' if you will, of the Cause which it had previously enjoyed." Nevertheless, the Sacred Congregation had deemed the guild "the legitimate representative of the Cause to the Holy See," and thus Burgio served as the proxy for Seton's spiritual daughters, whether they liked it or not.[35]

But Toohey was not entirely without recourse in her efforts to assert authority over Seton's life and legacy. In 1947 she asked John Tracy Ellis, a professor at the Catholic University of America and the era's leading Catholic intellectual, to write a new biography of Seton. Ellis, citing his need to finish what would become his magisterial biography of Cardinal James Gibbons, recommended instead one of his brightest graduate students: Annabelle Melville, who had recently produced a fine research paper on Seton and, as a married woman and a convert, shared a special affinity with her subject. Melville agreed, although she later admitted she had underestimated the challenges that awaited her. Among these was the need to tiptoe around Burgio, who demanded that all publications about Seton be channeled through him and whose offers of "help" masqueraded as thinly disguised attempts to monitor the book.[36]

Sister Isabel also devised other ways to circumvent Burgio. Seeking allies outside the Vincentian Family, she found a sympathetic ear in apostolic delegate Cicognani, who, after hearing her complaints about Burgio's excessive travel and financial mismanagement, raised these concerns with Burgio's superior at the Vincentian seminary in Philadelphia. Cicognani's queries prompted a sharp reprimand from Burgio's superiors, who reminded him on more than one occasion that despite being freed from other ministries he remained subject to his vow of obedience. Still unsatisfied, Cicognani approached Burgio personally and asked him to turn over an account of his expenditures and to explain the source of his dissension with Emmitsburg.[37] Responding in minute detail, Burgio portrayed himself, as he did in similar letters to Spellman and officials at the Holy See, as the savior of Seton's cause and Sister Isabel as its enemy. The closer he felt to his correspondent, the more shocking his accusations against Toohey, at one point even suggesting she was in league with the devil.

But Burgio did have Scognamillo's trust. The Roman postulator was particularly pleased with the way Burgio had organized a diocesan tribunal in New Orleans related to a possible Seton miracle.[38] On 27 December 1934, Sister

Gertrude Korzendorfer, a Daughter of Charity working in New Orleans, had been diagnosed with pancreatic cancer, a disease, Burgio explained, that was "100 percent fatal." Community tradition held that the Daughters of Charity had begun a novena to Seton "immediately" and that Korzendorfer's pain and nausea disappeared completely a day after doctors performed exploratory surgery on 5 January 1935. When Korzendorfer died of a pulmonary embolism seven years later, her autopsy revealed a normal pancreas, with neither traces of cancer nor scar tissue from the surgery.

Burgio spent the summer and fall of 1944 preparing for the investigation of the case. The medical testimony seemed convincing. One famous cancer specialist, described by Burgio as "a Jew-turned-agnostic," insisted that he himself did not believe in miracles but added that "if you mean by a miracle that it could not be explained in any scientific way, you have it here." This was sufficient from a medical point of view. The theological question, however, remained, and Burgio panicked when his detective work revealed that the Daughters of Charity had actually begun their novena on 8 January—three days after Sister Gertrude's surgery and two days after her cure. This would not work for purposes of the trial, and a "crestfallen" Burgio was preparing to close the case when a sister who had been working at the community's orphan home in New Orleans remembered that all the orphan girls had been praying for Seton to intercede on Korzendorfer's behalf. Burgio tracked down two of those girls, who later testified in the diocesan inquiry, and Burgio and Scognamillo were optimistic that the Sacred Congregation would eventually accept the cure as proof of Seton's sanctity.[39]

But the Sacred Congregation would not even review this testimony until after it had ruled on the question of whether Seton's virtues rendered her worthy of the title "Venerable," and the Historical Section's review of that supporting material seemed to be taking a long time. World War II was at least in part responsible for the delay. Burgio claimed, for example, that the 1944 Allied bombing of Italy's Monte Cassino, a monastery in which a consultant of the Sacred Congregation was examining key documents related to Seton's case, had "set [the cause] back for years."[40]

In his personal correspondence, Burgio seemed more distressed that the war had curtailed his once-regular trips to Rome. He returned to the Eternal City at the first opportunity after the war ended and, apart from his complaints about the scarcity and poor quality of the food, was happy to be back in the center of ceremonies at the Holy See.[41] Being in Rome also gave Burgio the upper hand in his conflict with Sister Isabel, as he could interact regularly with Scognamillo and other officials at the Sacred Congregation. The Roman postulator could hear only secondhand accounts of Sister Isabel's side of the story, and some of these reports were increasingly damning. The rector of Emmitsburg's Mount Saint Mary's Seminary, for example, warned Scognamillo that "the Holy Father himself" would have to mediate the conflict, as the pope was the only authority Toohey was likely to respect.[42]

One of Burgio's extended postwar visits put him in Rome in the summer of 1946 and present when the church celebrated Frances Cabrini's canonization on 7 July. Burgio managed simultaneously to diminish the significance of the event and to elevate his own importance at it.[43] As he had done in the aftermath of the 1939 conclave, Burgio used this and subsequent trips to capitalize on the combined symbolic and strategic opportunity presented by Cabrini's recent elevation and his own physical presence in Rome. Over the next year he met regularly with officials at the Sacred Congregation and had three separate audiences with Pope Pius XII, in which he lobbied assiduously on Seton's behalf, arguing that it was she, and not Cabrini, who would represent a *true* American saint. It was during this period that Burgio informed the pope that canonizing Seton was the least he could do to express his thanks to Americans.[44]

That a U.S. priest would speak so peremptorily to the pontiff—and later boast about it in print—suggests why, by 1947, Sister Isabel and her allies had begun to convince Burgio's superiors that something was indeed amiss. In fact, Burgio's efforts in Rome were focused not on advancing Seton's cause but on marshaling his own defense. Pleading his case with Scognamillo and Enrico Dante, the secretary of the Sacred Congregation and a friend of Dougherty's, Burgio fashioned himself as "martyr" to Seton's cause and complained that the people who should have been grateful to him were instead hampering his progress. Privately Burgio was more candid about his feelings toward Toohey, whom he referred to as a "battle-axe" and likened to "Uncle Joe" Stalin. "The Kremlin," he wrote to Dougherty, "has nothing on Emmitsburg." He offered repeatedly to resign as Seton's vice-postulator, should the Sacred Congregation ask him to do so—though he warned that her cause would founder without him at the helm.[45]

As the conflict worsened, it was drawn to the attention of New York's Archbishop Spellman. Like Burgio's, Spellman's story had begun to intersect with Seton's at the conclave of 1939, and the longer he presided over the Archdiocese of New York, the more vociferously he touted Seton as a saint who "belonged wholeheartedly to America."[46] Accustomed to leveraging his influence in Washington and Rome to support American Catholic priorities, Spellman would prove particularly adept in blending saint-seeking and American power.

Seton's Outstanding American Champion

A native of Boston, Francis Spellman studied at New York's Fordham University and at Rome's Pontifical North American College before being ordained a priest in 1916. In 1924, he became the first U.S. attaché to the Vatican secretary of state, a position through which he acquired a number of allies at the Holy See. Among them was Eugenio Pacelli, who consecrated Spellman in St. Peter's Basilica in 1932 when the American was named auxiliary to Boston's William O'Connell. Four years later, Spellman arranged Pacelli's itinerary for his historic visit to the United States (over the complaints of Cicognani, to whom protocol awarded official hosting duties).[47] Soon after Pacelli's election as Pius XII, he appointed his old friend to the coveted episcopal see of New York, which had been left vacant by Cardinal Patrick Hayes's death the previous summer. By virtue of that appointment, Spellman also served as head of the Military Ordinariate for the United States, which Hayes had created on the authorization of Pope Benedict XV during World War I.[48] The outbreak of World War II thus strengthened Spellman's influence at home and abroad.

Pius XII elevated Spellman to the cardinalate in 1946, a few months before Cabrini's canonization ceremony. New York's cardinal appreciated America's first "citizen saint" and often highlighted her connections to the United States. He lent his imprimatur to an image commemorating Cabrini's arrival in New York Harbor and often presided at Mass with the Missionary Sisters of the Sacred Heart in Upper Manhattan. On one of those occasions, he decided to honor Cabrini by delivering a homily in which he described her as having spoken four languages: English, Italian, "the language of the heart, and the language of prayer."[49] Still, no matter how effusively Spellman praised Cabrini, there was no question in his mind that Seton's story lent itself more easily to delivery in an American accent.

Spellman often described Seton in language that was more jingoistic than pious, touting her as "a down-to-earth woman who breathed American air, loved American town and countryside, enjoyed American pastimes, followed American conventions." Seton, he continued, had "battled against odds in the trials of life with American stamina and cheerfulness, worked and succeeded with American efficiency."[50] Seton's saintly triumph, he claimed, would translate into a victory for the American nation—and, not incidentally, for the city where she had been born. Given that "New York will always be [Seton's] Bethlehem," one Sister of Charity reminded Spellman, "it seems right that the crowning of her work should be so significantly linked to New York."[51] Spellman did all he could to make it so, and he was rightly acclaimed by other members of the U.S. hierarchy "as Mother Seton's outstanding American champion."[52]

As he lobbied to advance Seton's cause, Spellman was not about to let Burgio stand in Seton's way. By 1947, he had good reason to fear that the Vincentian's war with Emmitsburg was doing irreparable damage to her cause. Cicognani, too, had begun to fret that he would not live to see Seton beatified. Aware of Burgio's attempts to discredit Sister Isabel at the Holy See, the apostolic delegate was also concerned that the Vincentian had made so little progress in bridging the gap between the Daughters of Charity and the diocesan communities; if anything, Burgio's involvement appeared to have widened it. In April 1947, Cicognani approached Sister Isabel with a daring suggestion: that she create a loosely organized confederation of the Seton communities, united for the exclusive purpose of pursuing Seton's cause. Unless all of them were united behind the cause, he told her, Seton would never be canonized.[53]

Toohey was quick to recognize the brilliance of the strategy, which essentially would make an end run around Burgio. He could hardly continue to accuse the Daughters of Charity of trying to retain exclusive control over the cause if they themselves were making overtures to their separated sisters. Yet Toohey was also daunted by the prospect, for good reason. Though available sources offer little information about what happened next, oral tradition among the Daughters of Charity testifies that Sister Isabel traveled with Sister Rosa McGehee to each of the Seton communities, "begging their forgiveness" for past misunderstandings and enjoining them to move beyond their historic differences for the sake of Seton's cause. Details of these conversations remain murky; one memoir reported that an "uneven acceptance" of Toohey's proposal "created disappointment and suffering for all" and that it took years before "painful historical episodes" and "personal misunderstandings" were resolved and "trust could prevail." Mother Mary Josephine Taaffe, superior at the Sisters of Charity of New York—fittingly, the site of the original split from Emmitsburg—proved to be Sister Isabel's most crucial ally in the attempt to heal old wounds and to build new bridges.[54]

The firstfruits of Toohey's efforts were evident on 28 and 29 October 1947, when representatives from five diocesan Sisters of Charity communities and the two separate provinces of the Daughters of Charity gathered at Emmitsburg for the first Conference of Mother Seton's Daughters. Missing was a representative from Cincinnati—the superior had fallen ill—but she sent her warm greetings of support. Cicognani forwarded a blessing on the endeavor from Pope Pius XII, and Vincentian superiors in France also sent their best wishes. The sisters prayed together and discussed how to coordinate their efforts to make Seton's story better known and to advance her cause. Realizing that each community recited slightly different prayers for Seton's beatification, the delegates voted to adopt the version used by the Sisters of Charity in New York as their "uniform prayer."[55]

In retrospect, the most remarkable moment of the meeting occurred when Taaffe read a statement about the 1846 separation between the Emmitsburg and New York foundations. Forming a sustainable alliance between the Daughters and Sisters of Charity depended upon reaching a common understanding of the reasons behind that original split—reasons that, according to Taaffe, had long been misrepresented. "It is regrettable," she observed, "that the interest of persons outside the community, in this much discussed and greatly misunderstood question, has centered principally and even entirely on the heated correspondence of Bishop [John] Hughes and Father [Louis] Deluol [the Vincentian superior at Emmitsburg]," thereby overlooking the "real protagonists in the drama": the New York Sisters. Bishop Hughes had made clear to them that "there were no half measures." He had forced each sister to choose between two painful options: either to break the bond with Emmitsburg, the place that all of them considered their home, or to abandon the children under their care in New York "to a future—insecure and devoid of religious training."[56] But no matter which decision each sister had made in 1846, none had ever severed her connection to Mother Seton. As "incontrovertible proof" of this fact, Taaffe pointed out that the reconstituted diocesan community immediately had elected Mother Elizabeth Boyle, one of Seton's most intimate friends, as its first superior. The sisters' spiritual lives, moreover, had been formed under Seton's influence, and "even though physical separation takes place, a child does not relinquish the influence of its mother."[57]

Taaffe, lamenting "the myth that developed relative to an estrangement between the Communities," countered that historical sources revealed that communication among the various branches, while sporadic, had been cordial. Rumors of hostility, she maintained, "did not originate in either the words or actions of the Sisters, but in the minds of outsiders." The superiors of the various branches had always "worked in harmony whenever the need for concerted action arose." Now that Seton's beatification appeared to be drawing near, Taaffe argued, the need for concerted action among her progeny seemed "more urgent . . . than ever."[58]

Mother Mary Josephine's insistence that the sisters, and not their clerical advisers, had been the real protagonists in 1846 was echoed in the underlying resolve among participants in the 1947 Conference of Mother Seton's Daughters: to act as their own standard-bearers in advancing their spiritual mother's cause for canonization. They had not invited Burgio to join their gathering, and the Vincentian, predictably, was outraged. When the group also barred him from their second meeting, held at New Jersey's College of St. Elizabeth the following April, Burgio demanded that the Holy See force the sisters to include him, as doing otherwise, he insisted, would effectively "nullify" the office of vice-postulator and, by extension, challenge the authority of the Sacred Congregation itself.[59]

As the situation moved toward a crisis, Cicognani did not seem inclined to intervene directly in the conflict.[60] Perhaps the apostolic delegate may have preferred to work behind the scenes, or he may have wanted to avoid showing favoritism toward any of the candidates poised to become the next U.S. saint—a list that at the time, in his estimation, also included John Neumann, Tekakwitha, and Philippine Duchesne.[61] Cardinal Spellman, by contrast, had no such reservations—and he was anything but neutral on the question of who should be the next American saint. Quite apart from what was surely his own desire to bask in Seton's saintly glory, Spellman was acutely sensitive to the possibility of embarrassment at the Holy See, and he knew that the infighting did not reflect well on the American church.

Burgio appealed to Spellman directly in April 1948. In excluding him from the conferences, he charged, the sisters had effectively "erect[ed] an iron curtain between the Communities and the only legitimate authority in this Country on the Cause."[62] Spellman, having been apprised of the conflict by Cicognani, already had his suspicions about Burgio, and he made delicate inquiries at the Vatican. Writing to Cardinal Clemente Micara, Salotti's eventual successor as prefect of the Sacred Congregation of Rites, Spellman asked Micara to corroborate the terms of Salotti's 1941 declaration, noting that they struck him as "unusual in the power" awarded to a vice-postulator.[63] Micara reported that the Vincentian postulator "has repeatedly assured me that Father Burgio is discharging his task with zeal and rectitude."[64]

Nevertheless, neither Spellman nor Micara seemed reassured that this was the case, as they initiated separate investigations into "the Emmitsburg affair" in early summer 1948. In New York, Spellman asked Rev. Damian Blaher, a canon lawyer for the Military Ordinariate, to research the history of Seton's cause and the nature of the conflict between Burgio and the Daughters of Charity.[65] Meanwhile, in Rome, the prefect authorized Monsignor Enrico Dante, secretary of the Sacred Congregation, to review the documents related to the conflict, and after having done so Dante decided to stop in Maryland during a scheduled visit to the United States the following September.[66]

Meeting with Burgio and Toohey at Emmitsburg, Dante urged them to reconcile their differences: "Let the past be buried," he exhorted, "and start anew!" Dante agreed that Burgio's presence at the conferences would be appropriate if the sisters discussed anything that "pertained to the Cause proper," such as finances or concrete steps for advancing the cause, but that it was not required if the sisters discussed spiritual matters. Both Burgio and Toohey dug in their heels, however. The vice-postulator contended that his appointment entitled him to attend, while Toohey maintained that Burgio's presence would disrupt the purpose of the conferences, which was to strengthen relationships among the sisters themselves. The meeting ended in an impasse.[67]

At this point Spellman stepped in. Blaher's detailed report, which provided background and recommendations, had arrived in Spellman's office the day after negotiations at Emmitsburg failed. The good news, it revealed, was that Seton's cause itself was on sound footing, which had not always been the case. The bad news was that what it characterized as a "personality conflict" had jeopardized its success. Blaher noted that the dispute between the Daughters and Burgio was, strictly speaking, "extraneous to the cause itself . . . it is a real 'red herring' which is distracting everyone and focusing attention on the wrong place." Unless it was resolved, the investigation concluded, the cause would not succeed—both because of the time and attention it was taking away from the real work at hand and because the Holy See would not be likely to move forward with a beatification tainted by "scandalous overtones."[68]

On the question that had prompted the immediate crisis—the exclusion of Burgio from the meetings of Mother Seton's Daughters—Blaher allowed that the sisters were entitled to keep their meetings private if they so desired.

Nevertheless, he went on to say, if the stated purpose of the meetings was indeed the advancement of Seton's cause, they were being disingenuous in not inviting the vice-postulator, as the responsibility for moving that forward lay primarily with him. In essence, the canon lawyer affirmed Burgio's status as "the hub of the wheel," reiterating that Burgio answered only to the Sacred Congregation in Rome. Any refusal on Toohey's part to respect his authority, Blaher claimed, "showed a profound ignorance of canon law." He did allow that the sisters were free to ask the Sacred Congregation to appoint a new vice-postulator, but he cautioned them strongly against doing so. Not only would it take time for a new person to be appointed and to acquaint himself with the cause, but there was also no guarantee that the sisters would get along with the new person any better than with Burgio. Blaher advised Spellman to bring the opposing parties together in the presence of authorities from the United States and the Holy See. If they could be made to see the damage their "bickering" was doing to the cause, Blaher suggested, there was hope that Seton would someday be beatified; otherwise her cause was likely to languish in Rome forever.

Blaher's report spurred Spellman to action. A week later, the cardinal convened an "emergency meeting" at Mount St. Vincent in the Bronx, the motherhouse of the Sisters of Charity of New York. All of the principals were present at the gathering: Toohey of Emmitsburg, Taaffe of New York, and representatives from the Daughters of Charity in St. Louis and the Sisters of Charity of Cincinnati, Convent Station, Seton Hill, and Halifax. Joining Mother Seton's spiritual daughters were the archbishop of Baltimore; an auxiliary bishop of Washington, D.C.; Rev. Damian Blaher and a second canon lawyer; and two special guests from the Sacred Congregation of Rites: Monsignor Dante and Rev. Ferdinand Antonelli, the relator general of its Historical Section, who was overseeing the examination of the documents related to Seton's life and virtues. Also present, of course, was Burgio.

Presiding over the meeting, Spellman communicated the substance of Blaher's report and gave the sisters and Burgio an opportunity to air their grievances against each other. The minutes of the meeting reveal some tense moments, in which the entire history of the cause and the conflict—from the 1897 instruction to list the Daughters of Charity as sole petitioners to Burgio's exclusion from both the first and second meetings of the Conference of Mother Seton's Daughters—was rehashed. Spellman, displaying his diplomatic skills, informed the sisters that they were welcome to petition for another postulator but that doing so risked further delaying the cause. Given that "we are all anxious to submerge our own desires of furthering the Cause in our own way," the cardinal persuaded the sisters that it would be "prudent, tactful, and proper" to invite Burgio to future meetings. At the same time, Spellman also put Burgio on notice that, having been a persistent "source of irritation" to the sisters, it was now "up to him to get along" with them. He urged him to abandon what appeared to be a quest for "personal vindication" in the conflict and to concentrate instead on the cause itself. Burgio vowed "to bury the past in charity" (if only, he qualified, because any attempt to justify himself "would take too long, and would do no good"). As for the sisters, they invited Burgio to join their next scheduled conference in St. Louis. Delighted with the outcome of the meeting, Spellman apologized to Dante and Antonelli for the "spectacle" his compatriots had made.[69]

Aside from the apparent breakthrough at Mount St. Vincent, Antonelli's visit to New York yielded another victory for Seton's cause. In the company of Burgio, the relator general visited Trinity Church to conduct a fresh review of parish records, hoping to uncover confirmation of Seton's baptism. At last, he found the necessary proof that had eluded Seton's advocates for so long: the name "Eliza Ann Seton" appeared on a list of parish communicants dated January 1801, which, as Trinity's Rev. Charles Bridgeman later explained, was ample evidence that Seton had been baptized, as only the baptized were allowed to receive Communion.[70] Antonelli affirmed that the document would satisfy the Sacred Congregation on the question and departed New York with "a great store of new, profound impressions, and renewed assurance that we shall labor with all our energies for the advancement of the cause." He predicted that Seton would be declared venerable in three years.[71]

And so she might have been, had the peace Spellman brokered not turned out to be a fragile one. Before long, another conflict erupted over a new biography of Seton—or, rather, a reprint of Charles White's 1853 *Life of Mrs. Eliza A. Seton*. In this dispute, Burgio added the Sisters of Charity of New York to the list of nuns he had alienated. After having commissioned two of the sisters to edit White's original, Burgio then disregarded their changes and reserved the royalties for himself. When the sisters complained to Spellman, the cardinal wrote to Burgio demanding an explanation. Burgio's priorities were clear from his response: "In this affair, the publication of the book is of little consequence. What is ALL IMPORTANT is the disregard of some of those PRINCIPLES for which Your Eminence had been designated by the Eminent Cardinal Prefect of the S.R.C. to establish, defend and preserve, namely . . . the status and rights of the Vice-Postulator in his position."[72] Rather than address the issues raised by the cardinal—the content of the biography and concerns about his own profiteering—Burgio deigned to instruct the cardinal on his responsibility for safeguarding Burgio's authority.

The revised biography appeared in 1949 under a new title, *Mother Seton: Mother of Many Daughters*, and the content had been reshaped to reinforce the title's message. White's original had ended with a chapter that covered the period from 1821, when Rose White was elected Seton's successor to the 1850 alliance with the French Daughters, an event Reverend White had deemed "the most important event connected with the recent history of the society in this country."[73] The new edition lopped off that chapter and ended instead with Seton's death, a revision that made sense in light of efforts to emphasize that Seton was the founder of the diocesan Sisters of Charity as well as the present communities allied with France. In a preface to the new version, Cicognani referred diplomatically to the "various historical circumstances" that had led Seton's original community to be split into distinct branches but stressed that they were all one. In this context, White's earlier postscript about the union with France seemed superfluous.[74]

Burgio precipitated the biggest crisis yet between himself and the sisters the following year when he requested that the Daughters of Charity supply him with historical documentation on three subjects: negotiations about a possible alliance with France during Seton's lifetime, a comparison of the French rules and their American adaptation, and the "direct succession of Sisterhood at Emmitsburg to Mother Seton." The Daughters, interpreting this request as an attempt to impugn their connection to Seton, worried that Burgio had strayed so far from his stated original purpose of bringing the "Black Caps" into the sponsorship of the cause that he had carried it to the opposite extreme and was now attempting to assign sponsorship exclusively to the diocesan communities, excluding the Daughters of Charity entirely. Burgio maintained that he was merely complying with Antonelli's requests for clarification, yet his request prompted stern rebukes from Cicognani and other prelates.[75]

In response to Burgio's request, the Daughters produced a densely annotated thirteen-page document that emphatically declared their direct connection to Seton.[76] For Toohey, this episode seemed to have been the final straw. By 1950, her distrust of Burgio had risen to such a level that she decided to go to Rome herself and express her concerns about Burgio to the Sacred Congregation in person. News of Toohey's trip abroad alarmed Burgio, who warned Giuseppe Scognamillo that she would create "headaches" once "[she] gets into direct communication with the Sacred Congregation of Rites."[77] He had good reason to worry. During her face-to-face meeting with Cardinal Micara, soon-to-be prefect of the Sacred Congregation of Rites, and Monsignor Natucci, the Promoter of the Faith, Sister Isabel relayed her concerns about Burgio's mismanagement of the cause and his recent request to the Daughters of Charity to prove their connection to Seton. In the wake of that encounter, Scognamillo informed Burgio that Sister Isabel had convinced the prefect that the vice-postulator's behavior was untoward. In particular, the cardinal "was annoyed that you had come up with those questions causing distress to the Sisters." Faced with "a serious and delicate concern for Our cause," he wrote to Burgio, "I find myself in a state of uncertainty from which I would like to be released, before things get even more complicated." He asked Burgio to resign as vice-postulator.[78]

Burgio's reaction provides the clearest evidence that, despite his vehement insistence to the contrary, he was far more invested in personal vindication than he was in Seton's saintly success. On multiple occasions throughout the conflict, he had stated that were he ever asked to step down, he would sacrifice himself for the sake of Seton's progress. But when the opportunity arose to do just that, he decided to follow Dougherty's advice and "hasten to Rome" to defend himself.[79] Dougherty wrote immediately to his friends in Rome, including Monsignor Giovanni Battista Montini, an influential Vatican diplomat, and the day after he arrived in Rome, Burgio met with Montini, who "pledged his protection." The next day, Burgio met with Cardinal Micara, who had apparently found Sister Isabel's interpretation of events convincing. According to Burgio's transcript of the conversation, the prefect asked the Vincentian three times whether he had, in fact, "excluded the Emmitsburg Community from the Cause and turned it over to the Black Cap Communities." Burgio vehemently denied this. Montini intervened in support of Burgio, and as a result, Burgio reported to Dougherty, "the tide changed in our favor."[80] Thanks to Montini, Burgio would be "spared the executioner's axe."[81]

When Cardinal Micara advised Burgio to return to the United States and quietly resume his work, Burgio insisted that he would not leave Rome unless the prefect issued a "Declaration" that absolved him of guilt and stated his rights as vice-postulator. Micara acquiesced. "Information has reached this Sacred Congregation," he wrote to Scognamillo, "which indicates that not all persons interested in the Cause of Beatification of the Servant of God, Elizabeth

Ann Seton, have a precise idea of the functions which are the prerogative of the Postulation and Vice-postulation in the promotion of this Cause." Micara enclosed a declaration that reiterated the language of Cardinal Salotti's 1941 pronouncement on the subject of Burgio's authority and asked Scognamillo to share it with members of all the Seton communities. Each and every one of them, Micara emphasized, "can and must feel itself interested equally in the advancement and success of the Cause and all are obliged to work together with love and devotion."[82]

In his account of events, Burgio remembered 1950 as the "peak" of his feud, and Micara's declaration did seem to give him the unassailable authority he craved. But Dougherty's death in 1951 left him without a patron, and before long his own declining health rendered him more of a nuisance to the sisters than a threat to Seton's cause. Nonetheless Burgio did continue to challenge any effort he perceived as an attempt to subvert his position as the "hub of the wheel." In 1952, for instance, his target was the Mother Seton Committee of the International Federation of Catholic Alumnae. Asking the members to change the name of their fund-raising organization, he reminded them that there was only one "Seton Fund" and it was under his own control.[83] In 1954, Burgio drew up a last will and testament in which he apologized to his successor as vice-postulator for "the mess which I hate anyone to inherit" but instructed this person to insist on exclusive control, especially of Mother Seton Guild funds.[84] Burgio continued to attend meetings of the Conference of Mother Seton's Daughters, where he persisted in irritating the delegates. Indeed, his habit of overstepping his bounds at those meetings prompted Cicognani to ask him to absent himself from them voluntarily. Unsurprisingly, Burgio refused and appealed to Monsignor Montini to support him.[85]

In the midst of all this, however, it was clear that all of Mother Seton's spiritual daughters were indeed working together "with love and devotion." Annabelle Melville's biography of Seton, published in 1951, also helped bring the once-estranged siblings closer together. Melville's work testified to the rigorous historical training she had received from John Tracy Ellis, as she did not hesitate to set the record straight when historical evidence contradicted cherished oral traditions, even as she sought to protect them. When, for instance, a close examination of an 1809 community ledger controverted often-told stories about the meager first Christmas dinner the Sisters of Charity had at Emmitsburg, for example, she buried that information in a footnote. Melville, aware of expectations that her biography would support the widespread claim that

Seton had founded the parochial school system, diplomatically sidestepped the question and let the U.S. Congress provide a definition: tributes to the Mother Seton School read into the Record of the Ninety-Ninth Congress had called the institution a "precursor" to that system.[86]

Far and away, Melville's most significant achievement was her detailed and nuanced treatment of the question of her subject's original wishes regarding an alliance between the Emmitsburg Sisters and the French Daughters of Charity. Although "it has always been assumed," she wrote, citing White, "that the French women did not leave Europe because of obstacles thrown in the way by Bonaparte's government," Melville explained the complex considerations that had been present during the founding years and "may have played a larger part than has been hitherto suggested." She pointed out that Seton's clerical advisers had been divided on the question of whether it was wise for her to link her Sisters of Charity to the French Daughters in 1811, given their recent reestablishment in the wake of the French Revolution and the differences in each community's respective ministries: the American Sisters of Charity were focused at the time on education, while the French Daughters primarily cared for the sick and orphans. Melville also quoted Seton's two letters to Bishop John Carroll, written in the midst of the discussion of the French rules, in which she voiced her own misgivings about the prospect of having Frenchwomen join the fledgling community. She had questioned their potential impact on her own leadership role and on her responsibilities to her five dependent children, as the Daughters' rule could have compromised her ability to care for them. "How can they [the French sisters] allow me the uncontrolled privileges of a Mother to my five darlings?" she asked Carroll. Seton was willing to make sacrifices, she assured the bishop, as long as they were "consistent with my first and inseparable obligations as a mother."[87]

Melville's biography obviously could not settle definitively the question of what Seton would have thought of an alliance that took place almost three decades after her death. Nonetheless the book, in illuminating the various factors that had complicated the transatlantic relationship during the congregation's founding years, provided all the members of the Conference of Mother Seton's Daughters with a version of history they could accept. From the Daughters' perspective, Melville's account confirmed that Seton had modeled her congregation on the Vincentian rule. It also allowed them to infer that the circumstances that had militated against a formal union in Seton's lifetime might have shifted by the 1840s, thus leading Seton to make a different decision had she founded the congregation then. The Sisters, on the other hand, could continue to celebrate Seton's independent spirit and emphasize that she had founded a new religious family that had taken root in multiple dioceses. The first superiors in both New York and Cincinnati had been among Seton's original companions, and they, in turn, had become the progenitors of other diocesan communities. Seton was legitimately the "mother of many daughters," as she had once predicted she would be.[88]

Throughout the 1950s, the relationships between the various communities were strengthened by biennial meetings of the Conference of Mother Seton's Daughters, and the benefits of this collaboration would eventually extend far beyond Seton's cause. In a sense, the burgeoning alliance between the six Seton communities replicated larger-scale efforts of U.S. Catholic sisters to reach beyond their own congregational boundaries to cooperate with other vowed women. In 1954, for example, Catholic sister-educators founded the Sister Formation Conference to encourage communities to share information and resources offered in their own colleges with a view to shortening the length of time it took the average sister to complete a baccalaureate degree. In 1956, U.S. Catholic sisters established a second collaborative body, the Conference of Major Superiors of Women, which was intended "to facilitate dialogue and cooperation between superiors of women's congregations in the United States" and, like the Sister Formation Conference, built bridges across what had once been considered impenetrable barriers between religious congregations. While it had not been uncommon for sisters from different communities to offer each other hospitality and assistance for brief periods of time—such as that which Seton's spiritual daughters had offered Cabrini and her companions for their first weeks in New York City—sustained cooperative efforts were unprecedented until the mid-twentieth century.[89]

Isabel Toohey's extended conflict with Salvator Burgio marked a transitional moment in the history of U.S. Catholic sisters. On the one hand, Toohey had adopted strategies long relied upon by Catholic sisters to circumvent what they saw as unjust impositions of clerical authority. Mother Théodore Guérin, to cite only one example, had also cultivated sympathetic clerical and episcopal allies to help mediate her conflicts with the bishop of Vincennes. On the other hand, Toohey's decision to plead her case personally in Rome and her attempt to create a competing source of authority in solidarity with women outside of her particular religious community signaled a new chapter in that history. Apart from its other effects, developing an identity as sisters with a small *s* would soon lead Catholic sisters to become both increasingly insistent on representing themselves at the Holy See and more vocal in defying men like Burgio.

Meanwhile, Melville's biography had also boosted Seton's cause at the Sacred Congregation. Antonelli regarded it as "a serious historical work" based on "extensive and conscientious research" that confirmed that Charles White had indeed produced a sound biography that convinced members of the Historical Section that "nothing essential had escaped us." In December 1957, Antonelli appeared before a new prefect of the Sacred Congregation, Cardinal Gaetano Cicognani—Amleto's brother—to respond to the various doubts the "devil's advocate" had raised about Seton's cause. Most of them referenced documents related to the cause, but some concerned Seton's own apparent moral lapses. A few of these antedated her conversion to Catholicism, such as her intellectual flirtation with philosophers such as Jean-Jacques Rousseau and her possible romantic interest in Antonio Filicchi. Examiners also cited "the night spent in fitful terror," a reference to a dark period in her life when she may briefly have contemplated suicide. Other of Seton's "defects" included allegations that she had been "difficult to direct" and overly attached to her children. In the end, the judges determined that Seton's vices proved only that she had been human and that her virtues had indeed been extraordinary. Antonelli told the prefect that, after examining all the documents carefully, the consultors of the Historical Section had voted unanimously that she had practiced virtue to a heroic degree and that they "very much desire a good end to this Cause."[90]

Yet two more years would elapse before the entire Sacred Congregation—as opposed to the Historical Section—considered and voted on Seton's virtues. The reasons for the delay are not entirely clear, though some evidence suggests that Antonelli, still stung by Burgio's drawn-out conflict with the sisters, advised postponing the discussion. Whatever the case, on 18 December 1959, the Holy See pronounced Seton venerable. Toohey returned to Rome for the official pronouncement, as did representatives of all the other communities that considered Seton a founder. Toohey's "cornette," surrounded by the different styles of "black caps" worn by other sisters, made for a striking image in photographs of the occasion, in which Spellman was also prominent (figure 7).

Missing from the photographs was Burgio. He had died three months before the church pronounced Seton venerable. At Burgio's funeral in Manhattan's St. Peter's Church—the site of Seton's conversion to Catholicism—a eulogist had praised the Vincentian as a man with only one concern outside the salvation of his soul: "that personal predilections would be submerged in the all-important

FIGURE 7

Representatives of Seton communities in Rome when Seton was declared
venerable, 18 December 1959. *Left to right:* Mother Mary Omer Downing, SC
(superior, Cincinnati); Cardinal Francis Spellman; Mother Mary Fuller (superior
of the Sisters of Charity of New York); Sister Loretto Bernard Beagan (Fuller's
successor); Sister Isabel Toohey, DC (visitatrix, Emmitsburg); Mother Stella Maria
Reiser (superior of Sisters of Charity of Halifax); Mother M. Claudia Glenn,
SC (superior of the Sisters of Charity of Seton Hill). Not pictured: Mother
Joanna Marie Duffy (superior of the Sisters of Charity of Convent Station).
(Courtesy of Luigi Felici, Archivio Fotografico Felici, Roma)

business of praying God that Mother Seton would soon be canonized."[91] None
of his obituaries hinted at the rancor his reign as Seton's vice-postulator had
engendered; they instead emphasized the way he had worked tirelessly on her
behalf—and appeared to be continuing to do so in his own afterlife. "It was no
accident," the editor of the *Mother Seton Guild Bulletin* opined, "that—just
weeks after Father Burgio's death—Mother Seton's Cause *leaped* forward."[92]
The implication was that Burgio, now in God's presence himself, had used his

heavenly influence to propel Seton to venerable status. In reality, Seton's leap forward had stemmed from another death a year earlier, that of Pius XII in October 1958, and the subsequent strategic placement of a Seton supporter in Rome.

The 1917 Code of Canon Law prohibited brothers (or anyone else "related in the first or second degree of consanguinity to a living Cardinal") from serving simultaneously as cardinals.[93] Given that Pius XII had named Amleto's brother Gaetano a cardinal in 1953, it seemed the U.S. apostolic delegate would never receive the red hat. In December 1958, however, Pius XII's successor, John XXIII, made a dispensation and elevated Amleto Cicognani to the cardinalate, appointing him secretary of the Congregation for Oriental Churches. Now that Cicognani was stationed within whispering distance of the pope, Cardinal Spellman made certain he did not forget about Elizabeth of New York. Cicognani obliged. "His Holiness has been informed of our desire about the Cause of Mother Seton," he assured Spellman in June 1959, "and He intends to do something and take some steps." Cicognani promised to follow the matter attentively, "convinced that it will turn into a great good for America."[94]

Cicognani's vigilance at the Holy See had most likely provided the final push for the Sacred Congregation to finish its investigation of Seton's virtues and declare that she had indeed practiced them to a heroic degree.[95] As her long road to venerable status ended, Spellman and other Seton supporters looked to the next stage with confidence despite the almost universal consensus that authenticating miracles was extraordinarily difficult. As a candidate for whom no eyewitness testimony had been gathered, Seton officially needed four miracles to advance to beatification. Once the Sacred Congregation ruled on Seton's virtues, however, Spellman followed Cicognani's advice and submitted a request that the Holy See reduce the required miracles to two. The request was granted. As is usually the case with these exemptions, a stated rationale is not to be found—but it is certainly plausible that this particular one can be attributed to the standing of Cicognani and Spellman at the Holy See.[96]

Perhaps heartened by this success, Spellman also contemplated seeking other dispensations on Seton's behalf, but Cicognani warned him against doing so. Since Seton's was "the first American cause," he advised, "it is better to proceed regularly without having recourse to exceptions and favors."[97] Papal exemptions to canon law were hardly uncommon, as Cicognani well knew—having petitioned for at least one, with Cabrini's cause, and benefited from another, when he was elevated to the cardinalate. There were times, however, when it made sense to adhere strictly to the process, and in Seton's case to do otherwise may well have needlessly risked her saintly credibility in the eyes of European Catholics who already looked down at Americans enough in this regard. For a nation still awaiting the "joy and privilege" of being able to "look upon actual buildings or scenes that the saint actually saw," it made sense for the first native-born saint to receive the honors of the altar without too many strings attached.[98]

Cicognani's advice reflects the delicate dance that pursuing a cause for canonization entailed. Advocates could—and in fact needed to—exert a certain amount of pressure on behalf of a cause, but they had to do so inconspicuously and through the proper channels. Certain above-and-beyond measures seemed to be permissible. Spellman reported, for example, making "a contribution" to a consultor "so that he could work evenings in the promotion of this Cause," apparently in translating the material.[99]

Considering that the documentation on Sister Gertrude's 1935 cure was already assembled, Seton's supporters needed to find only one more credible miracle before Seton was beatified. They had good reason to believe the Holy See was prepared to move quickly on Seton's cause: Pope John XXIII had said as much in one of his first lengthy English-language speeches. Addressing Spellman, two other U.S. cardinals, and hundreds of U.S. bishops at the celebrations marking the centennial of Rome's Pontifical North American University, the pontiff had predicted that Seton's beatification would take place "in a relatively short time." American sources reported that the Sacred Congregation had sped up its work on Seton's cause "as a gesture to the visiting American hierarchy."[100] Overall, by 1959, Seton's supporters had ample reason to hope that Seton would soon be beatified—the first U.S. citizen so honored since Cabrini in 1938.

The drama of Seton's saintly journey, however, was far from over. Even as the curtain closed on Burgio, another player was waiting in the wings. Like Burgio, he had hailed from Philadelphia, and like Burgio, too, he compromised Seton's chances of becoming the next American saint—though from a decidedly celestial angle. John Neumann had been declared venerable in 1921, almost four decades before Seton reached the same milestone, but there had been almost no movement in his cause since then. Much to the chagrin of Spellman and other Seton advocates, Neumann's cause accelerated rapidly in the 1950s. It suddenly seemed possible that Seton's cause had survived Burgio's not-so-saintly machinations only to be subsumed in Neumann's holy shadow.

The Race for a Miracle

John Neumann had been "a boy of nine, with no thought of America," when Seton died. Still, their legacies had intersected in a number of ways in the United States. John DuBois, who had ordained Neumann in New York, had once been Seton's spiritual director, and the Redemptorists and Sisters of Charity had worked in close proximity in Philadelphia, Baltimore, and New York.[101] Seton and Neumann had overlapped as candidates for canonization from the beginning, and in the 1920s and 1930s they had competed for Cardinal Dougherty's patronage and for designation of parent of the Catholic school system. Thanks to the efforts of Dougherty's successor—ironically, one of Spellman's most successful former protégés—the "last lap" of their respective journeys to sainthood promised to end in a dramatic photo finish.[102]

John Francis O'Hara, a member of the Congregation of the Holy Cross, had been serving as president of the order's University of Notre Dame in 1939 when, on Spellman's recommendation, Pius XII appointed him administrator of the Military Ordinariate.[103] Spellman regarded O'Hara as "a most extraordinary man" and was influential in securing his appointment as bishop of Buffalo in 1945. In 1952, Pius XII named O'Hara Dougherty's successor in that archdiocese.[104] O'Hara, Philadelphia's ninth bishop, would be elevated to the cardinalate in the same consistory in which Cicognani received the honor. Cicognani, in fact, suggested to O'Hara that, given that his own installation in Philadelphia would occur exactly a century after Neumann's, it would present a good opportunity to promote Neumann's cause for canonization. O'Hara had already been familiar with Neumann's story before Cicognani's briefing, and once the apostolic delegate piqued his interest he became an ardent supporter of Neumann's cause. Though O'Hara's influence would never reach Spellman's heights, he did not need a national profile for Neumann's sake. He had plenty of power in Philadelphia, and that would be enough.[105]

O'Hara's support for Neumann seems to have been rooted in a genuine admiration and desire to hold up the immigrant bishop as a model for other priests. When Michael Curley's biography, *Venerable John Neumann, C.SS.R.: Fourth Bishop of Philadelphia*, appeared in 1952, O'Hara ordered 1,200 copies, one for each priest serving in the archdiocese.[106] O'Hara routinely mentioned Neumann in his official addresses to the archdiocese and renamed one of the city's oldest diocesan high schools his honor. O'Hara also relied on his Holy

Cross connections to generate devotion to Neumann and to advance his cause. In 1953, for example, he procured relics of the prospective saint for each member of the Notre Dame football team when they arrived in Philadelphia to play the U.S. Navy team.[107]

The archbishop also enlisted the help of confreres more familiar with the Holy See and its operations. Early in his tenure as Philadelphia's archbishop, O'Hara had been unimpressed when he met with Benedetto D'Orazio, the Redemptorist who had succeeded Claudio Benedetti as postulator in the 1920s and continued to shepherd Neumann's cause.[108] The postulator was "past his prime," he wrote to Edward Heston, CSC, and as a result, he "had done nothing in a long time to advance the Cause."[109]

In fact, nearly forty years had passed since young Eva Benassi's miraculous cure, and while reports of unofficial miracles had continued to flood the Philadelphia shrine, not a single one had been thoroughly investigated and sent forward to Rome. Until another promising cure could be paired with Benassi's, Neumann's cause would remain at a standstill. Consulting with his more experienced colleagues, O'Hara wondered whether the Benassi miracle could be sent to the Sacred Congregation alone, reasoning that a firm judgment in Neumann's favor on that case might generate the attention that could lead to a second miracle. O'Hara also suggested that perhaps the Redemptorists could make a stronger claim that Neumann was the *founder* of the Sisters of the Third Order of St. Francis in Philadelphia. "I am told," O'Hara wrote to Heston, "the Sacred Congregation is quite liberal in its definition of a founder."[110]

O'Hara's letter prompted Heston to do "a bit of sleuthing" in Rome, the results of which he shared with the archbishop. It was indeed true that the Benassi miracle was awaiting a companion; the Sacred Congregation would not commit to organizing a session to consider a single case. On the exemption question, Heston allowed that it was possible that O'Hara could petition the Holy Father to dispense Neumann from a second miracle, on the grounds that he had been a founder, although his inside sources suggested that the pope would be unlikely to grant it. "The only solution at the present time," Heston concluded, "is to prod the Servant of God into action."[111]

Heston's advice conformed to that given by the most experienced saint-seekers. Miracles, by definition, materialized in God's own good time. Nevertheless, there was plenty that human advocates could do to provide a nudge. Salvator Burgio, in fact, had written a helpful primer on how Seton's devotees could help generate the required miracle, including the advice that they should invoke Seton's intercession as frequently as possible, particularly for dire medical cases, and pay attention to the timing between the invocation and the healing. (He offered the lag time between Sister Gertrude's cure and the start of the Daughters of Charity's novena—a gap that had almost resulted in the miracle being shelved—as an example of what *not* to do.) Equally important was the need to invoke Seton exclusively. If at any point in the investigation it was revealed that a petitioner had invoked the intercession of more than one saint in requesting the miracle, the case could not move forward for approval. This was—and is—one of the points in the canonization process where institutional and personal perspectives seem especially detached from each other. For the beneficiary and his or her loved ones, a cure was a cure, and which saint received intercessional credit mattered little or not at all. For a postulator seeking an authenticated miracle, however, multiple intercessors incited a "war in the heavens" that could not be resolved to the satisfaction of Vatican investigators. And as Burgio had pointed out, "in war it is the united front that wins victories."[112]

Burgio's successor, John McGowan, CM, republished Burgio's guide and made certain that Seton's spiritual daughters were "storming Heaven" for a possible cure that could lead to her beatification.[113] Elements of a cure often evoked events or maladies in a saint's life, and because two of Seton's biological daughters had predeceased her, Seton's sisters often received prayer requests for sick children. One Sister of Charity, for example, assured a "heartsick and anxious" father from New York City that, because "the Lord had taken two of her own little girls to Himself," Seton understood his anguish and would be especially receptive to his prayers for the recovery of his sick daughter.[114]

In Philadelphia, meanwhile, Neumann's promoters were also doing all they could to prod the Servant of God to action. "The bishop needs a miracle," one Redemptorist publication announced.[115] After 1956, the task of vetting potential miracles fell to Rev. Francis Litz, a Redemptorist who became director of Neumann's shrine and his vice-postulator that year. For Litz, as for McGowan and other vice-postulators, this could be a frustrating task. The vast majority of reported cures—one seasoned vice-postulator estimated 75 percent—could easily be dismissed out of hand. Perhaps doctors had never been involved in the case, or there was no discernible causal relationship between invocation and cure. Even if a reported cure appeared to have a chance of meeting the criteria for a Vatican-sanctioned miracle, at any number of points things could go awry. The vice-postulator might fail in his attempt to follow up with the original correspondent, or the physician in charge of the case might ignore or deny requests for interviews. At any given moment, an alleged miracle could be tabled because the illness had returned.[116]

A vice-postulator's best hope was to generate as many reports of cures as possible, increasing the odds that one would succeed. Accordingly, Litz supplied hospital chaplains and nursing sisters with instructions on how to invoke Neumann's intercession. As many Philadelphia-based saint-seekers had done before him, Litz also sought to engage the interest of students enrolled in the archdiocese's vast network of Catholic schools. In this endeavor the Philadelphia Sisters of the Third Order of St. Francis, the community Neumann had helped to establish, and the Sisters, Servants of the Immaculate Heart of Mary, another local congregation he had helped introduce in Philadelphia, proved critical allies. Working closely with O'Hara and Neumann biographer Curley, Litz developed talking points that connected Neumann to the issues of the day.[117]

O'Hara also encouraged Neumann's promoters to renew their attempts to verify Neumann's U.S. citizenship. At his prompting, Curley visited the National Archives in 1959, hoping to find evidence of Neumann's naturalization on census data but locating it instead on a passenger list of the ship on which Neumann had returned from Europe in 1855; Curley later found Neumann's passport application in the same repository.[118] Though these discoveries reanimated Redemptorists' efforts to link Neumann to the nation's founding, Neumann's U.S. citizenship now mattered far less, in symbolic terms, than it had when his promoters had first sought to corroborate it in the 1920s. Arguably, the onset of the Cold War had made his birth in Bohemia—a region then under communist control—even more important in connecting Neumann to the tenor of the times. In a 1957 petition to the pope, in fact, U.S. bishops made a case for the "timeliness of honoring this Bohemian-born missionary in the midst of the persecution of the Church in the countries behind the Iron Curtain."[119]

The Cold War may have also compelled Amleto Cicognani to take a more active role in Neumann's cause. As secretary of the Eastern churches, Cicognani developed an expertise on communism and a commitment to halt its spread. This experience was undoubtedly a factor in his 1961 appointment as Vatican secretary of state—an honor Americans took as a national compliment. "For the first time in the history of the Roman Catholic Church, the second most important man in the Vatican is a Kentucky Colonel ... and an honorary chief of the Osage Indians," *Time* magazine observed, citing two of the local accolades Cicognani had acquired during his quarter century in the United States.[120] In his introduction to Curley's biography, Cicognani had written that "the Saints do not need us, but we need them," and his becoming more active in pushing Neumann's case when he returned to Rome suggests that he believed Americans needed Neumann more than ever during the Cold War.[121]

Back in Philadelphia, Litz was proving himself a resourceful advocate. In 1959, he approached O'Hara with a proposal that would channel more income for Neumann's cause and eventually connect him to another prospective Philadelphia saint. The story was this: In 1955, the Redemptorists had received an unexpected windfall following the death of Katharine Drexel, the former Philadelphia debutante who founded the Sisters of the Blessed Sacrament. To protect his three unmarried daughters from fortune hunters, Drexel's father, Francis Drexel, had stipulated in his will that the Drexel sisters would receive income from his estate for the duration of their lives and could pass the fortune on to their biological children. Should all three sisters die without heirs, however, the estate would be distributed among a list of beneficiaries named in the will. Katharine's two sisters died childless, and in her case, spiritual progeny did not count. After her death, all the capital and accumulated interest reverted to the beneficiaries on Francis Drexel's list, which did not include the Sisters of the Blessed Sacrament, as Katharine had not established the congregation until after her father's death. Two of these beneficiaries, however, were Philadelphia parishes staffed by Redemptorists and, according to an arrangement proposed by Litz and authorized by O'Hara, a portion of this bequest was allocated toward promoting Neumann's cause. The annual infusion of approximately $50,000—by one measure, over $400,000 in today's dollars—supported the printing of promotional material about Neumann and Litz's travel throughout the archdiocese and beyond.[122] Litz's annual report for 1959 shows that he preached about Neumann in 159 sermons that year, most of which were in greater Philadelphia but extending as far away as New Orleans and Toronto. He gave an additional twenty-eight talks at Communion breakfasts and other special events and hosted twenty-nine group visits at the shrine.[123]

That busy year also included a diocesan inquiry into a possible miracle, thanks to the efforts of Nicola Ferrante, a Redemptorist priest who became the congregation's postulator after D'Orazio died in 1958. Ferrante proved to be as enterprising as Litz. Taking a fresh look at the files of miracles that D'Orazio had rejected, Ferrante was drawn to one involving Kent Lenahan, a

Philadelphia teenager who had sustained catastrophic injuries in a 1949 automobile accident. Lenahan's parents attributed their son's unexpected recovery to Neumann's intercession, invoked through the application of Neumann's relics to his body. While the Lenahans had duly reported the cure to the Redemptorists, D'Orazio had demurred on the grounds of Lenahan's youth, concluding that "there may be unsuspected and untapped sources of energy in youthful constitutions, which provide an opportunity for unusual readjustments to otherwise desperate situations."[124] But Ferrante thought the cure was promising and pursued a diocesan inquiry. Its official transcript was paired with the Eva Benassi cure of 1923 and sent to the Holy See.[125]

The partnership among Ferrante, Litz, and O'Hara was disrupted by the cardinal's death in 1960. When John Krol succeeded O'Hara as Philadelphia's archbishop, he too became a major supporter of Neumann's cause, though Krol's episcopal style differed substantially from that of the obliging O'Hara. Whereas O'Hara had known how to be covert in his efforts to advocate for Neumann, as well as when to defer to Ferrante and other Redemptorists, Krol tended to be more outspoken in his support and more prone to interfering. Throughout the time they worked together on Neumann's cause, Ferrante often warned Krol and his associates that it was essential, in causes for canonization, to avoid making "unfavorable impressions" at the Holy See.[126]

Locally, Krol incited tensions with Redemptorists when rumors surfaced that the archbishop hoped to transfer Neumann's remains from St. Peter's to the crypt of Philadelphia's archdiocesan cathedral, where all the city's previous bishops except O'Hara (who was interred at Notre Dame) were buried. Hoping to forestall such a move, Litz wrote a polite but firm letter to the cardinal, explaining that at the time of Neumann's death Archbishop Francis Kenrick of Baltimore had granted special permission for Neumann to be buried at St. Peter's so that he could find "a resting place in death, where he could not find it in life," with his religious brethren. Litz also pointed out that transferring the body could "create confusion" among devotees, compromise the search for miracles, and be unfair to the Redemptorists, who had borne all of the responsibility for funding and promoting the cause.[127]

Tussles over saints' bodies are hardly uncommon, and at the same time the Daughters of Charity in Emmitsburg began to worry that Cardinal Spellman might have designs on Seton's remains. As they had done before, they appealed to Cicognani for help. With his assistance, and working through the archbishop of Baltimore, they petitioned the Holy See for special permission to build a new church at Emmitsburg where Seton's remains could be enshrined after her beatification; according to canon law, churches could be dedicated only to the canonized.[128] The Holy See granted the Daughters of Charity the dispensation through an official "rescript," a medium that, according to the archbishop of Baltimore, afforded the sisters "particular satisfaction."[129] As he told Cicognani, the sisters had heard rumors "that a national shrine is to be erected elsewhere, allegedly with the expectation that it might become the depository of Mother Seton's remains," and the wording of the rescript appeared to guarantee that Seton's body would rest in Emmitsburg in perpetuity.[130]

By then, Seton's spiritual daughters in Maryland could also claim another special honor: the long-awaited second miracle had occurred in their hospital in Baltimore in 1952. A four-year-old girl, Ann Theresa O'Neill, had been diagnosed with acute leukemia in January of that year and by April was on the brink of death. Already weakened by multiple blood transfusions, O'Neill contracted a particularly virulent case of chicken pox that intensified her pain and suffering. When she entered St. Agnes Hospital on Wednesday of Holy Week, her parents compared their daughter's agony to that of "Our Lord nailed to His cross" and prayed that God would release her from suffering into death. The next day, Holy Thursday, head pediatric nurse Sister Mary Alice Fowler asked the O'Neills to pray a different prayer, as Fowler had a feeling that the child's case might be a good one for "Mother Seton to show her power with God." Fowler affixed a ribbon that had once touched one of Seton's bones to O'Neill's tiny nightgown and, in unison with the O'Neills, recited a prayer that would soon be echoed by Daughters of Charity and their Catholic school pupils throughout the region: "O God, the giver of all good gifts, who has shown the power of Thy Grace in the life and virtues of Elizabeth Seton, deign to draw others to Thy Service, by the sweet influence of her example, and, if by Thy Holy will, hasten the Cause of her Beatification." By Easter, Ann had visibly improved, and soon all signs of her cancer had disappeared.[131]

O'Neill's cure was coupled with Korzendorfer's and sent on to the Holy See for investigation. In yet another coincidence in Seton's and Neumann's respective "last laps" in the race to sainthood, the Sacred Congregation approved those two cures within weeks of ruling positively on the Eva Benassi and Kent Lenahan miracles. The Sacred Congregation proposed that Seton and Neumann be beatified either jointly or on consecutive days in March 1963. Twinning the celebrations made practical sense, as U.S. bishops and pilgrims could celebrate two of their own new *beati* in a single trip.[132]

An "Ecclesiastical Coming-of-Age"

Yet it was not to be. The Sacred Congregation subsequently separated Seton's beatification from Neumann's, setting hers for 17 March and pushing his back to late June. The rationale for this decision was never explicitly stated. "June," Ferrante wrote hazily, "seemed to be more desirable." Yet several tantalizing clues suggest that Spellman, in a final dramatic flourish, lobbied to ensure that the first saint "born and bred" in the United States would not have to share the limelight with Neumann. Through Seton's vice-postulator, for example, the sisters conveyed their gratitude to the cardinal "that the cause will be separated from that of Bishop Neumann." Spellman's correspondence also suggests that he invoked an existing saint in his effort to give Seton her own day: petitioning the Sacred Congregation to have St. Patrick declared the patron of New York City, Spellman noted that it seemed fitting for Seton, "who belonged so much to New York," to be beatified on the Irish saint's feast.[133]

Cardinal Spellman led the official American pilgrimage to Seton's beatification. This time, the scene of departure was not New York Harbor but Idlewild Airport (now the John F. Kennedy International Airport), where two thousand U.S. travelers constituted "the largest air pilgrimage" to date. Cardinal Cicognani, by then secretary of state at the Holy See, was one of the Vatican dignitaries on hand to witness the moment when the papal brief declared "the name of Elizabeth Ann Bayley Seton be listed among the Blessed." When the pope himself paid his tribute to Seton later that afternoon, he paused to allow Spellman to read an English translation. "To the varied concept of the Church's holiness," said the Holy Father, "a new note has been added, bringing with it an element proper to [the] people" of the United States.[134]

For the next three evenings, pilgrims attended Solemn Triduum Masses—a series of three Masses over three days—at Spellman's titular church, Santi Giovanni e Paolo in Rome.[135] The cardinal hosted an elaborate dinner in the ballroom of Rome's Hotel Grande for the five hundred Daughters of Charity and Sisters of Charity who had made the journey. Sister Marie de Lourdes Walsh, a Sister of Charity of New York, rejoiced in these and other celebrations that marked "the Holy See's acceptance of this 'first flower of sanctity officially offered by the United States to the world.'" Sister Marie likely had no idea that she was misquoting the decree that had introduced Seton's cause in 1940; little could she have imagined that the Holy See had once ranked Seton behind Tekakwitha in the order of prospective American saints. Yet that was in the past. The multiple celebrations in Rome and at home suggested that Seton was second to none in the eyes of U.S. Catholics. According to Walsh, Seton's beatification signaled that "the American Catholic Church has reached spiritual maturity and is in a position to give not only generous material assistance, but also spiritual leadership in a crucial era of world history."[136] Secular publications also recognized the national momentousness of the event. Writing in the *Saturday Evening Post*, Thomas Congdon characterized Seton's beatification as an "ecclesiastical coming-of-age" on par with John F. Kennedy's election three years before.[137]

A month after Seton's beatification, her remains were enshrined at Emmitsburg, and pilgrims came "by the thousands" to venerate them.[138] While Seton stayed buried in Maryland, the Redemptorists also successfully fended off Krol's desire to transfer Bishop Neumann to Philadelphia's cathedral.

The competition between Seton and Neumann would persist after their beatifications. In the years to come, Ferrante would pepper letters to Litz, Krol, and other Philadelphia-based advocates with references to an ongoing sense of competition with Seton's promoters, reporting, for example, that he made a personal contribution to support the erection of a Neumann statue in Maryland, or "Seton country."[139] In one coup, Ferrante engaged Bishop Fulton Sheen, television star and a well-known adversary of Spellman, to give lectures about Neumann in Rome.[140] Francis X. Murphy, a Redemptorist priest teaching in Rome, openly described Seton's and Neumann's competition as "a contest between rival partisans," though he did so under a pseudonym and in a secular publication.[141]

Supporters of both candidates, aware that they would need evidence of new miracles to advance their causes to sainthood, began "storming heaven" once again with intercessory prayers. Seton's devotees were delighted to learn, just less than a year after Seton's beatification, that a promising cure had materialized at the congregation's hospital in Yonkers. As one Sister of Charity wrote to Spellman, "Wouldn't it be thrilling to have one of the miracles for the Canonization of Blessed Elizabeth Seton from New York?"[142] The prospect of a miracle from metropolitan New York would indeed complement the O'Neill miracle from Baltimore, as it could easily be interpreted as heavenly affirmation that both Maryland and New York could claim Seton as a citizen. Spellman, for his part, continued to foreground Seton's association with New York. In 1964, he authorized a weeklong celebration of Seton at the Vatican Pavilion at the New York World's Fair and dedicated a new shrine to Seton on State

Street in Lower Manhattan.[143] Though the New York shrine would not house Seton's remains, as the Emmitsburg sisters had once feared, the shrine would be recognized as the place "where a saint started."[144]

"It would be wonderful," one of Seton's devotees wrote to Spellman, "if our Holy Father Pope Paul could speed up the process of canonization dispensing with some of the legal formalities."[145] John XXIII had died less than three months after beatifying Seton, and there was reason to believe that his successor might be inclined to accelerate the final stage of her canonization process; the new pontiff was none other than the former Monsignor Giovanni Battista Montini, who had intervened at the height of the Burgio-Toohey feud in 1950. At the very least, Pope Paul VI had some appreciation of the complications that had prolonged Seton's journey to beatification, and, like his immediate predecessor, he also had reason to be positively disposed to extending a gesture of respect to the U.S. hierarchy—and hastening Seton's canonization might qualify as such.

However quickly either Seton or Neumann might be canonized, the more relevant question for this study was how long U.S. Catholics' excitement about their new blessed would last. Could their enthusiasm for holy hero of the hour extend into the next chapter of their American story, in a way that it had not done for either the North American martyrs or Cabrini? Or would the landscape of U.S. Catholicism be forever flooded by an overlapping cascade of saints, none of whom would wholly satisfy the original desire for a holy exemplar "sanctified . . . in our land, among circumstances familiar"? Was it possible that the familiar changed too rapidly for U.S. Catholics to sustain their ardor for an individual holy figure long enough to secure a national patron?

As Seton's supporters moved into the final stage of the canonization process, with Neumann's advocates close behind, few of them had an inkling that all that was familiar to them was about to change dramatically. Even as the candidates' partisans had been keeping watchful eyes on each other, an epochal event in Rome would soon lead the church to reform how it interpreted and evaluated sanctity. At the same time, developments at home would challenge the faithful to redefine their identities as Catholics and as Americans.

5

✦ *AGGIORNAMENTO* SAINTS ✦

The editors of the *Mother Cabrini Messenger* noted a striking trend in the years following Frances Cabrini's canonization: while her devotees continued to interpret her story in light of broader currents in American culture, such as anti-communism and concern over the nature of church-state separation, they also pleaded for more information about the saint's spiritual life. Odes to Cabrini's real estate prowess and her institutional legacy no longer sufficed. "Let us hear less about the buildings she erected and the journeys that she made," they asked. "Lift the veil, if possible, and reveal the intimacies of her soul that impelled the Church to pronounce her *Sancta*."[1] Into the 1960s and 1970s, a series of spiritual and cultural developments would continue to pique U.S. Catholics' curiosity about the inner lives of their holy heroes. Cabrini's first appearance in fiction illuminates the historic event at the center of these transformations and hints at the ways it would reverberate in the afterlives of the next American saints.

In 1965, Cabrini was one of a dozen saints featured in Joseph Tusiani's *Envoy from Heaven*. Cabrini was the novel's only character from the twentieth century, and her inclusion allowed Tusiani, an Italian-born naturalized U.S. citizen on the faculty at the College of Mount St. Vincent, to develop as a minor theme the trauma of the Italian emigrant experience. In the novel Cabrini assures the main protagonist that she understands the pain of Italian Americans who straddled two worlds, given that her time on earth had been "only yesterday." The novel's main narrative arc, however, centers on a contemporary event unfolding in Rome. *Envoy from Heaven* opens in April 1963, at a meeting of saints in paradise. They vote unanimously to send a delegate back to earth, assigned to report on the "Ecumenical Council of Our Church."[2] That event—the Second Vatican Council, known colloquially as Vatican II—was scheduled to begin its second of four sessions the following October.

The convocation of the council had itself come as a surprise. In October 1958, Cardinal Angelo Roncalli of Venice had been elected to succeed Pius XII, whose papacy had been long and momentous. Elected on the eve of the Second World War, Pope Pius XII had played a leading role in international relations and issued a number of landmark declarations with far-reaching implications for Catholics the world over. In Roncalli the College of Cardinals had chosen an elderly man who, many assumed, would serve the church as caretaker rather than as an agent of change. Yet in January 1959, less than three months after his election, the new pope, who took the name John XXIII, announced his intention to gather the world's bishops for an ecumenical council—the first such meeting in nearly a century and only the twentieth in the entire history of the church.[3] In his opening address to the council on 11 October 1962, John charged the assembled bishops with *aggiornamento*, an Italian word with no clear English translation that referred to an updating of the church to reflect the changed conditions of the contemporary world. Though the pontiff himself did not live to witness the aftereffects of Vatican II—his death from stomach cancer in June 1963 meant that he would preside over only the first of the council's four sessions—he had nonetheless set in motion monumental changes that would alter Catholics' understanding of themselves, both as men and women within the church and in relation to broader society, at a time of rapid social change.

Vatican II produced sixteen documents (four pastoral or dogmatic constitutions, three declarations, and nine decrees), the meanings of which have been subject to intense debate from their discussion in draft form on the council floor to this day. Yet, as Jesuit historian John O'Malley has warned, a "myopic" view that "focuses on the wording of documents without regard for contexts, without regard for before and after," risks failing "to see the Council as the new moment it wanted to be in the history of the Catholic Church."[4] Inspired to advance such broader understandings, scholars have made a powerful case that the most compelling answers to the question of "What happened at Vatican II?" can be found neither in the council's documents nor in the local histories of various dioceses but rather where the two converged in the *lives* of everyday Catholics.[5] From the vantage point of U.S. history, the *afterlives* of prospective saints also offer a gateway to the kind of beyond-the-document analysis O'Malley and others advocate—in large part because of the council's effort to reinterpret holiness in the age of *aggiornamento*.

Lumen Gentium (the council's "Dogmatic Constitution on the Church") reflected the council's new moment especially well. One of the council's most important documents, *Lumen Gentium* originated from an intervention made on the council floor by Belgium's Cardinal Léon-Joseph Suenens. Asked by Pope John XXIII to suggest a theme for the council, Suenens proposed that it be "the church of Christ, light to the world," and called upon the church to engage in dialogues with its own members, with "brothers and sisters not now visibly united with it," and, finally, with "the modern world." Suenens's speech set the overall agenda for the council and led the way for the call to holiness to become one of the great themes running through it. As O'Malley observes, *Lumen Gentium* said "explicitly, forcefully, and for the first time ever in a council that holiness is what the church is all about."[6]

Given the council's emphasis on holiness, it is unsurprising that its directives would shape the way the faithful interpreted and told stories of the saints, the men and women whose holiness had been confirmed by the institutional church through the canonization process and who the church encouraged the faithful to imitate. This, in fact, is the premise of Joseph Tusiani's novel: the "citizens of heaven" act on a strong premonition that the council's outcome would determine who would join their company in the future. The council's goals, St. Peter explains, are "of vital importance to us, who are waiting and hoping and praying that the light that unfolds our spirits may some day soon be shared by all mankind."[7] Peter and other saints had a stake in how holiness was defined, and if the criteria were up for reinterpretation, they wanted to return to earth to watch it happen. Tusiani's imagined dialogue captured what subsequent interpretations of the council would confirm: Vatican II represented a "new moment" not only in the history of the church but also in its understanding of holiness.

Had Tusiani been inclined to populate *Envoy from Heaven* with non-Italian saints, he could have easily incorporated the recently beatified Elizabeth Ann Seton—a local hero on his Bronx campus—as a Vatican II–era ambassador from heaven.[8] On Seton's beatification day in 1963, in fact, a priest at another U.S. Catholic college had described her in precisely that role. Presiding at a

Mass for Catholic sisters pursuing college degrees at the University of Notre Dame, Rev. Christopher O'Toole congratulated the Sisters of Charity in the assembly. He assured them that, though they were not physically present at the beatification Mass in Rome, the event was of immediate and vital importance to them. Only a select few could make a pilgrimage to the ceremony, but the new blessed was at that very moment making her own "pilgrimage into the hearts" of her spiritual daughters an ocean away—and indeed into the hearts of all Americans. The purpose of canonization, O'Toole reminded them, was "to place before us new and modern examples suited to our times and needs." Such models were eminently appropriate during this period of renewal, "when the entire church is astir with life and aglow with new vigor." Listen carefully, he advised, to the "accents of Mother Seton coming to you across the years." Her message would help them navigate the changes that lay ahead.[9]

Those attentive to Seton's story in the era of Vatican II would discern just how appropriate a model she was in light of the transformations the council inspired. John Neumann's devotees would also look to him for guidance. Echoing themes of Tusiani's novel and O'Toole's homily, Redemptorist leaders presented Neumann as a council-era envoy from heaven who could help guide U.S. Catholics through a period of dizzying change. Neumann's saintly trajectory would continue to parallel Seton's in a manner that, more often than not, exasperated his advocates. Postulator Nicola Ferrante and others may have accepted with aplomb the fact that Seton had been beatified before Neumann, but they were determined, as Ferrante put it, "to do our utmost in order not to remain behind" her in the final stage of the process. "Let us hope," he wrote to Francis Litz, Neumann's vice-postulator in Philadelphia, "that the canonization of our Blessed Neumann may take place before, or at least together with that of Servant of God Mother Seton."[10]

As Seton's and Neumann's fans wondered who would "win" the race to canonization, their stories and those of other prospective U.S. saints demonstrated how the council intersected with social change to reshape Catholicism in American life long after the last session ended in December 1965. Although Catholics had always reinterpreted their saints' stories in the light of contemporary events, the teachings of Vatican II gave them license to do so deliberately and explicitly in ways that helped mark this new moment in the church and society. By the time U.S. Catholics celebrated their next canonization, it was clear that the central dynamic in American saint-seeking still obtained: as U.S. Catholics changed, so, too, did the way they thought about their favorite saints.

Holiness in and beyond the Catholic Church

One of Seton's most ardent champions did not attend her beatification because he had been explicitly exiled from the normal life of the church. In the 1940s, Leonard Feeney had moved from *America* magazine to a Catholic center near Harvard University and had become an outspoken defender of a strict interpretation of the teaching that salvation was not possible outside the church. Feeney's refusal to recant provoked censure from the Vatican's Holy Office and led to his excommunication in 1963.[11] According to O'Malley, the Feeney controversy was only one instance of "the great interest in the church and the lively discussion about its nature and role in the decades immediately before the council opened." The episode thus helps to account for "the centrality that *Lumen Gentium* assumed in the Council and also for the vexed discussion of Catholicism's relationship to other Christian churches and other religions."[12]

In many ways Seton had been the perfect biographical subject for Feeney. The story of her conversion to Catholicism affirmed in a dramatic way the principle on which he had staked his ministry (and, given the eventual excommunication, his soul): the Catholic Church offered the only road to salvation. Vatican II's endorsement of religious liberty and a pluralistic society as well as its declarations on non-Christians would make Feeney's stance indefensible. The priest's continued interest in Seton offers trace evidence that council dialogues with members of other religions may have softened some of his views, albeit ever so slightly, but it would largely fall to future Seton biographers to write new narratives that reflected those theological transformations.[13]

Catholics' changing relationship with Protestants would have an even more immediate and visible impact on interpretations of Seton's life. In the interest of advancing dialogue with Catholics' "separated brethren," the council fathers had invited Protestants to join the proceedings as official observers—an overture with no precedent since the sundering of Christianity during the Reformation. As one Sister of Charity admitted, the new emphasis on ecumenism made it difficult "to examine the spirit and aims of a woman who named as the greatest blessing of her life her rejection of Protestantism." In the wake of the council, John Henry Hobart, the Episcopalian minister who had tried to dissuade Seton from converting and thereby a figure often demonized by her biographers, slowly evolved into a more sympathetic actor in her journey to Catholicism. In the wake of the council, Seton's devotees could acknowledge Hobart's positive influence on Seton in a way earlier generations could not. He had brought organization into her spiritual life and encouraged her to read the New Testament more assiduously. The brokenness that characterized Seton's life after her conversion—rejection by her family as well as her spiritual director, not to mention exile from her well-heeled social circles—likely would not have been inevitable had she lived after Vatican II.[14]

Just as the Protestant presence at Vatican II would have been inconceivable a century before, the U.S. Catholics who had first nominated Seton as a canonized saint could little have imagined that Protestants would also attend her beatification. Seton's early supporters may have hoped that Protestants would take a lively interest in the cause for canonization of a person who had started out as one of them, but they could not have predicted the investment some of them would develop for her cause in a more ecumenical era. When the archivist at New York's Trinity Church claimed for the Episcopalian parish partial credit for Seton's formal saintly success—by virtue of having supplied the crucial document that certified her baptism—he also emphasized the role the church had played in cultivating in Seton a life of holiness. Trinity, he reminded Catholics, had been the place that originally formed Seton in the faith and inspired her desire to care for the poor.[15]

U.S. Protestants also formed a sizable contingent among the pilgrims who traveled to Rome for the beatification of John Neumann. One Methodist bishop was particularly effusive in his praise of the elaborate ceremony. His own denomination, he marveled, had "much to learn from you Catholics, including the importance of pageantry.... We have to learn that people need the thrill of ceremony."[16] His observation ran directly counter to the sentiments expressed in the *Methodist Review* less than a century earlier, when the editors reacted in alarm to the very suggestion that there could ever be an American Catholic saint.[17]

Of course, the happiest attendees at Neumann's beatification were the Redemptorists. They had waited long enough. When Ferrante later described John Neumann's cause for canonization as the most difficult in the entire history of the Redemptorists, it is likely the first half of 1963 stood out as an especially maddening few months. First, the Sacred Congregation had pushed back Neumann's beatification from March until late June, very likely in deference to Cardinal Francis Spellman, the most influential of Seton's "partisans." Then, on 3 June, the death of Pope John XXIII postponed it once again, to the following October (figure 8).

FIGURE 8

Presentation of relics at John Neumann's beatification in October 1963.
Left to right: Monsignor Enrico Dante, Pope Paul VI, and Redemptorist
fathers Nicholas Ferrante, Francis X. Murphy, and Francis Litz.
(Courtesy of Redemptorist Archives of the Baltimore Province
of the Congregation of the Most Holy Redeemer)

Yet the rescheduling ensured that Neumann's beatification would take place
while Vatican II was in session. This timing may well have compensated for any
lingering frustration Redemptorists felt at the original deferral, as it permitted
more of the world's bishops to attend the ceremony and seemed to guarantee
more publicity than if it had been an exclusively U.S. affair. The Redemptorists
also had a ready-made publicity machine in place for Neumann in the person of
Rev. Francis X. Murphy, CSsR, an American teaching in Rome who served as
peritus (theological adviser) to fellow Redemptorist Aloysius Willinger, bishop
of Monterey-Fresno. Under the pseudonym "Xavier Rynne," Murphy published
a series of descriptive "Letters from Vatican City" in the *New Yorker*, thereby
becoming an important filter through which many Americans learned of the

council's proceedings. Both under the pseudonym and his real name, Murphy was an eloquent advocate for Catholic and secular audiences alike.[18]

The most meaningful intersection between Neumann's afterlife and Vatican II involved the council's dialogue not with those outside the fold but with its own members and particularly in discussions about the very nature of holiness. During the debate over *Lumen Gentium*, Belgium's Cardinal Suenens pointed out that 85 percent of recently canonized saints were members of religious orders and that more lay saints would better reflect the universal call to holiness.[19] This issue, like many others that surfaced during council proceedings, did not arise spontaneously at Vatican II. In the United States, for instance, Daniel Cantwell lamented in 1961 that "Steve the plumber or Mary the housewife with five young children" stood little chance of becoming a canonized saint according to present practice. Citing theologians Yves Congar and Pierre Teilhard de Chardin, Cantwell predicted that the church would soon search for heroic virtue among ordinary men and women.[20] In 1956, another writer had anticipated a "Saint in a Business Suit" and pictured "a statue of the first American-born saint, a smart, young business girl carrying a shorthand pad."[21]

Lumen Gentium nurtured this revised understanding of holiness. In defining the church as the "people of God," the document emphasized a horizontal rather than a vertical hierarchical structure, undermining the long-standing presumption that vowed religious were called to a holier life than that of the laity. If the call to holiness was universal, it suggested, so, too, should the church affirm it universally.

When it came to saints, *Lumen Gentium*'s most important chapter was its seventh, titled "Eschatological Nature of the Pilgrim Church and Its Union with the Church in Heaven." One of the chapter's principal authors was Jesuit Paolo Molinari, another *peritus* at the council who had served since 1957 as postulator for causes for canonization of members of the Society of Jesus. In 1961, Molinari published theological reflections on the "function of saints in the Church" that captured the attention of Pope John XXIII. The pontiff, stressing the subject's importance for the work of the council, urged Molinari to expand these reflections in book form and later appointed the Jesuit to the theological commission charged with writing the council's dogmatic constitution. Molinari recalled the pope insisting that the document devote an entire chapter to saints: How could the church understand itself, the pontiff had asked, "without referring to that part of the church which is in heaven?" Molinari and others drafted the chapter mindful of the church's need to explain the vital connection between believers on earth and those who were "perpetually united" to God. According to Molinari, it was "the first time in the history of the Church that this doctrine, so intimately related to her life and therefore to her practices from the very first centuries of Christianity, has been set forth positively and systematically by her supreme teaching authority."[22]

Molinari, a fluent English speaker, would figure very prominently in the canonizations of U.S. saints after the council, along with his protégé and fellow Jesuit Peter Gumpel. During the preparation of *Lumen Gentium*, Molinari became especially familiar with the story of one U.S. candidate for canonization. In seeking to explain saints' function in the church, the constitution's seventh chapter cited models for holiness. From its earliest days, the document specified, the church had believed that "the apostles and Christ's martyrs, who had given the supreme witness of faith and charity by the shedding of their blood, are closely joined with us in Christ, and she has always venerated them with special devotion." The document went on to stipulate that the church also recognized the holiness of those who had lived their faith in less dramatic ways. To the witness of the martyrs was added those "whom the outstanding practice of the Christian virtues and divine charisms recommended to the pious devotion and imitation of the faithful."[23]

It was in this context that John Neumann's pedestrian virtues, once a serious liability for his cause, became an asset. To support the above statement, *Lumen Gentium* referenced Benedict XV's 1921 decree on Neumann's heroic virtue, in which he had praised his ordinariness.[24] Thus Neumann's afterlife intersected with what John Courtney Murray identified as the key "issue-under-the-issues" at the council: "the development of doctrine," or, as O'Malley elaborated, "the problem of change in an institution that draws its lifeblood from a belief in the transcendent validity of the message it received from the past, which it is duty-bound to proclaim unadulterated."[25] Neumann's ordinary holiness became part of the council's argument that its proclamations were entirely consistent with past teaching.

Although Redemptorists made little of the fact that Neumann had surfaced in Vatican II's most significant document, their new crafting of his story clearly reflected a more pronounced emphasis on his spiritual life and holiness. Francis Murphy, writing under his own name rather than as Xavier Rynne, published a biography of John Neumann in which, while not ignoring Neumann's external accomplishments, he exhorted Neumann's devotees to imitate the bishop in his cultivation of interior spirit. "The most important thing about Bishop Neumann's life," Murphy insisted, "was not that he was a priest or a prelate nor that he instituted the Catholic elementary school system, or that he introduced the Forty Hours Devotion . . . or gave new impetus to a number of congregations of nuns." Despite Murphy's parroting of the message of decades of promotional material about the Bohemian missionary, his claim that Neumann's most important achievement had been his "inner self" signaled that he was writing for a new era.[26]

Litz and Ferrante, too, continued to focus on the ways that Neumann's sanctity had radiated outward into the local culture—so long as "local" meant the United States. When a bishop in Germany, for example, expressed his wish that Neumann's canonization take place in 1973 to coincide with the millennium of the introduction of Catholicism into Bohemia, Ferrante chided him for "his inclination to mix politics just a little with the canonization of Blessed John." Yet Ferrante had no reservations about pairing Neumann's canonization with the bicentennial of the American Declaration of Independence, and he often indulged Litz as well as Cardinal John Krol in their hopes that Neumann's cause would succeed by the U.S. bicentennial in 1976. From their perspectives, a double church-state celebration would represent the perfect cap to a cause that had long fused holiness and patriotism in the nation's birthplace.[27]

Despite the heavy emphasis on local concerns, Ferrante and Litz also remained attuned to the center, where it was becoming clear that the spirit of *aggiornamento* would affect the canonization process. Some attempts at modernization were incidental, if welcome, such as the Sacred Congregation's 1965 decision to allow postulators to submit typewritten material for the first time.[28] There were plenty of signs that more substantive changes to the canonization process were on the way. The council's commitment to collegiality—the notion that the world's collected bishops, or college, exercised supreme authority in unity with the pope—prompted Suenens to question whether the Roman center should have as much authority over naming saints as it had for the past three centuries. He suggested that the church revert to its former practice of allowing local bishops to beatify saints, while leaving the final stage of the process in the hands of the bishop of Rome.[29]

The presence of so many non-European cardinals at the council also helped to make clear that the church's canonization procedures were set up in a way that seemed to guarantee little geographical breadth among canonized saints. Suenens, pointing out that 90 percent of canonized saints came from just three European nations, suggested that the church redesign the process so that the roster of saints would reflect the church's truly global reach.[30] Channeling Edward McSweeny, the U.S. priest who in 1890 had urged the Holy See to validate the "hidden saints" from countries "too poor to stand all the necessary expense," Suenens criticized the process as "too burdensome and expensive." Although revising the process was not on the conciliar agenda, Pope Paul VI took tentative steps in that direction in 1969, when he made some minor adjustments to the procedures and renamed the Sacred Congregation of Rites the Congregation for the Causes of Saints.[31] More sweeping revisions would not take place until the 1980s.

But another intervention made by Suenens during the council, while unrelated to canonization, would nonetheless have a more immediate and dramatic impact on the way one segment of the U.S. Catholic population approached saint-seeking in the years to come. In October 1963, during the council's second session, Suenens asked the assembled bishops how they could reasonably deliberate the future of the church when half of it was missing: no women had been invited. In response, Pope Paul VI appointed fifteen female "auditors" to attend the council beginning with its third session in September 1964.[32] Among these was Sister Mary Luke Tobin, superior of the Kentucky-based Sisters of Loreto and chair of the Conference of Major Superiors of Women, the umbrella organization founded in 1956 to facilitate cooperation among women's religious congregations in the United States. In the wake of the council, Tobin became one of many U.S. Catholic sisters who would spearhead a wholesale transformation of religious life. Suenens himself had argued for many of these changes in his book *The Nun in the World*, which first appeared in English in 1962. Insisting that all religious had an obligation to spread the gospel by direct personal action, he encouraged sisters to reform structures and patterns of religious life to engage more completely with the world beyond convent walls.[33] These proposals were incorporated into conciliar and postconciliar decrees on religious life, and the changes they inspired would prompt many sisters to question their identities as citizens of the United States and as women in the church. And as they did so, they increasingly looked to their favorite saints as signposts in an unfamiliar world and as vehicles to express a new understanding of their place in it.

Sisters and Their Saints in the Council Era

In 1977, Rev. Joseph Kerins, superior of the Redemptorists of the Baltimore Province, spoke to women who belonged to two Philadelphia congregations associated with John Neumann: the Sisters of the Third Order of St. Francis and the Sisters, Servants of the Immaculate Heart of Mary (IHMs). Kerins reminded the sisters of their historic links to Neumann. To the Franciscans, he emphasized the bishop's role as their founder—a role that Redemptorists had recently enlarged in their efforts to claim for him the miracle exemption. To the IHMs, Kerins spoke of the way Neumann had "saved" the congregation by welcoming members from the original Detroit-based community to Philadelphia during a particularly complicated period in its history. Kerins's reflections on the past, however, merely served as a preface to more extended musings on the future. Whatever assistance Neumann had offered sisters during his lifetime, the superior argued, it was dwarfed in significance by the ways he could help contemporary sisters from his heavenly perch. Neumann's own experience in adapting to an unfamiliar environment rendered him a particularly effective guide through a tumultuous era of change. Indeed, Kerins argued, sisters' "traumatic transition" from the old world of the pre-council era to the new one it created rivaled in scale the adjustment Neumann had made in his migration from Bohemia to the United States over a century before.[34]

It was an evocative comparison. Neumann's passage through the final stages of the canonization process did overlap with a period of perplexing change for U.S. Catholic sisters. As with other reforms associated with the council, the restructuring of religious life had been under way in the decades before it opened. In particular, U.S. sisters' growing awareness of an identity beyond their particular communities—nourished in the Sister Formation Movement, in the Conference of Major Superiors of Women, and in colleges like Notre Dame and other Catholic universities where sisters studied together—shaped the way they responded to the transformations of the council era.

Nevertheless, *Perfectae Caritatis*, the council's "Decree on the Adaptation and Renewal of Religious Life,"[35] prompted what seemed a rapid transformation, by turns exciting and unsettling to many Catholics. Promulgated in 1965, the decree stipulated that congregations should "renew" themselves by engaging in extended reflection on how the original vision of their founder would translate into the modern world. It directed each community of men and women to convene a special general chapter meeting (or legislative assembly) within three years, to engage in designated periods of experimentation, and to rewrite their constitutions to permit them to respond to the call of the gospel in the contemporary world. In a dramatic departure from past practice, all members of the community were to be consulted in preparation for this. The search for renewal prompted most communities to implement a variety of structural changes. The strict rules that governed convent life became much less rigid, and community members were permitted more latitude in choice of ministry, living arrangements, and dress.

Vatican II's broader message about the whole church also transformed the way religious life was lived and perceived by Catholics.[36] *Lumen Gentium's* invitation to universal holiness undermined the two-tiered spirituality that had long placed ordained and vowed Catholics a plane above the non-ordained and non-vowed laity. Seeking to identify with members of the Catholic laity (which, as non-ordained members of church, they had technically always been), many individual sisters and communities made decisions that reoriented religious life. They chose, for example, to live in apartments rather than convents, to revert to their given names (to emphasize their baptismal rather than vocational call), and to modify or even abandon the habit (which had established a visible distinction between sisters and the rest of society). Given the council's emphasis on the call to holiness of all the baptized, the document instructed, "religious life could no longer be understood as an elite vocation to a 'life of perfection' that made its members superior to other Christians."[37]

Gaudium et Spes, the council's "Pastoral Constitution on the Church in the Modern World," was equally influential in renewing and changing religious life. Although the document runs to over thirty thousand words, its essence is communicated in its first line: "The joys and the hopes, the griefs and the anxieties of the men of this age, especially those who are poor or in any way afflicted, these are the joys and hopes, the griefs and anxieties of the followers of Christ."[38] The document's strong social content prompted many American sisters to choose new forms of ministry and inspired them toward a commitment to civil rights and other social justice movements.[39] In 1965, a number of U.S. sisters converged on Selma, Alabama, to join civil rights activists under the leadership of Dr. Martin Luther King Jr. on a march to the state capital of Montgomery to protest restrictions on African American voting rights. Selma not only represented the first mass movement of whites into the civil rights movement but also served as a highly visible marker of the church's engagement with the most pressing social problem of the day. Selma's white marchers were disproportionately Catholic, and habited nuns attracted a great deal of media attention.

Sister Mary Peter Traxler (or Margaret Ellen Traxler, as she was known after she reverted to her birth name in the late 1960s) found the Selma experience to be so powerful that she was compelled to redefine her life as a woman religious. In an article titled "After Selma, Sister, You Can't Stay Home Again!," Traxler urged Catholic sisters to step outside the classroom and convent and work for justice in the world.[40] Many Catholic sisters did indeed leave the classroom. As scholar Michael Novak described in his 1966 report on the "new nuns," sisters could be found working in urban renewal programs, advocacy, addiction counseling, chaplaincy, and government posts. Within Lyndon B. Johnson's Great Society, for example, American sisters worked with Head Start, Job Corps, and VISTA.[41]

The combination of new ministries and the disappearance of the habit and other traditional hallmarks of religious life prompted debate, conflict, and soul-searching within and beyond religious communities. Sisters' gravitation from traditionally female ministries of teaching and nursing in favor of other ministries had dramatic consequences for church-sponsored institutions. It particularly affected the Catholic parochial school system, which had long depended on the subsidized labor that women religious provided. Compounding the problem was a precipitous decline in the overall numbers of Catholic sisters. In the aftermath of the council, many men and women left religious life either because they felt the reforms had gone too far or had not gone far enough. In addition to these massive departures, the number of new vocations plummeted. The cumulative drop in numbers forced many Catholic schools to close. Others remained open, with only a handful of vowed religious on staff, as lay Catholics stepped in to fill roles traditionally occupied by priests, brothers, or sisters.

This reality formed the backdrop of Joseph Kerins's 1977 message to the Philadelphia Franciscans and IHMs, communities whose members long had helped to sustain the archdiocese's vast parochial school system. Some, Kerins conceded, believed that Neumann, surveying recent changes in religious life, "would throw up his hands in dismay—and run away in desperation." But the superior dismissed out of hand those who sounded a note of despair, insisting that Neumann would take, on the whole, an optimistic view of the transformations in religious life. True, Neumann would admit to some challenges, but he would focus on the "flowers, blooming bright in religious life," such as loosening authority structures, flexibility in living arrangements, and greater range in ministries. Neumann would recognize that this "new freedom" would "enable Catholic sisters to make better use of "the talent, judgment, vision, and grace of the Holy Spirit." In Kerins's view, even Neumann, long lionized as the founder and champion of the school system, would be heartened, rather than disturbed, at sisters' efforts today to "animate" institutions rather than being content with merely "staffing" them. (Kerins here was using a descriptive term intended to convey the effort of vowed religious remaining on staffs of congregational-sponsored institutions to empower their lay partners and infuse them with the congregational charism or spirit). The shuttering of some Catholic schools and decreased representation of sisters on the faculty of others was a small price to pay, Kerins insisted, for the sisters' greater commitment to the poor and op-pressed. Now channeled to more urgent pursuits, sisters' energy exhibited the "mobility and flexibility" that would be their key words in responding to the signs of the times.

The same themes surfaced among the Sisters of Charity as they, too, reflected on Elizabeth Ann Seton's meaning in a new world. In a homily delivered to the sisters in New Jersey, Sister Francis Maria Cassidy argued that Seton would have responded to the council's decree on adaptation and renewal (whose of-ficial name, after all, translated to "Perfect Charity") with a hearty "Amen." Remembering Seton's "invincible faith in and devotion to the living church" and her "determination to be an instrument of love and service . . . especially here in America," Cassidy exhorted the members of the New Jersey–based Sisters of Charity to pray for guidance about how to translate Seton's vision to the contemporary United States. Continuity derived not from the sisters' specific ministries but rather from their response to the most urgent needs of the church and the nation. The important point, Cassidy contended, was that "John Carroll [bishop of Baltimore when Seton founded the Sisters of Charity] needed Catholic schools for America as desperately as Terrence Cook [*sic*] [Ter-ence Cooke, Spellman's successor as archbishop of New York] needs a working anti-poverty program for New York."[42]

John Tracy Ellis, the historian who had recommended Annabelle Melville as Seton's biographer, echoed Cassidy in his post–Vatican II reflections on Seton. Ellis had retained an avid interest in Seton's cause for canonization. On the eve of the council, in fact, Ellis had told an international group of Catho-lic laywomen that he could "think of few more appropriate undertakings in the realm of the spirit" than "an energetic campaign of prayers" on behalf of Seton's beatification.[43] Fifteen years later, Ellis speculated that Seton would have sympathized with "certain aims of the Women's Liberation Movement" or the leadership of the National Organization of Women. If "every age in recorded history" required heroes and heroines to whom others could turn to shape their thoughts and actions, Ellis argued, Seton's guidance and example were especially welcome in the 1970s, "an age of ceaseless change and bewildering complexity."[44]

If the transformations of the council era turned Neumann and Seton into figures who could offer wisdom and consolation on the cusp of their canonizations, they also affected causes that were far less advanced. For many Catholic women's religious communities in the United States, the call to reexamine their founding charism in the light of the contemporary world reinvigorated a number of causes for canonization that had lost momentum in the era of the nation saint. One such example was the Italian-born missionary Samuel Mazzuchelli. The Sinsinawa Dominicans read in the council directives a mandate to press forward on the cause for canonization of the man they revered as their founder. Archbishop John Ireland and the sisters had nominated "the Apostle of the Midwest" as a prospective saint in the early days of the quest for a native patron, though they had taken no formal steps. While Amleto Cicognani's promotion of Mazzuchelli, as well as the centennial of his arrival in the United States, inspired modest publicity in the 1930s, the story of his evangelization on a massive swath of the midwestern frontier never quite meshed with the decade's "new ideal of sainthood." Mazzuchelli's lack of broad appeal and the disruptions of World War II, combined with the sisters' obligation to rely on Dominican priests to act in their stead, forcing them to work on the case only at some remove, were all probably factors that delayed a formal opening of a cause on his behalf. By the late 1940s and 1950s, the Sinsinawa Dominicans and their clerical representatives were gathering documentation and cataloging it meticulously, preparing it to meet rigorous Roman standards, and in 1964 the bishop of Madison, Wisconsin, officially opened Mazzuchelli's ordinary process by appointing a commission to review all documents: 1,130 in total, including 417 written by Mazzuchelli himself.[45] The evidence suggests that the sisters' renewed appreciation of their founder in the light of Vatican II gave the cause added impetus. "Something beautiful is happening in the Congregation now," one sister observed in 1972, "in that there are Sisters asking for and feeling the need for more information about Father Samuel."[46]

The teachings of the Second Vatican Council not only motivated the Sinsinawa Dominicans to pursue Mazzuchelli's cause more energetically but also inspired them to assume more visible roles as they did so. The sister most closely associated with Mazzuchelli's cause was Mary Nona McGreal, who served as president of Edgewood College in Madison from 1950 until 1968 and as leader of the Sinsinawa Dominicans from 1968 until 1977. Even though McGreal neither marched at Selma nor eschewed the congregation's traditional ministry of education, she nonetheless was a "new nun" who harnessed the mobility and flexibility of the council years to serve in a number of innovative capacities—and to advance Mazzuchelli's cause. As a founding member of the Mazzuchelli Guild, McGreal adopted the language of Vatican II to make Mazzuchelli's story relevant to a new generation of Catholics, touting the founder as a visionary with regard to lay involvement in the church. Well over a century before the council was convened, she argued, Mazzuchelli had shown a deep "appreciation of lay catechists" and relied on them "all his priestly life." McGreal and others also suggested that Mazzuchelli's outreach to various groups on the frontier prefigured modern movements designed to promote ecumenism and improve race relations.[47]

The cause for canonization of Mother Théodore Guérin unfolded along much the same pattern. Like Mazzuchelli, Guérin had emerged as a candidate for canonization in the late nineteenth century, when saint-seekers had foregrounded European missionaries' civilizing influence on the American nation. In the 1930s, Cicognani's interest in Guérin's cause had helped complete the ordinary process that had begun in 1913, but decades would pass before there was any more official movement.[48] As was the case with other missionaries whose stories did not evoke urban immigration, skyscrapers, or U.S. citizenship, Guérin could not generate enough national attention in those decades to compete with figures like Frances Cabrini. A frequent turnover of male postulators did not help matters. After Vatican II, however, as the Sisters of Providence sought to adapt Guérin's founding charism to the modern age, Guérin's cause attracted renewed interest. It, too, would be shaped by a nascent female activism, mostly in the person of Sister Josephine Ryan, who began to work on the cause full time in 1978.[49]

While Vatican II propelled forward a number of causes sponsored by U.S. Catholic sisters, it sent at least one moving in the opposite direction. When it came to promoting the cause for canonization of their American founder, Philippine Duchesne, the Society of the Sacred Heart interpreted the council's teachings differently than either the Sisters of Providence or the Sinsinawa Dominicans had done. Duchesne, like Guérin and Mazzuchelli, had been a

European missionary in the American Midwest in the nineteenth century who had emerged as one of the first prospective U.S. saints. Unlike Guérin and Mazzuchelli, however, Duchesne had advanced to beatification by 1940, in part because the renowned experts in canonization, the Jesuits, directed her cause. While Duchesne's beatification may not have attracted much national attention, a lack of broader interest had not lessened the Society of the Sacred Heart's eagerness to see her canonized. Working through their male proxies, the RSCJs had submitted two miracles to the Sacred Congregation in the mid-1950s.[50] Neither of them held up to the scrutiny at the Sacred Congregation, but in 1961, the congregation submitted a third, very promising case, involving a cure that had taken place approximately a decade before. In September 1951, Mother Marguerite Bernard, a French-born RSCJ serving in Shanghai, had arrived in San Francisco seriously ill with a cancerous lump in her neck. The RSCJs in San Francisco, and subsequently the entire congregation, began a novena to Philippine on Bernard's behalf. By the following spring, the missionary returned to Asia much improved. Bernard's new assignment was in Tokyo, and after doctors deemed her completely cured, it was there that an official investigation into the miracle was undertaken.[51]

The strength of the Bernard miracle contributed to the RSCJs' sense of optimism about Duchesne's prospects for canonization in the early days of the council. Believing that the event was "imminent," RSCJ leaders had even petitioned the Holy See to delay their 1964 General Congregation (chapter meeting) so that it might coincide with Duchesne's canonization. They also began to publish a *Duchesne Guild Bulletin* to publicize the cause, one section of which included testimonials of prominent U.S. churchmen. One of the first people they approached, naturally, was Cardinal Spellman. Though he retained his singleness of focus on Seton's candidacy, Spellman did agree to endorse Duchesne's cause—though he outsourced the actual crafting of the statement to his good friend Kathryn Sullivan, an accomplished RSCJ biblical scholar on the faculty of Manhattanville College in Purchase, New York. Sullivan, who also served as an editor of the *Duchesne Guild Bulletin*, supplied Spellman with the requisite statement, which appeared in the publication's winter 1964 issue.[52]

Sullivan and Spellman's more sustained interaction concerned another subject. At Manhattanville's commencement ceremonies in 1964, Spellman proposed that Sullivan pursue advanced study in the Holy Land. Such an experience, he wrote in a follow-up letter, would enable Sullivan to be "of even greater

service to the Church than you have been up to the present." When Sullivan demurred, citing the congregation's inability to fund such an endeavor, Spellman
offered to cover the costs. As was the custom, he submitted an official request to
Mother Beatrice Brennan, Sullivan's immediate superior at her Manhattanville
convent, who then passed it on to Sabine de Valon, the RSCJs' mother general
in France. Valon's answer arrived in August: a firm "no." Informing Spellman
of the mother general's decision, Brennan expressed "deep and heartfelt gratitude for the kind and generous offer" but explained that Sullivan was needed
at the college. Giving voice to the rapid pace at which religious life was changing, Brennan continued, "I am sure your Eminence will understand how Our
Mother General is being asked for so many dispensations at this time that it is
not possible for her to accept all of them." Spellman expressed his "amaze[ment]
at the disappointing answer to my proposal" and contemplated sending "various comments and answers" but in the end decided—uncharacteristically for
the outspoken cardinal—to "keep silent."[53]

On 15 October 1964, the RSCJs convened for their General Congregation;
the Holy See had not, after all, granted them permission to delay it until Duchesne's canonization. It would be a historic meeting. Valon, who had by that
point been serving along with Mary Luke Tobin as an auditor at Vatican II
for two weeks, had this to say to the delegates: "We are at an important hour
where the religious life, by the voice of the Church, is doubtless going to take a
different orientation." Citing the provisions in the rule that applied to cloister,
or the separation of the sisters from the world, she explained that it was time
"to go more towards the world, because the Church requests it." Referencing
the text of *Perfectae Caritatis*, then in the discussion stage at the council, Valon
appealed to the society to maintain "the spirit of cloister," even as she effectively
abolished it in practice. Also at the 1964 chapter, the RSCJs agreed to adopt
a simplified habit and identified three major priorities: experiments in education, a strong missionary thrust, and an energetic response to the cry for social
justice. On the latter issue, the congregation called for greater presence in inner
city areas and a gradual assimilation of social classes in the schools.[54]

The changes implemented at the 1964 General Congregation would transform the religious lives and ministries of the RSCJs. Mother Kathryn Sullivan
would make an especially brisk transition from the old world to the new world.
The General Congregation closed on 15 November. When Spellman renewed
his "wonderfully generous" offer soon after that, Sullivan responded jubilantly

that that "the spirit of aggiornamento" made it possible for her to accept it, making the upcoming Thanksgiving holiday "one of the happiest of my whole life."[55] Sullivan went to the Holy Land and would return often as she became an even more renowned scholar and experienced congregational leader.[56]

If the "spirit of aggiornamento" had led to an abrupt pivot in Kathryn Sullivan's life, it precipitated an equally sudden reversal in the afterlife of the woman she and other RSCJs regarded as their spiritual mother. For the RSCJs, the mandates of Vatican II diminished, rather than magnified, their enthusiasm for their founder's cause. They were no less confident in Philippine's holiness; they were simply less inclined to expend the resources required to prove it. In November 1967, the *Duchesne Guild Bulletin*, launched in the heady early days of Vatican II, when Duchesne's canonization had seemed imminent, announced that it would cease publication. Although it had become apparent by 1967 that the event was "not in the foreseeable future," the RSCJs did not explicitly abandon Duchesne's cause, and there is no evidence that they ever formally renounced their position as petitioners. They did judge, however, that devoting the necessary time, personnel, and money toward canonizing Duchesne was no longer justifiable in light of the congregation's renewed commitment to the poor. Such an endeavor, according to one member of the congregation, did not seem "in keeping with the spirit of Philippine herself."[57]

Members of the Society of the Sacred Heart were not the only Americans to express concerns about the expense and labor involved in pursuing canonization. In 1975, the *Wall Street Journal* published an article about Elizabeth Ann Seton's cause that alleged that the Sisters of Charity had spent "millions" of dollars in its pursuit. According to "Rev. Francis X. Murphy, an authority on sainthood," the article reported, finding out exact costs or anything about the selection of new saints was as impossible as discovering the details of Cold War diplomacy: "It's like trying to find out how a missile is put together and fired off." The article also quoted Joel Wells, editor of the Chicago-based liberal Catholic magazine *The Critic*, who consigned canonization's significance "to the past" and argued that "there is a lot more the church could do with the money spent on it."[58]

In a response later published in the *Wall Street Journal*, the archivist of the Sisters of Charity of Seton Hill rebutted the article's claim that pursuing the cause had incurred "crippling deficits" for the congregation. After a brief sketch of the six communities that traced their ancestry to Seton, she explained that, in response to a request from the vice-postulator in 1939, each community had contributed a hundred dollars per month to Seton's cause. These funds had placed the cause on such a sound financial footing that the present vice-postulator, Sylvester Taggart, had removed the assessment in 1971. Anyone familiar with the background of the relationship between the sisters and the original vice-postulator, who had raised such an enormous furor in imposing his "tax," would have savored the delicious irony: a Sister of Charity was actually awarding Salvator Burgio public credit for financial solvency! Nevertheless, the letter set the record straight: promoting Seton as a saint had not bankrupted her spiritual daughters.[59] Privately, Sisters of Charity embraced the advertising adage that there was no such thing as bad publicity. The article had garnered more attention for Seton's cause than her promoters could have generated through their own efforts, even, as one observed pragmatically, "if we had gone into the multimillion dollar PR campaign implied in the story."[60]

The *Wall Street Journal* article also elicited other spirited defenses of canonization-related expenditures. Writing in *Columbia* magazine, Jesuit Robert Graham argued that to faithful Catholics—unlike denizens of "the world of finance . . . who, when seeing a masterwork of art, immediately ask how much it cost"—the prospect of raising one of their own to the honors of the altar was priceless. Long and precise processes always required money, Graham pointed out, and canonizations resembled "extended litigation in secular courts," in that they went all the way "up to the 'Supreme Court,' the pope."[61] Francis Litz also went on the record defending the material resources required to honor a saint, estimating that the Redemptorists had spent approximately $35,000 to stage Neumann's beatification ceremony. In comparison, he pointed out, "it cost $6 million to inaugurate Richard Nixon, and who's more important?"[62]

Litz was especially cognizant of the time, expense, and labor a cause for canonization entailed: by that point, he was overseeing not only John Neumann's cause but also that of a second prospective saint from Philadelphia: Katharine Drexel. The most revelatory causes are not necessarily those that move forward—or as Duchesne's did during Vatican II, backward—during a particular era but those that originate during it. In many ways, the most illustrative cause of the council era belonged to a woman who, coincidentally and posthumously, cemented John Neumann's connection to a third local congregation of Catholic sisters.

An "Unmistakably American" Saint

Almost a quarter century after Frances Cabrini's canonization, poet Phyllis McGinley was one of the midcentury Americans who resented Rome's petulant refusal to canonize a "truly native candidate." McGinley also complained about the outsize attention paid to Cabrini's external accomplishments; one would think, McGinley wrote in 1969, that Cabrini had been "canonized as much for her business acumen as for her holiness." McGinley was even more dismissive of those who would claim the Italian-born woman as a U.S. saint. McGinley pinned her hopes for an American patron not on the recently beatified Seton or Neumann but on a newly minted U.S. Servant of God: Katharine Drexel, the Philadelphia heiress and founder of the Sisters of the Blessed Sacrament. In McGinley's view, Drexel had combined "holiness with indigenous Yankee know-how" in a manner that made her "as unmistakably American as Catherine of Siena, say, was Italian." While that Catherine had been "the most powerful woman in Europe," Drexel had been similarly influential in the United States. McGinley mainly admired Drexel for her generosity, but she also included a tongue-in-cheek homage to her stamina. She playfully suggested that Drexel had lived almost ninety-seven years solely because, knowing that the income from her family's fortune would revert to other beneficiaries after her death, she wanted to prolong the period in which her wealth would flow to Native Americans and African Americans. "Never underestimate," McGinley warned, "the stubbornness of a woman or a saint."[63]

McGinley was neither the first nor the last Drexel supporter to compare her hero to St. Catherine of Siena. Writing to Drexel before she entered her novitiate, James O'Connor, formerly of Philadelphia and then bishop of Omaha, Nebraska, sent her feast day greetings: "May your patroness obtain for you the grace to be a peacemaker among the races, as she was among the nationalities." Drexel's spiritual daughters evoked O'Connor's salute in the first issue of *The Peacemaker*, the quarterly bulletin used to promote Drexel as a saint that appeared for the first time in 1964.[64] The official launch of Drexel's cause followed a five-year effort undertaken by Mother Mary Anselm, the superior general of the Sisters of the Blessed Sacrament, who with other members of the community had begun to contemplate nominating Drexel for canonization soon after the founder's death. A flurry of new biographical information convinced them there was support beyond Drexel's immediate circle. In 1957, Katherine Burton, who had also produced biographies of both Elizabeth Ann Seton and Mother Théodore Guérin, published an account of Drexel's life that portrayed her as a patriotic as well as a pious hero—"an American in the real and abundant sense of the word."[65]

In 1959 Mother Anselm approached Cardinal John Francis O'Hara to ask for his help in initiating a cause for Drexel. The cardinal had already proven to be a valuable ally to the sisters in the wake of Katharine's death four years before. Recognizing their precarious financial position without income from Drexel's inheritance, O'Hara had directed a number of the Philadelphia entities on Francis Drexel's original list of beneficiaries—Redemptorists among them—to donate a portion of their windfall to the Sisters of the Blessed Sacrament.[66] O'Hara had also been amenable to helping the congregation promote Drexel as a saint, but he had died soon after his conversation with Mother Anselm. But Krol, O'Hara's ambitious successor, embraced the prospect of a second Philadelphia saint and by 1964 had authorized the opening of Drexel's process. Whereas Krol hoped local Jesuits would act as the necessary proxies for Drexel's congregation, the sisters preferred to work with the Redemptorists. They may well have been encouraged by Litz and Ferrante's triumph in securing Neumann's beatification the previous year, but they also cited historical precedent as a rationale for this collaboration: when Drexel had gone to Rome to secure pontifical approval for her congregation, a Redemptorist canon lawyer had helped her navigate the Roman bureaucracy. Notwithstanding Krol's tempestuous relationship with Ferrante, the archbishop eventually agreed to the arrangement, and Ferrante became Drexel's postulator and Litz her vice-postulator.[67]

Drexel's family fortune had allowed the Sisters of the Blessed Sacrament to sidestep the question of whether pursuing a cause for canonization represented the best use of congregational resources. In 1927, Drexel's sister Louise Morrell had established a special fund for the Sisters of the Blessed Sacrament from which the superior could draw at her discretion to support any "extraordinary work." After Mother Anselm decided that Drexel's canonization fit these criteria, the income from that original fund covered all expenses related to Drexel's cause.[68] The sisters paid Litz a nominal fee and worked with him to develop promotional material explaining Drexel's relevance in a post–Vatican II church. "The present stress of ecumenism," Litz argued, had been evident in Drexel's openness to Protestants in all schools run by her congregation. In naming her congregation after the Blessed Sacrament, and in recognizing the Eucharist as "the source and summit" of her life, Drexel had "lived and believed in a Eucharistic orientation not verbalized by the Church until Vatican II."[69]

In seeking to connect Drexel to prominent issues of the day, Litz and the Sisters of the Blessed Sacrament were doing nothing other than what U.S.-based petitioners had been doing since they nominated their first candidates for canonization in the 1880s: projecting what they saw as the best and brightest part of their American stories onto their prospective saints. Yet Drexel's case brought with it a new challenge. During the council era, the darkest and most divisive aspects of American culture would increasingly encroach on U.S. Catholics' efforts to present candidates for the church's highest honor. In retrospect, Drexel's real claim to being "unmistakably American" may lie not in the innovation or stamina she had displayed during her lifetime but in the degree to which the fractures of the 1960s and 1970s intruded upon her afterlife.

As the founder of a congregation dedicated to ministering to African Americans, the most glaring such issue in Drexel's case involved race. After presiding at Drexel's reception into the Sisters of Mercy (the congregation with whom she had prepared for religious life) in 1889, Archbishop Patrick Ryan of Philadelphia had proclaimed her a "prophetess of reparation and conciliation between the races." Throughout the 1960s and 1970s, Drexel's promotional material frequently referred to her as a prophet, arguing that in founding a congregation "devoted completely to the welfare of the Indians and Blacks" Drexel had "provided a viable means for carrying on a continual battle against racial injustice."[70] On the face of it, the 1960s and 1970s appeared to be an auspicious time to present Drexel as a crusader for racial justice. But however prophetic Drexel's approach to race relations may have appeared in the 1890s, aspects of it appeared decidedly paternalistic in the context of the civil rights movement. Drexel's supporters would have to contend with accusations that Drexel, far from having been a visionary, had been rooted all too firmly in her time and subject to all of its biases. Sister Mary Elise, a Sister of the Blessed Sacrament who had worked with Drexel, "took [the backlash against the congregation] in stride." It was understandable, she maintained, that learning about the "the suffering, the unfairness," in their past made African Americans angry. "And in their anger they lashed out at the most accessible target—us."[71]

But while coming to terms with the present-day consequences of Drexel's choices was one thing, preventing them from interfering with the case for her sanctity was another, and that task fell to Litz and other promoters. The most seemingly damning evidence against Drexel centered on her refusal to accept African American women into the Sisters of the Blessed Sacrament. Those close to Drexel insisted that her refusal to accept black aspirants had stemmed not from her racial prejudices but instead from a desire to support all-black congregations such as the Baltimore-based Oblate Sisters of Providence and the Sisters of the Holy Family in New Orleans. Accepting African American women into the Sisters of the Blessed Sacrament would have siphoned candidates away from them. According to Sister Juliana Haynes, "Mother Katharine did not want to hurt the all-black orders by drawing vocations away from them."[72]

Members of those "all-black" congregations corroborated such claims. Testifying on behalf of Drexel's cause, Sister Marie Enfanta Gonzales, superior general of the Oblate Sisters of Providence, offered her own life story as a defense of Drexel's decision. Educated by the Sisters of the Blessed Sacrament in grade school, Gonzales had become aware of her vocation and contemplated entering the congregation. Drexel directed her instead to the Oblate Sisters of Providence, as she had done in many other cases. Gonzales contended that the rationale was not racism: Mother Katharine's "real and only reason was that we had our two Black communities [the Oblate Sisters of Providence and the Sisters of the Holy Family]. Mother Katharine really felt that it would have taken away from our Black Community."[73]

Drexel's supporters, aware of the potential for controversy, sought to avert it by crafting a narrative that focused on what she had done rather than on what she had failed to do for African Americans. The bedrock of their argument rested on Drexel's "Eucharistic-centered" spirituality, which led her to recognize racial equality in the eyes of God. Whereas belief in the real presence of Christ in the Eucharist had been the deciding factor in Seton's conversion to Catholicism, for Katharine Drexel, belief in the Eucharist as a source of unity for all Catholics had inspired her to devote her family's fortune to ensure that underserved populations within the church could receive the sacrament. To that end, Drexel subsidized the establishment of black churches, supported religious congregations engaged in missionary activity, and nurtured black vocations. In this last respect, Drexel had been ahead of her time in recognizing that people of color could have a vocation to religious life—a principle that had been far from universally accepted when she had founded the Sisters of the Blessed Sacrament. In 1898, Drexel had explained why she believed African American girls should be permitted take religious vows. "Why should they not be religious?" Drexel asked Rev. J. R. Slattery, a member of an order of priests who ministered to African Americans. "As I understand they are sent to do the work of religious without the graces or the protection of religious. . . . If it be possible—as seems to be the case—that the Colored girl may live in religion, why should she not do so, and enjoy its advantages?"[74]

Testimony from prominent African American Catholics buttressed the case that Drexel was ahead of her time on race relations. Litz's file of promotional material on Drexel included quotes from Rev. Augustine Tolton, the first black priest ordained in America, who had drawn parallels between himself and Drexel: "As I stand alone as the first Negro priest of America," he told her, "so you stand alone as the first one to give your whole treasury for the sole benefit of the Colored and Indians."[75] Drexel's ovations also came from more contemporary sources. In 1966, Judge Raymond Pace Alexander, the first black graduate of Wharton, went so far as to claim that "it does not require the profound imagination of the prophet to believe firmly that had the conscience of the great Protestant establishment of wealth and church been as shaken about the condition of African-Americans after the Civil War" as had Mother Drexel's, "the bitter conflicts of the last century between the races, more particularly the explosive events during the last decade, would never have taken place."[76]

The majority of acclamations on Drexel's behalf came from African American leaders who had been educated in institutions established by her congregation. Among the most effusive was Ellen Tarry, an African American children's author and figure in the Harlem Renaissance who had been personally handed her diploma by Drexel when she graduated from the Sisters' St. Francis de Sales School in Rock Castle, Virginia. According to Tarry, though, the founder had given her something more meaningful: the gift of faith.[77]

Another vocal Drexel supporter was Norman Francis, the president of Xavier University in New Orleans, the nation's first college for black Catholics and the institution understood to be the "crowning point" of Drexel's educational mission. Echoing Tarry and others, Francis characterized Drexel as a "heroine" who had "national influence" among black Catholics. In an age when most church leaders had ignored them, he argued, Drexel had devoted her life to alleviating their suffering and in so doing was singlehandedly responsible for ensuring that African American Catholics did not leave the church. Drexel had been an exception among Catholic leaders, Francis allowed, but she had been "enough of an exception for us to keep the faith."[78] Francis expressed what many of Drexel's devotees identified as her most significant spiritual legacy:

through her spiritual and material support, Drexel had given black Catholics a reason to stay in the church.

Sister Marie Gonzales, the superior of the Oblate Sisters of Providence who defended Drexel's decision not to accept black women into her congregation, was an alumna of Xavier who also believed that Drexel's ministry had made a lasting difference in race relations. At Xavier, Gonzales claimed, she and other future African American leaders learned that they "did not have to be afraid of White people." The presence of Sisters of the Blessed Sacrament had made a lasting difference throughout the South. "Every place where Mother Katharine and her sisters have not been in the church," Gonzales testified, "the people are different. I noticed that." Asked whether pursuing Drexel's canonization was "worthwhile," Gonzales quoted Sargent Shriver at a meeting of Head Start, the early intervention program for young children. According to Gonzales, Shriver had called Drexel "the first Head Start director of the United States, because she was the first one to go help the children of the poor and go do something about it."[79]

Other admirers of Drexel also praised her in the parlance of the day, characterizing her as a woman who moved easily between the "affluent society" and "other Americans" or as a person who "had plunged into the black liberation movement decades before it was a hip thing."[80] A bishop from Louisiana who had worked with the Sisters of the Blessed Sacrament supported the founder's canonization because her love for "the most neglected of God's people" bore witness to the Catholic Church's commitment to civil rights for African Americans. "The Protestants had their Martin Luther King," he said, but Catholics had Katharine Drexel—a woman who had a reputation "of goodness, of service, of generosity" that surpassed, he claimed, even that of Mother Seton.[81]

Litz and other Drexel promoters had apparently been less concerned about the possibility that indigenous people might object to Drexel's canonization, despite the fact that Drexel's practices and attitudes toward them had also been consistent with those of most Americans of her time. Perhaps they did not anticipate backlash from Native Americans because Drexel had admitted a few native women into the Sisters of the Blessed Sacrament. They may have also realized that, whatever Drexel's limitations had been, her case was unlikely to inspire indigenous protests to the same degree European missionaries to the colonial United States had begun to do. In the 1960s, Junípero Serra, the Spanish-born Franciscan whose cause formally opened after the North

American Jesuits' canonization, emerged as a particular flash point for native protests. Serra's supporters insisted it was misguided to make Serra a scapegoat for the misdeeds of European colonizers and sought to counter negative publicity by framing him as a perfect saint for the modern age. The bishop of San Diego, for instance, suggested that Serra had a future as the "patron saint of ecologists," given his work in "the development and preservation of natural beauty in California." In 1969, Rev. Neil Moholy, Serra's vice-postulator, looked beyond earthly boundaries to emphasize his timeliness, drawing "a tremendous parallel between Serra's time and ours. He closed the era of (Spanish) exploration and we have crossed the threshold of the space age." Serra's promoters also had their eyes on the looming U.S. bicentennial. Moholy, recognizing that Pope Paul VI wanted to "promote national heroes" in conjunction with the celebration, argued that Serra, unlike John Neumann and other saints from the Eastern Seaboard, would call attention to Catholicism's long presence in the American West. "As people are more familiar with the 13 colonies," the Franciscan observed, "many don't realize that a culture possessing similar values was flourishing, thanks largely to Serra, at the time of the Revolutionary War."[82] Yet Serra's legacy would elicit more heated protests as his cause for canonization progressed.

As for Drexel, the question of whether her practices and attitudes regarding African Americans complicate her sanctity remains an open one that has begun to capture the interest of scholars.[83] Far less attention has been paid to the intersection between Drexel's cause and a second social movement that converged with the mandates of Vatican II to reshape U.S. Catholicism and American life: feminism. As noted by Mary Luke Tobin, the U.S. sister who was one of fifteen women at the council's third and fourth sessions, Vatican II offered "an opening, although just a tiny crack in the door, to a recognition of the vast indifference toward women and the ignoring of their potential within the whole body of the Church."[84] Carol Coston, a Dominican sister from Adrian, Michigan, who was one of many U.S. sisters sent to serve the developing world in the 1960s, observed that while Vatican II had opened "windows" into the renewal of religious life, the women's movement had opened doors, leading Catholic sisters to cultivate "a feminist perspective that recognized and critiqued domination wherever it operated—men over women, whites over blacks, U.S. over Third World countries, military over civilians, [and] hierarchy over religious."[85]

The growing feminist awareness among Catholic sisters led to highly publicized clashes between specific congregations and their clerical superiors in dioceses throughout the United States. It also generated conflict at the national level. By 1970, the term "women's liberation" appeared regularly in memos, correspondence, and published documents of the Conference of Major Superiors of Women.[86] Feminist concerns inspired the organization to change its name to the Leadership Conference of Women Religious in 1972, arguing that the word "superior" in the former title had emphasized hierarchy and unilateralism rather than inclusion and collaboration and that the incorporation of "women religious" emphasized their identity as women. From the perspective of the Vatican's Congregation for Religious and for Secular Institutes,[87] which had to approve the change, however, the word "leadership" became the primary sticking point. After three years of debate, the congregation eventually approved the new name on the condition the title be followed by a clarifying sentence: "This title is to be interpreted as: The Conference of Leaders of Congregations of Women Religious of the United States of America" and not, in other words, leaders in any other realm.[88]

The most pressing question of Catholic women's leadership within the church involved their admission to the ordained ministry. In 1963, St. Joan's International Alliance, an organization of Catholic women named in honor of the French saint, began to submit an annual petition to the Vatican in support of women's ordination. They initially cloaked this radical request in deferential language: "St. Joan's international alliance reaffirms its loyalty and filial devotion and asks that should the Church in her own wisdom and in her good time decide to extend to women the dignity of the priesthood, women would be willing and eager to respond."[89] Such submissiveness would not survive the resurgence of feminism. In 1974, the Leadership Conference of Women Religious passed a resolution to support women's ordination; the next year, twelve hundred Catholics gathered in Detroit for the Women's Ordination Conference.

Canonization represented another arena in which a blossoming identity as feminists among Catholic women—and in particular, among Catholic sisters—affected their relationships with local clerics and Vatican officials. The alliance between Redemptorists and the Sisters of the Blessed Sacrament on Drexel's behalf, for example, looked much more like a partnership than many previous relationships established between female saint-seekers and their male proxies. Francis Litz oversaw the components that entailed direct interaction with the Holy See, while the sisters published *The Peacemaker*, kept track of potential miracles, and solicited monetary contributions to support the cause. Practical considerations may well have prompted this division of labor;

advancing Neumann's cause, with its idiosyncratic complications, certainly kept Litz busy enough. Litz's personality was also a factor; sensitive and kind, he appears to have deferred to Drexel's spiritual daughters to the extent canon law permitted. Litz was certainly no Salvator Burgio. Nevertheless, it was also clear that activism on the part of the Sisters of the Blessed Sacrament fit into a larger pattern. As Sisters Mary Nona McGreal and Josephine Ryan were doing on behalf of Mazzuchelli and Guérin, Mother Anselm and other Sisters of the Blessed Sacrament were taking up Isabel Toohey's mantle. Toohey's attempts to wrest control from Burgio had foreshadowed the transformations of the council era. As consecrated Catholic women sought more control over their own lives, they would also claim more authority over the afterlives of their spiritual ancestors.

Not all U.S. Catholic sisters embraced feminism. Notably, Mother Claudia Honsberger, superior of the Philadelphia IHMs, was among those who believed the new direction of U.S. religious life reflected a misinterpretation of the council's teaching. Honsberger and others formed an organization in 1971, the Consortium Perfectae Caritatis, that would rival the Leadership Conference of Women Religious.[90] As the afterlife of another Philadelphia sister was helping to make clear, cross currents of anti-feminism would also turn canonization into contested terrain. In addition to touting Drexel as a prophet in terms of race relations, her promoters also suggested she had been a visionary in terms of women's leadership within the church. Litz argued that Drexel had called attention to the role of women "a hundred years before the actualization of those concerns in the Church as we see them emerging today."[91] In the petition they sent to the Holy Father in 1975, U.S. bishops similarly cited Drexel's "prophetic interest" in expanding "THE ROLE OF WOMEN IN THE CHURCH one hundred years before these concerns reached the current level of interest." They added, however, a telling qualification: Drexel had been "AN ECCLESIAL WOMAN, ALWAYS SENSITIVE TO THE MIND OF THE CHURCH AND TO THE AUTHORITY WITHIN THE CHURCH."[92] The emphasis underscored the message: just as Drexel had obeyed orders from the pope and her episcopal advisers, so, too, should contemporary Catholic women listen to what Catholic leaders were telling them about their proper roles in the church. One year after the U.S. bishops submitted Drexel's petition, the Vatican definitively declared that women could not be ordained in the Catholic Church.[93] Drexel's obedience to church authorities would subsequently become a theme of the testimony gathered in her apostolic process. Asked to speak about Drexel's relationship with the Catholic hierarchy, the bishop who had delivered the homily at her funeral responded that he had never heard of any "controversy" between Drexel and the bishops. It had been "quite the opposite with Mother Cabrini," he opined, who had "fought with every bishop along the line."[94]

The need for women to obey church authorities also surfaced in the causes of other U.S. candidates for canonization. In reference to Neumann, for instance, Kerins's otherwise optimistic address to Catholic sisters associated with the bishop made clear that the "new freedom in religious life" had definite limits. While vague about what those limits were, Kerins urged Catholic sisters to be "most exact in following the guidance of the Church," as Neumann always had been. "As religious today," he told his audience, which included members of Mother Claudia's IHMs, "we will walk a safe path in transition only under the guidance of the church."[95] John Tracy Ellis saw in Seton's story a similar message for Catholic women of the 1970s. According to the historian, Seton would have eventually overcome her "natural modesty" and been comfortable reading the scriptures at Mass, a liturgical innovation of the council era that Ellis deemed entirely appropriate. He was sure, however, that Seton would have firmly resisted "the insistence of some women on the right to ordination."[96]

Such cautions were hardly new; church leaders had long marshaled Seton and other saints to support traditional female roles. In the context of the 1970s, however, such efforts would elicit more active resistance from some Catholic women. As they began to chafe under male clerical authority, some sisters shied away from direct engagement with church leaders; as one Sister of Charity put it, "In a post–Vatican II climate, the term 'hierarchy' can raise, even in sympathetic circles, controversial hackles."[97] Such perceptions obviously bled over into canonization processes, which depended on interaction with church authorities first at the diocesan levels and finally at the Vatican. One Sinsinawa Dominican bristled, for example, at a priest's suggestion that the congregation appoint a "promoter" of Mazzuchelli's cause within each of its provinces. "The word *Cause* to many of our Sisters means formal legalistic procedures in Rome," she explained. Such formal language was "completely disassociated with the man, Father Samuel." It would be better, she advised, for Mazzuchelli's champions to emerge at "the grass roots level" rather than be imposed from the top down.[98]

For many Catholics sisters in the years to come, emerging feminist sensibilities would also magnify their financial-based reservations about pursuing causes for canonization. Though the Sisters of Charity had traveled too far with Seton's cause to develop any such misgivings, they nonetheless allowed that feminism complicated Seton's story. Sister Patricia Noone, a member of the Sisters of Charity of New York, explained that it would be inaccurate to label Seton a feminist, because "she had largely responded to the direction of men." Still, Noone—a feminist herself—suggested that Seton had prefigured the movement by having "stood up to [men] when she had to" and having been "a woman in touch with herself." In identifying the sources of Seton's strength, Noone continued, contemporary feminists might find their own.[99] Noone and other Catholic feminists became even more hopeful about Seton's ability to reflect a new moment in American womanhood as she stood on the verge of what some understood—a bit too optimistically—as a feminist victory.

The Lady Won?

Seton's advocates continued to maneuver behind the scenes, with concrete results. Spellman and Cicognani, two of her staunchest advocates, had been powerful actors at the Second Vatican Council, and in its wake they continued to leverage their influence to move her cause forward. In 1973, the Congregation for the Causes of Saints certified that another cure—the one that had occurred at the Yonkers hospital in 1963—qualified as a miracle and could be credited to Seton's intercession. Although Spellman had died in 1967, Cicognani, in one of his last acts before his death in December 1973, appealed to the Holy See to exempt Seton from the second required canonization miracle. The request was granted.[100]

Meanwhile, the final stage of John Neumann's canonization process was doing nothing to counter his postulator Ferrante's claim that it was the most difficult in Redemptorist history. The authenticated miracles that had been so difficult to secure during the beatification phase once again proved elusive. Litz continued to keep track of reported cures, but Ferrante deemed few of them likely to withstand scrutiny. Reading between the lines of Ferrante's correspondence with Krol, who was named a cardinal in 1967, it is also evident that the Roman postulator spent a great deal of time struggling, usually in vain, to prevent Krol from engaging in unseemly lobbying on Neumann's behalf. When Seton's exemption was granted, it ensured that her "partisans" would defeat Neumann's champions in the race for canonization as they had in beatification. As Neumann's advocates continued to wrestle with frustrating medical cases, Seton's canonization was scheduled for September 1975. "The lady won," Francis Murphy grudgingly conceded.[101]

An array of signs and symbols displayed during Seton's canonization painted her elevation as an all-American triumph. Thousands of pilgrims "flocked" to Rome for a celebration that was "a thoroughly American affair," complete with U.S. flags and strains of "The Star-Spangled Banner."[102] Pope Paul VI, quoting Spellman in his homily at the canonization Mass, characterized Seton as a "wholly American" woman. He exhorted U.S. citizens to "Rejoice!" The inclusion of the nation's "first flower" in the calendar of the saints, he told them, proved that "your land too, America, is indeed worthy of receiving into its fertile ground the seed of evangelical holiness."[103] An image on a giant tapestry hanging behind the specially constructed outdoor altar in St. Peter's Square reinforced the pope's message: it depicted Seton hovering above a globe with the United States in its foreground.

Pope Paul VI's homily also alluded to the significance of Seton's canonization occurring during the United Nations–sponsored International Women's Year. Like the UN initiative, the pontiff suggested, Seton's elevation both called attention to the role of women in the world and sought to further "their authentic advancement in society." Going even further, *Time* magazine dubbed Seton's canonization "a nod to women's lib, for Mother Seton was a spirited and independent woman."[104] Though the Vatican had most assuredly not envisioned Seton's canonization in such a manner, the liturgy did incorporate a modest gender innovation: for the first time, a woman read from scripture at a papal Mass. Chosen for this honor was Sister Hildegarde Mahoney, a Sister of Charity from the New Jersey branch of Seton's religious family who was then serving as the leader of the Federation of Mother Seton's Daughters, as the former conference established in 1947 had been renamed. The once-distant siblings had continued to grow closer through their annual meetings and other collaborative ventures.[105]

In later years, when Sister Hildegarde contemplated writing a history of the federation, her review of historical documents convinced her that Spellman had rendered Seton's cause "a great service" by facing the problems caused by Burgio "head-on" and convening the emergency meeting with Seton's spiritual daughters and representatives of the Sacred Congregation at Mount St. Vincent in 1948. Mahoney awarded most of the credit for Seton's canonization and the federation's success, however, to Sister Isabel Toohey. Had Toohey not already convened the Conference of Mother Seton's Daughters on two previous occasions, thereby laying the foundation for collaboration, Spellman's intervention might have been "injurious rather than helpful" to Seton's cause.[106] From the perspective of hindsight, Mahoney could rejoice in the fruit of Toohey's efforts and marvel at her courage in uniting the Seton communities under the auspices of the conference, an alliance that has since become ever more critical to the ministries and mission of Seton's spiritual daughters. As membership declined within the Seton communities, as it did in most U.S. congregations of women, there was a strength in union impossible for individual communities alone.

Mahoney's perspective is interesting. It had taken far longer for Seton to become a canonized saint than Archbishop James Gibbons would have supposed back in 1882, or even than Spellman would have guessed when he became head of the Archdiocese of New York in 1939. With what Mahoney called "the benefit of hindsight," however, the Sisters of Charity could see the hand of God at work in Seton's slow journey. Had Seton been canonized more speedily, or had Salvator Burgio's machinations not forced Sister Toohey's hand, the branches of Seton's spiritual family might never have been reunited. Mahoney's reflections suggest that, however complicated by imperfect human actors, a canonization process always unfolds in God's time. From the perspective of her spiritual daughters, at least, Seton had been canonized at exactly the right moment.

Viewed from other angles, however, the timing of Seton's canonization was less optimal—or at least more ironic. As Jesuit Robert Graham observed, Seton's canonization had occurred in the midst of a de-emphasis on saints in post–Vatican II worship, making it "rather paradoxical to speak of the 'honors of the altar' at a time when statues of saints long canonized are being removed from the proximity of the Eucharistic table."[107] Although some commentators have referred to this element of liturgical reform that had swept through American Catholicism after Vatican II as a fresh "stripping of the altars"—Eamon Duffy's characterization of the cataclysmic changes in English religious life during the Reformation under Henry VIII and Edward VI—the comparison is extreme.[108] It was true, however, that the council's emphasis on the importance of the Mass (especially in *Sacrosanctum Concilium*, the council's "Constitution on the Sacred Liturgy") affected devotions like the rosary, novenas in honor of the saints, the benediction of the Blessed Sacrament, Forty Hours, and stations of the cross. Though never prohibited in the post–Vatican II era, they were not strongly promoted and "pushed to the margins of Catholic life."[109]

More important to our story was a second irony in the timing of Seton's triumph. By 1975, U.S. saint-seekers' original objectives—cementing a connection to the Holy See and affirming Catholics' place in the nation—had already been secured, without the help of a native patron. U.S. Catholic leaders' prominence at the Vatican, beginning with Spellman's episcopal appointment and consolidated in the later stages and in the wake of the Second Vatican Council, had testified to American influence in Rome. The GI Bill, the onset of the Cold War, and demographic change had steadily erased differences between U.S. Catholics and their fellow citizens, and the 1960 election of John F. Kennedy to the U.S. presidency had symbolically affirmed Catholics' ability to be loyal American citizens fifteen years before the church added Seton's name to the roster of canonized saints. In light of these developments, the arrival of the first "wholly American" saint seemed somewhat anticlimactic. Seton's supporters, of course, insisted that U.S. Catholics should not view it that way. U.S. Catholics' joy in Seton's elevation, according to one U.S. priest, should be absolute, rather than "mechanical or polite . . . or quickly fleeting." Through her, God had touched the United States in a special way. The nation's Catholics should, therefore, "hitch their wagon to Mother Seton's star" and realize that under her patronage "a new, endless day has dawned for the American Church."[110]

Whether or not U.S. Catholics would revel in Seton's patronage, it soon became clear that American saints would no longer be the "rare birds" they had once been. Seton's canonization had been only the third in nearly a century of U.S. saint-seeking. The pace would soon pick up dramatically, and by 2015, the church would have raised another eight Americans to the honors of the altar. This rapid acceleration at the center was partly explained by changes on the periphery. The U.S. church, no longer disorganized at home and without influence in Rome, was far better positioned to support saints' causes throughout this period than it had been when U.S. bishops had proposed Tekakwitha and the martyrs in 1884, or even when petitioners had muddled their way through the process in the mid-twentieth century. Even so, the rising numbers of new saints was a universal phenomenon in the church, driven primarily by the man who led it between 1978 and 2005. More than Seton's canonization, it was John Paul II's elevation to the papacy that, combined with cultural change, signaled a new day in the story of sanctity in America.

✦ PAPAL SAINTS ✦

To the relief of his long-suffering Redemptorist advocates, John Neumann became the next American canonized saint. The final phase of
Neumann's canonization process had also been marked by drama and
difficulty. Neumann's third miracle—the recovery of a young Philadelphia
man from a rare cancer—had originally generated an inconclusive medical
verdict in Rome. Postulator Nicola Ferrante advised submitting an entirely
new case, but Cardinal John Krol overrode him, instead prevailing upon local
Catholic doctors to review the file and soliciting additional medical experts to
testify in support of a miraculous outcome. Though Ferrante seemed to have
been appalled by the breach of tradition, the postulator had to concede that the
strategy worked: the Holy See affirmed that miracle, dispensed Neumann from
a fourth one, and canonized him on 19 July 1977.[1]

In the years to come Neumann's devotees continued to report a flurry of
miracles attributed to the intercession of the new saint, noting that many involved happy outcomes for dangerous pregnancies or premature deliveries.
Neumann's interventions on behalf of "unborn babies" were interpreted as a
sign that he, from heaven, was teaching Americans "that human life is invio-
lable from the moment of conception to the moment of natural death."[2] Like
so many other saintly stories, Neumann's reinvention as a "pro-life bishop" reveals far less about the age in which he had lived than it does about the age in
which he was canonized. After the passage of *Roe v. Wade* in 1973, opponents
of legalized abortion—or, as they would come to define themselves, members

of the "pro-life" movement—increasingly made the case that "the sanctity of life" was the most pressing moral issue of the day. U.S. Catholic bishops were at the forefront of efforts to recriminalize abortion: in 1973 alone, the Catholic Church spent $4 million in lobbying members of Congress for restrictions on abortion, and the following year Krol was one of four U.S. cardinals to testify before a Senate subcommittee in favor of a constitutional amendment banning abortion in all circumstances.[3] In championing the pro-life movement, U.S. bishops had the full support and encouragement of Pope John Paul II, who throughout his long papacy urged Catholics to resist legalized abortion and other practices that contributed to a "culture of death." As Neumann's "pro-life" credentials suggest, saints were enlisted in efforts to defend the sanctity of life—and no one called upon them to greater effect than the man who would be known as the saint-making pope.

John Paul II canonized 482 people—more saints than all of his predecessors combined.[4] He beatified almost three times that many, for a total of 1,341. The pontiff himself framed the proliferation of new saints and blesseds as a response to Vatican II, claiming that the council had affirmed that holiness was "the essential note of the church" and that the rising number of saints simply reflected an acknowledgment of the abundant and diverse channels through which that holiness flowed.[5] Other interpreters, however, have attributed John Paul II's fondness for canonization to his intuitive grasp of its symbolic power. This was certainly evident in 1994, when he beatified Gianna Molla, an Italian pediatrician diagnosed with a uterine tumor during her fourth pregnancy. Having forsworn treatment to protect the fetus, Molla died soon after delivering a healthy baby girl.[6]

If John Paul II used the elevation of Molla to galvanize pro-life activists around the world, he also looked to prospective saints as an avenue to implement his vision of a Roman-centered global church. More than any of his predecessors, he sympathized with the longing that U.S. Catholics had first articulated in the 1880s: for the Holy See to acknowledge, first through beatification and finally through canonization, persons "who lived and labored and sanctified themselves in our land, among circumstances familiar." Never before in history had a pontiff been more committed to extending to Catholics throughout the world the "joy and privilege" of encountering canonized saints in the places where they lived.[7] In naming saints from among regions or nations that did not previously have one, he also bound those communities more closely to the universal church.[8]

Causes introduced from the United States constituted only a fraction of those that succeeded during John Paul II's papacy: he canonized two Americans and beatified an additional six (five of whom would be canonized by his two immediate successors). This relatively tiny contingent is nonetheless illuminating, especially when examined along with a sampling of the dozens of U.S. causes that were initiated during his papacy—as well as a few that, quite deliberately, were not.[9]

Many of John Paul II's U.S. saints and blesseds had emerged as candidates for canonization in the early days of U.S. Catholics' quest for a national patron. Some of these would reach the final stage having a much different meaning for believers than when they had first been proposed, while others arrived with virtually no meaning at all, at least beyond their immediate circle of supporters. John Paul II's enthusiasm for naming saints did introduce a few fascinating twists into this story, but what really made this era a new chapter in American sanctity was not the saint-making pope but rather U.S. Catholics' new perspectives on canonization. For nearly a century, they had sustained the search for a national patron, and it had sustained them. As they struggled to gain influence in their church and a comfortable place in their nation, saint-seeking had afforded them opportunities to defend, celebrate, assert, challenge, and understand their identities as Americans. By the last quarter of the twentieth century, the divisions among U.S. Catholics became much deeper than those that had once distanced them from Rome and from their fellow citizens. Canonization reflected those dynamics. In Rome, American allies and insiders at the Vatican increasingly determined which U.S. candidates would move forward. At home, the faithful would become less likely to project their American stories on their favorite saints and more inclined to use saints' stories to express where they positioned themselves as Catholics, especially on divisive issues involving gender and sexuality.

John Paul II's First U.S. Saint

Having "lost" to Elizabeth Ann Seton, Neumann's promoters had also missed the next milestone on which they had set their sights. The U.S. bicentennial had passed in 1976 without offering Redemptorists a chance to celebrate Neumann's canonization in tandem with national commemorations in Philadelphia.[10] In October 1979, however, Pope John Paul II's first pastoral visit to the United States afforded them a second opportunity to highlight their confrere

FIGURE 9
Cardinal John Krol and Pope John Paul at St. John Neumann Shrine in
Philadelphia, 1979. (Courtesy of Redemptorist Archives of the Baltimore Province)

while the city and the nation watched. The pope's American tour included a
day in Philadelphia, and the pontiff came to the shrine at St. Peter's Church to
pray before Neumann's tomb (figure 9).[11]

By the time of John Paul II's visit, however, his Philadelphia host, Cardinal
Krol, cared less about the most recently canonized American than he did about
the person he believed should be the next one: Katharine Drexel. The cardinal
was delighted at the prospect of presiding over the only U.S. archdiocese with
both a male *and* a female saint and hoped Drexel's cause would gather momentum from Neumann's success.[12] But the Redemptorist's elevation would
indirectly slow Drexel's progress when Francis Litz was reassigned to parish
ministry outside of Philadelphia and Monsignor James McGrath, Krol's archdiocesan chancellor, replaced him as Drexel's vice-postulator. Although the
cardinal assumed that McGrath's involvement would bring Drexel's cause more
solidly into his orbit and work in its favor, Krol had not taken into account

that it would further alienate Nicola Ferrante. Without Litz's mediating influence, the relationship between McGrath and the Roman postulator grew even frostier, especially as both the chancellor and Krol blamed Ferrante for what they regarded as Drexel's maddeningly slow progress.

For Krol, then, John Paul II's 1979 visit offered an opportunity to work around Ferrante by enlisting the pontiff's direct support. The Polish American cardinal shared ideological sympathies as well as an ethnic bond with the former cardinal-archbishop of Krakow. Hoping to use this friendship to Drexel's advantage, Krol tried to interest the pope in her story and to convince him to intervene on her behalf. Even at this early stage of his papacy, John Paul II had proven himself amenable to nudges on causes for canonization, and it initially seemed that Krol's effort had borne fruit; one month after his return to Rome, John Paul II authorized the "introduction" of Drexel's cause. The apostolic phase, the Roman review of the ordinary process, took place during 1980 and 1981.

Drexel would be one of the last saints to undergo such a review. In January 1983, John Paul II promulgated the apostolic constitution *Divinus Perfectionis Magister*, the first comprehensive revision of the canonization process in centuries, and one that would have a momentous impact on causes introduced from the United States and elsewhere. As experienced postulators like Paolo Molinari observed, this reform "did not come down from Heaven in 1983" but rather had been inherited from Paul VI, who had appointed a commission charged with updating the canonization process to reflect innovations in historical scholarship—a trend that had begun in 1930 with Pius XI's creation of the Historical Section. Members of the commission were also urged to consider how Vatican II's teaching on collegiality might prompt the Holy See to share the responsibility for evaluating sanctity with the world's bishops.[13]

Paul VI died before the commission completed its work, but decentralization and historical consciousness remained guiding principles of *Divinus Perfectionis Magister*. The reforms combined the ordinary and apostolic processes into a single diocesan phase in which testimony about the candidate's virtues was gathered under the exclusive authority of the presiding bishop. The new system gave local bishops authority to introduce a cause. The reforms also created a new consultant within the Congregation for the Causes of Saints, a "relator" who, in collaboration with a person from the candidate's local diocese, produced a detailed historical document (called a *positio*) that situated the prospective saint in his or her historical context.[14]

Divinus Perfectionis Magister also substantially reduced the role of the Promoter of the Faith, popularly known as the devil's advocate. As a result, the promoter would raise objections only during the final stage, an adjustment consistent with the emphasis on a historical as opposed to an adversarial approach. This elimination of the multiple volleys between the advocate and the postulator, along with a number of other modifications, shortened the average length of the canonization process. In particular, the new procedure reduced the postmortem waiting period from fifty to five years. Even more significantly, the new constitution halved the number of required authenticated miracles: one for beatification (except in the case of martyrs, for whom no miracles were required at this stage) and one for canonization.[15]

Here again the revision did not arise spontaneously. By the late 1960s, members of the Congregation for the Causes of Saints had been debating the necessity of the miracle requirement. Some had questioned it on theological grounds: were miracles strictly necessary to prove sainthood, once the virtues were established? Other considerations were more practical: as modern medicine reduced the realm of the medically inexplicable, was it even realistic to expect that a sufficient number would make it through such a stringent process?[16] Reformers were also aware of the potential that new medical research could uncover scientific explanations for cures that the Holy See had already judged miraculous. (In 2015, this is exactly what happened with the miracle that had made Seton's beatification possible. Advancements in immunotherapy suggested that Ann Theresa O'Neill's 1952 recovery from leukemia may not have been medically inexplicable after all; it was possible that the onset of her chicken pox triggered a reaction that killed not only that infection but also the life-threatening disease.)[17]

In revising canonization procedures, John Paul II was also acting out of his vision of the global church—a reality the contemporary canon of the saints did not reflect. By streamlining the process, *Divinus Perfectionis Magister* made it more feasible for less wealthy and more distant "local churches" to sponsor and promote their own saints. In effect, John Paul II adopted a version of the strategy Father Edward McSweeny had recommended in 1890, when he urged the Holy See to make it easier to validate the "hidden saints" from countries "too poor to stand all the necessary expense." By 1983, of course, the United States was no longer in that position, and its wealth and influence had helped to create a cozy relationship between the Holy See and U.S. Catholic leaders, even as the Cold War continued to strengthen the relationship between the Vatican and the United States. In 1984, the two governments, both led by fervent anti-communists, established official diplomatic relations.

Soon after the promulgation of *Divinus Perfectionis Magister*, Cardinal Krol traveled to Rome to ascertain what impact these reforms would have on Katharine Drexel's cause. Krol directed his inquiries to two English-speakers at the Congregation for the Causes of Saints: Peter Gumpel, SJ, a German Jesuit who had been assisting Paolo Molinari in his duties as postulator since 1960, and Robert Sarno, a diocesan priest from Brooklyn who became the first American to work at the Congregation for the Causes of Saints in 1982.[18] Sarno and Gumpel not only explained the new process to the impatient cardinal but also tried to temper his expectations; according to Gumpel, Krol demanded that Drexel be beatified within two years, an impossible task given the amount of work involved. Nevertheless, Gumpel promised Krol that he would work as quickly as he could and that the reforms in the process would "energize" Drexel's cause.[19]

Krol arranged for Peter Gumpel to serve as Drexel's relator. In that capacity, Gumpel requested a collaborator from the United States, a "first-class historian" ideally based in Philadelphia, who would be charged with writing her *positio* under the new guidelines.[20] Although many U.S. bishops, faced with increasing shortages of personnel, might have been reluctant to release priests for full-time work on a cause for canonization, Krol was not one of them. He and Gumpel selected one of Krol's diocesan priests, Joseph Martino, who had written his doctoral dissertation at Rome's Pontifical Gregorian University on Philadelphia's Archbishop Patrick Ryan, who had been presiding over the archdiocese when Drexel had founded her congregation. By his own account, the diocesan priest had passed a miserable two years teaching at a local Catholic high school. When the cardinal asked him if he would like to go back to Rome, he could not say yes fast enough. The cardinal freed him from all duties, though as a diocesan priest he continued to earn a full salary, while the Sisters of the Blessed Sacrament reimbursed him for travel and expenses.[21]

Paolo Molinari replaced Nicola Ferrante as Drexel's postulator upon the Redemptorist's death in 1985. It was not a surprising choice, as Molinari and Peter Gumpel were close friends and worked well together, and it proved a fortuitous one for the advancement of Drexel's cause. Molinari matched Ferrante in brilliance and experience, and he also had a gentle demeanor that did not lend itself to reproducing the fractious relationship between archdiocesan officials and his predecessor. Molinari, Gumpel, and Sarno made an effective triumvirate, and their cumulative experience helped compensate for considerable technical mistakes that had already been made in Drexel's cause. Gumpel, later admitting his "strong impression that Americans have never understood what was required for canonization," cited the testimony gathered on Drexel's virtues as a case in point, claiming that hers "was one of the poorest processes I have ever had the misfortune to examine."[22] Ninety years after officials at the Sacred Congregation had criticized the procedural errors, improperly formulated questions, and vague answers in John Neumann's material, officials at the Holy See still marveled at the incompetence of U.S. saint-seekers.

Martino finished writing Drexel's *positio* in 1986. A "hybrid" document containing elements of both the old and new procedures, it was the first of its kind to be submitted to the Holy See entirely in English; the 1983 reforms had eliminated the need for translation into Italian.[23] Regarding the question of whether Drexel's failure to accept African American women into the Sisters of the Blessed Sacrament undermined her reputation for sanctity, Martino simply provided a historical overview of race relations in North America and portrayed Drexel as a woman constrained by the limits of her time: Drexel, he argued, had accepted the laws of segregation and admitted black sisters as soon as she was able.[24]

Martino's argument was buttressed by the fact that, by this point, the Sisters of the Blessed Sacrament had a tangible rebuttal of the alleged racism of their founder in the person of Sister Juliana Haynes, then president of the congregation. Haynes, a native of Roxbury, Massachusetts, entered the Sisters of the Blessed Sacrament in 1952 and became the first African American professed by the order. During those early years, Haynes and another novice, a Navajo, presented Mother Katharine with "spiritual bouquets" on her birthday and on Christmas.[25] Their superiors had chosen them for this honor to make sure that Drexel, then in her nineties and bedridden, "knew she had a black novice and an Indian novice." Sister Juliana taught at St. Peter Claver's school in South Philadelphia before moving to Washington, D.C. It was only after joining the faculty of Xavier University, however, that Haynes began to appreciate the range of Drexel's influence, especially on the U.S. South. She met "black professionals, principals, doctors—people who had gone to rural schools established by Mother Katharine" and who, Haynes believed, "started her cause [for canonization] long before the Church did."[26] In 1974, Sister Juliana left Xavier and returned to Philadelphia to serve on the congregational council. Ten years later, the Sisters of the Blessed Sacrament elected her president.

After Pope John Paul II proclaimed Drexel venerable in January 1986, Robert Sarno confided to his American contacts that he planned to work through his channels of influence to persuade the pope to mention Drexel during his second extended papal trip to the United States, scheduled for September 1987. The visit included a stop at New Orleans, where he would address representatives of Catholic colleges and universities at Xavier University, the college founded by Drexel and the perfect setting to reference her.[27] Preparations for the pope's 1987 visit did in fact prompt the next advancement in the history of American sanctity—though that development would most pointedly not involve Katharine Drexel.

Scholars who study John Paul II and canonization have focused on the ways he decentralized the process, viewing it as a mechanism to lift up local churches throughout the world. Less explored are the ways in which he also increased the Holy See's involvement in the process. The case of the first U.S. saint challenges John Paul II's own insistence that his approach to naming saints flowed from a desire to implement the teachings of Vatican II. Not only did his actions in this instance undermine collegiality through an extraordinary assertion of papal power, but they also controverted a decision one segment of the local church had made during the council era.

In October 1986, Anne O'Neill, RSCJ, provincial superior at the Sacred Heart house in St. Louis, Missouri, was nonplussed by a telephone conversation with the city's Archbishop John May, who had recently returned from a visit to Rome with some startling news to share: the Vatican had approached him about the possibility of canonizing Philippine Duchesne. According to May, a person from the Congregation for the Causes of Saints had told him "we need somebody, not from Philadelphia, to be canonized in the United States and a woman and a religious would be helpful."[28] This remarkable statement testified to the lengths John Paul II was willing to go to secure local saints. In 1925, when Pius XI had asked the prefect of the Sacred Congregation why he could not give him an American saint, the response had been, "I can't give you one until they give me one." By contrast, when John Paul wanted to canonize an American saint, he told the prefect to go out and find one.

Robert Sarno, Paolo Molinari, and Peter Gumpel all took part in the discussions about who the new American saint would be, and given their involvement in Drexel's cause, the inclusion of the stipulation that the new saint not be from Philadelphia is fascinating.[29] It very likely reflects a strategic decision on the part of Drexel's Rome-based promoters. Sarno, for example, later revealed that although he personally viewed Drexel's cause as a "shoo-in," he fretted that "people would say that we have a big lady from a big city with a big Cardinal and we are going to rush her right through."[30] It made sense to adhere scrupulously to the process and wait for Drexel to be canonized after her cause proceeded through normal channels, without asking for special favors. On the other hand, the qualification "not from Philadelphia" may also suggest that Cardinal Krol's efforts to appeal directly to John Paul II's support had, at best, failed and, at worst, backfired spectacularly. Material related to the Drexel cause suggests that Krol continued to make "unfavorable impressions" at the Holy See; one report cites fears that the cardinal would be "screaming up and down the hallway about it" as soon as he arrived in Rome.[31] At the very least, the specification for a saint "not from Philadelphia" suggests a lack of enthusiasm for Drexel on John Paul II's part. When it came to naming saints, he could, and in many cases did, accelerate the process in any manner he chose, and he evidently did not want to do so in Drexel's case. Tellingly, he did not reference her in his formal comments during his visit to Xavier University.[32]

Another tantalizing element to Anne O'Neill's conversation with Archbishop May was the preposition she used in recounting to the Society's superior general: the Holy Father, O'Neill wrote, needed a person "to be canonized *in* the United States." This hint that John Paul II wanted to canonize the next saint on American soil conforms to another of his innovations. During a visit to the Philippines early in his papacy, he had presided at the beatification of Lorenzo Ruiz, who became the first Filipino to be so recognized. In his homily on that occasion, John Paul II made clear that he saw naming saints as an instrument of evangelization and Ruiz's entrance into the ranks of the blessed as signaling the "harmonious mingling of faith and culture" in the Philippines, the only predominantly Catholic nation in eastern Asia.[33] The setting of the ceremony accentuated the pope's message. Ruiz's was the first beatification in church history to have occurred *fuori sede* or outside Vatican walls. By the end of his long papacy, John Paul would preside at a total of sixty-one *fuori sede* beatifications that were scheduled to coincide with his pastoral visits throughout the world. Three years after Ruiz's beatification, another Asian nation became the site of the first canonization ceremony outside of the Vatican when, during a visit to Seoul, John Paul II canonized en masse 103 Korean victims of anti-Christian persecution in the nineteenth century. John Paul II ultimately presided at fourteen *fuori sede* canonizations.[34]

These *fuori sede* beatifications and canonizations also demonstrate that John Paul II's saint-making initiatives both diminished and increased the role of the Roman center. Whereas a beatification or canonization that took place in situ allowed witnesses to see "heaven touching earth" on their own soil, the star of the show was not the new saint but the charismatic pope. In the case of beatifications, this dynamic obtained even at the ceremonies held at the Vatican. Traditionally, popes had not presided at beatifications, both to distinguish them from canonizations and to allow the local church to shine. Though Paul VI had made an exception to this rule in 1971 when he presided at the beatification of Maximilian Kolbe, during his time as pope John Paul II presided at beatifications as standard practice.

In a 1987 interview with Kenneth Woodward, Paolo Molinari confirmed that John Paul II had indeed hoped to schedule a canonization in the United States in conjunction with his U.S. visit, and he had asked the prefect of the Congregation for the Causes of Saints to help him find an appropriate candidate. "The pope was going to the U.S.," Molinari recalled, and "he asked the cardinal [Pietro Palazzini, prefect of the Congregation for the Causes of Saints from 1980 until 1988], are there any causes that could come to a head so that I could have the opportunity of presenting this person among the people?"[35]

What prompted the Congregation for the Causes of Saints to suggest Philippine Duchesne in response to the pope's request? The French missionary met all the specifications: she was a woman and a religious, and she had no real connection to Philadelphia. According to Molinari, a miracle-in-waiting was the decisive factor weighing in Duchesne's favor.[36] Molinari had reviewed documents related to the 1951 cure of Mother Marguerite Bernard, the RSCJ missionary to Japan whose recovery had elicited such optimism within the Society of the Sacred Heart on the eve of the council. Although a previous postulator had not believed the case had much merit, Molinari disagreed. Such a reversal itself was not unprecedented; Ferrante's fresh perspective on one of John Neumann's tabled miracles, after all, had paved the way for his beatification. The difference was that in Neumann's case, the reviewer had been the postulator specifically assigned to his cause, whereas in this instance, Molinari agreed to review the Bernard miracle in response to the specific request of the prefect, by way of the Holy Father. According to Gumpel, the miracle of Mother Bernard "had been lying there," simply waiting for an expert such as Molinari, who could "see at a glance" what could have been done years before. By that point, the Jesuit had been reviewing miracles for thirty years and could instantly spot ways that a medical review could result in a different verdict. Molinari consulted with doctors with whom he had already worked and requested the proper documents from the San Francisco hospital where Bernard had recovered.[37]

While the miracle review was in the works, the only question was whether the RSCJs would agree to rededicate themselves to Duchesne's cause. Moving forward without the congregation's cooperation would have been counterproductive and may well have been impossible. Archbishop May informed the Society of the Sacred Heart that the new procedures ensured Duchesne could proceed to canonization with only one miracle and that Molinari, based on his review of the Bernard cure, was confident that it would pass medical and theological scrutiny. He also assured them that the remaining costs would not be onerous, which made the decision to proceed. The congregation believed its limited material resources should support its priorities, and the canonization of Duchesne had not been among those since the late 1960s, when the sisters had decided that pursuing her cause past beatification would drain valuable resources from their mission.[38]

By the 1980s, it had become increasingly evident that the Society of the Sacred Heart's misgivings about pursuing Duchesne's cause were also rooted in a second source: their feminist-based resistance to the patriarchal structure of the Catholic Church. Canonization always required direct and repeated engagement with the male hierarchy of the church, and for most American women religious during this period, relationships with church authorities at all levels had by then become increasingly fraught. Many of the seeds of conflict planted during the era of Vatican II had led to memorable clashes between American Catholic sisters and the hierarchy in the United States and Rome. During Pope John Paul's visit to the United States in 1979, for example, Theresa Kane, RSM, president of the Leadership Conference of Women Religious, welcomed him on behalf of all American Catholic sisters in a statement that included a controversial plea for the church to consider opening all of its ministries to women—including the ministerial priesthood. Throughout John Paul II's papacy, the church often disciplined Catholic sisters for openly dissenting from church teaching, especially on issues relating to homosexuality and abortion. Feminism was becoming an increasingly divisive issue between the many American women religious who embraced it and the many church leaders who viewed it as a social evil on par with abortion.[39]

Although details about how the Society of the Sacred Heart came to terms with canonizing Duchesne are scant, Helen McLaughlin, then the congregation's superior general, acknowledged to Anne O'Neill that she could see some "tremendous possibilities" in renewing Philippine's cause. In a letter announcing the news to all the members of the Society, timed to arrive just before the feast of the founder, Madeleine Sophie Barat, herself a canonized saint and Philippine's "much-loved friend," McLaughlin claimed that the while the news "has come as a complete surprise to us," she welcomed it as a joy and an invitation to self-examination:

> I feel it is important for each one of us to take up Philippine's life and to reflect on her message. She has surprised us now by stirring the surface of our immediate consciousness with extraordinary energy! What is she trying to communicate to us today? Who is she for us: a courageous, sensitive woman; a deeply prayerful religious; a lover of poverty and simplicity; a loyal, suffering daughter of the Church; a pioneer into the future who dared to go where few had gone before? She is saying something to us with urgency and insistence, and I am certain that during our preparation for her feast, Saint Madeleine Sophie will help us to be open to Philippine's challenges and inspirations to be authentic Religious of the Sacred Heart.[40]

In short, the RSCJ leadership decided to do what people had always done with their beloved saints: listen to the messages Duchesne might be sending them about their contemporary lives and ministries.

Sources are silent as to why Duchesne's canonization did not take place in the United States during the pope's visit in September 1987, as he had apparently wished. Yet many members of the congregation traveled to Rome for Duchesne's canonization the following year, which was preceded by its General Chapter meeting. Anecdotal evidence also suggests that however cool they may have initially felt toward the prospect of the canonization, most of Duchesne's spiritual daughters had resigned themselves to it and rejoiced at the chance to celebrate her life and mission on a grand scale.

In a biography of Duchesne published soon after the canonization, however, one RSCJ did go on the record with her feminist-based ambivalence about the event. Noting the uptick in the number of new female saints in the twentieth century, Catherine Mooney suggested that most of their stories reflected "traditional and sometimes antiquated assumptions about activities appropriate to women." Mooney offered Elizabeth Ann Seton as an example: "Seton's authority, and the perception of holiness her contemporaries formed about her,"

Mooney pointed out, "clearly derived from her admirable commitment to the womanly task of nurturing."[41] Seton continued to be revered for her traditionally feminine attributes; one assessment of Seton's significance for "modern women" portrayed her as a source of inspiration for women "trying to raise a family while beset with illness and financial problems." The same article also praised Seton as an accomplished pianist, who "saw not only to her children's education but to their entertainment as well."[42]

A new moment for women demanded new models of womanhood. Where, Catherine Mooney asked, were the canonized female saints who "exercised religious leadership outside the bounds of the traditional cultural constraints? To what extent might the models of female holiness being chosen today by the papal curia subtly skew or constrict our notions of what constitutes women's holiness?" Expressing her hope that the church would not shoehorn Duchesne into narrow models of womanhood, Mooney reimagined Duchesne as a feminist heroine: "Philippine was a woman in a world and a Church run largely by men." While her life reflected the reality of women's roles in the nineteenth century, Mooney wrote, Duchesne could speak to modern women struggling to overcome sexism and narrowly defined gender roles. "As a woman on the frontier," she argued, Duchesne "has something to say to women who find themselves on frontiers of another sort."[43]

The occasion of Duchesne's canonization also demonstrated that gender was not the only category of identity that would make canonization much more complicated in the 1980s than it had been a century before. The first U.S. saint-seekers had not troubled themselves over the imbalance of power between European Catholic missionaries and indigenous people; neither had they considered the church's complicity in suppressing native cultures and traditions. By the 1980s, however, Americans' attitudes toward Catholic missionaries were increasingly inflected by an awareness of the oppressive legacy of European colonization. Among the RSCJs, a desire for racial inclusivity led them to welcome Native Americans to Duchesne's canonization. A prominent guest was Bishop Charles Chaput, OFM, Cap., of Rapid City, South Dakota, who had become only the second Native American bishop when John Paul II had appointed him a bishop earlier that year. Chaput was a member of the Prairie Band of the Potawatomi tribe, and late in her life Philippine Duchesne had lived for a brief time at a Potawatomi mission in Sugar Creek, Kansas. As John Paul intimated in his homily, the presence of Chaput and other Native

American Catholics posthumously honored the desire that had led Duchesne across the Atlantic in the first place. The "nun who desperately wanted to give her life to the Native Americans" had not been able to do so during her life on earth, but Native Americans celebrated her at the most pivotal moment in her afterlife.[44]

Back at home in the United States, the *Bureau of Catholic Indian Missions Newsletter* ended its coverage of Duchesne's canonization with a plea to its readers to pray that the newly minted "St. Rose" would intercede on behalf of an intention even more dear to the hearts of Chaput and other native Catholics: that "Blessed Kateri" would soon be canonized. Tekakwitha has garnered more attention from scholars than any other of John Paul II's U.S. saints or blesseds, largely because they interpret her beatification as an example of the pope's commitment to inculturation, the idea that Catholic beliefs and rituals can find expression in native cultures throughout the world.[45]

More telling for our story, however, are the parallels between John Paul II's first U.S. saint and his first U.S. blessed. Both the Rose of Missouri and the Lily of the Mohawks had blossomed as candidates for canonization in the late nineteenth century, nourished by U.S. Catholics' desire to present the Holy See with a saint of their own. Ardor for both women had first wilted at home during the era of the nation saint and had been redirected in the wake of Vatican II. While Duchesne's congregation had lost enthusiasm for pursuing her cause, Tekakwitha's cause would increasingly be spearheaded by indigenous supporters. Though indigenous Americans had always supported Tekakwitha's cause, it had been sponsored first by the Jesuits and, after 1939, by the Tekakwitha Conference, which was open only to missionary priests until the 1970s. As in Duchesne's case, John Paul II had provided the stimulus to advance Tekakwitha to the next stage in the process. Though her promoters had not submitted a miracle to the Holy See since 1955, John Paul II waived this requirement and beatified Kateri in Rome in July 1980.[46]

As organizations such as the Bureau of Catholic Indian Missions and the Tekakwitha Conference promoted devotion to Blessed Kateri among indigenous Catholics, these members of her primary constituency hoped and prayed that John Paul II, perhaps with prompting by a newly interpreted St. Rose Philippine Duchesne, would canonize her before too long. By the late 1980s, they certainly had reason for optimism in this regard, as new saints seemed to be emerging at unprecedented speed.

More Saints, New Meanings

Indeed, this was a pace that disturbed some Vatican leaders. During a conference held near Milan in 1989, Cardinal Joseph Ratzinger, prefect of the Congregation for the Doctrine of the Faith, raised eyebrows when he appeared to question the theological justification for the increase in canonizations and beatifications. Arguing that the recent saints and blesseds "may have some meaning for a limited group of people" but did not mean much to "the vast majority of believers," he suggested that it was perhaps time to give priority to causes of people who offered the faithful "a truly universal message."[47]

Newspapers described Ratzinger's statements as criticism of the "inflation" in saints, a term that seemed to apply to the situation in the United States. Within four months of Philippine Duchesne's canonization, two more U.S. causes reached beatification. One of them, to Krol's delight, was Katharine Drexel. The new norms required only one miracle for beatification, and, as had been the case with two of John Neumann's three miracles, the new cure attributed to Drexel involved a young person from the Philadelphia area. In 1974, fourteen-year-old Robert Gutherman had developed a life-threatening ear infection that, even in the best-case scenario, was expected to result in complete hearing loss. The Guthermans had lived close to the Sisters of the Blessed Sacrament's convent in Bensalem and Robert had often served as altar boy for Masses held there. After his mother followed a sister's advice to "pray directly to Mother Katharine and Mother Katharine alone," Gutherman recovered from his illness, with "perfect hearing." Under Molinari's expert guidance, the miracle passed medical and theological scrutiny.[48]

Gutherman, by then a grown man, joined a thousand other Americans who traveled to Rome for Drexel's beatification in November 1988. Cardinal Krol led the group, though he was no longer presiding over the Archdiocese of Philadelphia; Anthony Bevilacqua had succeeded him the previous winter. New York's Cardinal John O'Connor also attended, both in his capacity as the head of the Bureau of Catholic Indian Missions and as a former neighbor of the Drexel family in his native Philadelphia. O'Connor was poised to become as energetic a saint-seeker as Cardinal Francis Spellman had been. One of O'Connor's first acts was to initiate the cause for canonization of his immediate predecessor as New York's archbishop, Cardinal Terence Cooke.

Like the Sisters of Charity in Seton's case, Sister Juliana Haynes and the Sisters of the Blessed Sacrament viewed Drexel's beatification as an unparalleled opportunity to further the congregation's mission. "REMEMBER," the sister in charge of public relations for the entire congregation wrote to sisters designated for that role in each convent, "WE COULD NEVER AFFORD TO PAY FOR THIS TYPE OF PUBLICITY. WE HAVE AN OPPORTUNITY NOW WE MIGHT NOT HAVE AGAIN FOR A LONG TIME." Recommended responses to media inquiries included statements such as, "The reason the Church selects individuals to be canonized is to provide us with models we can imitate. Mother Katharine believed we are all brothers and sisters in Christ, and for this reason was a civil rights activist long before this was popular."[49] Envisioning the event as a chance to advance social justice and to celebrate "the spirituality and culture of the Black and Native Americans," Haynes authorized a gift of $10,000 to Pope John Paul II to be distributed among the poor, as well as an additional $15,000 to sponsor black and Native American participants in the celebrations in Rome.[50]

At the beatification Mass, the prayers of intercession were read in Navajo by Marie Tso Allen, who had been educated by the Sisters of the Blessed Sacrament. This was the first time that language had been spoken in St. Peter's. Eagle dancers from Laguna Pueblo, New Mexico, performed at a prayer service, and the day after the beatification a Mass of Thanksgiving took place at the Basilica of St. Mary Major. The Xavier University of Louisiana Choir sang "Mass for an American Saint," composed especially for the occasion by a Xavier alumnus, and the call to worship included the Prayer of the Four Directions—a native prayer for peace, reconciliation, and thanksgiving—by Deacon Victor Bull Bear from South Dakota. Also present were Norman Francis, president of Xavier University; Ellen Tarry, the African American writer who had defended Drexel's decisions on race; and members of the Oblate Sisters of Providence, the African American congregation to whom Drexel had directed many black vocations. Drexel's official beatification portrait featured her superimposed on a map of the United States, standing next to an African American and a Native American. (figure 10).[51]

That Drexel's beatification appears to have generated no protests from African Americans or Native American groups may have resulted from the sisters' success in promoting Drexel as a model of inclusivity. On the other hand it may simply reflect that the event had not captured much attention at all. Whichever the reason, Drexel's beatification stood in marked contrast to the other U.S. beatification of the autumn of 1988, which elevated Junípero Serra.

The cause of the Franciscan missionary, which been launched in 1931 in part as a Franciscan rejoinder to the North American Jesuits, had begun to move

FIGURE 10
Katharine Drexel official beatification portrait.
(Sister M. Lurana Neely, SBS, SBS centennial drawing;
courtesy of the Archives of the Sisters of the Blessed Sacrament)

forward during the late 1960s, when his promoters billed him as the perfect saint for the "space age" and the putative patron of ecologists. In the summer of 1987, Vatican officials attributed the recovery of a Franciscan sister in St. Louis from a mysterious and life-threatening illness to Serra's intercession.[52] The timing of this announcement raised expectations that John Paul II would sidestep the remaining hoops—a plenary session of cardinals of the Congregation for the Causes of Saints followed by official papal sanction—and beatify Serra on American soil the following September, when he would be in Monterey, California, during a visit to the United States. A month before the scheduled arrival, however, a Vatican spokesman announced that because the "normal procedures" had not yet been completed, the trip would not include the beatification. The pope did, however, visit Mission San Carlos in Carmel, where Serra was buried, and hail the "Apostle of California" as the "defender and champion" of Native Americans.[53]

Native Americans themselves had begun to argue the opposite in the 1960s, accusing Serra of complicity in the extinction of native peoples and traditions. Writing at the time of beatification, Monsignor Paul Lenz, the executive director of the Bureau of Catholic Indian Missions, dismissed such criticism as "nonsense," arguing that it was unfair to hold Serra accountable for the sins of California's Spanish colonizers. Lenz allowed that the Spanish had done "much damage to the daily living, health, and culture of the California Indians." But the fact that Serra was Spanish, Lenz argued, should not make him automatically guilty. Lenz hoped the "exhaustive study" undertaken to support Serra's beatification would settle the matter.[54]

It did not. The year of the beatification, native activists protested at Serra's burial site in Carmel, and vandals defaced a statue of Serra at the San Diego mission, scrawling phrases such as "genocidal maniac" and "enslaved Indians" at its base. Such demonstrations appalled Serra supporters, including Monsignor Francis Weber, a historian and an archivist who had published a book about Serra and believed that "the attempts to discredit Serra . . . constitute an attack on the whole mission of evangelization."[55]

Faced with depictions of Serra as a "Killer Saint," the Franciscans decided in the late 1990s not to comment on stories of native protests, perhaps believing that no publicity was better than the alternative, and by 2000 the congregation's enthusiasm for actively pursuing the cause seemed to have wavered; a draft of a letter from U.S. bishops to John Paul II in support of Serra's cause was never sent. Although the Franciscans certainly did not renounce Serra's cause, they, much like the Society of the Sacred Heart had done in the council era with Duchesne, appeared to have resigned themselves to the probability that Serra would remain permanently a "blessed."[56]

Promoters of the woman from Philadelphia took an opposite tack. Throughout the 1990s, Drexel's supporters developed an "aggressive agenda" for marketing her cause in the United States and in Rome, seeking to capitalize on anniversaries such as the centennial of the founding of the Sisters of the Blessed Sacrament and the fortieth anniversary of Drexel's death.[57] Priests and bishops from the Archdiocese of Philadelphia remained heavily involved in her cause, and their partnership with Drexel's congregation, though not without tension, continued to function relatively smoothly. Had Sister Juliana Haynes been less willing to allow Monsignor McGrath to take credit for "carrying" the cause, and to compensate him handsomely for doing so, the relationship may well have been more strained.[58] Paolo Molinari's sensitivity to this issue seems also to have helped; on at least one occasion, the postulator reminded Philadelphia's cardinal that, considering the sisters were the "Attori della Causa," they should be kept informed of all developments related to it.[59]

As it was, concerns over what author Bill Briggs would refer to as "men and money" were giving many other women's religious communities pause about pursuing causes for canonization.[60] Many members of such congregations, echoing Catherine Mooney's concerns about Duchesne, were determined that their saints would not be co-opted by male church leaders who recognized only limited roles for women. In theory, this became marginally easier under the revised norms, which contained no provision that female petitioners could petition the Holy See only through male proxies. Isabel Toohey's dream had technically been realized: women could at last represent their founders in causes for canonization. In 1982, Angela Bolster, an Irish Sister of Mercy working on the cause of congregational founder Catherine McAuley, became the first woman recognized as a vice-postulator by the Congregation for the Causes of Saints.[61] In the United States, the Sinsinawa Dominicans claimed another first with Sister Mary Nona McGreal, who, with the publication of Samuel Mazzuchelli's *positio* in 1989, was the first woman to be acknowledged as the author of such a document.[62]

Yet despite women's increasing prominence in the process, canonization would effectively remain a male affair. The vast majority of people who worked at the Congregation for the Causes of Saints, as in other Vatican dicasteries, were priests—by definition, men. According to Peter Gumpel, personal decisions made by women, rather than structural impediments, made female absence particularly glaring at the Congregation for the Causes of Saints in the 1980s. Despite no formal prohibition against women serving as postulators, very few of them were interested in doing so. Successful postulators needed to acquire years of experience, and few qualified women religious from the United States, Gumpel explained, "were willing to spend the whole of their lives on this work."[63] There were obvious reasons why most sisters would be disinclined to enter the saint-making business full time. For many, their vows of poverty and commitment to social justice ministries made a posting in Rome seem an unjustifiable diversion of their labor from higher priorities at home, especially as an aging population and an overall decline in the membership created a massive personnel problem in sister-sponsored institutions. Most sisters may have been reluctant to accept even a short-time appointment for a cause, as had Father Martino from 1984 until 1986. As feminism increasingly influenced the choices of women religious, it was difficult for many of them to see the appeal of immersing themselves in the overwhelmingly clerical environment of the Holy See.

Male or female, U.S. vice-postulators needed the help of clerics working at the Congregation for the Causes of Saints to move causes forward—or more precisely, they depended on Monsignor Sarno, who since his arrival in 1982 proved "extremely helpful" in determining which causes did so.[64] Soon after Duchesne's canonization, the Brooklyn priest made a key intervention in the cause of another French-born missionary to the Midwest, Mother Théodore Guérin. By 1989, Guérin's cause was represented by a vice-postulator from within the Sisters of Providence, but she and other congregational leaders were frustrated with their postulator in Rome—Guérin's eighth—who did not communicate often or well with them. When the Holy See pronounced Guérin venerable in 1992, the Indiana sisters learned of it only when Belgian-based members of their community read it in their local newspaper. After they turned to Sarno for help, he connected them to Andrea Ambrosi, an enterprising Italian who had established himself as a postulator after the revisions of 1983 opened that position to members of the laity. Ambrosi agreed to review a miracle that one of Guérin's previous postulators had discarded: the apparently spontaneous cure of Mother Theodosia Mug, Guérin's biographer, from stomach cancer in 1908. Much as Molinari had done for Mother Bernard's miracle, Ambrosi's experience and a practiced eye convinced him that the original judgment that it was not worthy of consideration was wrong.[65]

When Vatican approval of the Mug miracle led to Guérin's beatification in Rome in 1998, however, some Sisters of Providence expressed misgivings about pursuing her cause further. At a celebration of Guerin's beatification held in Indiana, Sister Nancy Nolan acknowledged the "anti-cause" members of her community and tried to appease them by ruminating that all members of a group of highly educated women could hardly be expected to agree on everything. Nolan evoked the spirit of the congregation's founder as she assured the naysayers that they were entitled to their opinion. As Mother Théodore had done in her lifetime, each of her spiritual daughters had to stand up for what she believed in, and all members of the community would respect her decision. Sisters who supported pursuing Guérin's cause, such as Nolan and Sister Marie

Kevin Tighe, who served as Guérin's vice-postulator between 1996 and 2006, reminded skeptics that "canonization merely called attention to the kind of woman [Mother Théodore] was—which is the kind of woman we are all striving to be."[66]

For other U.S. Catholic sisters, concerns over the costs of canonization, combined with reservations about the imbalance of power in their interactions with male church leaders, led them to resist pursuing processes altogether—especially when the request to do so came from an outsider to the community. Throughout this era, Andrea Ambrosi's resourcefulness, like John Paul II's activism, often reversed the initiative in canonization, which had historically flowed from periphery to center. After accumulating some notable saintly successes, the Roman postulator promoted not only his candidates but also his own services. In 2002, for example, he approached Anthony Pilla, bishop of Cleveland, Ohio, asking for more information about Sister Mary Ignatia Gavin, a Sister of Charity of St. Augustine who had died at the congregation's motherhouse in 1966. Gavin, working as director of admissions at a Catholic hospital in Akron in the 1930s, had collaborated with Robert Smith and Bill Wilson to treat alcoholism as a medical condition and to develop the twelve-step program of recovery known as Alcoholics Anonymous. Ambrosi told the bishop he was "honestly very impressed" with Gavin, finding her uncommon moral qualities equal to "many other Servants of God that I brought to the altar as Postulator." Ambrosi inquired whether the bishop had ever thought to "start a cause of Beatification and Canonization" on her behalf. Pilla forwarded the letter to Gavin's congregation, but the sisters demurred. Though they encouraged people to honor her as a "saint" informally, they were not interested in opening an official cause. "Besides the issue of formal canonization for another nun," one member of the congregation explained, "there is the very real $$ issue."[67]

But Ambrosi's overtures to other prospective petitioners in the United States met with more success, and he would go on to represent some of the most high-profile American causes, such as that of Knights of Columbus founder Rev. Michael McGivney and of Bishop Fulton Sheen, the radio and television star whom Nicola Ferrante had once engaged to speak about John Neumann. One U.S. cause that did not need Ambrosi's assistance was Katharine Drexel's, which continued to rest in Molinari's capable hands. The Jesuit postulator repeatedly relied on his own prudence and familiarity with the process to temper the enthusiasm and ambition of Drexel's Philadelphia-based supporters. When

Philadelphia archdiocesan officials, citing John Paul II's interest in naming saints among the married laity, proposed initiating a cause for Drexel's father, stepmother, and sister, Molinari concluded that none of them had enjoyed "an authentic and widespread fame of sanctity" required for canonization, and therefore it would not be worthwhile to carry the matter further.[68] Similarly, when Drexel's Philadelphia-based advocates proposed taking advantage of a liberal interpretation of the rules regarding miracles—they wanted to move forward with a potential miracle that had taken place after the pope announced Drexel's beatification but before the elevation ceremony—Molinari advised patience. "Until and unless" a new prefect at the Congregation for the Causes of Saints developed a "greater familiarity with the intricate matters" about miracles, he cautioned, it was better to wait.[69]

Under Molinari's tutelage, it appeared that Philadelphia saint-seekers had finally learned—a century after opening John Neumann's cause—how not to make "unfavorable impressions" at the Holy See. In 1993, concerns that James McGrath "was not acting in accordance with the norms" of the Congregation for the Causes of Saints prompted his removal as Drexel's vice-postulator.[70] McGrath's successor, another diocesan priest named Alexander Palmieri, adhered closely to procedure, although lapses occurred despite his scrupulousness. In 1998, for instance, the president of Philadelphia's Drexel University (an institution founded by Katharine's uncle) committed a public relations blunder when he mentioned in media interviews that he had used a recent audience with Pope John Paul II to "advocate" for Drexel's canonization. Palmieri sent him a harsh rebuke: "No one can give the impression that anyone is 'advocating' with the Pope or with any Vatican official to have Blessed Katharine canonized a saint. The Vatican does not look kindly upon any semblance of outside pressure in what is an extremely objective process of canonization."[71]

Inside pressure, of course, was another matter altogether, and when it came to causes introduced from the United States, much of that was applied by Sarno. He fielded correspondence from and offered detailed advice to many U.S. saint-seekers, including Cardinal John O'Connor. Soon after his return from Drexel's beatification, O'Connor launched the cause of Haitian-born Pierre Toussaint, who had arrived in New York as an enslaved man in the early nineteenth century and died there in 1853. Toussaint's owner—whose social set, incidentally, included the Seton family—had apprenticed him as a hairdresser. Working in what was then a lucrative field, Toussaint accumulated a great deal of wealth, and eventually he gained his freedom and became one of

Catholic New York's most significant benefactors, supporting, among other institutions, an orphanage and school established by Elizabeth Ann Seton's Sisters of Charity.[72]

O'Connor, presiding over the exhumation of Toussaint's body from the cemetery at Old St. Patrick's Cathedral in 1990, suggested that the canonization of "this man, God's reflection in ebony," would be "a wonderful thing for the city of New York" that would "restore some pride in the city. It will be a great thing for the church. It will be a fine thing for the black community."[73] Ellen Tarry and other African American Catholics readily agreed. Rev. G. Augustus Stallings, president of the National Black Catholic Clergy Caucus, expressed the organization's strong support for Toussaint, whom he called a "saint for our times and people." Pointing out that the church "raises to her altars men and women who have specific importance at critical moments of history," Stallings posited that Toussaint would be the perfect saint for a society plagued by racial divisions, poverty, and a decline in family values.[74]

Not everyone thought that the creation of saints had much actual spiritual or social significance for contemporary Americans, however. Another New Yorker took exception to O'Connor's grandiose claims about what Toussaint's canonization would mean, writing angrily to the cardinal, "Would the average New Yorker care more or less if the Catholic Church canonizes another saint? I THINK NOT. Would the canonization of another saint be a source of New York City pride? My God, who even thinks of Mother Cabrini or Mother Seton who toiled through the streets of this city, except those in their congregations, and those close to those religious communities?"[75] The increasingly circumscribed celebrations surrounding John Paul II's U.S. blesseds suggested that O'Connor's cranky correspondent had a point. The level of secular and Catholic media coverage of the beatifications of Tekakwitha, Drexel, and Guérin never came close to rivaling that of either Cabrini's in 1938 or Seton's in 1963, whereas Serra's beatification had been notable primarily for the negative attention it captured.

John Paul II's three remaining U.S. blesseds had even more limited national appeal. The saintly trajectory of Francis Xavier Seelos followed a recognizable pattern in the history of U.S. saint-seeking. Proposed in the early days of the quest, Seelos's cause had originally been paired with that of John Neumann, with whom he had once lived. Archbishop Amleto Cicognani had been interested in it in the 1930s, but it had since languished for reasons that his biographers insisted were "not clear even to expert students of the canonization process of Father Seelos."[76] In the context of this study, however, they become quite apparent. Seelos's story, unlike that of his Redemptorist confrere, had not translated very well to the "new ideal of sainthood" of the 1930s.[77] Yet congregational interest in Seelos's cause had revived in the late 1960s, as the centennial of his death approached and as Neumann's cause was inching toward completion.[78] After the reforms of 1983, the congregation assigned one of its historians to the task of writing Seelos's *positio,* which was finished in in 1998 and approved the following year by the Congregation for the Causes of Saints. Seelos's postulator had a miracle, dating back some thirty-odd years, ready to propose, and it, too, was approved quickly.[79] John Paul II beatified Seelos in Rome in April 2000.

John Paul II's next U.S. blessed, Marianne Cope, was also loosely connected to John Neumann, though in her case the link was established retroactively. German-born Marianne Cope had been a young child when her family settled in Syracuse, New York, where she entered a Franciscan community of sisters. By the time of her beatification, that community had merged with three other Franciscan congregations who traced their roots to the Philadelphia community founded under Neumann's guidance in 1855. Many other women's religious congregations were following suit, consolidating their resources by merging with other congregations that shared a similar charism. This was necessary as their membership continued its downward trend. The consortium that included Marianne Cope's congregation named itself the Sisters of St. Francis of the Neumann Communities.

As for Cope herself, she had worked in the community's Syracuse hospital until 1883, when she had answered a call to minister to the lepers of Molokai, where she remained until her death in 1918. There are no signs that Cope's community considered opening her cause until the 1970s. [80] It is likely their decision to do so then stemmed from the publicity surrounding Father Damien de Veuster, a Belgian-born missionary who lived and worked among the leper colony of Molokai between 1873 and his own death from Hansen's disease (leprosy) in 1889.

Though Hawaiians have long celebrated Damien's legacy (the anniversary of his death is an unofficial state holiday), Damien has not yet entered this story, for a simple reason: just as he had bypassed the United States entirely in his lifetime, having died nine years before Hawaii was incorporated as U.S. territory, so, too, did his cause for canonization largely skirt the United States until its final stages. De Veuster's cause was introduced from the Archdiocese of

Malines, Belgium, in 1938, where most of his remains currently lie. The church declared him venerable in 1977.[81] Damien did not become widely identified as an *American* saint in the continental United States until the onset of the AIDS crisis in the 1980s. As Catholics and non-Catholics ministered to victims of another disease that led to societal and religious ostracism, they adopted Damien as a model of compassionate care.[82] John Paul II beatified Damien in 1995, in a ceremony held in Brussels, Belgium.

Once Cope's cause was introduced, Sarno took an avid interest in it, claiming to have been motivated by a quest for gender parity; he bristled that Cope had received so much less attention than Damien had. Gumpel, who served as Cope's relator, testified in his affirmative report to the Congregation for the Causes of Saints that "in the work for the lepers, Father Damien did nothing that Mother Marianne did not do likewise."[83] The combination of Gumpel's expertise and Sarno's careful attention helped move Cope's cause swiftly through the process.

When John Paul II declared Cope blessed in 2004, she became the first U.S. missionary sent *from* the United States so designated—though, of course, by the time of her death, Hawaii had become U.S. territory. Unlike Cope, who died of natural causes, most of the missionaries beatified and canonized by John Paul II had died as martyrs. In his efforts to create more models of holiness, the pope adopted a more generous definition of martyrdom than had been used in the past, which encompassed not only those who perished because of hatred of the faith but also those who died defending truth and human dignity. Of John Paul II's saints, 83 percent were considered martyrs, as were 77 percent of his blesseds.[84]

Yet U.S. Catholics were conspicuously absent among this total, even though several likely candidates emerged during his papacy. Perhaps the best known of these are Maryknoll missionaries Maura Clarke and Ita Ford, lay Maryknoll missioner Jean Donovan, and Ursuline sister Dorothy Kazel, who have become collectively known as the "four churchwomen of El Salvador" since their murder in that country in December 1980. Although these women have been hailed as modern martyrs and considered unofficial saints, no steps have been taken to open formal causes on their behalf.[85] Though the region in which the women died is surely a factor—John Paul II was far less attentive to candidates who died in Central American civil wars than he was to prospective saints who perished under communist regimes—it appears that gender has also played a part, given that by the end of John Paul's papacy, the faithful were pursuing such honors for many of the sisters' male counterparts. These efforts led to the 2016 beatification of El Salvador's Archbishop Oscar Romero, killed while celebrating Mass in March 1980, as well as the beatification the following year of Stanley Rother, an Oklahoma-born priest killed while on mission in Guatemala in July 1981. Most open causes of modern U.S. martyrs involve men: Bishop Francis Xavier Ford, a cousin of Ita Ford's who was killed by Chinese communists in 1952; Emil Kapaun, a military chaplain who died as a Korean prisoner of war in 1953; and Vincent Capodanno, a priest and navy lieutenant who died serving with the marines on a Vietnam battlefield in 1967.[86] The interest in martyrs has also breathed new life into a more geographically concentrated subset of the long-forgotten "Martyrs of the United States of America." The Diocese of Pensacola-Tallahassee has proposed 43 prospective saints, many of whom appeared on the list of the original 119 men championed by Bishop John Mark Gannon in the 1930s and 1940s, as the "Martyrs of La Florida."[87]

The lack of movement for martyred churchwomen suggests that the misgivings of the Society of the Sacred Heart about pursuing Duchesne's cause, internal disagreements within the Sisters of Providence about Guérin's canonization, and the disinclination of the Sisters of Charity of St. Augustine to propose Sister Mary Ignatia Gavin may reflect more than idiosyncratic decisions made by individual communities. Instead they appear to point to a more systematic and decisive shift in U.S. saint-seeking: an aversion to formal canonization among sisters who reevaluated their ministries and relationships to the hierarchy in the aftermath of Vatican II. When a group of Ursuline sisters were asked whether they planned to open a cause on Dorothy Kazel's behalf, for example, one member of her congregation responded cagily, "I was at Romero's beatification, and it was very male. That's all I will say."[88] A similar wariness seems to be evident among the Adorers of the Blood of Christ, a religious order of women based in Ruma, Illinois, who lost five members on mission to Liberia during its civil war in 1992. Though the murdered sisters could easily fit the criteria for modern martyrs, their sisters have not asked that they be formally recognized as such, and at least one member expressed the opinion that the resources used to pursue a cause would be better spent on educating women.[89]

As noted above, the unwillingness to pursue formal canonization is also fueled by feminists' belief that doing so would force the candidates into clergy-defined gender roles. Such fears are not unfounded, as attested to by the most controversial cause launched by New York's Cardinal O'Connor: that of Dorothy Day. Day's singular achievement was founding the Catholic Worker movement in 1933, and to many of her devotees and admirers, the case for her holiness rests on her fierce commitment to social justice. In announcing the opening of her cause for canonization, O'Connor, by contrast, foregrounded Day's pre-conversion abortion, positing her as a model for women who had had or were considering abortions. "It is a well-known fact," the cardinal said, "that Dorothy Day procured an abortion before her conversion to the faith. She regretted it every day of her life."[90] Day's appropriation as a pro-life saint has outraged critics who claim that church leaders are attempting to tame Day's message by recasting her in the familiar trope of the "fallen woman" rather than grappling with the radical challenge that her life and example pose to the Catholic Church. Echoing the concerns of many Catholic sisters, other admirers of Day object to her formal canonization on the grounds that resources would be better spent on helping the poor.[91]

Dorothy Day had been inspired to establish the Catholic Worker movement when she was reading the life of Rose Hawthorne Lathrop, daughter of author Nathaniel Hawthorne and founder of a congregation of Dominican sisters dedicated to Rose of Lima. In her autobiography, Day recounted reading that Hawthorne had started "a chain of cancer hospitals in a four room tenement such as the one I was living in" and wondering, "Why not start a newspaper the same way?"[92] Lathrop and Day, linked by a common mission in their lifetimes, are also bound in their afterlives as prospective pro-life saints.[93] While Lathrop's spiritual daughters—known since her death as the Hawthorne Dominicans—had for decades disavowed any interest in opening a cause on her behalf, they changed their minds in the era of John Paul II.[94] Lathrop's cause, they believed, would help advance "the dignity and sanctity of human life" by promoting the value of keeping the incurable comfortable in their final days rather than advocating euthanasia or assisted suicide. Hawthorne's care for "the most untouchable terminally ill of her day," her supporters argued, would provide a strong witness in an age when "human life is often ignored or denied."[95] Such a platform marks an interesting divergence between Lathrop and Elizabeth Ann Seton, the woman to whom she had been so often compared in life. As converts from elite American families, Seton and Lathrop both had stories tailor-made to underscore Catholic compatibility with U.S. citizenship. While Seton's supporters made the most of such claims, Hawthorne's devotees have not emphasized this angle, a difference explainable by the time frames in which they emerged as candidates. Seton had become a holy hero during a period in which U.S. Catholics were seeking to affirm their place in the nation's history, whereas Lathrop's cause was opened at a time when Catholics were secure in their sense of national belonging but often criticized American culture from a faith perspective.

Gender and feminism have shaped Lathrop's cause as well. The Hawthorne Dominicans belong to the Council of Major Superiors of Women Religious, the smaller and more traditionally minded of the two umbrella organizations that represent Catholic sisters in the United States. The CMSWR developed from Consortium Perfectae Caritatis, the group that had splintered from the Leadership Conference of Women Religious in the early 1970s. Members of the CMSWR are more likely to wear habits, engage in traditional female ministries of teaching and nursing, and have less charged relationships with members of the male hierarchy than the members of congregations that belong to the Leadership Conference of Women Religious. Like these general characteristics, a willingness to pursue causes for canonization is not an absolute differentiator between the two organizations, but it is a useful one.[96]

In eschewing canonization processes, Catholic sisters who identify as feminists may be inadvertently ensuring that the holy women who lived among them will be lost to history. However tedious and costly, canonization does lead to permanent memorialization. A century after her death, will Dorothy Kazel be as unfamiliar to Catholic believers as Leo Heinrichs, the Denver priest killed at the altar in 1908, or other long-defunct candidates for canonization? Will future U.S. Catholic parishes honor only St. Stanley Rother, St. Emil Kapaun, or St. Francis Xavier Ford? Will photographs of future female American saints feature only habited nuns, performing traditionally female tasks?

Abdication also runs the risk of appropriation. In the case of Sister Mary Ignatia Gavin, for instance, Alcoholics Anonymous has presented itself as the sponsor of her cause.[97] In a less benign example, an organization that calls itself the Father Mazzuchelli Society has proposed wresting control of the sponsorship of Father Samuel's cause from the Sinsinawa Dominicans, maintaining that the sisters' "estrangement" from the church after Vatican II and their adoption of "beliefs quite at odds with the Catholic faith" are a betrayal of their founder's legacy.[98] While this particular fringe group stands little chance of pushing the Sinsinawa Dominicans out of the process, as the community's enthusiasm for Mazzuchelli's cause continues unabated, the potential of similar groups to usurp other founders' causes is a warning to those familiar with the decades-long struggle of Seton's spiritual daughters to gain control over her life and legacy. Women who forswear canonization entirely may be transforming a hard-won victory into a hollow one, neglecting an opportunity to reshape canonization as a vehicle for creating models of Catholic womanhood that fully reflect the broadened roles of women in modern life.

Yet even Seton's canonization could be considered a hollow victory itself. Developments in the decades that followed suggested that U.S. Catholics had found their all-American saint at the precise moment it ceased to matter. Admittedly, the symbols that had united U.S. Catholics to Rome and to their fellow citizens at Seton's canonization in 1975 — the enthusiastic Protestant presence, Pope Paul extolling the American spirit in his homily, and the banner that emphasized Seton's dual citizenship in heaven and in the United States — had indeed been powerful. The cooler reception of John Paul II's U.S. saints and blesseds, however, suggested that U.S. Catholics would attach far less meaning to such symbols in the decades that followed. This dynamic is particularly well illustrated by a reversal in the afterlife of the only American to be both beatified and canonized by John Paul II.

Katharine Drexel was canonized on 1 October 2000. Drexel's second authenticated miracle, like her first, involved a local child's recovery from hearing loss.[99] When asked to explain the significance of this coincidence — elements of a saint's miracles often correspond to aspects of his or her life or ministry, and ears had not figured prominently in either of Drexel's — Drexel's supporters speculated that she might be advising Americans to listen more carefully to what she was telling them about how to be holy.[100] Whatever message Drexel might have been sending about holiness, however, it had little to do with the unique ways it had manifested itself in America. While a few devotees implied that Drexel, who had been born a U.S. citizen, had a slight patriotic edge over Seton, who had been born a British subject, these isolated and half-hearted attempts to present Drexel as a quintessential American were a far cry from the ambitious national claims her supporters had made on her behalf when she had emerged as a candidate in the 1960s. Claims that Drexel had been "unmistakably American" or the founder of the first Head Start program did not resonate in an era when U.S. Catholics no longer needed their saints either to stake their claim in American culture or to remind the Vatican of their unique national "brand." Instead, Drexel's devotees celebrated her canonization as a spark for the "new evangelization," John Paul's call to renew Catholics' missionary fervor throughout the world, especially among peoples who had heard the gospel proclaimed but had forgotten its message.[101]

From an American Brand to a Catholic Brand

No other U.S. causes for canonization had reached either their penultimate or final stage by the time John Paul II died in April 2005. Crowds at his funeral chanted "santo subito," a phrase that roughly translates into "sainthood immediately," and invoked an early practice of the church—long before there was such a procedure as a canonization process—when saints were proclaimed by popular acclamation. The new pope, the former cardinal Joseph Ratzinger, decided not to forgo the entire process, perhaps subscribing to the same philosophy Cicognani had embraced with regard to Seton about the importance of maintaining the integrity of the process. Pope Benedict did waive the five-year waiting period, however, and opened his predecessor's cause for canonization just days after his death. It would succeed in record time: John Paul II was beatified in May 2011 and canonized in April 2014.[102]

Meanwhile, many Vatican watchers wondered whether Benedict would modify his predecessor's canonization practices, especially after he reiterated his concerns about the inflation in the number of saints in a 2006 interview on Vatican Radio. "The large number of beatifications was almost overwhelming," he had said, and perhaps it was time to be "more selective, choosing figures that entered our consciousness more clearly."[103] Nonetheless, Pope Benedict did not substantially adjust the canonization process, though he did reverse one innovation made by John Paul II: except in unusual circumstances, the pope would not preside at beatifications.[104]

Whatever Benedict's reservations about the increasing number of saints, there was little he could do to stop momentum that had been building during John Paul II's papacy on a number of causes, including those of several Americans. Three weeks after his interview on Vatican Radio, he canonized Mother Théodore Guérin as the next U.S. saint. Celebrations of Guérin's canonization were clustered in the state of Indiana, where representatives of both church and state commemorated the first Hoosier saint. When Mitch Daniels, then Indiana's governor, unveiled a sign dedicating a section of U.S. 150 to Guérin, he observed, "We've named roads, bridges and other facilities for sports heroes, military heroes and politicians. . . . That's all well and good, but we've had many of those and only one saint."[105]

On a national scale, Guérin did gain some traction as a model of independent womanhood in the face of entrenched male authority. In a *New York Times* op-ed published on the Catholic Feast of All Saints, Catholic commentator James Martin, SJ, recounted Guérin's struggles with the bishop of Vincennes and saucily wondered what the bishop made of her recent canonization as he watched "from his post in heaven—or wherever he is today." Martin linked Guérin's story to those of Joan of Arc and Mary MacKillop, the latter another of John Paul II's blesseds who had founded a religious community in Australia and had often been at odds with local bishops—and unlike Guérin had actually been excommunicated. All three of them, according to Martin, were independent women who offered proof that saints were not models of compliance but occasionally "noisy prophets" who spoke truth to power and examples of "faithful dissent" from church authority.[106]

Three years after Guérin's canonization, the church declared Damien of Molokai a saint. U.S. celebrations were largely contained to the fiftieth state, though the event did register briefly in the nation's capital, albeit through the efforts of a non-Catholic. President Barack Obama, then in his first year in the White House, issued a public statement expressing his deep admiration for the saint who "had earned a special place in hearts of Hawaiians."[107]

In October 2012, the canonization of Damien's female counterpart, Marianne Cope, received marginally more attention, if only because the event marked a double triumph for North Americans: Kateri Tekakwitha was canonized on the same day. Although John Paul II had beatified Tekakwitha in 1980 without an authenticated miracle, his more discriminating successor waited until one materialized. It arrived with poignancy. In 2006, Jake Finkbonner, a five-year-old member of the Lummi tribe, had incurred a facial injury that led to a serious bacterial infection that left him close to death. After his parents placed a relic of Kateri's on his pillow, he recovered rapidly. The case easily passed Vatican scrutiny and to some seemed especially heaven-sent. Unlike Katharine Drexel's auditory miracles, Jake's cure connected petitioner and intercessor: like Tekakwitha, Jake was both young and native, and his permanent facial scarring evoked her smallpox-scarred countenance.[108]

Jake Finkbonner was an honored guest at a reception sponsored by the Canadian Embassy to the Holy See after Tekakwitha's canonization Mass. Also attending was Phil Fontaine, the former chief of the Canadian Assembly of First Nations, who had been an outspoken critic of the church's complicity in abuse of native children in Canadian residential schools. Three years earlier, Fontaine had led a delegation to Rome to receive an official apology from Pope Benedict, and in his speech at the post-canonization reception, he described his two visits to the Vatican as bookends in a journey of healing and reconciliation between church leaders and indigenous people. "They have acknowledged their sins," he said, "and we have forgiven them. Today, they canonize one of our daughters, and we walk forward together into the future."[109]

At the time of the two women's canonizations, the church in the United States was also grappling with the consequences of a devastating clergy sexual abuse crisis. Tekakwitha's elevation, in fact, represented a bright spot in a bleak year for her longtime devotee Charles Chaput, who in 2011 had become Philadelphia's thirteenth bishop and the first Native American to preside over a U.S. archdiocese. Attempting to deal with the moral, legal, and financial implications of the crisis, Chaput announced in January 2012 his plans to close dozens of archdiocesan institutions that faced declining enrollments and crumbling infrastructures. The optimism of Joseph Kerins and others who had hoped that John Neumann's canonization would inspire enough vocations to shore up a crumbling school system had been misplaced.

Chaput attended the canonizations of Cope and Tekakwitha in October 2012, and the following January he presided at a Mass for the two new American saints, held at the Basilica of the National Shrine of the Immaculate Conception in Washington, D.C. In his homily, Chaput spoke of his common ethnic heritage with Tekakwitha but also reminded the congregation that he felt a double affinity with Cope. Not only were they both Franciscans, but they were also linked through John Neumann: Chaput as one of Neumann's successors as Philadelphia's bishop, and Cope as a member of a community that had traced its roots to the congregation he had founded.[110]

Less than three years after Chaput delivered that homily, he would gather with his fellow U.S. bishops at the same basilica for a momentous event: the first *fuori sede* canonization celebrated on American soil. And a new pope would preside. In a move that astonished the Catholic world, Benedict had resigned three months after Cope's and Tekakwitha's canonizations. Equally surprising, to some, was the honoree at the 2015 canonization. Pope Francis, Benedict's successor, had announced aboard a flight from Sri Lanka to the Philippines that he planned to canonize Junípero Serra during his upcoming visit to the United States. The vice-postulator for Blessed Serra's sainthood cause, Franciscan father John Vaughn, told the Catholic News Service that he had been taken completely by surprise by the pope's announcement. "I was the last to know," Vaughn said.[111]

Though the Franciscan friars had not anticipated the papal decision, they made the most of it and, as the RSCJs had done with Duchesne in 1988, celebrated their new saint. An earlier generation of their confreres, who had nominated Serra in part out of a desire to give Franciscans their due in the aftermath of the North American martyrs' canonization, might have appreciated the irony: the "Apostle of California" was canonized by a Jesuit. Francis's unilateral decision to elevate Serra, though not in keeping with his image as a populist pope, underscores that canonization remains a papal prerogative.

As had been the case with his beatification in 1988, Serra's canonization elicited fierce protests from Native Americans. One wonders whether the pope was at all familiar with the story of Francis Xavier Seelos, or if he had even discussed open causes with the prefect of the Congregation for the Causes of Saints as John Paul II had done in advance of his second U.S. visit. Had Francis chosen to elevate the Redemptorist missionary instead of Serra, he would have forfeited the opportunity to call attention to holy heroes of the West and Southwest—admittedly a welcome development, as U.S. canonized and prospective saints remain concentrated in the Northeast. Nevertheless, canonizing Seelos would have allowed Francis to emphasize the same themes of evangelization without accentuating the harsh legacy of colonialism to the extent Serra's canonization had done.[112]

Pope Francis gave U.S. Redemptorists a more obvious reason to feel affronted during his U.S. trip. It was very plausible that Francis would visit John Neumann's shrine while he was in Philadelphia, the final leg of his U.S. trip. Not only had John Paul II visited St. Peter's in 1979, but Benedict XVI had also done so in 2008. Moreover, Neumann's reputation for humility seemed to make it even more likely that he would attract notice from a pontiff who deliberately shunned the luxurious trappings of the papal office. Nevertheless Francis's Philadelphia sojourn passed without either a scheduled or spontaneous stop at St. Peter's, despite his appearance at nearby Independence Hall.

Frances Cabrini's sisters in Upper Manhattan also had grounds for disappointment. When the papal visit was announced, they had expressed their hopes that the pope would visit their newly restored shrine in honor of Cabrini, and there were reasons enough to suppose he might. The shrine was in a neighborhood filled with immigrants, a population especially dear to Francis's heart. Moreover, the former cardinal Jorge Bergoglio was already familiar with the Cabrini sisters, attributing his own vocation to the congregation's work around his native Buenos Aires. Finally, for the Argentinian-born grandson of Italian immigrants making his first visit to the United States, it would be hard to imagine a more relevant figure than Cabrini, whose life had revolved around the same geographical triangle.[113] Yet Francis did not stop by, even though he was in the vicinity, and he did not mention Cabrini at all. This omission should not be interpreted as a slight but instead as another instance of how American exceptionalism has shaped the way U.S. Catholics tell Cabrini's story. For Pope Francis, as for most of Cabrini's admirers born outside the United States, her holiness derived from her multiple border crossings, not from the time she spent within U.S. boundaries.[114]

Aside from Serra, the American saint whose star shone most brightly during Pope Francis's visit was Elizabeth Ann Seton. Not only did President Obama single Seton out as an iconic American during the visit by presenting the pope with the key to her Emmitsburg home, but the pontiff himself recalled Seton's heroic charity and extraordinary sacrifice as part of his prepared remarks at New York's St. Patrick's Cathedral. Seton's holiness, he observed, had helped Catholicism and its institutions—particularly schools—to flourish in the nation's founding period and beyond.[115]

Elizabeth Ann Seton had remained a "wholly American saint" in the sense that a viable challenger for that title had not emerged in the four decades that followed her canonization. But while U.S. Catholics would not suggest that another candidate could better embody homegrown holiness, as earlier generations had done in the case of both the North American martyrs in 1930 and Frances Cabrini in 1946, there is no evidence that Seton's devotees ever took the additional step of petitioning the Holy See that she be named patron of the United States. The only geographical area under her patronage is the state of Maryland—a designation that surely would have disappointed those who had championed her as "Elizabeth of New York."[116] By any measure, U.S. Catholics certainly had not "hitched their wagon to Mother Seton's star," as the priest had advised them to do after her canonization.

For almost a century, the story of canonization in the United States had skewed heavily toward the pursuit of an American brand of holiness. By the time Seton was elevated in 1975, however, the narrative had begun to tilt in the opposite direction, becoming a function of intra-Catholic debates that only intensified throughout John Paul II's papacy. In 1998, journalist Paul Elie wrote about this dynamic in reference to the divisiveness surrounding the cause of Dorothy Day. Elie paraphrased a lament by Jesuit Thomas Reese that "conflicts among Catholics often seem like quarrels over a brand-name, with the players so worked up over what it means to be Catholic that they lose sight of the holy."[117] This accusation is a serious one to levy against Catholics, whose religious practices and sensibilities testify to a palpable sense of the sacred, to an acute awareness of the ways heaven touches earth through objects, sacraments, and saints.

Reese's criticism misses the larger point: U.S. Catholics have not so much lost sight of the holy but rather have become far less likely to rely on saints to define holiness for them. In part this is a theological phenomenon, rooted in a greater emphasis on saints' human qualities. Robert Ellsberg, an expert on saints and a supporter of Dorothy Day's cause, made this point dramatically in his 2017 cover story in *America* magazine, which appeared under the headline "SAINTS NOT SUPERHEROES."[118]

The more important takeaway for our narrative is that U.S. Catholics no longer rely on saints to define their place in America. Once again, where U.S. Catholics went, they took their saints with them. As polarization within the church supplanted marginalization in America as the keynote of U.S. Catholicism, the faithful became less inclined to view prospective saints as they had once viewed the Jesuit martyrs, Cabrini, Seton, Neumann, and others. No longer outward expressions of a deep yearning for holy heroes who sprang from their own time and place, favorite—or relentlessly "informal"—saints have become signifiers of where Catholic individuals and groups position themselves within the church, often on issues related to gender, sexuality, and social and racial justice. The search for a holy American hero had begun as an effort to define and articulate an American Catholic identity to outsiders to the faith and to the United States. It ended when canonization evolved into one of the most telling wedge issues, if not necessarily the most obvious, among U.S. Catholics.

American saints are now anything but rare, and considering the plethora of open U.S. causes, they will be even less so in the future.[119] But holy heroes have become far less meaningful than they once were, not only theologically but also culturally, as U.S. saint-seekers, influenced by papal initiatives, globalization, and the nation's culture wars, have abandoned their pursuit of an American brand of holiness in favor of fragmented efforts to define what they envision as an authentically Catholic one.[120] And thus we arrive at what may be the most revealing aspect of U.S. Catholics' search for a saint of their own: it was not the outcome of the search that showed that Catholics, despite their ties to the

Holy See, were an essential part of the American story but rather the pattern in which that search ran its course. Launched just as the United States announced its intention to become one of the world's most powerful nations, the quest for a wholly American saint reached it apex just as those aspirations were attained, and unraveled as social and cultural change prompted all Americans to question whether they could be said to share one common identity.

The Next American Saints

Prospective saints from the United States continue to reveal a great deal about the priorities and perspectives of their devotees, as a few examples drawn from the many open U.S. causes show. The muscular adventures of "Kapaun's Men," for instance, a Kansas-based group devoted to the cause of the Korean War chaplain, speak volumes about some Catholics' desire to defend the masculinity they believe to be under assault.[1] The argument that Sister Blandina Segale—a Cincinnati Sister of Charity who, coincidentally, traveled on the 1931 International Federation of Catholic Alumnae pilgrimage to support Elizabeth Ann Seton's canonization—models a saint who "leaned in" evokes Facebook's executive Sheryl Sandberg's clarion call to American women and highlights ongoing struggles about women's leadership within the church.[2] The causes of Pierre Toussaint, Augustus Tolton (the first black priest in the United States who had complimented Drexel's racial sensitivity), and several other African American Catholics reflect the church's efforts to come to terms with its complicity in slavery and racial discrimination.[3]

Many LGBT Catholics, meanwhile, find solace in devotion to Father Mychal Judge, OFM, the New York City firefighter chaplain killed on 11 September 2001 who had served as "unofficial chaplain" to New York's gay community and whose own homosexuality became public shortly after his death.[4] The causes of Knights of Columbus founder Michael McGivney and Bill Atkinson, a quadriplegic Augustinian priest who has become the most recent candidate for canonization to emerge from Philadelphia, are two of the many open ones attached to "good priests" who defend that calling in the aftermath of the clergy sex abuse scandal.[5] Both McGivney and Atkinson, as well as recent U.S. blesseds Stanley Rother and Solanus Casey, are also viable contenders for the elusive honor of the first U.S.-born male canonized saint. Had it not been for a remarkably public internecine conflict, the church may have already awarded that distinction to Fulton Sheen, but the legal battle between Cardinal Timothy Dolan of New York and Bishop Daniel Jenky of Peoria over which diocese should house Sheen's remains has stalled the cause.[6]

The causes for canonization of these and other prospective American saints can serve, as those of the past have done, as valuable interpretive tools. Unlike their predecessors, however, contemporary candidates for canonization belong to a new story in American sanctity whose themes differ substantially from the ones examined in these pages. One thing is certain: the next Americans to be canonized are likely to highlight the complexity of the U.S. Catholic experience to a degree the first twelve U.S. saints do not. As we have seen, the stories U.S. Catholics tell about saints often correlate to the stories they tell about their experience in America. Causes such as those attached to Carlos Rodríguez of Puerto Rico or the New Mexican native and Sacramento bishop Alphonse Gallegos will expose the fallacy, presumed by many contemporary historians as well as saint-seekers of the past, that "American Catholic" is a stand-in for "European Catholic." As this book has shown, hagiography and historiography are closely entwined, and in orienting American saint-seeking away from the urban Northeast, Rodríguez and Gallegos, as well as other prospective saints such as Samuel Mazzuchelli and Emil Kapaun, may signal corresponding changes in narratives of U.S. Catholicism. Pursuing the causes of Augustus Tolton and other African American Servants of God, meanwhile, may have a scholarly impact as well as a pastoral one, as incorporating them as subjects can help historians move black Catholics from the margins of the American experience to its center. Attention to Tolton, for example, would add an important layer to any analysis of U.S. Catholics' relationship to Rome; he traveled there to be ordained because no seminary in the United States would accept a black man.

Questions of gender and sexuality will continue to be thorny, but Pope Francis's 2018 apostolic exhortation on holiness suggests that the church may be poised to broaden its interpretations of female sanctity. *Gaudete et Exsultate* foregrounded women more than most previous papal documents, referencing a number of uncanonized and canonized women saints. It also addressed many of the factors complicating the cause of Dorothy Day, a figure whom the pope referenced admiringly in his 2015 address to the joint session of the U.S. Congress. Not only did the pope urge that any evaluation of holiness should take into account the "totality" of saints' lives, "their entire journey of growth in holiness," but he also defined "the lives of the poor, those already born, the destitute, the abandoned," and other vulnerable members of society as "equally sacred" as the lives of the unborn.[7] Throughout the document, Pope Francis cited national bishops' conferences, a testament to his support for collegiality that could conceivably lead him to implement a recommendation of the council years and delegate beatification to leaders of local churches. Of course, Pope Francis may also act on his own and decide to bypass the process entirely for an American candidate he deems worthy of universal veneration—a possibility that could conceivably result in formal sanctity for someone like Dorothy Stang, an Ohio Sister of Notre Dame de Namur who was murdered in Brazil in 2005 for her advocacy on behalf of the poor and the Amazon rain forest.[8]

Whatever actions Francis may take regarding canonization will certainly shape the future of saint-seeking in the United States. Nonetheless, it will continue to unfold as an American story that does not, after all, resemble very closely the history of European sanctity. While many of the original goals of the first U.S. saint-seekers have been realized—U.S. Catholics feel no need to prove they belong in America, and neither do they lack for influence at the Vatican—they are still missing what the first saint-seekers had hoped to secure: an American equivalent of France's Louis or Genevieve or Ireland's Patrick or Bridget. In this respect, the wide variety of U.S. prospective saints reflects the diversity of the U.S. Catholic experience, which, contrary to the expectations of the first U.S. saint-seekers, could never be represented by any single holy hero.

SELECT TIMELINE OF EVENTS AND MILESTONES
IN U.S. CAUSES FOR CANONIZATION

1884   Third Plenary Council of Baltimore; petition sent for Isaac Jogues, René Goupil, and Tekakwitha

1886   John Neumann's ordinary process begins in Philadelphia

1903   Leo XIII dies; Pius X is elected

1907   Elizabeth Ann Seton's ordinary process begins in Baltimore

1908   Holy See removes "mission territory" designation of the United States

1914   Pius X dies; Benedict XV is elected

1917   Frances Cabrini dies in Chicago

1921   Neumann is declared venerable

1922   Benedict XV dies; Pius XI is elected

1925   Jogues, Goupil, and the other North American martyrs are beatified

1926   International Eucharistic Congress in Chicago

1928   Cabrini's ordinary process begins in Chicago

1930   North American martyrs are canonized

1933   Amleto Cicognani is appointed apostolic delegate to the United States

1938   Cabrini is beatified

1939   Pius XI dies; Eugenio Pacelli is elected Pius XII

1940   Philippine Duchesne is beatified; Seton's cause is introduced at the Holy See

1944   Pius XII signs Cabrini's decree of canonization (official elevation ceremony is postponed until 1946)

1955   Katharine Drexel dies

1958   Pius XII dies; John XXIII is elected

1959   Seton is declared venerable

1962   Second Vatican Council opens

1963   Seton and Neumann are beatified

1965   Second Vatican Council closes

1975   Seton is canonized

1977   Neumann is canonized

1978   John Paul II is elected pope

1979   John Paul II visits United States; Drexel's cause is introduced at the Holy See

1980   Tekakwitha is beatified

1983   Reform of the canonization process

1988   Duchesne is canonized; Drexel is beatified; Junípero Serra is beatified

1995   Damien of Molokai is beatified

1998   Mother Théodore Guérin is beatified

2000   Francis Xavier Seelos is beatified; Drexel is canonized

2004   Marianne Cope is beatified

2006   Guérin is canonized

2009   Damien of Molokai is canonized

2012   Cope and Tekakwitha are canonized

2013   Benedict XVI resigns; Francis is elected

2015   Francis visits the United States; Serra is canonized

ACKNOWLEDGMENTS

I have been looking forward to writing this section so much! Now that the time has arrived, though, doing so is mostly making me sad—not because the book is finished but because I'm painfully aware that my words cannot convey the depth of my gratitude to the many colleagues and friends who have helped make it so. At the top of the list is everyone associated with the Cushwa Center, including its previous directors Jay P. Dolan, R. Scott Appleby, and Timothy Matovina; former staff members Paula Brach, Heather Grennan Gary, and Pete Hlabse; and current staff members MaDonna Noak and Shane Ulbrich. I'm especially grateful to Pete, who helped me in countless ways large and small, and to Shane, whose stellar performance as Cushwa's assistant director over the last few years freed up a great deal of mental space for me to think and write. Thanks go, too, to Catherine Osborne, Cushwa's postdoctoral fellow from 2014 to 2017, for reading drafts of several chapters, and to Valentina Ciciliot, our Marie Curie Fellow in residence from 2016 to 2018, whose own study of canonization has helped me understand the topic better. Thanks also to the members of Cushwa's Advisory Board, all treasured colleagues: Scott Appleby, Darren Dochuk, Tom Guinan, Tom Kselman, John McGreevy, Mark Noll, and Valerie Sayers. Warmest thanks go to Luca Codignola, Cushwa's Senior Fellow in Rome, for his collegiality and guidance and to Matteo Sanfilippo for accompanying me on my first visit to the Vatican Secret Archives and for all our collaborations since. Appreciation is also due to Matteo Binasco, Cushwa's postdoctoral fellow in Rome from 2014 to 2017, both for the assistance he provided me personally and for his brilliant *Roman Sources for the Study of American Catholicism*, which will help other scholars navigate archives at the Holy See and in Rome for years to come. Finally, I am grateful to the Cushwa family, especially Bill and Anna Jean, whose intellectual curiosity is as boundless as their generosity.

This book has benefited from many generous and thoughtful colleagues at Notre Dame. Over the time I was writing it, I received considerable support and encouragement from chairs of the Departments of American Studies and History: Erika Doss, Bob Schmuhl, Tom Tweed, and Patrick Griffin. Tom and Patrick went above and beyond; each of them read drafts and made recommendations that improved it substantially. I am also grateful to John T. McGreevy both for his insightful critique of my manuscript and for his own studies of American Catholicism, from which I have learned a great deal.

My thanks go to Theodore Cachey and Heather Hyde Minor, visionary directors of Notre Dame's Rome Global Gateway, and to Demetrio Yocum for teaching me to read and speak Italian. Jason Ruiz is the best next-door office neighbor ever. Sarah McKibben gave an impromptu pep talk in Purple Porch, and Karen Graubart coached me through my first transatlantic research trip. Mary Ellen Koniezcny has been my friend and sounding board; I miss her terribly. Jane Doering translated from French Sister Isabel's crucial letter and the biographical material on Ellen McGloin. Words fail me when I contemplate trying to thank Jean McManus for all she has meant to me as a colleague and a friend. The same is true for Angie Appleby Purcell, who inspires me personally and professionally, and for Tami Schmitz, who is the best running (now walking) partner, confidante, and friend anyone could ever ask for.

I am extremely grateful for the doctoral students who have assisted me with research over the years, including the late Jeff Bain-Conkin, Catherine Godfrey, Josh Kerschmar, Andy Mach, and Natalie Sargent. In a class by himself is Dr. Michael Skaggs, who for several years now has served as research assistant, editor, and conversation partner all wrapped up in one. I am also lucky to have learned from so many talented undergraduates enrolled in my Sanctity and Society seminar, especially Mary Carroll, Darcy Dehais, Bridget Hart, Margaret Moran, Garett Rethman, and Jacqueline Winch, whose final papers led me to helpful sources.

One of the unique pleasures of writing about women and men who were members of religious communities is the opportunity to interact with and learn from their spiritual descendants. Betty Ann McNeil, DC, and Regina Bechtle, SC, scholars and spiritual daughters of Elizabeth Ann Seton, match their founder in heroic virtue; they read my manuscript, saved me from embarrassing errors, and kept me in their prayers. Sister Mary Ellen Gleason, SC, invited me to give a talk at the College of St. Elizabeth, thus facilitating my discovery of critical documents in the congregation's archives. Archivists Noreen Neary, SC, and Louise Grundish, SC, supplied crucial information.

Writing this book also brought me, delightfully, into Frances Cabrini's spiritual circle. I am especially grateful to her direct successor, Sister Barbara Staley, superior general of the Missionary Sisters of Cabrini, for her prayers and support. Special thanks go to Maria Williams, both for her scholarly work, which helped me understand Cabrini as a transnational figure, and for her constant prayers and encouragement. I have come to appreciate the wisdom and grace of Philippine Duchesne through encounters with Carolyn Osiek, RSCJ, archivist of the U.S.-Canada Province, and Margaret Phelan, RSCJ, archivist at the congregation's generalate in Rome. Confreres of John Neumann, especially Matthew Allman, CSsR, and Gilbert Enderle, CSsR, have shown me characteristic Redemptorist hospitality in Philadelphia, Brooklyn, and Rome.

I owe an immense debt of gratitude to Catherine Brekus, who made very helpful suggestions at the proposal stage and even better ones after reading the penultimate draft; they all improved the final version substantially. Maggie McGuinness read several versions and is as unparalleled a commentator as she is a friend. Ellen Skerrett deployed her prodigious research skills on my behalf and supplied me with crucial sources on the North American martyrs and Cabrini. Patrick Hayes not only provided me with access to sources on Neumann but was always willing to listen to me talk about this book and add his own insights. If Patrick learns even one new thing from this book, I will count it as a success.

My thanks go to all the archivists and librarians who made my research possible: John Carven, CM, archivist of the Eastern Province of the Congregation of the Mission; Kevin Cawley of the University of Notre Dame Archives; Denise Gallo of the Daughters of Charity Archives; Anne Schwelm at Cabrini University; Kate Feighery at the Archives of the Archdiocese of New York; Mary Flynn of the Sisters of Charity of Halifax; Lois Hoh of Sinsinawa Mound; Stephanie Morris of the Sisters of the Blessed Sacrament; and Shawn Weldon at the Catholic Historical Research Center of the Archdiocese of Philadelphia.

Many colleagues and friends invited me to give talks and workshops while the book was in progress: Andrew Barlow, Chris Burke, Francesca Caddedu, Ed Hahnenberg, Patrick Hayes, Alberto Melloni, Kyle Roberts, Stephen Schloesser, Ann Taves, Sam Thomas, and Judith Weisenfeld. Judith merits special mention for her encouragement very early on in this project and for her mentorship. Ken Woodward made his papers available, introduced me to Peter Gumpel, SJ (who in turn led me to Paolo Molinari, SJ, and Monsignor Robert Sarno), and read the manuscript.

Warmest thanks go to Elaine Maisner at the University of North Carolina Press for always believing in me and my projects, ever since we first met for coffee in San Francisco in 2002. I am grateful to the entire team at the University of North Carolina Press, especially Dino Battista, Anna Faison, Cate Hodorowicz, Jay Mazzocchi, and Andrew Winters. Jeanne Barker-Nunn and Mary Reardon proved to be expert editors. I am grateful to the National Endowment for the Humanities for a sabbatical fellowship in support of this project in 2010–11. The Institute for Scholarship in the Liberal Arts in the College of Arts and Letters at Notre Dame provided both a research grant that permitted a two-week research trip to Rome and a subvention grant to the University of North Carolina Press for this book.

I appreciate all who have given me moral support over the many years I was writing this book, including Erin, Owen, and Alex Akel; Dominique Bernardo; Kathleen Brannock; Chris Cervanek; Annie Crew-Renzo; Caitlin Fitzpatrick; Kevin Grove, CSC; Carla Ingrando; Paul Kollman, CSC; Jody Vaccaro Lewis; Mary Lynch, SSJ; Bernard McIlhenny, SJ; John and Alicia Nagy; Elizabeth O'Reilly; Steve Reifenberg; Barbara Searle; Colleen Seguin; and Sister Janet Welsh, OP. Special thanks to my mother-in-law, Elaine A. Cummings, for her encouragement and her own fervent devotion to the saints. I am so very grateful to my Sunnymede family, especially Marie Harrer, whose companionship always lifts my spirits, whether we are at the Y or the Colosseum. My thanks also go to Erin Seeley, who in the last seventeen years has gone from student to neighbor to treasured friend, and to Lyn Caponigro, Steve and Erin Camilleri, Carl Loesch, Becky Reimbold, Cathy Stapleford, Leanne Suarez, and Bryon Thomas. Thanks are due to all my partners in mothering throughout South Bend, especially Christina Wolbrecht (maybe once Annie and Jane leave for college, we could publish a book in the same year?). I am also grateful to Denise Beidinger, Laurie Bulaoro, Kris Choinacky, Jenica Cory, Margie Griffith, and Kristin Pruitt.

Far away in miles but close in heart are my Delco friends and family. My thanks go to Tom and Kathy Sprows for making me an expert on Catholicism in the Archdiocese of

Philadelphia long before I ever set foot in an archive; to Teresa Calkins Hollingsworth for never failing to get me #backontrack; to Wendy Winchester Bonner for providing comic relief since kindergarten, and to our other O'Hara friends, Gina Evangelista, Eileen Murphy Costanzo, Jen Rankin, and Chris Stango for our long friendship; to Jack Betzal for helping me get permission to access the restricted material in the Philadelphia archdiocesan archives; to Pat Betzal, Jack Betzal Jr., and Pat Betzal Truede for the laughter and the memories; to Karen Rodemer for all our conversations at the shore; to Will McDowell for promising to buy the book; and to Tom, Mala, Lauren, Jonathan, Evan, and Ryan Sprows for your love and support. My most effusive thanks go to my sister Marybeth Sprows, my first friend and loudest cheerleader.

My thanks go to my husband, Thomas Cummings, for absolutely everything; he is my hero. Annie's creativity and energy delights me every single day. I am so proud of the young man T. C. has become, even as I savor the memories I have of him as a little boy. Among these is the time I was struggling to write at the dining-room table on a snow day, when he told me that he had trouble believing I was writing a book because I seemed just like a regular mom. I especially thank my eldest child, Margaret Grace Cummings, to whom this book is dedicated. Margaret was born on 1 October 2000, and when I called my dad with the news he told me excitedly that Katharine Drexel had been canonized in Rome earlier that morning. Though the significance escaped me at the time—I was too overwhelmed by my beautiful baby to care much about a new saint—as Margaret has grown into a young woman, I see in her the same combination of grace, tenacity, and faith that helped Drexel make the world a better place. I know Margaret will do the same.

NOTES

ABBREVIATIONS

AANY   Archives of the Archdiocese of New York, Yonkers, N.Y.

ADSH   Archives of the Dominican Sisters of Hawthorne, Hawthorne, N.Y.

AGSSC   Archivio Generale Società del Sacro Cuore (General Archives of the Society of the Sacred Heart), Rome

APSL   Archives of the Daughters of Charity, Province of St. Louise, Emmitsburg, Md.

ARSCJ   Archives of the Society of the Sacred Heart, United States–Canada, St. Louis, Mo.

ASBS   Archives of the Sisters of the Blessed Sacrament, Philadelphia, Pa.

ASCNY   Archives of the Sisters of Charity of New York, Bronx, N.Y.

ASCSE   Archives of the Sisters of Charity of St. Elizabeth, Convent Station, N.J.

ASV   Archivio Segreto Vaticano (Vatican Secret Archives), Vatican City

CHRCAP   Catholic Historical Research Center of the Archdiocese of Philadelphia, Philadelphia, Pa.

CKLW   Kenneth L. Woodward Collection

CLWR   Leadership Conference of Women Religious Collection

CR-CU   Cabriniana Room, Holy Spirit Library, Cabrini University, Radnor, Pa.

CRP   Congregatio Riti Processus (Processes, Congregation of Rites)

DA-EPCM   Ducournau Archives of the Eastern Province of the Congregation of the Mission (Vincentians), Germantown, Pa.

EASC   Elizabeth Ann Seton Collection

GA-CM   Archivio Generale della Congregazione della Missione (General Archives of the Congregation of the Mission), Rome

GA-CSSR   Archivio Generale della Congregazione del Santissimo Redentore (General Archives of the Congregation of the Most Holy Redeemer), Rome

KDC   Katharine Drexel Collection

MSGB   *Mother Seton Guild Bulletin*

NYT   *New York Times*

RABP   Archives of the Baltimore Province of the Congregation of the Most Holy Redeemer (Redemptorists), Philadelphia, Pa.

SBMAL   Santa Barbara Mission Archive-Library, Santa Barbara, Calif.

SDA   Sinsinawa Dominican Archives, Sinsinawa Mound, Wis.
SJNC   St. John Neumann Collection
UNDA   University of Notre Dame Archives, Notre Dame, Ind.
UNDL   University of Notre Dame Libraries, Notre Dame, Ind.

INTRODUCTION

1. "Eucharistic Prayer III," no. 113.

2. McGinley, "Easiest to Love," 52.

3. "Reminiscences of Sr. Ursula Infante MSC, and Mother Ignatius Dosini MSC from Queen of Heaven in Denver," in folder 24, "Accounts of Beatification Ceremony, 1938 and Reminiscences, 1941," File H: Beatification and Canonization Processes, CR-CU.

4. McGinley, *Saint-Watching*, 44.

5. Attwater, *Saints Westward*, 6, 7–8, 9.

6. The total includes canonized saints who lived and died within the present-day boundaries of the United States according to the latest statistics of the United States. See "American Saints and Blesseds." Note that this list includes only eleven canonized saints, but the feast of St. Isaac Jogues and Companions also includes René Goupil, who, as we will see, has been understood as a U.S. saint since his cause was first proposed. John LaLande was also a companion of Jogues who died in what became the United States, but he has not been conventionally included in lists of U.S. saints.

7. Robert Seton to William Seton, 26 and 27 June 1858, CSET-II-1-a7, UNDA. The 2016 *Official Catholic Directory* shows ninety-six Catholic parishes in the United States named for St. Elizabeth Ann Seton. The second and third most popular U.S. saints, Frances Cabrini and John Neumann, each have, respectively, fifty-one and forty-two parishes named for them. As for schools, approximately eighty are named for Seton. See Skaggs, "Seton Schools," for a map showing their locations throughout the country.

8. Spellman, foreword, ix, xi.

9. For two particularly instructive examples, see Vauchez, *Sainthood in the Later Middle Ages*; and Burke, "How to Be a Counter-Reformation Saint." Vauchez analyzes all the canonization processes conducted between 1181 and 1431, including unsuccessful ones, while Burke's prosopography considers fifty-five saints formally canonized between 1588 and 1767. For a brilliant analysis of saints as interpretive tools, see Ditchfield, "Thinking with the Saints."

10. Burke, "How to Be a Counter-Reformation Saint," 162. There have been several excellent studies of devotion to non-American saints in the United States, including Robert Orsi's *Thank You, St. Jude* and Margaret McCormack's edited collection *Saints and Their Cults in the Atlantic World*.

11. For studies of multiple causes of canonization in New France and New Spain, see Greer and Bilinkoff, *Colonial Saints*; and Pearson, *Becoming Holy in Early Canada*. For studies of single causes for canonization that have included the United States to

greater or lesser degrees, see, notably, Greer, *Mohawk Saint*; and Cussen, *Black Saint of the Americas*.

12. Tweed, "After the Quotidian Turn," 379, 384.

13. Dolan, *American Catholic Experience*, 9, 10; Dolan, *Immigrant Church*.

14. Tweed offered another compelling model for such scholarship in *America's Church*, in which he used the National Shrine of the Immaculate Conception in Washington, D.C., "as a vantage from which to combine the insights generated by the quotidian turn and the fruits of the scholarship that preceded it." Tweed, "Catholic Studies after the Quotidian Turn," 83.

15. Cummings, "Frances Cabrini, American Exceptionalism, and Returning to Rome." See, for other examples, D'Agostino, *Rome in America*; and McGreevy, *American Jesuits and the World*.

16. There were exceptions to this rule. See, for example, Fogarty's *Vatican and the American Hierarchy*. Other scholars, many of whom were also ordained or members of a religious community, also consulted Roman sources. A more representative example, however, was Jay P. Dolan, the preeminent historian of his generation, who emphasized the autonomy of the U.S. church both in his pioneering study of New York's Irish and German Catholics and in his survey of the American Catholic experience, cited above.

17. Burke, "How to Be a Counter-Reformation Saint," 158.

18. Burke, 155; for a comprehensive history of the process, see Woodward, *Making Saints*.

19. A novena is "a nine days' private or public devotion . . . to obtain special graces." Hilgers, "Novena."

20. St. Christopher is probably the best-known example of a saint who was based on legend. Pope Paul VI dropped him from the liturgical calendar in 1969. Woodward, *Making Saints*, 18, 104.

21. Donoghue, "How the Pope Makes Saints," 319–20.

22. Notes on Woodward interview with Gumpel and Molinari, May 1987, box 5, folder 19, CKLW, UNDA. I interviewed Peter Gumpel in Rome in May 2013 and found him to be as charming as he was informative. Even more helpful, though, were transcripts of interviews Kenneth Woodward conducted with Gumpel, his mentor Paolo Molinari, SJ, and Gumpel's doctoral student Robert Sarno in the 1980s as Woodward was researching his book *Making Saints*. I am grateful to Ken for depositing his material in the archives of the University of Notre Dame. For those interested in a detailed analysis of the process and a wider lens on canonization, his *Making Saints* remains the standard book on the subject.

23. "Relation, Elizabeth Ann Bayley widow Seton," in *Beatificationis et canonizationis servae Dei Elisabeth Annae Bayley viduae Seton fundatricis Congr.nis sororum a charitate sancti Joseph in America septentrionali: Nova positio super virtutibus*, GA-CM.

24. This latter tradition prompted Monsignor Robert Sarno, a U.S. priest at the Congregation for the Causes of the Saints since 1982, to characterize canonization as "one of the most democratic processes in the church." Quoted in Higgins, *Stalking the Holy*, 30.

25. Testimony of Sister Benedicta Burns, Elizabeth Ann Bayley, ordinary process on fame of sanctity, 1907–1911, vol. 1, pp. 161–62, 6057, CRP, ASV.

26. "A Report on the Exhumation of the Remains of the Venerable Elizabeth Seton and the Location and Status of her Relics," box 4, folder 2, 2D.4, DA-EPCM.

27. Congregational annals, 3 August 1882, APSL; see, for example, "An Editorial," 3.

28. Shea, "Holy Personages," 183. Emphasis added.

29. O'Toole, *Faithful*, 138–39.

30. For one recent study, see Rowe, *Saint and Nation*.

31. L. Taylor, *Virgin Warrior*, esp. epilogue.

32. "Decree in the Baltimore Case Concerning the Beatification and Canonization of the Servant of God, Widow," 28 February 1940, copy in box 5, folder 2, EASC, ASCSE.

33. Orsi, *History and Presence*, esp. chap. 2.

34. Gallo, "Unlocking the Archival Legalities."

CHAPTER 1

1. Clarke, "Beatification Asked," 808.

2. Gibbons, "Pastoral Letter to the Archdiocese of Baltimore," 111; "A Great Catholic Council," *NYT*, 28 March 1884, 5.

3. Fogarty, *Vatican and the American Hierarchy*, 31.

4. "Letter Petitioning for the Introduction of the Cause of the Servants of God, Isaac Jogues and Rene Goupil, of the Society of Jesus, also of the Virgin Katharine Tekakwitha," 6 December 1884, document 20, in *Positio of the Historical Section on the Virtues of Katharine Tekakwitha*, New York, 1940, 445.

5. Chauchetière, *La vie de la B. Catherine Tegakoüita*; a modern edition of Cholenec's biography, edited by William Lonc, is *Catherine Tekakwitha: Her Life*.

6. Greer, *Mohawk Saint*, esp. chap. 1, "Beautiful Death."

7. Greer, *Mohawk Saint*; Clarke, "Beatification Asked," 809.

8. "Letter Petitioning," 445, 446.

9. "Catherine Tegakwitha [*sic*]," 87.

10. Rose of Lima had been declared patroness of the Americas in 1670, and U.S. bishops petitioned the Holy See to approve the decree recognizing the Blessed Virgin Mary, under the title of the Immaculate Conception, patroness of the United States. Guilday, *History of the Councils of Baltimore*, 149; MacLeod, *Devotion to the Blessed Virgin Mary*, 28–29.

11. Byrne, "Catholic Education in the United States: Foundations," 55.

12. "American Bishops and Pastoral Care of Italians," 163–64.

13. Gleason, *Contending with Modernity*, 8–12; Thomas, "American Press and the Church-State Pronouncements of Pope Leo XIII," 18.

14. Clarke, "Beatification Asked," 808, 809.

15. Shea, "Holy Personages," 183. Emphasis added.

16. Shea, 100.

17. Holweck, "American Martyrology," 495.

18. McSweeny, "Hidden Saints," 535.

19. "American Saints," 716–17.

20. "Venerable Mother Mary of the Incarnation," 608.

21. Holweck, "American Martyrology," 495.

22. F. G. H., "S. Rosa de Lima, Virgo," 91–92; Storm, *Life of Saint Rose*, 201–2.

23. Meagher, "Sheaf of Letters," 311.

24. F. G. H., "S Rosa a S. Maria," 335.

25. Emery, "Mother Duchesne," 687.

26. "Kateri Tekakwitha," 776; E. Walworth, *Life and Times of Kateri Tekakwitha*; review of *The Life and Times of Kateri Tekakwitha*, by Ellen Walworth, 318.

27. Lowth, "Philippine-Rose Duchesne."

28. Sarah Ann Curtis presents Duchesne as a prominent example of a Catholic female missionary whose overseas adventures proved critical to the establishment and consolidation of France's Second Empire. See Curtis, *Civilizing Habits*.

29. Lowth, "Philippine-Rose Duchesne"; G. E. M., *Venerable Philippine Duchesne*, ii.

30. Duchesne, ordinary process on fame of sanctity, 1895–96, 5248, CRP, ASV.

31. Details of the early efforts to initiate Duchesne's cause were recounted as part of an official investigation into her reputation for sanctity conducted in St. Louis in 1895 and 1896. Philippine Duchesne, Society of Sisters of the Sacred Heart of Jesus, ordinary process on fame of sanctity, St. Louis, 5251, CRP, ASV.

32. McSweeny, "Hidden Saints," 536–37.

33. See E. McGloin to Rev. Mother, 7 July 1898 and 23 December 1898, in "Unofficial Letters about Cause," 2b, C-VII, Philippine Duchesne, AGSSC.

34. E. McGloin to Very Rev. Mother, 19 September 1901, in "Unofficial Letters about Cause," 2b, C-VII, Philippine Duchesne, AGSSC. For more on McGloin's life and her time in Rome, see *Lettres Annuelles de la Société du Sacré Coeur*, 1918–1920, Eden Hall, vol. II, 67–71, ARSCJ.

35. The general consensus is that Martin of Tours (d. 397) was the first non-martyr to be canonized.

36. "Venerable Mother Mary of the Incarnation," 608.

37. Wynne, *Our North American Martyrs*, 18.

38. Donnelly, *Thwaites' Jesuit Relations*, 9–10.

39. Anderson, *Death and Afterlife*, 7, 52–53.

40. Anderson, 9.

41. "Our Lady of Martyrs: Father Walworth's Poems," 62.

42. On 1 December 1885, Loyzance wrote a letter to George R. Peck, editor of the *Daily Advertiser*, in which he notes "our present work" in the beatification of Jogues and Goupil (Joseph Loyzance, SJ, to Mr. Geo. R. Peck, 1 December 1885, in *Collections of the Cayuga County Historical Society* 4 [1887]: 81); "A Holy Place in New York State," *New York Freeman's Journal*, 13 December 1884, 4; *Pittsburgh Catholic*, 3 January 1885, 5; *Catholic Review* (Brooklyn), 22 August 1885, 117; "The Shrine on the Mohawk," *New York Freeman's Journal*, 22 August 1885, 1; "Catholic Church Matters," *NYT*, 10 August 1885, 2.

43. "Origin and Design of the Pilgrimage," 5–6.

44. "First Religious Pilgrimage in the Country Largely Attended," *Pittsburgh Catholic*, 29 August 1885, 4; "An American Sanctuary," *Catholic Review*, 29 August 1885. The pilgrimage was held at least for another year. "Five Thousand Pilgrims Visit the Shrines of the Martyrs in the Mohawk Valley," *Pittsburgh Catholic*, 21 August 1886, 5; *Baltimore Catholic Mirror*, 28 August 1886, 5; *New York Freeman's Journal*, 4 September 1886, 1; Wilbur, "American Lourdes," 278.

45. McDannell, *Material Christianity*, esp. chap. 5, "Lourdes Water and American Catholicism."

46. "Origin and Design of the Pilgrimage," 6.

47. Promoters of other holy sites in the United States also claimed for them the distinction of the "American Lourdes." See McDannell, *Material Christianity*, chap. 5, on Notre Dame's grotto; and Tweed, *America's Church*, on the Basilica of the National Shrine of the Immaculate Conception in Washington, D.C.

48. "Domestic Religious Intelligence," 450. Emphasis in original.

49. Shea, "Holy Personages," 179.

50. Breckinridge, *Papism in the XIX Century*, 60.

51. "Domestic Religious Intelligence," 449.

52. "Is the Church of Rome Idolatrous?" 264–65; Jane Addams to Sarah Alice Addams Haldeman, 12 February 1888, in Bryan, Bair, and Angury, *Selected Papers of Jane Addams*, 2:570; Severance, "Beatification and Canonization," 62.

53. Barrett, "Word about the Old Saints," 269–70.

54. Shea, *Our Faith and Its Defenders*, vi. For more on Shea's approach to integrating Catholics into American history, see, "Catholic Church in American History."

55. Parkman, *Jesuits in North America*, 304. For examples of Catholics' use of the quote, see Murray, *Popular History of the Catholic Church*, 117; "In Memory of a Martyr," *New York Herald*, 16 August 1885, 7; Donohoe, *Iroquois and the Jesuits*, 48; "Father Jogues Died, 1646," *Irish World and American Industrial Liberator*, 27 October 1900, 8; and "Father Isaac Jogues Martyred, 1646," *Irish World and American Industrial Liberator*, 17 October 1903, 7. Catholics used Bancroft's history to similar effect. Bancroft had written that "the history of Jesuit mission is connected with the origin of every celebrated town in the annals of French-America. Not a cape was turned, not a river entered, but a Jesuit led the way." Bancroft, *History of the United States*, 122. Writers in Catholic newspapers presented Isaac Jogues and his companions as members of "that famous band of heroic missioners and explorers who the Protestant historian Bancroft and other historians have so unstintedly praised." This was repeated in "Father Jogues, Martyr, 1646," *Irish World and American Industrial Liberator*, 12 October 1901, 6.

56. "St. Ignatius Starts the Order of Jesuits, 1534," *Irish World and American Industrial Liberator*, 10 August 1901, 8; "Our Lady of Martyrs," 62.

57. See Cummings, *New Women of the Old Faith*, 28–38.

58. Ireland, "Jeanne d'Arc," 58, 60, 64.

59. John Ireland to R. A. [Ferdinand] Litz, 4 August 1892, "Letters: Cause of Beatification," box 5, SJNC, RABP.

60. "The Saints of America," *Daily Inter Ocean*, 11 August 1896, 12.

61. Greer has traced her reinvention as "Kateri" Tekakwitha to the publication, in 1891, of Ellen Walworth's *The Life and Times of Kateri Tekakwitha*. Greer, *Mohawk Saint*, 193–94; Greer, "Natives and Nationalism."

62. "Domestic Religious Intelligence," 449.

63. As Anderson points out, the early U.S. saint-seekers reproduced the biases of their culture. Apart from Tekakwitha, they put forward no other indigenous candidates for canonization. This lacuna has since led native advocates and interpreters to question the imperialist assumptions behind the distinction that names the eight French missionaries "martyrs" while describing native converts who perished in the same decade as merely having been "slain," a term without the heavy theological implications of martyrdom. Anderson, *Death and Afterlife*, 360.

64. Wynne, *Jesuit Martyrs*, vii; Conde Pallen, untitled poem, in Wynne, *Our North American Martyrs*, 26.

65. Shea, "Holy Personages," 129–32; Murray, *Lives of the Catholic Heroes and Heroines*, 478–89, 563–81; see also Greer, "Colonial Saints."

66. See, for example, Emery, "Mother Duchesne."

67. Ordinary process on Guérin's fame of sanctity, 9165, CRP, ASV; J. White, "Path to Sainthood," 73.

68. *Irish World and American Industrial Liberator*, 4 November 1893, 3.

69. See chapters 20–25 of Mug, *Life and Life-Work of Mother Theodore Guérin*; J. White, "Path to Sainthood," 74.

70. Gibbons, introduction, xx.

71. Ireland, "Rt. Rev. Mathias Loras," 721.

72. Turner, "Significance of the Frontier"; Turner, "Problem of the West"; "Current Religious Comment," 267; "The Gifts of the West," *Catholic Journal* (Rochester, N.Y.), 17 January 1903, 8.

73. Nelson, "Apostle of the Midwest," 23.

74. Eckert, "Missionary in the Wilderness," 590; "TJC," review of *Memoirs of Father Mazzuchelli*, 378.

75. Eckert, "Missionary in the Wilderness," 590.

76. Nelson, "Apostle of the Midwest," 23.

77. Stadick, "Saint Patrons," 127.

78. Ireland, introduction, xv.

79. A. Waible, "A Centenary Sketch," in "Liturgical Celebrations," box 5, SJNC, RABP.

80. Ireland to Litz, 4 August 1892, "Letters: Cause of Beatification," box 5, SJNC, RABP.

81. John Nepomucene Neumann, bishop of Philadelphia, C.SS.R., ordinary process in Philadelphia on fame of sanctity, 1886–1888, p. 212., 3984, CRP, ASV.

82. Cicognani, *Sanctity in America*, 54; Elliott, "Bishop Baraga," 78.

83. For more on missions see Dolan, *Catholic Revivalism*.

84. Ordinary processes on Seelos's reputation for sanctity and absence of a cult were

conducted in Pittsburgh, Baltimore, and New Orleans between 1900 and 1902. See 5664–68, CRP, ASV; and Cicognani, *Sanctity in America*, 95.

85. Cicognani, *Sanctity in America*, 37–41, 77–82.

86. Quoted in Melville, *Elizabeth Bayley Seton*, 71.

87. Elizabeth to Cecilia Seton, 6 October 1808, in Seton, *Collected Writings*, 2:34.

88. Robert Seton to William Seton, 26 and 27 June 1858, CSET-II-1-a7, UNDA.

89. Seton was titular archbishop of Heliopolis in Phoenicia. "Archbishop Robert John Seton."

90. Two of her daughters predeceased her and the third, Catherine, entered the Sisters of Mercy. One son, Richard, died at sea without heirs at the age of twenty-five, but the other, William, married and had seven children. James Roosevelt Bayley was the son of Elizabeth's half-brother, Guy Charleton Bayley.

91. Elliott, "St. Vincent de Paul and the Sisters of Charity," 13.

92. Conway, "Individual Catholic Women," 386.

93. Parton, "Our Roman Catholic Brethren," 447.

94. T. Taylor, "Sisters of Charity," 55.

95. Elliott, "St. Vincent de Paul and the Sisters of Charity," 28.

96. Quoted in Cummings, *New Women of the Old Faith*, chap. 1.

97. Jameson, "American *Acta Sanctorum*," 290, 292, 295, 296.

98. Wynne, *Jesuit Martyrs*, 231.

99. "News Items," box 5, SJNC, RABP.

100. The *Catholic Encyclopedia* of 1907 listed no fewer than twenty separate steps to advance to the penultimate stage of beatification. Beccari, "Beatification and Canonization." For the Code of Canon Law in English, see canons 1999–2141 in E. Peters, *1917 Pio-Benedictine Code of Canon Law*. These norms were revised in 1983 by John Paul II, as I discuss in chapter 6.

101. Halley, "How Saints Are Canonized," 342.

102. Amato, "Prolusione."

103. Wüst [Wuest], "John N. Neumann," 322. Neumann's ordinary process on fame of sanctity was conducted in Philadelphia between 1886 and 1888 and in Budweis during the same period. The process on the absence of cult was completed in Philadelphia in 1888. The ordinary process on Neumann's fame of sanctity in Rome was completed in 1891. See 3984, 3985, 4014, and 5443, CRP, ASV.

104. "Present Stage of the Inquiry"; "Present Status of the Canonization Process."

105. Ferrante, "John Nepomucene Neumann," 40–44.

106. Ferrante, 46–49; Rev. John Doherty, "Summary of John Neumann's Process for Beatification," December 1963, in "Cause History," RABP.

107. Vico, "Beatificationis et Canonizationis," *Analecta Congregationis Sanctissimi Redemptoris* 1 (1922): 12–22.

108. E. Weigel, "New Glory of the American Hierarchy."

109. Ferrante, "John Nepomucene Neumann," 39.

110. Bechtle, "1846 Separation."

111. Metz, "Sisters of Charity," 226.

112. McNeil, "Sulpicians and Sisters of Charity."

113. See "History of the Sisters of Charity of Cincinnati," Sisters of Charity website, 18 July 2018, http://www.srcharitycinti.org/about/history_sc.htm.

114. O'Gallagher, "Sisters of Charity of Halifax"; "Our Beginnings"; and "Sisters of Charity—Halifax." In 1911, the Daughters of Charity in the United States split into two provinces, based in Emmitsburg and St. Louis. This explains why, at times, the total number of Seton communities is listed as seven.

115. C. White, *Life of Mrs. Eliza A. Seton*, 296, 462.

116. "History of the Sisters of Charity of Seton Hill"; "Short History of the Sisters of Charity."

117. Original account written by Rev. Robert Lennon, box 7, folder 8, 2D.4, DA-EPCM. The account states that Lennon visited the superior general of the Congregation of the Mission as well as the congregation's postulator in May 1897. Cardinal Gibbons directed him to "ascertain from him what course should be followed in the United States for the inauguration of this work." In particular, Lennon was to find out what organization should officially be appointed to assume the responsibility of carrying out the work of the cause in the United States. Lennon was asked to wait a few days for his answer. It arrived in the second interview.

118. This is the conclusion reached by a canon lawyer in his detailed investigation into the history of Seton's cause in 1948. "Rev. Damian J. Blaher, O.F.M., to Spellman," 7 September 1948, with attached report, Blaher, "To His Eminence Cardinal Spellman Pro Memoria on the Cause of Elizabeth Ann Seton," folder 5, S/C-71, AANY.

119. Testimony of Esther Kearney Barry in Seton, ordinary process, vol. 1, p. 144. 6057, CRP, ASV.

120. *Beatificationis et canonizationis servae Dei Elisabeth Annae Bayley viduae Seton fundatricis Congr.nis sororum a charitate sancti Joseph in America septentrionali: Positio super virtutibus ex officio disposita 18 giugno 1957*, GA-CM.

121. Robert Sarno draws on the texts of Vatican II to explain that "the Holy Father proposes those canonized for the imitation—by a life and faith and charity toward God and neighbor—veneration, i.e., cult, and therefore for the invocation by prayer of the people of God with an act of public ecclesiastical cult." "Theological Reflection on Canonization," 9.

122. Park's response to this question appears in Seton's process on the absence of cult, p. 68, 6063, CRP, ASV. Responses of Lagarde and O'Keefe appear in volume 4 of Seton's ordinary process on fame of sanctity, p. 980, 1042, 6060, CRP, ASV.

123. Gibbons's testimony in Seton's ordinary process on fame of sanctity, vol. 1, pp. 124–25, 6057, CRP, ASV.

124. Gibbons's testimony, p. 123.

125. See, for example, the testimony of Sister Benedicta Burns in volume 1 of the testimony on Seton's fame of sanctity (6057, CRP, ASV), who prefaced many of her answers with "I know from Dr. White . . ." Burns and other witnesses often cite the page number of White's *Life of Mrs. Eliza A. Seton*.

126. Articles 54 and 68, James Hayden, CM, "Positions and Articles Proposed for the

Beatification and Canonization of the Servant of God Elizabeth Ann Seton, Foundress of the Congregation of Sisters of Charity of St. Joseph's in America," enclosure, in 6057, CRP, ASV.

127. See, for example, testimony of Sister Benedicta Burns in Seton's ordinary process, vol. 1, 216, 6057, CRP, ASV.

128. McCann, *History of Mother Seton's Daughters*, 2:119; 1:xviii.

129. Giuseppe Scognamillo explains the need to incorporate the Sisters of Charity as petitioners in order to claim the miracle exemption in a letter he wrote to Amleto Cicognani, 19 April 1947, box 7, folder 3, 2D.4, DA-EPCM. Original in Italian; translated by Demetrio Yocum.

130. See testimonies of Sister Ambrose Callahan and Sister Benedicta Burns, Seton's ordinary process on the absence of a cult, Baltimore, 1914–1920, pp. 55 and 62, 6063, CRP, ASV.

131. Clipping, "Archbishop Seeks Writings of Mother Seton," *Baltimore Catholic Review*, 29 June 1923, "Advancement of Cause to Venerable," box 2, 100.150, ASCNY.

132. Souvay, "Questions anent Mother Seton's Conversion." See also "Research on EAS Baptism," box 1, 100.150, ASCNY.

133. Charles L. Souvay, "History of Mother Seton's Daughters," in "St. Elizabeth Ann Seton, 1900–1959," box 5, folder 11, EASC, ASCSE.

134. Souvay used this phrase in a postulatory letter sent to the Holy Father in 1936, which was reprinted in "Editorial Notes," 2. His admission that Seton "never actually belonged to the Religious Family of St. Vincent de Paul" was controversial at the time, and a French sister advised that the phrase be excised when it was reprinted: "I have a suggestion to make, in regard to Our Most Honored Father's letter to the Holy Father. It seems to me it would be well to leave out the part which tells that Mother Seton never belonged to the religious family of Saint Vincent de Paul, etc. There has been so much controversy in regard to the Union, etc, I think it would be well not to publish this portion of the letter." Sister (name unclear) to Father Hoctor, 12 January 1936, "Important Letters Concerning Cause," RG 1-3-5-8 ("Cause"), APSL. The phrase was left in, however, and it remains a contentious one.

135. Souvay to Wynne, 22 June 1933, "History of the Process," ASCNY.

136. Issues of the *Pilgrim of Our Lady of Martyrs* typically listed contributions to the shrine of Our Lady of Martyrs in Auriesville.

137. Jean Brebeuf and seven members of the Society of Jesus, ordinary process, Quebec, (on martyrdom), 4755, CRP, ASV; Wynne is quoted in "New York May Have a Saint," *Wilkes-Barre Times*, 6 August 1904.

138. Sacred Congregation of Rites, "Decree of Beatification for the North American Martyrs," copy in Dougherty Correspondence, 80.8481, CHRCAP; Clarke, "Beatification Asked," 820.

139. "Our American Beatified Martyr Priests," 76; Wynne to Dougherty, 25 September 1925, Dougherty Correspondence,80.8481, CHRCAP.

140. Quoted in Dolan, *American Catholic Experience*, 343.

141. Quoted in Hennesey, *American Catholics*, 241.

142. Contemporary regulations on conclaves required the cardinal electors to begin the process no more than ten days after the previous pope's death. Pope St. Pius X, *Vacante Apostolica Sede*, nos. 33 and 34.

143. Fogarty, *Vatican and the American Hierarchy*, 220.

144. Walsh, *Our American Cardinals*; Hennesey, *American Catholics*, 240.

145. Wynne to Dougherty, 25 September and 18 November 1925, and Dougherty to Wynne, 4 December 1926, Dougherty Correspondence, 80.8481, CHRCAP. In 1927, Wynne was able, first, to convince the Sacred Congregation to permit one U.S. archbishop to submit the petition on behalf of all the American hierarchy and, second, to persuade New York's Cardinal Hayes to do so. "Communications," 354.

146. Lyons, "Saints of the United States," 188; Souvay "Word of Superiors," *The Echo of the Motherhouse*, January 1935, in "Important Letters Related to Cause," RG 1-3-5-8, APSL; Clemens, "On the Hill of the Martyrs"; Lux, "Chicago's First Saint," 4.

147. Lyons, "Saints of the United States," 188.

148. See pamphlet, *Novena in Honor of the Only Saints of North America*, copy in Dougherty Correspondence, 80.8482, CHRCAP; "To Honor Jogues Today," *NYT*, 26 September 1927, 39; Lombardo, "Founding Father," 128.

149. *Novena in Honor of the Only Saints of North America*, copy in Dougherty Correspondence, 80.8482, CHRCAP.

CHAPTER 2

1. Miccinelli, "Postulators," 5.

2. LaFarge, "Blessed Martin," 484.

3. The 1917 Code of Canon Law remained in effect, with some piecemeal modifications, until Pope John Paul II's massive reform effort that resulted in the 1983 Code. The only English translation of the 1917 Code is Edward Peters's curation *The 1917 Pio-Benedictine Code of Canon Law*. The pope's ability to dispense with the waiting period was a curiosity not only of beatification and canonization procedure: under canon 218 and the ecclesiological notion of each pope as the direct successor of Saint Peter, the pontiff enjoys supreme authority over every aspect of canon law.

4. Pope Pius XI, "*Già da qualche tempo*," 6 February 1930, Vatican website, https://w2.vatican.va/content/pius-xi/it/motu_proprio/documents/hf_p-xi_motu-proprio_19300206_sezione-storica.html.

5. Antonelli, "Commentary," in "Process," box 19, SJNC, RABP; Veraja, "Genesis and Structure of the New Legislation," box 7, folder 1, CKLW, UNDA; Sarno, "Diocesan Inquiries," 17.

6. *NCWC News Sheet*, 19 May 1925, 1.; *Catholic Herald* (St. Louis), 24 May 1925, 1.

7. D'Agostino, *Rome in America*, 158.

8. Quoted in Congdon, "Making of a Saint," 75; "Catholic Editors Hear Bias Scored," *NYT*, 24 June 1939, 21. On Pius XI's eagerness to canonize an American saint during the Holy Year of 1925, see Francis Litz to O'Hara, 12 May 1958, box 19, SJNC, RABP; and Ferrante, "John Nepomucene Neumann," 51.

9. John Farley died in 1918, and Gibbons died in 1921.

10. For biographical profiles of these men, see Walsh, *Our American Cardinals*; and Hennesey, *American Catholics*, 240.

11. Cicognani, *Sanctity in America*, 2.

12. "American Indian Woman May Be Named a Saint," 5; on the reported 1931 cure of John Szymanski from a head injury, see LaRosa, "Saint Kateri."

13. "American Indian Woman May Be Named a Saint," 5.

14. Addendum, John J. Wynne to Dougherty, 25 May 1939, Dougherty Correspondence, 80.8483, CHRCAP.

15. Feldberg, "American Heretic."

16. "Priest Sees a Need for American Saint," *NYT*, 21 December 1936, 6; "Catholics Told to Pray for U.S. Modern Saint," *New York Herald Tribune*, 21 December 1936, 3.

17. "Catholics Told to Pray for U.S. Modern Saint."

18. "Priest Sees a Need for American Saint," *NYT*, 21 December 1936, 6.

19. Cicognani, *Sanctity in America*, 2; Cicognani to Andrew Kuhn, 2 June 1933, in "Letters: Cause of Beatification," box 5, SJNC, RABP. Five volumes related to the cause of Seelos were deposited in the Sacred Congregation of Rites in 1902 and 1903; see 5664–68, CRP, ASV.

20. Mug's testimony, as well as an account of her cure, a letter to Mother Mary Cleophas Foley, 21 November 1908, appears in Guérin's ordinary process on fame of sanctity, Indianapolis, 1915, 1937, 9165–66, CRP, ASV.

21. Cicognani, *Sanctity in America*, 146–47.

22. Habig, *Heroes of the Cross*, 16.

23. Charles F. Lummis to Zephyrin Englehart, 1 April 1909, and Lummis to Englehart, 28 April 1927, in Series 8 Serra Cause Historical Collection, *Serrana* anthology, vol. 2, nos. 45 and 46, US-CaStbMAL, SBMAL; Cadorin, "Father Junipero Serra."

24. "May Be First American Saint," 25 December 1927, *Washington Post*, SM5. An ordinary process on Heinrich's martyrdom was conducted in Newark, New Jersey, between 1926 and 1929. See 6289, CRP, ASV.

25. Documents related to this cause were later published in Gannon, *Martyrs of the United States of America*.

26. See also correspondence between Wynne and Dutton, box 1, folder 13, Joseph Dutton Collection, UNDA.

27. Gannon, *Martyrs of the United States of America*, 9, 195.

28. Gannon to Dougherty, 26 September 1941, Dougherty Correspondence, 80.5641, CHRCAP; Gannon, *Martyrs of the United States of America*. Two copies of the original report can be found in the Dougherty Correspondence, CHRCAP.

29. Quoted in "Catholic Editors Hear Bias Scored," *NYT*, 24 June 1939, 21.

30. See chapter 6, "Papal Saints," for the story of how some of these causes have recently been revived.

31. Gannon, *Martyrs of the United States of America*, 193–94.

32. Morris, *American Catholic*, 164; "57th Annual Report of the Superintendent of Schools," 9, CHRCAP.

33. Quoted in Mize, "'Catholic Way,'" 50.

34. Halsey, *Survival of American Innocence*.; LaFarge, "Blessed Martin," 484. The advocacy of LaFarge and other racial reformers was one reason why devotion to de Porres's cause revived in the mid-twentieth century. He was canonized in 1962. See Cussen, *Black Saint of the Americas*, 4–5, 187–96, 200–205.

35. "Little Flower and the Nation," 281–82.

36. Fogarty, *Vatican and the American Hierarchy*, 299; McGuinness, "Let Us Go to the Altar," 187; Morris, *American Catholic*, 137.

37. Dolan, *American Catholic Experience*, 350. In 1924 the town of Area, just outside Chicago, was renamed Mundelein in the cardinal's honor. See "Mundelein."

38. Gannon, *Martyrs of the United States of America*, 193–94.

39. Hughes, "Saints of To-morrow," 941, 943.

40. "Religion: St. Knute, St. Joyce?," 22.

41. Clipping, *Baltimore Catholic Review*, n.d., box 4, SJNC, RABP.

42. Waible, "A Centenary Sketch," box 5, SJNC, RABP.

43. Ireland to A. Litz, 4 August 1892, "Letters: Cause of Beatification," box 5, SJNC, RABP.

44. Duchesne's ordinary process on fame of sanctity was conducted in 1895 and 1896, while the process on the absence of cult was finished in 1900. See 5251 and 5248, CRP, ASV.

45. Francis Xav. Wernz to Reverend Mother General, 1 February 1912; Miccinelli to Revda M. Ferri, 21 November 1931; Miccinelli to Revda Madre, 13 July 1930, all in "Unofficial Letters about Cause," 2b, C-VII, Philippine Duchesne, AGSSC.

46. Ferrante, "John Nepomucene Neumann," 39, 51. See apostolic processes on Neumann's miracles conducted in Philadelphia in 1919 and in Regii Lepidi in 1924, 5439, CRP, ASV.

47. Cicognani, *Sanctity in America*, 129. For information on Duchesne's miracles, see apostolic processes conducted in Tauriana, Italy, in 1927 and in Rome in 1932–33, 5240 and 5241, CRP, ASV.

48. Shaw, "Some Heroines," 627.

49. M. G. Will to Rev. and dear Father, 5 March 1932, box 5, SJNC, RABP.

50. Waible, "A Centenary Sketch," box 5, SJNC, RABP; H. A. F., "Cause of the Ven. Bishop Neumann," 11.

51. For more on Dougherty, see Morris, *American Catholic*, esp. chapter 7, "God's Bricklayer."

52. Dougherty to William T. McCarty, 2 January 1940, "Beatification Cause Correspondence," box 5, SJNC, RABP.

53. Ferrante, "John Nepomucene Neumann," 53.

54. Code, "Contribution of Europe," 1218.

55. "Bohemians Hold Bishop Neumann in Reverence," *Baltimore Catholic Review*, 15 January, 1932, 2.

56. "Italians," box 19, SJNC, RABP.

57. John F. Byrne to A. H. Bleistein, 16 September 1935, "Beatification Cause Corre-

spondence," box 5, and "Languages," box 19, SJNC, RABP. The actual number of Neumann's spoken languages fluctuated between eight and twelve. The discrepancy likely resulted from how many "Slavic dialects" were considered as "full" languages. MacKinnon, "Voices for Philadelphia," 20.

58. Wüst [Wuest], "John N. Neumann," 323.

59. MacKinnon, "Voices for Philadelphia," 18.

60. E. Weigel, "New Glory of the American Hierarchy," 439.

61. "Neumann, St. John."

62. Waible, "Venerable John Neumann," 32; *Metropolitan Catholic Alumnae*.

63. E.g., Curley, "A Real Philadelphia Story," in "Tributes," box 19, SJNC, RABP.

64. In his letter to a "confrère," dated 19 June 1940, Redemptorist historian Michael Curley admitted that "you can safely say that John Neumann's work in this field has been exaggerated. The report that only three schools existed in 1852 and one hundred when he died probably comes from Father Berankek. Father Byrne wrote on this subject to Bishop McDevitt of Harrisburg (formerly Superintendent of Schools in the Archdiocese of Philadelphia) some years ago, and he wrote that there has been much overstatement regarding schools. The correspondence is at Esophus." See "Education," box 19, SJNC, RABP.

65. E. Weigel, "New Glory of the American Hierarchy," 439.

66. "57th Annual Report of the Superintendent of Schools," 9, CHRCAP.

67. M. Agatha Scott to My dear Father Wuest, 5 January 1911, box 5, SJNC, RABP.

68. Three German-speaking women had been preparing for religious life under the guidance of one of Neumann's fellow Redemptorists. While he was in Rome in 1854, Neumann received permission from the Franciscan superior general to receive them into religious life, and they were professed the following year. Curley, *Venerable John Neumann*, 250, 261. See also chap. 1 in this volume, "North American Saints."

69. Glennon, introduction, vii; Garraghan, "Holiness on the Frontier," 203.

70. Behrman, "Valiant Woman," 6, 20; Kurth, "Holiness Chez Nous," 85; Gilmore, "Mother Duchesne's Progress to Sanctity," 211; Windeatt, "Gemma and Euphrasia," 93.

71. McGreevy, *American Jesuits and the World*, esp. chap. 3, "Westphalia, Missouri: Nation."

72. Maynard, *Too Small a World*, 299.

73. Garraghan, "Holiness on the Frontier," 203.

74. Correspondence related to this extensive search, and Curley's find, is in "JNN Citizenship Documents," oversized box, SJNC, RABP.

75. Lyons, "Saints of the United States," 188.

76. See, for example, an advertisement titled "One-Day Pilgrimage to Bishop Neumann's shrine in Philadelphia, June 10, 1934," SJNC, RABP.

77. Schreck, manuscript, later published under the title *Written in Letters of Gold* by *Our Sunday Visitor* as a pamphlet, clippings file, SJNC, RABP.

78. Mecklin, "Passing of the Saint," 353.

79. Heiermann, "Sainthood," 34, 36–37.

80. Review of *Mother Philippine Duchesne*, by Marjory Erskine, 333.

81. Glennon, introduction, vii.

82. See program for "'A Daughter of Dauphiny, 1769–1852,' Triduum in honor of the beatification of Blessed Philippine Duchesne," San Francisco College of Women, Lone Mountain, San Francisco, California, February 6, 7, 8, 1941," and other examples in "Tridua celebrating her beatification—U.S.A.," 2b, C-VII, Philippine Duchesne, AGSSC.

83. Maynard, *Too Small a World*, 299.

84. Glennon, introduction, ix; "Two Americans May Be Added to Catholic Saints," *Springfield Sunday Union and Republican*, 6 March 1938, 6A.

85. Feeney, *Elizabeth Seton*, 2, 6.

86. Rev. Charles Souvay, "Word of Superiors," *The Echo of the Motherhouse*, January 1935, in "Important Letters Related to Cause," RG 1-3-5-8, APSL.

87. Meehan, "Repaying Our Debt to Italy," 4, 25.

88. "Pilgrims Carry Mother Seton Plea to the Vatican," *NCWC Bulletin*, 13 July 1931, 4.

89. The National Basilica of the Shrine of the Immaculate Conception, which opened in Washington, D.C., the same year as the celebration at St. Peter's, was the most ambitious such attempt. See Tweed, *America's Church*.

90. "An American Saint," 333–34; "Pilgrims Carry Mother Seton Plea to the Vatican."

91. Souvay, "Word of Superiors."

92. O'Donnell, *Elizabeth Ann Seton*.

93. Peter Guilday to Salvator M. Burgio, 15 November 1940, 80.5964, CHRCAP.

94. Hoare, *Virgin Soil*.

95. Wedge, "Saint from the Sidewalks of New York," 15.

96. Melville, *Elizabeth Bayley Seton*, 63n2.

97. So called because, at that point, Catholics were obligated to fast from midnight before receiving communion. E. Peters, *The 1917 Pio-Benedictine Code of Canon Law*, no. 858. "Communion breakfasts" were thus an opportunity to enjoy a longed-for meal and commemorate festive occasions.

98. Burns, "New Light on Mother Seton," 93.

99. Hughes, "A New York Saint," clipping, box 2, 100.150, ASCNY.

100. "Cardinal Pacelli, indeed, is himself considered one of the most likely candidates for St. Peter's throne upon the death of the present pope." Cortesi, "Pacelli Reported Seeking Aid of U.S. in Anti-Red Drive," *NYT*, 2 October 1936, 13.

101. Cicognani wrote that, after his election as Pope Pius XII, Pacelli recalled "how I had spoken to him of Mother Seton during his visit to the United States. His Holiness even indicated to me the exact time of our conversation, the evening of October 21, 1936, when I had the honor of motoring with him from Baltimore to Washington." *Sanctity in America*, 16.

102. The "New Woman" represented a significant emotional and spiritual threat to no few American Catholics. See Cummings, *New Women of the Old Faith*, 5–6.

103. Feeney, *Elizabeth Seton*, 17.

104. Marie, "Three Nun Converts of the Last Century."

105. According to some interpreters, young "Rosebud's" chance encounter with Pope Pius IX in the Vatican gardens during the family's sojourn in Rome foreshadowed her subsequent conversion to Catholicism. Hanley, "Rose Hawthorne Story," 73–74.

106. When Rose's husband, George Parsons Lathrop, died in 1898 as a result of his alcoholism, the couple had been estranged for several years.

107. Griffin, "The Lives of Elizabeth Ann Bayley and Rose Hawthorne Lathrop," box 12-A, folder 13, ADSH.

108. Clara Douglas (Mrs. James) Sheeran to "the Hierarchy of the United States," 23 October 1933, 80.6387, CHRCAP.

109. "150,000 Urge Mother Seton Be Named Saint: American Women Carry Petition to the Vatican," *Chicago Daily Tribune*, 23 July 1931, 13.

110. Clara Douglas (Mrs. James) Sheeran to "the Hierarchy of the United States," 23 October 1933, 80.6387, CHRCAP.

111. Burgio to Slattery, n.d., box 2, folder 17, 2D.4, DA-EPCM.

112. Souvay, "Word of Superiors."

CHAPTER 3

1. John LaFarge, "Jesuit—West Park, N.Y. Death of Cabrini (Eng. & Ital.) 1-2-1918," in "Eulogies 1917–1918," in "Cabrini's Death," CR-CU; LaFarge, *The Manner Is Ordinary*, 198; LaFarge, "Blessed Frances Cabrini," 124; LaFarge, "Mother Cabrini's Requiem," 304.

2. Simoni, introduction, ix.

3. Dailey, *Citizen Saint*, n.p. (chap. 3, "Expansion").

4. "'If God Wills It.'"

5. Cabrini's momentous audience with Leo did not take place during her first visit to Rome in 1887, as Dailey's essay suggests. In a letter written in October 1888 she refers to not being able to get an audience with the pope despite support from various members of the hierarchy. She grew more confident by December of that year, securing an audience in early January 1889. See the following in *Epistolario, vol. 1*: Cabrini to Sr. Maddelena Saveré, 1 October 1888, 69; Cabrini to Serafina Tommasi, 19 December 1888, 398; Cabrini to Suore della Casa di Castel San Giovanni, 21 December 1888, 401; and Cabrini to Prevosto, 17 January 1889, 413, the latter of which refers to an audience the week before. I am grateful to Maria Williams for helping me assemble this chronology.

6. Della Casa, "Distanze percorse," 271–72, in Cabrini's ordinary process on fame of sanctity, Chicago, 1928, 5636, CRP, ASV.

7. Salotti's address was published as a preface to de Maria, *La Madre Francesca Cabrini*. Salotti, prefazione, xiv. For another example of an account of Cabrini "abandoning" her dreams of China, see her *To the Ends of the Earth*, xvii.

8. Sullivan, *Mother Cabrini*, 45.

9. Quoted in M. Sullivan, *Mother Cabrini*, 79.

10. "Zeal for Souls Motivated Mother Cabrini's Life Work," *Chicago New World*, 18 November 18, 1938, 3.

11. "Recollections of Sr. Gabriella Linati," folder 3(a); "Memorie: Sister Umilia Capietti one of the 6 sisters who came to America with Cabrini 1899–1914," folder 3(b); folder 3(c); all in file D, CR-CU.

12. Fitzgerald, *Habits of Compassion*, 1–2.

13. M. Sullivan, *Mother Cabrini*, 80–81.

14. See Moreau, "Rise of the (Catholic) American Nation."

15. M. Sullivan, *Mother Cabrini*, 107.

16. Choate, *Emigrant Nation*, 1.

17. Choate, 23.

18. Cabrini to "my dearest Brother [Giovanni Battista Cabrini]," 27 June 1894, folder 1(a), file D, CR-CU.

19. According to one estimate, between 1907 to 1911, of every 100 Italians who arrived in the United States, 73 returned to Italy. See Foerster, *Italian Emigration*, 32.

20. Quoted in M. Sullivan, *Mother Cabrini*, 115.

21. *Canonizationis servae Dei Catharinae Mariae Drexel: Fundatricis Congregationis Sororum a SS. Sacramento pro Indis et Colorata Gente (1858–1955). Vol. I: Expositio historica et documenta* (Rome: Congregatio pro Causis Sanctorum, 1986), p. 733, KDC, CHRCAP.

22. *Canonizationis servae Dei Catharinae Mariae Drexel*, 733–34.

23. M. Sullivan, *Mother Cabrini*, 62, 121.

24. De Maria, *Mother Frances Xavier Cabrini*, 101, 341.

25. *In Memoria della Rev.ma Madre Francesca Saverio Cabrini*.

26. Malak, *Theresa of Chicago*, 113. An ordinary process on Dudzik's virtues was conducted in Chicago between 1979 and 1981, 9556–64, CRP, ASV.

27. Simoni, introduction, ix.

28. "Notes taken from material at Apostolic Delegation (Wash. DC) SML 1973," folder 141, in file E, CR-CU; "Bonzano eulogy (Apostolic Delegate 1-2-1918)," in "Correspondence U.S.A. Apostolic Delegates," folder 144(b), file E, CR-CU.

29. Salotti, preface, xv; Bonzano to Mundelein, December 1926, 13 1926 M 300; Salotti to Mundelein, 21 June 1928, 16 1928 M 202; Mundelein to Salotti (copy), 2 July 1928, Mundelein Correspondence, Archdiocese of Chicago's Joseph Cardinal Bernardin Archives and Records Center, Chicago, Ill.

30. "Account of Exhumation Cabrini's body 10-3-1993 and newspaper clippings," folder 14(b); "Letter: Cicognani to Sisters about Exhumation of S.F.X. Cabrini 10-19-33—other correspondence," folder 14(c), file H, CR-CU.

31. Amleto Cicognani to Antonietta Della Casa, 10 June 1935; "Letter from Cicognani to Sisters about Exhumation of S.F.X. Cabrini 10-19-33—and other correspondence," folder 14(c), file H, CR-CU.

32. See, for example, nos. 52–54 of Cabrini, *Journal of a Trusting Heart*.

33. Cited in M. Sullivan, *Mother Cabrini*, 36.

34. "Saint Frances Xavier Cabrini," 325. In 1952, the American Committee on Italian Migration proclaimed Cabrini the "Italian immigrant of the century," and four decades later Cabrini's most recent U.S. biographer, Mary Louise Sullivan, adopted that as the subtitle of her biography. See also Donato, *Immigrant Saint*.

35. "Cardinal Mundelein Calls Blessed Francis Cabrini a Real Christian Heroine," *New World*, 18 November 1938, 2.

36. "Zeal for Souls Motivated Mother Cabrini's Life's Work," *New World*, 18 November 1938, 3.

37. "Memorie," 26 February 1908, quoted in M. Sullivan, *Mother Cabrini*, 228.

38. Maynard, *Too Small a World*, 298.

39. Walsh, "Mother Cabrini," 232.

40. M. Sullivan, *Mother Cabrini*, 104.

41. LaFarge, "Blessed Frances Cabrini," 125.

42. "First American Saint," 264.

43. Walsh, "Mother Cabrini," 232.

44. Louisiana Works Progress Administration, "Poem of Holiness (Mother Cabrini)."

45. "Two Americans May Be Added to Catholic Saints," *Springfield Sunday Union and Republican*, 6 March 1938, 6A; "Sainthood Urged for 2 Nuns," *Boston Globe*, 6 March 1938, B40; "Causes of Mother Cabrini, Mother Duchesne Advance," *Catholic Action of the South*, 23 June 1938, 1, 5.

46. This quote appears on commemorative posters of the Smith mural, one of which hangs in the Cabriniana Room at Cabrini University. Stritch's comments on the twenty-fifth anniversary of Cabrini's death appear in Stritch, "Christian Perfection," 2.

47. O'Reilly, "Saint over the Hudson," 66–67.

48. Photographs, CR-CU.

49. Logan, "Recollection," 9.

50. M. Sullivan, *Mother Cabrini*, 246.

51. Lux, "Chicago's First Saint," 4; Dailey, *Citizen Saint*, epilogue; Maynard, *Too Small a World*, 298.

52. "Cardinal Mundelein's Address," *NYT*, 14 November 1938, 9.

53. Cicognani, *Sanctity in America*, 111.

54. Mons. C. Salotti, "La Madre Cabrini," speech on 4 January 1930, Rome, 17, translation from original Italian by author, Archivio Generale delle Missionarie del Sacro Cuore di Gesù (General Archive of the Missionary Sisters of the Sacred Heart of Jesus), Rome; Salotti, prefazione, xiv–xv.

55. See, for examples, obituaries titled "Una grande italiana" by A. Grossi-Grondi in *L'Osservatore Romano* and by Maddelena Patrizi in *Il Bollettino dell'Unione fra le Donne Cattoliche d'Italia*, reprinted in *In Memoria della Rev.ma Madre Francesca Saverio Cabrini*, 317–21 and 337–38.

56. See *Epistolario*, vol. 1: Cabrini to Sr. Maddalena Savaré, June 1889, 465. This line is quoted in D'Agostino, *Rome in America*, 58.

57. Maynard, *Too Small a World*, 300. For more on Maynard see Hendriks, "Theodore Maynard"; and Maynard, *Catholic Church*.

58. Gilbert and Maloney, "Reporter at Large," 36, 38.

59. LaFarge, "Blessed Frances Cabrini," 125.

60. Gerard, "Mother Cabrini," 591.

61. McCormick, "Current Events," 362–63.

62. See testimony of J. Willard Newman in apostolic process on Cabrini's virtues, 5639, CRP, ASV.

63. O'Sullivan, "St. Frances Xavier Cabrini," 351.

64. Ordinary processes on Cabrini's reputation for sanctity and absence of cult were conducted in Chicago in 1928, and another ordinary process was conducted in Lodi in 1929. Apostolic processes on her virtues were conducted in Chicago, New York, Lodi, and Rome in 1933. See 5636–41, CRP, ASV.

65. M. Sullivan, *Mother Cabrini*, 142.

66. Flatley, "Martin Scorsese's Gamble," *NYT*, 8 February 1976, SM9. The "Movie Script 'The Trial of Francesca Cabrini' (Savage-Scorsese)," which should be in folder 34(b), in "Movie Script and Times Article," file H, CR-CU, is missing. The only connection I have been able to find is a book published by Ronald Blake, which has no footnotes: *The Trial of Mother Cabrini*.

67. "1937 Cabrini declared Venerable (Letter M. Grazia) (Beatification Process)," folder 16(b), in "Beatification & Canonization Processes," file H, CR-CU.

68. Miller, "Miracle for the Bishop," 42.

69. All information about the miracles can be found in 5639, CRP, ASV.

70. M. Josephine to Reverend dear Mother, 1 February 1926, folder 12(d), file H, CR-CU.

71. See 5639, CRP, ASV.

72. After she was notified on 30 June, Mother Antonietta passed the notice on to superiors at MSC institutions throughout the world. See, for example, telegram sent from Grazia to Reverenda Madres, 8 July 1938, folder 18(a), file H, CR-CU.

73. Gilbert and Maloney, "Reporter at Large," 34.

74. "Facts Concerning Mother Seton's Cause," box 5, folder 10, 2D.4, DA-EPCM.

75. "Cardinal Mundelein in Interview," *New World*, 18 November 1938, 2.

76. Pamphlet, *Pilgrimage to Rome on the Occasion of the Beatification of the Venerable Mother Frances Xavier Cabrini, November 13, 1938*, folder 18(b), file H, CR-CU.

77. "Reminiscences of Sr. Ursula Infante MSC, and Mother Ignatius Dosini MSC from Queen of Heaven in Denver," folder 24, file H, CR-CU; "Name of Mother Cabrini Is Equal to a Poem." *New World* (Chicago), 18 November 1938, 3.

78. "Cardinal Mundelein Calls Blessed Frances Cabrini 'A Real Christian Heroine,'" *New World*, 18 November 1938, 2; "Mundelein Officiates at Cabrini Ceremony," *Chicago Evening American*, 14 November 1938.

79. "Reminiscences of Sr. Ursula Infante MSC, and Mother Ignatius Dosini MSC from Queen of Heaven in Denver," folder 24, file H, CR-CU.

80. Gilbert and Maloney, "Reporter at Large," 43.

81. "Reminiscences of Sr. Ursula Infante MSC, and Mother Ignatius Dosini MSC from Queen of Heaven in Denver," folder 24, file H, CR-CU.

82. "Millions Hear Beatification Broadcast," *New World*, 18 November 1938, 1; "Cardinal Mundelein's Address," *NYT*, 14 November 1938, 9.

83. "Cardinal Mundelein's Address," *NYT*, 14 November 1938, 9.

84. Lux, "Chicago's First Saint," 4.

85. See McCarthy, "Mother Cabrini: An Appreciation of Her Life's Work," PGEN 2/32, UNDA; and "Mother Cabrini Leaves Four Monuments Here: Southland Charitable Institutions Attest to Nun's Benevolent Activities," *Los Angeles Times*, 20 November 1938, A2.

86. "Cardinal Spellman—1st anniversary of the beatification of M. Cabrini," folder 26, file H, CR-CU.

87. Lux, "Chicago's First Saint," 4; Dorn, "New Missioner Saint," 16.

88. Simoni, "Mother Cabrini's Secret," 2.

89. Apostolic processes on these miracles were undertaken in 1940 and 1941. See 5642, 5643, CRP, ASV.

90. Salvator Burgio to Dennis Dougherty, 12 July 1947, Dougherty Correspondence, 80.2192, CHRCAP.

91. Quoted in Molloy, "Canonization of Mother Cabrini," 467.

92. Russ Vincent composed a tune, "Saint Frances Cabrini," which received a favorable review in a 1950 issue of *Billboard*, a popular entertainment weekly. "Billboard Music Popularity Charts," 35.

93. "First American Saint."

94. O'Sullivan, "St. Frances Xavier Cabrini," 351.

95. "Saint Frances Xavier Cabrini," 325.

96. Fremantle, "Sacred and Profane Success," 361.

97. Simoni, introduction, x.

98. Stritch, "Christian Perfection," 2.

99. Labella, "Day . . . in the Citadel of God," 54.

100. "In Memoriam," 2.

101. "Statue of St. Frances Cabrini," 4.

102. Farley, *Saints for the Modern Woman*, 37.

103. Even Cabrini's modern biographer, Mary Louise Sullivan, MSC, who was fluent in Italian, translates "Breve Ponteficio che Proclama S.F.S. Cabrini 'Patrona Degli Emigranti'" into "Patroness of Immigrants." M. Sullivan, *Mother Cabrini*, 285–86. For examples of British uses of the title, see [A Benedictine of Stanbrook Abbey], *Frances Xavier Cabrini*; and M. Williams, "Mobilising Mother Cabrini's Educational Practice."

CHAPTER 4

1. "Pope Urges Prayers for Miracles," 2.

2. Gannon's audience with Pope Pius XII took place on 14 September 1948. He recounts the meeting in *Martyrs of the United States of America*, 192–93.

3. McGinley, *Saint-Watching*, 44.

4. "Some Day, Perhaps . . . 'Elizabeth of New York'" [1939], clipping, box 2, 100.150, ASCNY; see also "Mother Cabrini to Be the First U.S. Saint: Her Beatification in Rome Today Stirs Hope of Other Elevations," clipping, *Chicago Herald and Examiner*, 13 November 1938, folder 25(a), file H, CR-CU.

5. Spellman, foreword, ix; Cooney, *American Pope.*

6. Pius XI, *Cum Proxime.* The fundamental motivation beyond Pius's extension, to a maximum of eighteen days (from the previous ten), remains murky. "Pius Says Conclave Must Wait for U.S.," *NYT*, 1 March 1922, 4. See also Castagna, *Bridge across the Ocean*, 78.

7. Cicognani, *Sanctity in America*, 16.

8. Biographical information on Burgio is found in box 1, folder 1, IH.2, DA-EPCM. See also "Blessed Are Those Who Die in the Lord," 1, 4.

9. Burgio's transcripts record a meeting with Cardinal Rossi on 21 February 1939 and Cardinal Salotti on 22 February. See Burgio, "Facts Concerning Mother Seton's Cause," box 5, folder 10, 2D.4, DA-EPCM.

10. Burgio, "Facts Concerning Mother Seton's Cause," box 5, folder 10, 2D.4, DA-EPCM.

11. A *New York Times* article that ran two weeks before the start of the conclave explained in great detail the methods used to sequester the cardinal electors, for the purpose of ensuring "that no mundane considerations should enter into such a vital function as the election of the head of the Roman Catholic Church." "Vatican Prepared to House Conclave," *NYT*, 14 February 1939, 8.

12. Burgio, "Facts Concerning Mother Seton's Cause," box 5, folder 10, 2D.4, DA-EPCM; Burgio, "Essential Requisites for Miracles," *MSGB*, October 1949, 1, 3.

13. Scognamillo to Cicognani, 19 April 1947, box 7, folder 3, 2D.4, DA-EPCM, translated from Italian by author.

14. Copy, Sister Hildegarde Marie Mahoney to Sister Elizabeth Vermaelen, 6 March 1991, in "Special Meeting, 1948," box 5, folder 20, EASC, ASCSE.

15. Dougherty made the remark during a visit to the Leonine College (the Vincentian college in Rome) on 25 February 1939, as reported in Burgio, "Facts Concerning Mother Seton's Cause," box 5, folder 10, 2D.4, DA-EPCM.

16. "Decree in the Baltimore Case Concerning the Beatification and Canonization of the Servant of God, Elizabeth Ann Bayley Seton, Widow, Foundress of the Congregation of the Sisters of Charity of St. Joseph," 28 February 1940, copy in box 5, folder 2, EASC, ASCSE.

17. "Decree in the Baltimore Case."

18. Copy, Sister Hildegarde Marie Mahoney to Sister Elizabeth Vermaelen, 6 March 1991, in "Special Meeting, 1948," box 5, folder 20, EASC, ASCSE; note by Rev. Robert Lennon, box 7, folder 8, 2D.4, DA-EPCM.

19. Burgio, "Story of the Dissension between the Emmitsburg Community of the Sisters of Charity and the Rev. Salvator M. Burgio," box 7, 2D.4, DA-EPCM.

20. *MSGB*, 8 December 1941, 1.

21. Burgio to Dougherty, 30 June 1939, Dougherty correspondence, 80.2121, CHRCAP.

22. Burgio, "Story of the Dissension between the Emmitsburg Community of the Sisters of Charity and the Rev. Salvator M. Burgio," box 7, 2D.4, DA-EPCM; copy, Mother Marie Vincentia McKenna, SC, to Rev. John F. Brady, 14 March 1924, in "History of the Process," ASCNY.

23. Circular letter #9, Salvator Burgio to Reverend Mothers General, Sisters Visitatrix and Sisters Secretary of the Sisters of Charity, 26 September 1941, box 5, folder 6, 2D.4, DA-EPCM.

24. Mother Maria's letter is quoted in Dorothy Stoner to Joanna Marie [Duffy], 28 October 1960, box 8, EASC, ASCSE.

25. In a letter dated 10 February 1971, Rev. Sylvester Taggart, CM, informed Mother Josephine Marie at St. Elizabeth's Convent, New Jersey, that, in light of a favorable financial situation, "I have decided that, as of December 31, 1970, it will no longer be necessary for your Community to send any money by way of 'Tax,' as it has been listed in our financial account over the years." Box 8, EASC, ASCSE.

26. Copy, Burgio to Sister Paula, 20 April 1940, box 5, folder 10, 2D.4, DA-EPCM.

27. Copy, Sister Paula to Burgio, 19 June 1940, box 5, folder 10, 2D.4, DA-EPCM.

28. Translation of letter from Carlo Salotti, 30 May 1941. See, for example, Burgio to Dante, 22 June 1948, in box 7, folder 3, 2D.4, DA-EPCM. I am uncertain whether Burgio remained at the same location in Emmitsburg after this. It is possible he moved to another location in the town that was not on Daughters of Charity property.

29. Burgio's side of the story is preserved in his extensive correspondence with Dougherty, Burgio's Vincentian superiors, and Vatican diplomats, as well as an eighty-four-page *apologia* he wrote near the end of his life. Sister Isabel did not leave much of a written record; she destroyed most of her correspondence related to the controversy and, even today, Daughters of Charity who remember the conflict remain reluctant to discuss it. Toohey's position and perspective, nonetheless, are easily inferred, both from Burgio's rendition of the story and from the correspondence that survives in the Spellman collection in AANY and in correspondence by Sister Hildegarde Mahoney in ASCSE.

30. Copy, Burgio to Slattery, 15 April 1946, box 7, folder 3, 2D.4, DA-EPCM. Emphasis in original.

31. Sister Isabel estimated that by 1948 the Daughters had contributed $6,000 to the cause. Minutes of Emmitsburg meeting, 6 September, APSL.

32. Sister Isabel to Scognamillo, 25 January 1945, multiple copies in DA-EPCM, translated from French by E. Jane Doering. This is the only extant source written from Sister Isabel's perspective.

33. E. Peters, *1917 Pio-Benedictine Code of Canon Law*, no. 2004.

34. Scognamillo to Toohey, 31 May 1945, copy in DA-EPCM.

35. Scognamillo to Cicognani, 19 April 1947, box 7, folder 3, 2D.4, DA-EPCM, translated from Italian by author.

36. Melville, "Writing a Saint's Biography," 71–77.

37. See seven letters between Cicognani and Burgio's provincial, Daniel M. Leary, 21 June 1946–30 November 1946, box 5, folders 10 and 11, 2D.4, DA-EPCM; Burgio to Cicognani, 2 February 1947, DA-EPCM.

38. Copy (original in Italian), Scognamillo to Cicognani, 19 April 1948, S/C-71, AANY.

39. Baudier, "Apostolic Court Meets to Study Remarkable Case of N.O. Sister,"

clipping, *Catholic Action of the South*, 30 November 1944, enclosed with Burgio's letters of 21 September and 20 November 1944, Dougherty Correspondence, 80.2148, CHRCAP. For Burgio's summary of the Korzendorfer case, see Burgio, "Essential Requisites for Miracles," *MSGB*, October 1949, 1, 3.

40. *MSGB*, October 1947, 2.

41. Burgio to Dougherty, 3 June 1946, Dougherty Correspondence, 80.2174, CHRCAP.

42. Copy, Francis Desmond to Scognamillo, 21 June 1946, DA-EPCM. Scognamillo's trust of Burgio is confirmed by the fact that he forwarded copies of these and other letters to Burgio.

43. He reported that Cabrini's congregation had pressured a reluctant Pius to schedule the canonization so soon after the war, as well as that U.S. attendance had been appallingly light. He also explained that he had used his Roman connections to secure choice seats for U.S. pilgrims. Burgio to Dougherty, 3 June 1946, Dougherty Correspondence, 80.2174, CHRCAP; Burgio to Gerald O'Hara, June–July 1946, DA-EPCM.

44. "Pope Urges Prayers for Miracles," 2.

45. Burgio to Dougherty, 8 May 1947, Dougherty Correspondence, 80.2190, CHRCAP.

46. Spellman, foreword, xi.

47. Hutton, "Future Pope Comes to America."

48. "Military Services, USA," 618.

49. "Cardinal Spellman, First Anniversary of Beatification of M. Cabrini," folder 26, file H, CR-CU.

50. Spellman, foreword, xi.

51. Mother Claudia to Spellman, 24 November 1959, folder 13, S/C-71, AANY.

52. McNamara to Spellman, 12 October 1959, folder 13, S/C-71, AANY.

53. Provincial annals, 13 April 1947, APSL.

54. Anonymous sister to Denise Gallo, "Remembrance of Sr. Rosa McGehee: Sr. Isabel Toohey and the start of the Seton Federation," January 2016, in author's possession.

55. "Minutes, First Conference of Mother Seton's Daughters, Saint Joseph's, Emmitsburg, Maryland," folder 2, S/C-71, AANY.

56. "Notes of Mother Mary Josephine," appended to "Minutes," folder 2, S/C-71, AANY.

57. "Notes of Mother Mary Josephine."

58. "Notes of Mother Mary Josephine."

59. Burgio to Dante, 22 June 1948, box 7, folder 3, 2D.4, DA-EPCM.

60. Cicognani told Daniel Leary that he had set up a meeting with Salotti in Rome to discuss the matter, but the prefect's illness had caused it to be postponed. There is no evidence that the conversation took place. Leary to Cicognani, 29 June 1946, and Cicognani to Leary, 22 July 1946, box 5, folders 10 and 11, 2D.4, DA-EPCM.

61. Cicognani, *Sanctity in America*, 16.

62. Burgio to Spellman, 12 and 15 April 1948, folder 4, S/C-71, AANY.

63. Copy, Spellman to Micara, 15 April 1948, folder 4, S/C-71, AANY.

64. Copy and translation, Micara to Spellman, 13 July 1948, box 2, folder 3, 100.150, ASCNY.

65. "Rev. Damian J. Blaher, O.F.M., to Spellman," 7 September 1948, folder 5, S/C-71, AANY.

66. Burgio to Spellman, 14 June 1948, folder 4, S/C-71, AANY.

67. Minutes of meeting, 6 September 1948, APSL.

68. Blaher, "To His Eminence Cardinal Spellman Pro Memoria on the Cause of Elizabeth Ann Seton," folder 5, S/C-71, AANY.

69. Sister Elizabeth [Vermaelen] to Sister Hildegarde [Mahoney], 6 March 1991, encl. "Minutes of a Special Meeting, of the Members of the Mother Seton Conference convened by His Eminence Cardinal Francis Spellman, September 13, 1948, Mount St. Vincent-on-Hudson," box 5, folder 20, EASC, ASCSE.

70. Rev. Charles T. Bridgeman, letter to the editor, *Jubilee*, November 1960, 7.

71. Antonelli to McNamara, 27 September 1948, "Miscellaneous Letters, 1922–1959," box 5, EASC, ASCSE.

72. Burgio to Spellman, 19 January 1949, box 2, folder 17, 2D.4, DA-EPCM. Emphasis in original.

73. C. White, *Mother Seton*, 462.

74. Cicognani, foreword to *Mother of Many Daughters*, xvi.

75. Burgio to Cicognani, 2 November 1953, box 7, folder 2, DA-EPCM. The Daughters may well have overreacted, as it is unclear how any interpreter—even Burgio—could have argued that the union with France abrogated their connection to Seton. Nevertheless, there is some evidence to suggest that rumors to that effect lingered among the diocesan sisters. See, for example, letters from McGowan to sisters from Convent station in 1962, in which he dismisses such suggestions as "nonsense." Box 8, EASC, ASCSE

76. "Facts Concerning the Sisters of Charity, Emmitsburg, Maryland, in Reply to Questions Presented by Reverend Salvator Burgio, C.M., Vice Postulator," APSL 13 16 2 (#3); Burgio to Cicognani, 2 November 1953, box 7, folder 2, DA-EPCM.

77. Burgio to Scognamillo, 13 October 1950, box 7, folder 2, 2D.4, DA-EPCM.

78. Scognamillo to Burgio, 27 October 1950, box 7, folder 2, 2D.4, DA-EPCM.

79. Scognamillo to Burgio, 27 October 1950.

80. Burgio to Dougherty, 11 December 1950, Dougherty Correspondence, 80.2204, CHRCAP.

81. Burgio to Cicognani, 2 November 1953, box 7, folder 2, 2D.4, DA-EPCM.

82. Micara to Scognamillo, 18 January 1951, "Translation of Declaration and Mandate," box 7, 2D.4, DA-EPCM.

83. Copy, Burgio to Hannan, 4 August 1952, box 5, folder 15, EASC, ASCSE.

84. "Will, 1954," folder 10, IH.2, DA-EPCM.

85. Burgio to Cicognani, 2 November 1953, box 7, folder 2, 2D.4, DA-EPCM; Burgio to Montini, 12 September 1953, box 7, folder 2, 2D.4, DA-EPCM.

86. Melville, "Writing a Saint's Biography," 75–76. On 20 February 1985, tributes to Seton were read out in both the U.S. House and Senate. Congresswoman Beverly Byron called Seton's school "the original parochial school"; Senator Paul Sarbanes specifically

called it "the precursor of the American parochial school system." Byron, "Mother Seton School"; Sarbanes, "Mother Seton School," 2761.

87. Seton to Carroll, 13 May and 5 September 1811, quoted in Melville, *Elizabeth Bayley Seton*, 160–61.

88. Elizabeth Seton to Cecilia Seton, October 1808, quoted in Melville, *Elizabeth Bayley Seton*, 141. Since the publication of Melville's biography, other historians, including several of Mother Seton's daughters, have further illuminated the story of the founding years. See, for example, McNeil, "Sulpicians and Sisters of Charity"; and Metz, "By What Authority?"

89. McGuinness, *Called to Serve*, 158–60.

90. Detailed accounts of Antonelli's testimony can be found in two documents deposited in the General Archives of the Congregation of the Mission in Rome, *Positio super virtutibus ex officio disposita*, 18 June 1957, and *Relazione presentata all'E.mo Sig. Card. Gaetano Cicognani prefetto della S. Congregazione dei Riti dal Rev.mo P. Relatore Generale sulla seduta della sezione storica del 13 Novembre 1957*. For *animadversiones* (objections) raised before the cause was introduced, see Natucci, *Relazione sommaria presentata all'E.mo Signor Card. Carlo Salotti, 14 Agosto 1939*. All in Seton canonization material, GA-CM.

91. Code, "Eulogy Preached," reprinted in *MSGB*, September 1959, 2.

92. "An Editorial," 4.

93. E. Peters, *1917 Pio-Benedictine Code of Canon Law*, no. 203.

94. Cicognani to Spellman, 11 June 1959, folder 13, S/C-71, AANY.

95. After the discussion in 1957, the Sacred Congregation needed to vote on Seton's virtues in three separate sessions, called "antepreparatory," "preparatory," and "general" congregations. Correspondence between Spellman and Cicognani reveals that these took place in October and November 1959.

96. Spellman to McNamara, 6 October 1959, folder 13, S/C-71, AANY.

97. Cicognani to Spellman, 19 September 1959, folder 13, S/C-71, AANY.

98. Attwater, *Saints Westward*, 6, 7–8, 9.

99. Spellman to Enrico Galeazzi, 16 June 1959, folder 13, S/C-71, AANY.

100. Clipping, *Philadelphia Inquirer*, box 5, folder 12, 2D.4, DA-EPCM.

101. Dirvin, "Three Saints," 1.

102. Francis X. Murphy, "Sainthood and Politique," *The Tablet*, 18 June 1977, 574.

103. "Military Services, USA," 618.

104. Fogarty, *Vatican and the American Hierarchy*, 268.

105. Copy, O'Hara to Rev dear father, 1 February 1952, 107.25, CHRCAP. "The exhortation of his Excellency the Apostolic Delegate to further the cause of Venerable John N. Neumann, former bishop of Philadelphia, deserves our earnest attention. This year, 1952, marks the centenary of the consecration of this venerable prelate as Bishop of Philadelphia, so our prayers for the advancement of his cause should be given without stint."

106. O'Hara to Curley, 15 December 1952, box 3, Correspondence, Michael J. Curley Papers, RABP.

107. O'Hara-Missig correspondence, 6 November 1953, 107.32, CHRCAP.

108. Boland, *Dictionary of the Redemptorists*, 453.

109. Copy, O'Hara to Heston, 14 May 1958, in "Process," box 19, SJNC, RABP.

110. Based on Curley's findings that Neumann had received permission to establish the Philadelphia Franciscans, had written its rule, and received its first members into religious life, O'Hara thought there was a chance Neumann could be recognized as the founder of the community. Copy, O'Hara to Heston, 14 May 1958, in "Process," box 19, SJNC, RABP. O'Hara's letter reproduced the content of the letter Francis Litz had written to him two days earlier. Litz to O'Hara, 12 May 1958, 107.48, O'Hara Correspondence, CHRCAP.

111. Heston to O'Hara, 24 May 1958, box 19, SJNC, RABP.

112. Quoted in Gallese, "The Good Fight," *Wall Street Journal*, 25 June 1975, clipping in "Process," box 19, SJNC, RABP; Burgio, "Essential Requisites for Miracles," *MSGB*, October 1949, 6.

113. "Father Burgio's Address"; McGowan to Johanna Maria, 4 January 1962, box 7, EASC, ASCSE.

114. Johanna Maria to Ernest O'Brien, 27 January 1964, box 7, EASC, ASCSE.

115. Miller, "Miracle for the Bishop," 42.

116. See, for example, "Recoveries Whose Documentation Has Been Forwarded to Rome" and "Summary of Cures as of May, 1970," in "Cures," box 19, SJNC, RABP.

117. Litz, "Meet Bishop Neumann," November 1957, presentation to the Catholic Libraries Conference, in "Sermons and Lectures," box 19, SJNC, RABP.

118. "JNN Citizenship Documents," oversized folder, and "Allied Documents I," box 19, SJNC, RABP. The date on which Neumann became a citizen was 10 February 1848.

119. Copy, petition of U.S. bishops to Most Holy Father, 13 November 1957, in SJNC, GA-CSSR.

120. "Vatican's No. 2," 52.

121. Cicognani, foreword to *Venerable John Neumann*, vii. Cicognani's name appears frequently in Ferrante's correspondence after 1959, and it seems that Cicognani discussed the cause with his brother Gaetano during the latter's tenure as prefect of the Congregation of Rites.

122. O'Hara to Litz, 30 March 1959, "Drexel Fund," RABP. Litz's report of Bishop Neumann's activities for 1959 shows that O'Hara authorized a trust fund of $50,000 for the cause, established from Drexel's bequests from St. Peter's and St. Boniface's. "Bishop Neumann Activities—1959," box 19, SJNC, RABP.

123. "Bishop Neumann Activities—1959," box 19, SJNC, RABP.

124. O'Hara to Heston, 24 May 1958, box 19, SJNC, RABP.

125. Ferrante, "John Nepomucene Neumann," 53–54; "Cures," box 19, SJNC, RABP.

126. Ferrante's frustration with Krol's behavior is a running theme throughout Ferrante's correspondence, but the phrase "unfavorable impressions" appears in Ferrante's letter to Litz in reference to a scheme proposed by archdiocesan chancellor Monsignor James McGrath, 15 January 1976, in "Postulator," box 19, SJNC, RABP.

127. Copy, Litz to Krol, 7 February 1962, and attached "Memorandum," in "Chancery," box 19, SJNC, RABP.

128. E. Peters, *1917 Pio-Benedictine Code of Canon Law*, no. 1168.3: "Churches cannot be dedicated to Blesseds without an indult of the Apostolic See."

129. According to the 1911 *Catholic Encyclopedia*, "Rescripts are responses of the pope or a Sacred Congregation, in writing, to queries or petitions of individuals. . . . Rescripts have the force of a particular law, i.e., for the persons concerned." A. Meehan, "Papal Rescripts." Contemporary canon law defines a rescript generally as the granting of a favor or dispensation directly from the Holy See. E. Peters, *1917 Pio-Benedictine Code of Canon Law*, no. 35.2.

130. Copy, Shehan to Cicognani, 21 May 1963, APSL. See also Shehan to Cicognani, 25 April 1963, APSL. A copy of the rescript, dated 2 May 1963 and issued by the Sacra Rituum Congregatio, Prot. Num. B. 22/963, as well as an English translation by Rev. Daniel Nusbaum, are in APSL. Though the location of the proposed shrine was not named in this correspondence, it was almost certainly the one Spellman had in mind for New York, which opened in 1964.

131. Burgio, "Case of Acute Leukemia"; Congdon, "Making of a Saint," 77; Briggs, "For Mother Seton, Sainthood Crowns Career in Church," *NYT*, 13 December 1974; Barthel, "A Saint for All Reasons," *NYT*, 14 September 1975, 13F; Boursiquot and Reddoch, "Approved Miracle of Saint Elizabeth Ann Seton."

132. McGowan to Spellman Correspondence, folder 14, S/C-71, AANY.

133. McGowan to Spellman, 16 June 1962, and Larraona to Spellman, 17 June 1962, folder 14, S/C-71, AANY.

134. "Mother Seton Beatified," 2; de Lourdes, "Travelogue to Beatitude," 57.

135. Wynne, "Triduum." Cardinal priests and deacons are all assigned "titles" or diaconates in the City of Rome; Peters, *1917 Pio-Benedictine Code of Canon Law*, no. 231. Spellman, as a cardinal priest, held the title of Santi Giovanni e Paolo, as did all his successors in New York through Cardinal Edward Egan.

136. De Lourdes, "Travelogue to Beatitude," 53.

137. Congdon, "Making of a Saint," 75.

138. "Blessed Mother Seton's Remains Enshrined," 1.

139. Ferrante to Litz, 23 June 1974, SJNC, GA-CSSR.

140. Sheen to Ferrante, 18 September 1963, Ferrante Papers, SJNC, GA-CSSR.

141. Rynne, "Saint," 26.

142. Bernard to Spellman, n.d. [before 10 November 1964, when he replied], folder 15, S/C-71, AANY.

143. McGowan to "My Dear Confrere" [circular letter], copy in box 8, EASC, ASCSE.

144. Pronechen, "Where a Saint Started," *National Catholic Register*, 4–10 July 1999, 11.

145. Matthews to Spellman, 22 February 1964, folder 15, S/C-71, AANY.

CHAPTER 5

1. Slominski, "Mother Cabrini," 1.

2. Cipolla, "Francesca Cabrini"; Tusiani, *Envoy from Heaven*, 131, 6.

3. While there is wide disagreement among Christian denominations over the validity of certain ecumenical councils, the Roman Catholic Church and churches in communion with it counted twenty at the time John convoked Vatican II.

4. O'Malley, *What Happened at Vatican II*, 12.

5. Cummings, Matovina, and Orsi, *Catholics in the Era of Vatican II*.

6. O'Malley, *What Happened at Vatican II*, 12, 51, 175–76.

7. Tusiani, *Envoy from Heaven*, 6.

8. The Sisters of Charity at Mount St. Vincent had hired Tusiani in 1948—coincidentally, just a few weeks before Cardinal Spellman hosted the "emergency" meeting at the college.

9. "Homily of Christopher O'Toole," University of Notre Dame, 17 March 1963, "Beatification Homilies," box 8, folder 2, EASC, ASCSE.

10. Ferrante to Litz, 13 August 1972, SJNC, GA-CSSR.

11. For a detailed history, see F. Sullivan, *Salvation outside the Church?*

12. O'Malley, *What Happened at Vatican II*, 85.

13. When he re-released his biography—newly subtitled *St. Elizabeth of New York*—Feeney revised one passage to refer more politely to Orthodox Jews. Feeney, *Mother Seton*, 120; Rousseau, *Du contrat social*, UNDL. The University of Notre Dame holds a copy of Rousseau owned by Seton; a note from her grandson Robert inside reads, "My grandmother . . . used this volume at a period of her early married life when she was so unfortunate as to become somewhat enamored of the French infidel literature. I had it rebound in 1875, the old binding being much damaged." In a post–Vatican II climate, for example, Seton's preconversion literary interests appeared less as flirtations with what her grandson once called "infidel literature" and more as evidence of her spiritual openness and breadth. See O'Donnell, *Elizabeth Ann Seton*.

14. See, for examples, Flanagan, "Influence of John Henry Hobart"; and Cassidy, "Address Given," in "Beatification Homilies," box 8, folder 2, ASCSE.

15. Rev. Charles T. Bridgeman, letter to the editor, *Jubilee*, November 1960, 7.

16. "Protestant Leaders Praise Canonization of Neumann," *Our Sunday Visitor*, 3 July 1977.

17. "Domestic Religious Intelligence," 449–50.

18. Though Murphy refused—until 1989—to admit to being Rynne, even to his Redemptorist superiors, most suspected it. Hayes, "'Bless Me Father.'"

19. Rynne, *Third Session*, 12; "Fathers End Talk on Chapter 7," *Catholic Messenger* (Davenport, Iowa), 24 September 1964, 6.

20. Cantwell, "World Has Its Saints, Too," 1–2.

21. Lind, "Wanted," 55.

22. Transcript of Woodward interview with Molinari, box 5, folder 19, 14, CKLW, UNDA; Molinari, *Saints*, v.

23. Second Vatican Council, *Lumen Gentium*, para. 50.

24. See Second Vatican Council, chap. 7, footnote 9; Abbott and Gallagher, *Documents of Vatican II*, 82n236; and Rush, "Second Vatican Council," 183–90.

25. O'Malley, *What Happened at Vatican II*, 9.

26. Murphy, *John Nepomucene Neumann*, 91.

27. "Conditions favoring Canonization," n.d., in 1968 folder, Ferrante Papers, SJNC, GA-CSSR.

28. Litz to Ferrante, 23 December 1965, Correspondence, SJNC, GA-CSSR.

29. "Role in Canonizing Urged for Bishops," *NYT*, 17 September 1964, 1, 4.

30. Rynne, *Third Session*, 12; "Fathers End Talk on Chapter 7," *Catholic Messenger*, 24 September 1964, 6.

31. Veraja, "For the Causes of the Saints: Commentary on the New Legislation," box 7, folder 1, CKLW, UNDA; Antonelli, "Commentary," *L'Osservatore Romano*, 17 April 1969, clipping, in "Process," box 19, SJNC, RABP. It is more precise to say that Paul VI suppressed the Sacred Congregation of Rites and created two new, separate dicasteries: the Congregation for Divine Worship and the Congregation for the Causes of Saints.

32. Suenens argued, "*Women* too should be *invited* as auditors; unless I am mistaken, they make up half of the human race." Suenens, "Charismatic Dimension," 34, emphasis in original; John L. Allen, Jr. "Remembering the Women of Vatican II," *National Catholic Reporter*, 12 October 2012, https://www.ncronline.org/blogs/ncr-today/remembering-women-vatican-ii.

33. Suenens, *Nun in the World*.

34. Kerins, "Homily on Women Religious at the Mass in St. Mary Major, Rome, in Honor of St. John Neumann, C.S.s.R., June 20, 1977," in "Homilies," box 8, SJNC, RABP.

35. Second Vatican Council, *Perfectae Caritatis*.

36. Schneiders, *Buying the Field*, 599–600.

37. Schneiders, 603.

38. Second Vatican Council, *Gaudium et Spes*, para. 1.

39. For valuable perspectives on the intersection between social change and council mandates in the lives of American sisters, see Ware, *Midwives of the Future*, especially essays by Mary Luke Tobin, SL, Margaret Ellen Traxler, and Jeannine Grammick.

40. Traxler, "After Selma."

41. Muckenhirn, *New Nuns*, esp. chap. 1; Novak, "New Nuns"; Koehlinger, *New Nuns*, 57, 59, 60, 101, 109, 142, 199, 216.

42. Cassidy, "Address Given," in box 8, folder 2, EASC, ASCSE.

43. Ellis, "The Catholic Laywoman and the Apostolate of Our Time," address to the Nation Council of Catholic Women, 6 November 1962, NCCW (10), box 24, American Catholic History Research Center and University Archives, Washington, D.C.

44. Ellis, "Saint Elizabeth Ann Seton in 1977," address delivered at the Seton Founder's Award Convocation, 14 May 1977, Pamphlet Collection, UNDL.

45. Stadick, "Saint Patrons," 130.

46. Sister Marie Amanda, "Minutes of the Mazzuchelli Commission Meeting, May

1972," "Mazzuchelli Guild Bulletins/Mazzuchelli Guild Meetings/Mazzuchelli Guild," drawer 1, Cabinet 9, SDA.

47. "Minutes of the Mazzuchelli Guild," April 1964, May 1972, SDA; [McGreal], "Possible Topics for Mazzuchelli 'Briefs,'" n.d., in "Mazzuchelli Guild Bulletins/ Mazzuchelli Guild Meetings/Mazzuchelli Guild," drawer 1, cabinet 9, SDA; Pat Marrin, "Sr. Mary Nona McGreal, Historian and Educator, Dies," *National Catholic Reporter*, 27 March 2013, https://www.ncronline.org/news/people/sr-mary-nona-mcgreal -historian-and-educator-dies. McGreal was involved in the ordinary processes conducted in Madison and Milwaukee on Mazzuchelli's virtues and absence of cult in 1966 and 1967. See 9326–29, CRV, ASV.

48. For Guerín's ordinary processes in Indianapolis on fame of sanctity (1915, 1937) and absence of cult (1930), see 9165–67, CRP, ASV.

49. Apostolic processes on Guerín's virtues were undertaken before Vatican II: in Indianapolis between 1956 and 1958 and in the Diocese of Saint-Brieuc (France) in 1958. See 9168–80, CRP, ASV. See also Briggs, *Third Miracle*, 44–46.

50. Apostolic processes on miracles attributed to Duchesne were conducted in St. Louis in 1954 and in Gratianopolitan (a now-defunct Roman Catholic diocese in the Maghreb desert that is now a Latin titular see) in 1955. See 7814–16, CRP, ASV.

51. Thanks to Patricia Byrne for the citations related to Mother Bernard's cure and the novena undertaken on her behalf: San Francisco College for Women, House Journal entry for 27 September 1951, VIII G 1 b, ARSCJ; D'Avrack, "Account of M. Bernard's illness and cure," 20 November 1959, I D 1 b 10) e) (28), ARSCJ. The official testimony on the miracle was gathered in 1961. See 7818–21, CRP, ASV.

52. Copies of the *Duchesne Guild Bulletin*, box 3, folder 2, packet 2, Duchesne Collection, ARSCJ. See also Osiek, *Kathryn Sullivan, RSCJ*, 55.

53. Spellman to Sullivan, 25 September 1964, S/R-11, AANY.

54. Patricia Byrne, SSJ, helped me understand the significance of the 1964 chapter and supplied the following citations: Clôture (Conférence de Notre T. R. Mère de Valon), *Directives et Décisions du 26me Chapitre Général, 15 Octobre–15 Novembre 1964*, Nouvelle édition, Décembre 1967, 26–33; and Byrne, "Change in the Society of the Sacred Heart: Cloister," paper given at the Conference on the History of Women Religious, University of Scranton, 27–30 June 2010 [excerpt].

55. Sullivan to Spellman, 3 December 1964, S/R-11, AANY.

56. Osiek, *Kathryn Sullivan*, esp. chap. 3.

57. Mooney, *Philippine Duchesne*, 10. I am grateful to Margaret Phelan, RSCJ, archivist at the congregation's generalate in Rome, for confirming that, contrary to Mooney's claim that the "Society of the Sacred Heart decided not to promote her cause beyond beatification," the council minutes suggest a more gradual falling away from pursuit of the cause, as opposed to an explicit resolution not to move forward. Council minutes, 1 May 1968, AGSSC.

58. Gallese, "The Good Fight," *Wall Street Journal*, 25 June 1975, clipping in box 23, folder 10, "Federation Canonization Committee," EASC, ASCSE.

59. Sister Teresa [surname unclear], "Mother Seton's Canonization," *Wall Street Journal*, 15 August 1975, clipping in box 23, folder 10, EASC, ASCSE.

60. Valli Ryan to Sister Patricia Noone, 6 August 1975, box 23, "Federation Canonization Publicity Committee," EASC, ASCSE.

61. Graham, "Are Canonizations an Unnecessary Expense?," 23.

62. Quoted in Gallese, "Good Fight."

63. McGinley, *Saint-Watching*, 44.

64. "Reverend Mother M. Anselm's Invitation," *The Peacemaker*, April–June 1964, Drexel Beatification file, ASBS.

65. Burton, *To the Golden Door*; Burton, "Mother Katharine Drexel," 260.

66. Margaret Kuehmstedt, secretary to the Sisters of the Blessed Sacrament for over thirty years, provided details and amounts in a confidential letter to Alexander Palmieri, 22 March 2000, box 1, folder 4, 2000.051, KDC, CHRCAP.

67. Martino to Palmieri, 3 January 1994, KDC, CHRCAP.

68. Juliana Haynes to Kenneth Woodward, 5 March 1990, box 1, folder 2, CKLW, UNDA.

69. "Mother M. Katharine Drexel (1858–1955)," in "Drexel," box 19, SJNC, RABP.

70. *The Peacemaker*, April–June 1964; "Mother M. Katharine Drexel (1858–1955)," and "Copy of Petition, Joseph L. Bernardin, President, National Conference of Catholic Bishops to His Holiness Pope Paul VI," 12 February 1975, in "Drexel," box 19, SJNC, RABP.

71. Quoted in Brown, "Does Mother Drexel Deserve to Be a Saint?," *Philadelphia Inquirer*, 6 October 1974, in "Drexel," box 19, SJNC, RABP.

72. Quoted in Brown, "Does Mother Drexel Deserve to Be a Saint?"

73. Testimony of Marie Enfanta Gonzales, 9 February 1981, in *Philadelphien. Canonizationis servae Dei Catharinae Mariae Drexel: Fundatricis Congregationis Sororum a SS. Sacramento pro Indis et Colorata Gente (1858–1955). Vol. II: Summarium depositionum testium* (Rome: Congregatio pro Causis Sanctorum, 1986), 320–24, 1992.013, KDC, CHRCAP.

74. Drexel to J. R. Slattery, 12 December 1898, 14-E-8 H10A box 26, Slattery, Fr. JR MMK letters, ASBS.

75. "Mother M. Katharine Drexel (1858–1955)," in "Drexel," box 19, SJNC, RABP.

76. Alexander, "A Tribute to Mother Katharine Drexel," 10 February 1966, box 1, 2010.083, KDC, CHRCAP, later published in the *Negro History Bulletin* 29 (Fall 1966): 181–82, 184, 189, 191–92.

77. Tarry, *Katharine Drexel*, ix, x.

78. Testimony of Dr. Norman Francis, 9 February 1981, reprinted in *Philadelphien. Canonizationis servae Dei Catharinae Mariae Drexel. Vol. II: Summarium depositionum testium*, 363–73, 1992.013, KDC, CHRCAP.

79. Testimony of Marie Enfanta Gonzales, 323.

80. Ledoux, "Mother Drexel Overcame Long before It Was Fashionable," *Morning Star* (New Orleans), 25 March 1976, clipping in Drexel Beatification file, ASBS.

81. Testimony of Warren L. Bordreaux, 10 February 1981, reprinted in *Philadelphien. Canonizationis servae Dei Catharinae Mariae Drexel. Vol. II: Summarium depositionum testium*, 352–62, 1992.013, KDC, CHRCAP.

82. Bishop Leo T. Maher, quoted in "Father Serra Foreseen as a 'Saint' for Ecologists," *Our Sunday Visitor*, 31 August 1975, 12; Moholy, quoted in Ursula Vils, "Padre Lives by Spirit of Serra," *Los Angeles Times*, October 1969, clipping in "Vice-Postulator Neil Moholy scrapbook," 115, Serra Cause Historical Collection, SBMAL; Moholy, quoted in Taylor, "Serra Almost a Saint," *Peninsula Herald Weekend Magazine* (Monterey), 20 October 1974, clipping in "Moholy scrapbook," 130–32.

83. Journalist Kenneth Woodward provided a detailed analysis of this issue in *Making Saints*, his book-length study of the canonization process; more recently, historians have turned their attention to Drexel's racial attitudes as well. See the work of Shannen Dee Williams on race in American women's religious life: *Subversive Habits* (forthcoming) and "Desegregating the Habit" (under review).

84. Tobin, "Women and the Church," 244.

85. Coston, "Open Windows," 147.

86. See, for examples, "Memo for Congregation for Religious on Sisters' Survey, June 1969," box 10, folder 15; Haughey, "Where Has Our Search Led Us," box 10, folder 18; and "Proposed Name Changes to CMSW," CLCW, UNDA.

87. In 1988, John Paul II changed the title to Congregation for Institutes of Consecrated Life and Societies of Apostolic Life.

88. "Proposed name changes to CMSW," October 1970, box 10, folder 18; press release, 23 August 1971, box 10, folder 22, CLCW, UNDA; Quiñonez and Turner, *Transformation of American Catholic Sisters*, 28.

89. Quoted in Ruether and McLaughlin, *Women of Spirit*, 374.

90. "Proposed name changes to CMSW," October 1970, box 10, folder 18; press release, 23 August 1971, box 10, folder 22, CLCW, UNDA. Now known as the Council of Major Superiors of Women Religious, this organization was granted canonical recognition in 1992. "Council of Major Superiors of Women—Canonical Status—1983, 1992," box 9, folder 36, Consortium Perfectae Caritatis Collection, UNDA; "Years of the Second Vatican Council."

91. "Mother M. Katharine Drexel (1858–1955)," in "Drexel," box 19, SJNC, RABP.

92. "Copy of Petition, Joseph L. Bernardin, President, National Conference of Catholic Bishops to His Holiness Pope Paul VI," in "Drexel," box 19, SJNC, RABP. Emphasis in original.

93. Sacred Congregation for the Doctrine of the Faith, "Declaration *Inter Insigniores*."

94. Testimony of Most Reverend Joseph McShea, 4 May 1981, reprinted in *Philadelphien. Canonizationis servae Dei Catharinae Mariae Drexel. Vol. II: Summarium depositionum testium*, 228, 1992.013, KDC, CHRCAP.

95. Kerins, "Homily on Women," in "Homilies," box 8, SJNC, RABP.

96. Ellis, "Saint Elizabeth Ann Seton in 1977," Pamphlet Collection, UNDL.

97. Cassidy, "Address," box 8, folder 2, EASC, ASCSE.

98. Sister Marie Amanda, "Minutes of the Mazzuchelli Commission Meeting, May

1972," "Mazzuchelli Guild Bulletins/Mazzuchelli Guild Meetings/Mazzuchelli Guild," drawer 1, Cabinet 9, SDA.

99. Quoted in Barthel, "A Saint for All Reasons," *NYT*, 14 September 1975, 13F.

100. See correspondence between Taggart and Rev. James D. Collins, CM, April 1972–December 1973, box 5, folder 3, EASC, ASCSE.

101. Murphy, *John Nepomucene Neumann*, 5.

102. See various articles in clippings file, box 6, folder 5, 2D.4, DA-EPCM.

103. Paul VI, "Canonization of Elisabeth [*sic*] Ann Seton."

104. "Saint for America," 59.

105. Paul VI, "Canonization of Elisabeth Ann Seton."

106. Copy, Sister Hildegarde Marie Mahoney to Sister Elizabeth Vermaelen, 6 March 1991, in "Special Meeting, 1948," box 5, folder 20, EASC, ASCSE.

107. Graham, "Are Canonizations an Unnecessary Expense?," 23.

108. Duffy, *Stripping of the Altars*.

109. Dolan, *In Search of an American Catholicism*, 238.

110. Dirvin quoted in D. Peters, "What Does Seton Say to Modern Women?," 29.

CHAPTER 6

1. Information related to the Michael Flanagan miracle is in SJNC, GA-CSSR. See also "Canonization," box 19, SJNC, RABP. As for the exemption, neither the Sacred Congregation nor the Redemptorists made the reason public. It could well have been that the Sacred Congregation had finally agreed to acknowledge Neumann as the "founder" of the Philadelphia Franciscans and awarded him exemption on those grounds. The sisters certainly accepted him as their founder; they celebrated his canonization enthusiastically and renamed their Aston college in his honor. Ferrante's correspondence hints that he and other influential Redemptorists pressured the Sacred Congregation to canonize Neumann under the same conditions it had Seton.

2. Byerley, *St. John Neumann*, 1.

3. Griffith, *Moral Combat*, 202, 226.

4. Since 1588, the year the Sacred Congregation was established by the constitution *Immensa æterni Dei* of Pope Sixtus V. Ott, "Pope Sixtus V."

5. For a list of saints canonized by John Paul II, see "Canonizzazioni del Santo Padre Giovani Paolo II," Vatican website, http://www.vatican.va/news_services/liturgy/saints/index_saints_en.html; John Paul II, "Discorso di Giovanni Paolo II ai Cardinali di Tutto il Mondo Convocati in Vaticano per il Concistoro Straordinario," Vatican website, http://w2.vatican.va/content/john-paul-ii/it/speeches/1994/june/documents/hf-jp-ii_spe_19940613_concistoro-straordinario.html; "Why John Paul II Proclaimed So Many Saints: Interview with Cardinal Saraiva Martins," Zenit, 4 April 2006, https://zenit.org/articles/why-john-paul-ii-proclaimed-so-many-saints/.

6. John Paul II canonized her in 2004. Cummings, "American Saints," 203; Higgins, *Stalking the Holy*, 68–72.

7. John Paul also applied this principle to regions underrepresented in the canon of

the saints, including those within Italy—hardly a country with a shortage of saints. See Ciciliot, "'Heritage Talks'"; and Catanoso, *My Cousin the Saint*, esp. chap. 1.

8. Woodward, "Slow Up on Saint-Making," *The Tablet*, 13 November 1999, quoted in Higgins, *Stalking the Holy*, 34.

9. This total does not include U.S. *beati* whose causes were introduced from the unincorporated territories of Guam and Puerto Rico. It does include the cause of Marianne Cope, whose decree of beatification was promulgated by John Paul II shortly before his death. Benedict XVI presided over the actual beatification ceremony. "St. Marianne Cope."

10. The Redemptorists, with the help of "an urgent request" from Krol to Pope Paul VI, had targeted 26 September 1976 as the date for the canonization, but earlier that summer they learned that "it was not possible to complete the necessary details prior to the general summer exodus from Rome." Adam Otterbein to "confreres," 24 July 1976, in "Various Articles, Clippings, etc.," box 15, SJNC, RABP.

11. "The Pope at St. Peter's and the Shrine of St. John Neumann," *Catholic Standard and Times*, 11 October 1979, 19; "Pope John Paul II's Day in Pictures," *Mobile Register*, 5 October 1979, 3F.

12. Quoted in Corr, "Philadelphia Nun Closer to Sainthood," *Philadelphia Inquirer*, 10 December 1987, 1A, clipping, box 5, folder 38, CKLW, UNDA.

13. Sarno, "Diocesan Inquiries"; Veraja, "Commentary on the New Legislation for the Causes of Saints," box 7, folder 1, CKLW, UNDA; transcript of Woodward interview with Molinari and Gumpel, May 1987, box 5, folder 19, CKLW, UNDA.

14. Veraja, "Commentary on the New Legislation for the Causes of Saints," box 7, folder 1, CKLW, UNDA.

15. Veraja, "Commentary."

16. Woodward to "Paul" [Molinari], n.d. ("Sunday"), box 2, folder 1, CKLW, UNDA.

17. Apple, "At the Vatican."

18. Sarno's doctoral dissertation, written under Gumpel's direction at Rome's Pontifical Gregorian University, offers the most comprehensive English-language summary of the reforms of 1983. He remains the reigning U.S. expert on the canonization process. See "Diocesan Inquiries."

19. "Katharine Drexel," box 2, folder 1; notes on Woodward interview with Gumpel and Molinari, May 1987, 30, box 5, folder 19; "Martino on Drexel, November 9," 6, box 5, folder 38; "Financial Report—Cause & Beatification of Blessed Katharine Drexel—1965–1989," box 2, folder 1, all CKLW, UNDA. Author interviews with Peter Gumpel, Rome, May 2013 and December 2017.

20. Joseph Martino to Alexander Palmieri, 3 January 1994, box 1, folder 23a, "Drexel Canonization Cause—Correspondence, 1993–1995," 2000.051, KDC, CHRCA.

21. Martino to Palmieri, 3 January 1994.

22. Quoted in Woodward, *Making Saints*, 105, 237.

23. Untitled notes on interview with Martino, n.d., 5, box 5, folder 38, CKLW, UNDA.

24. Untitled notes from Martino on Drexel, n.d., 1; "Martino on Drexel, Nov. 9," 6, both box 5, folder 38, CKLW, UNDA; chap. 1, *Philadelphien. Canonizationis servae*

Dei Catharinae Mariae Drexel: Fundatricis Congregationis Sororum a SS. Sacramento pro Indis et Colorata Gente (1858–1955). Vol. I: Exposito historica et documenta (Rome: Congregatio pro Causis Sanctorum, 1986), 1992.013, KDC, CHRCAP.

25. In Catholic devotional life, a "spiritual bouquet" is a list of prayers, often counted, offered for the intentions of a person or on that person's behalf.

26. Baldwin, "Carrying a Saintly Vision into the Future," *Catholic Standard and Times*, n.d., "Clippings file, Beatification," ASBS.

27. "Phone Interview in Rome day Drexel Cause was Discussed," n.d. [1987], 1, box 5, folder 38, CKLW, UNDA.

28. Anne O'Neill to Helen McLaughlin, 30 October 1986, ARSCJ.

29. Sarno referenced by name in O'Neill's letter to McLaughlin. Peter Gumpel remembers the original conversation, and his name and Molinari's appear in conjunction with Duchesne's cause in Woodward's interviews.

30. "Phone Interview in Rome day Drexel Cause was Discussed," n.d. [1987], 1, box 5, folder 38, CKLW, UNDA.

31. "Phone Interview," 1.

32. "Phone Interview," 2; John Paul II, "Address of His Holiness John Paul II," Vatican website, 12 September 1987, http://w2.vatican.va/content/john-paul-ii/en/speeches/1987/september/documents/hf_jp-ii_spe_19870912_xavier-university.html.

33. John Paul II, "Homily of the Holy Father John Paul II," Vatican website, 18 February 1981, https://w2.vatican.va/content/john-paul-ii/en/homilies/1981/documents/hf_jp-ii_hom_19810218_beatificazione-ruiz.html.

34. For a list of saints canonized by John Paul II as well as the locations of the ceremonies, see Ufficio delle Celebrazione Liturgiche del Sommo Pontefice, "Canonizzazioni del Santo Padre Giovanni Paolo II"; for *beati*, Ufficio delle Celebrazione Liturgiche del Sommo Pontefice, "Beatificazioni del Santo Padre Giovanni Paolo II."

35. Notes on Woodward interview with Gumpel and Molinari, May 1987, 26, box 5, folder 19, CKLW, UNDA.

36. Notes on Woodward interview, 26. While this interview suggests that Duchesne was chosen because the miracle-in-waiting brought her so close, Robert Sarno emphasizes that the person who pointed him in Duchesne's direction was Monsignor Charles Burton Mouton, a diocesan priest from Lafayette, Louisiana, who had a long career as a Vatican diplomat. The RSCJs had educated Mouton, and his sister belonged to the congregation. "Mouton, Monsignor Charles Burton Canon." I had heard this rumor from members of the RSCJs, but Sarno confirmed this in an interview with me on 12 June 2017 at the Congregation for the Causes of Saints.

37. Notes on Woodward interview with Gumpel and Molinari, May 1987, 26–27, box 5, folder 19, CKLW, UNDA.

38. Anne O'Neill to Helen McLaughlin, 30 October 1986, ARSCJ.

39. McGuinness, *Called to Serve*, esp. chap. 8, "Serving Today"; Griffith, *Moral Combat*, 228.

40. Helen McLaughlin to Ann O'Neill, 26 November 1986, I.A.13a; Helen McLaughlin to the Society, 1 May 1987, IX.B.1, both ARSCJ.

41. Mooney, *Philippine Duchesne*, 26.

42. D. Peters, "What Does Mother Seton Say to Modern Women?," 29.

43. Mooney, *Philippine Duchesne*, 31.

44. John Paul II, "Omelia di Giovanni Paolo II," Vatican website, 3 luglio 1988, https://w2.vatican.va/content/john-paul-ii/it/homilies/1988/documents/hf_jp-ii_hom_19880703_santi-rojas-duchesne.html, esp. paras. 6 and 7.

45. John Paul II, "Address of John Paul II to the Indians of North America." See Holmes, "Narrative Repatriation of Blessed Kateri Tekakwitha."

46. Apostolic processes on miracles attributed to Tekakwitha were undertaken in Marquette in 1944 (no. 6149, 6151, CRP, ASV), in Hamilton in 1943 (6148, CRP, ASV), and in Siopolitan in 1955 (6152, CRP, ASV).

47. Ricci, "Discussioni: Troppi Santi?," 18. See also Woodward, *Making Saints*, 377–79.

48. Box 1, folder 8, "Case of Robert Gutherman," 2000.051, KDC, CHRCAP.

49. Copy, Faith to "Public Relations Sister," 15 April 1988, Drexel Beatification File, ASBS. Emphasis in original.

50. Haynes to Woodward, 5 March 1990, box 2, folder 6, CKLW, UNDA.

51. The archives suggest that this image was actually painted in preparation for the centennial of the congregation's founding, which would have made it 1991, three years after the beatification. But it appears on the cover of the beatification booklet, and a sister who attended the canonization describes it perfectly.

52. See 9401, CRP, ASV.

53. Schanche and Pinsky, "Pope Won't Beatify Serra during Visit, Vatican Says," *Los Angeles Times*, 8 August 1987, http://articles.latimes.com/1987–08–08/news/mn-478_1_papal-visit.

54. Lenz, *Bureau of Catholic Indian Missions Newsletter*, vol. 7 (July–August 1988), copy in Drexel Beatification File, ASBS.

55. Sandos, "Junípero Serra," 311–12; Weber to Lenz, 5 October 1988, "Native American Controversy, 1986–2002," drawer 10, Serra Cause Historical Collection, SBMAL.

56. "Father Serra: Killer Saint," *Orange County Weekly*, 17–23 March 2000, clipping in "Native American Controversy, 1986–2002," SBMAL. In an email response to the account of one incident sent by the archives of the Archdiocese of Monterey, "Friar Tim" wrote that "our executive Board decided years ago not to reply to stories." "Indian Controversy Drawer," SBMAL.

57. O'Neill to Palmieri, 14 July 1994, box 1, folder 23a, "Drexel Canonization Cause—Correspondence, 1993–1995," 2000.051, KDC, CHRCAP.

58. One such tense moment was when McGrath and Krol's successor, Anthony Bevilacqua, compelled her to reveal the exact amount spent on the cause to journalist Kenneth Woodward. See Bevilacqua to Woodward, "Important Letters on Saints Book," box 2, folder 6, CKLW, UNDA. For an example of McGrath taking credit for Drexel's cause, see Corr, "Philadelphia Nun Closer to Sainthood," *Philadelphia Inquirer*, 10 December 1987, clipping, CKLW, UNDA. On the question of compensation, McGrath commanded a much higher fee than his predecessor, Francis Litz, and the same was true

of Molinari compared to Ferrante. Sister Juliana Haynes reveals the exact figures in a letter to Kenneth Woodward, 5 March 1990, box 2, folder 1, CKLW, UNDA.

59. Molinari to Bevilacqua, 12 January 1994, box 1, folder 23a, "Drexel Canonization Cause—Correspondence, 1993–1995," 2000.051, KDC, CHRCAP.

60. The phrase "men and money" comes from Bill Briggs, who used it to refer to the divisions pursuing Mother Théodore Guérin's cause within the Sisters of Providence. It may be flippant, but it is accurate. Briggs, *Third Miracle*, 157.

61. "Angela Bolster rsm RIP."

62. McGreal, *Madisonen. Canonizationis servi Dei Caroli Samuelis Mazzuchelli.*

63. Notes on Woodward interview with Gumpel and Molinari, May 1987, 25, box 5, folder 19, CKLW, UNDA.

64. Author's interview with Monsignor Robert Sarno, 12 June 2017, Vatican City. American sociologist Gordon Zahn, who was active in the cause for canonization of World War II–era conscientious objector Franz Jägerstätter, wondered about the extent of Sarno's influence as early as 1990. In a letter to Woodward dated 13 September 1990, Zahn wrote, "Since, as you point out more than once, it is this Pope's established practice to 'find' a local hero to honor, some search must have been made. What role your 'saint makers' (and Sarno in particular?) may have played in the circulation of those 'rumors' interests me greatly." Box 2, folder 10, CKLW, UNDA.

65. When I interviewed Ambrosi at his office in Rome in October 2010, I asked him what criteria he looked for in a miracle. He listed three: a certainty of diagnosis (in that all consulted medical experts agree); an initial prognosis of death (a cure from, say, deafness, may qualify as miraculous but lacks the drama inherent in avoiding apparently certain death); and proximity of the invocation to the saint and the healing (almost immediate, rather than drawn out over weeks or months). Cummings, "Doorway to Sainthood." For details of the revaluation of the Mug miracle, see Briggs, *Third Miracle*, 31–38.

66. Quoted in Briggs, *Third Miracle*, 159. I have also drawn information about intracongregational tensions from my extended conversations with Sister Marie Kevin Tighe at Notre Dame in October 2006 and at St. Mary of the Woods in July 2008.

67. Anonymous Sister of Charity of St. Augustine to author, n.d., 2010; she enclosed a copy of a letter from Andrea Ambrosi to Anthony Pilla, 8 November 2004.

68. The proposal appears to have originated with Lou Baldwin, a reporter at Philadelphia's *Catholic Standard and Times* who had written a biography of Drexel, in a letter to Cardinal Bevilacqua dated 1 September 1995. Drexel's vice-postulator, Alexander Palmieri, followed up with Rev. James J. Fitzpatric on 8 September 1995 and wrote to Molinari a week later. Molinari's response to Palmieri, dated 26 September 1995, both affirmed John Paul II's interest in canonizing members of the laity and pointed to the reason why doing so was so difficult. The above letters are in box 1, folder 23a, "Drexel Canonization Cause—Correspondence, 1993–1995," 2000.051, KDC, CHRCAP.

69. Details related to the cure can be found in box 1, folder 8, "Case of Kathleen M. Dean," 2000.051, KDC, CHRCAP. Correspondence related to the proposal to move forward and Molinari's response: Palmieri to Fitzpatrick, 13 June 1995; Molinari

to Palmieri, 26 September 1995, box 1, folder 23a, "Drexel Canonization Cause—Correspondence, 1993–1995," 2000.051, KDC, CHRCAP.

70. Though the official explanation given was McGrath's move to Florida, correspondence between Molinari and the archdiocesan chancery reveals that the real reason was concerns over "irregularities" in the preparation of documentation and Molinari's long-standing suspicion of him. See, for example, a letter from Cardinal Bevilacqua to Monsignor Cullen, 20 July 1993, in which the cardinal reports on a recent meeting with Molinari about McGrath. Box 1, folder 23a, "Drexel Canonization Cause—Correspondence, 1993–1995," 2000.051, KDC, CHRCAP.

71. Palmieri to Joseph Cascerceri, 2 March 1998, box 1, folder 23b, "Drexel Canonization Cause—Correspondence, 1996–2000," KDC, CHRCAP.

72. O'Connor, "A Christian, a Gentleman . . . Pierre Toussaint," clipping in "Causes of Saints (Possible)," Cardinal O'Connor Collection, A-42, AANY.

73. O'Connor's quote appears in Anne Marie Calzolari, "Church Identifies Remains as Haitian Slave Pierre Toussaint," 17 November 1990, written for the Associated Press.

74. On Tarry's support, see her letter to O'Connor, 17 December 1989, and her quote in Arthur Jones, "Pierre Toussaint, a Slave, Society Hairdresser, Philanthropist, May Become the Nation's First Black Saint," *National Catholic Reporter*, 25 August 2000. Copy, Augustus Stallings to Michael Wrenn, 17 September 1987, "Causes of Saints (Possible)," Cardinal O'Connor Collection, A-42, AANY. For a more critical read of Toussaint's cause, as well as those of canonized saints Martin de Porres and Peter Claver, see Grimes, *Fugitive Saints*.

75. Michael Geraghty to O'Connor, 20 November 1990, in "Causes of Saints (Possible)," Cardinal O'Connor Collection, A-42, AANY. Emphasis in original.

76. Hoegerl and von Stamwitz, *Life of Blessed Francis Xavier Seelos*, 89.

77. Verification of Seelos's U.S. citizenship did not surface until 2009, though it mattered little by that point. "Seelos Citizenship Finally Discovered!," *Seelos Center News*, November 2009, 1. Verification came in the form of a petition for citizenship from October 1852.

78. Redemptorists established a shrine near Seelos's tomb in New Orleans and began to publish a monthly newsletter. Neumann's biographer Michael Curley published a study of Seelos's life in 1969. Nothing further was done until after the reforms of 1983.

79. An ordinary process on a miracle attributed to Seelos was conducted in New Orleans between 1973 and 1979. 10363, 10364, CRP, ASV.

80. The Sisters of St. Francis of the Neumann Communities provide a detailed timeline of Cope's cause, although the website is currently defunct: http://blessedmarianne cope.org/history_cause.html.

81. Ordinary processes on Damien's virtues were conducted in Malines and Honolulu in 1956 and 1957, and investigations into miracles attributed to him were undertaken in 1956 and 1988. See 8230–39, CRP, ASV.

82. In 1987, for example, an Episcopalian minister named Earl Connor established the Damien Center in Indianapolis as a coordinated community response to those infected

with HIV. With support from local Episcopal and Catholic churches, the center was founded to meet Damien's standard for compassionate care. See "Our History."

83. Author's interview with Robert Sarno, 12 June 2017, Vatican City; quoted in Matt Sedensky, "Canonization Is Pushed for Molokai's Other Saint," *Honolulu Star Bulletin*, 25 May 2003, http://archives.starbulletin.com/2003/05/25/news/story5.html.

84. Cunningham, *Brief History of Saints*, 115–18, 122; the exact percentages are cited by Ciciliot in *Donne sugli altari*, 251.

85. Markey, *Radical Faith*. A parish in Medina, Ohio, describes the four church-women as "modern-day martyrs." Holy Martyrs Catholic Church, "Our El Salvador Connection," http://www.holymartyrs.net/el-salvador/. 18 July 2018.

86. G. Weigel, "Why Hasn't Francis Ford Been Beatified?"

87. A 501(c)3, the Martyrs of La Florida Missions currently promotes the martyrs' canonization. See "About Us." I am grateful to Deandra Leiberman for informing me that the cause was revived in this manner.

88. LANACC Panel Discussion, "Romero Days," 1 April 2016, University of Notre Dame. https://kellogg.nd.edu/about/outreach-initiatives/latin-americannorth-american -church-concerns-lanacc.

89. Email from a member of the Adorers of the Blood of Christ to author, 18 May 2011. The same sister left open the possibility that causes for these women could be initiated in the places where women died. "We would do it for the people of Liberia. It would mean so much to them." For more on the martyred Adorers, see Boehmer, *Echoes in Our Hearts*.

90. O'Connor, "Dorothy Day's Sainthood Cause Begins."

91. For a detailed critique of this appropriation, see Fessenden, "Worldly Madonna."

92. D. Day, *Long Loneliness*, 169; Meagher, "Sheaf of Letters," 311.

93. Theodore Maynard, who had written a biography of Frances Cabrini, published a biography of Lathrop, as did Katharine Burton, an author who turned hagiography into a cottage industry. "Theodore Maynard," box 4, folder 13, series 2, Mothers General Correspondence, ADSH.

94. See, for example, letter to Gordon Gaskill, 8 November 1958, in "Letters Regard-ing Mother M. Alphonsa Lathrop," box 5, folder 9, series 2, Mothers General Corre-spondence, ADSH.

95. "Canonization Cause Opened for Rose Hawthorne in New York Archdiocese," *National Catholic Register*, 16–22 February 2003, 3; O'Donnell to Egan, 30 October 2001, reprinted on pages 24–25 of Hawthorne's positio, AANY; Short, "Rose Haw-thorne," 20–21.

96. Cummings, *Understanding US Catholic Sisters Today*, 11–12.

97. See, for example, "Sister Ignatia Gavin—Cause for Canonization," a Facebook page dedicated to the "Angel of the Alcoholics," https://www.facebook.com/Sister-Ignatia -Gavin-Cause-for-Canonization-149044051830333/.

98. "Sinsinawa Dominican Sisters."

99. For documents and correspondence related to the cure of Amanda Wall, see box 1, folders 1–4, KDC, CHRCAP.

100. Martino memo, n.d., in box 1, 2010.083, KDC, CHRCAP; Garneau, "Saint Katharine Drexel," 131.

101. Garneau, "Saint Katharine Drexel," 123, 130. On John Paul II and the "new evangelization," see John Paul II, *Redemptoris Missio*, esp. para. 30.

102. Kerr, "Pope Benedict Said to Have Declined Immediate Canonization for Pope John Paul II"; John L. Allen, Jr. "With Beatification of John Paul II, What Makes a Fast-Track Saint?," *National Catholic Reporter*, 1 February 2011, https://www.ncronline.org/news/vatican/beatification-john-paul-ii-what-makes-fast-track-saint.

103. "Interview with Benedict XVI."

104. While there would be exceptions, such as the beatification of John Henry Newman in 2010, presided over by Pope Benedict during his visit to the United Kingdom, the Congregation for the Causes of Saints provided a nuanced rationale for the new procedures. Beatifications by local bishops would "give greater emphasis . . . to the substantial difference between Beatification and Canonization" and "involve the particular Churches more visibly in the Beatification rites of their respective servants of God." Yet the ceremony at the periphery retained an intimate connection to the Roman center: "Wherever Beatifications take place, in Rome or elsewhere, it is necessary to show clearly that every Beatification is an *act of the Roman Pontiff*, who thus permits . . . the local cult of a Servant of God." Martins, "New Procedures in the Rite of Beatification."

105. E.g., "St. Theodora Guérin: A Journey of Providence," http://www.archindy.org/criterion/files/2006/pdfs/20061020-guerin.pdf; Daniels is quoted in Crystal Garcia, "St. Mother Theodore Guerin," *Indianapolis Star Tribune*, 29 December 2006, http://www.tribstar.com/news/local_news/st-mother-theodore-Guérin-brought-inspiration-motivation-to-wabash-valley/article_4a42119d-2257-5498-870c-9e5ea8c02b86.html.

106. Martin, "Saints That Weren't," *NYT*, 1 November 2006, A23.

107. The president also conveyed his "best wishes to the Kingdom of Belgium and his people, who are proud to count Father Damien among their great citizens." Gilgoff, "Obama Weighs In on New Saint."

108. Hagerty, "Vatican Declares Boy's Recovery a 'Miracle.'"

109. Fontaine, spoken comments, 21 October 2012, North American College, Vatican City.

110. Chaput, "Homily at Mass of Thanksgiving."

111. Quoted in Patricia Zabor, "Serra Announcement Surprised Everyone," *The Tablet*, 22 January 2005, https://thetablet.org/serra-announcement-surprised-everyone/.

112. Holson, "Sainthood of Junípero Serra Reopens Wounds of Colonialism in California," *NYT*, 30 September 2015, https://www.nytimes.com/2015/09/30/us/attack-on-statue-of-new-saint-junipero-serra-digs-up-old-conflicts.html?mcubz=3.

113. Luongo, "In Upper Manhattan, Restoring the Golden Halo of Mother Cabrini," *NYT*, 8 February 2015, MB1.

114. Pope Francis is an admirer of Cabrini. During his Angelus on World Day for Migrants and Refugees on 14 January 2017, Pope Francis cited "the example of Saint Francesca Cabrini, patron of migrants, the centenary of whose death occurs this year. This courageous Sister dedicated her life to bringing the love of Christ to those who were far

from their native land and family." See Vatican website, http://w2.vatican.va/content /francesco/it/angelus/2017/documents/papa-francesco_angelus_20170115.html; and Brockhaus, "Mother Cabrini's Care for Immigrants."

115. Gallo, "Unlocking the Archival Legalities"; Francis, "Homily of his Holiness Pope Francis." Pope Francis also mentioned John Neumann in the same homily.

116. In 2006 that dicastery named her patron of Maryland. See "Elizabeth Named Patron Saint of Maryland."

117. Elie, "Patron Saint of Paradox."

118. Ellsberg, "Treating Saints Like Superheroes." This article appeared on the cover of the print edition on 20 March 1917.

119. For a list of open causes, see "Dozens of Causes Underway in the United States," *National Catholic Reporter*, 21 November–5 December, 2014, p. 3a; O'Neel, "The Spirit of 79," *National Catholic Register*, 25 February 2017, http://www.ncregister.com/daily -news/spirit-of-79-the-number-of-americans-proposed-for-sainthood.

120. Cressler, *Authentically Black and Truly Catholic.*

EPILOGUE

1. "Kapaun's Men." I am very grateful to Notre Dame students Darcy Dehais and Garrett Rethman for all they taught me about Kapaun and this organization.

2. Vaccariello, "Sister Who Leaned In," 70.

3. O'Neel, "African-American Sainthood Causes: Everyday Holiness," *National Catholic Register*, 5 February 2017, http://www.ncregister.com/daily-news/african-american -sainthood-causes-illustrate-the-beauty-of-everyday-holiness.

4. DeBernardo, "It's Time to Canonize Fr. Mychal Judge."

5. Patti Mengers, "Journey to Sainthood begins," *Delaware County Daily Times* (Pa.), 22 November 2015, 4–5, 8.

6. Otterman, "Tug of War for Bishop's Body, or at Least Its Parts, Delays Sainthood," *NYT*, 14 September 2014, https://www.nytimes.com/2014/09/14/nyregion/archbishop -sheens-corpse-is-subject-of-long-running-dispute.html?mcubz=3&_r=0.

7. Pope Francis, *Gaudete et Exsultate*, Vatican website, 19 March 2018, paras. 22, 101 http://w2.vatican.va/content/francesco/en/apost_exhortations/documents/papa -francesco_esortazione-ap_20180319_gaudete-et-exsultate.html.

8. This is exactly the argument advanced by Bridget Hart in "Dorothy Stang: A Saint the World Needs," unpublished paper, May 2018, in possession of author. Hart argued that Stang's commitment to the poor and the environment would help Francis foreground his own priorities in those arenas, and that declaring her a saint by proclamation would render moot any misgivings her community had about devoting resources to her cause.

BIBLIOGRAPHY

ARCHIVES CONSULTED

American Catholic History Research Center and University Archives, Washington, D.C.

Archdiocese of Chicago's Joseph Cardinal Bernardin Archives and Records Center, Chicago, Ill.

Archives of the Archdiocese of New York, Yonkers, N.Y.

Archives of the Baltimore Province of the Congregation of the Most Holy Redeemer (Redemptorists), Philadelphia, Pa.

Archives of the Daughters of Charity, Province of St. Louise, Emmitsburg, Md.

Archives of the Dominican Sisters of Hawthorne, Hawthorne, N.Y.

Archives of the Sisters of Charity of New York, Bronx, N.Y.

Archives of the Sisters of Charity of St. Elizabeth, Convent Station, N.J.

Archives of the Sisters of the Blessed Sacrament, Philadelphia, Pa.

Archives of the Society of the Sacred Heart—United States and Canada, St. Louis, Mo.

Archives of the University of Notre Dame, Notre Dame, Ind.

Archivio Generale della Congregazione della Missione (General Archives of the Congregation of the Mission), Rome

Archivio Generale della Congregazione del Santissimo Redentore (General Archives of the Congregation of the Most Holy Redeemer), Rome

Archivio Generale Società del Sacro Cuore (General Archives of the Society of the Sacred Heart), Rome

Archivio Segreto Vaticano (Vatican Secret Archives), Vatican City

Cabriniana Room, Holy Spirit Library, Cabrini University, Radnor, Pa.

Catholic Historical Research Center of the Archdiocese of Philadelphia, Philadelphia, Pa.

Ducournau Archives of the Eastern Province of the Congregation of the Mission (Vincentians), Germantown, Pa.

General Archives of the Missionary Sisters of the Sacred Heart of Jesus, Rome

Santa Barbara Mission Archive-Library, Santa Barbara, Calif.

Sinsinawa Dominican Archives, Sinsinawa Mound, Wis.

University of Notre Dame Libraries, Notre Dame, Ind.

NEWSPAPERS

Baltimore Catholic Mirror
Baltimore Catholic Review
Boston Globe
Catholic Action of the South
Catholic Herald (St. Louis)
Catholic Journal (Rochester, N.Y.)
Catholic Messenger (Davenport, Iowa)
Catholic Review (Brooklyn)
Catholic Standard and Times (Philadelphia)
Chicago Daily Tribune
Chicago Evening American
The Criterion (Indianapolis)
Daily Inter Ocean (Chicago)
Delaware County Daily Times (Pa.)
Honolulu Star Bulletin
Irish World and American Industrial Liberator
Los Angeles Times
Mobile Register
National Catholic Register
National Catholic Reporter
NCWC News Sheet
New World (Chicago)
New York Freeman's Journal
New York Herald
New York Herald Tribune
New York Times
Our Sunday Visitor
Philadelphia Inquirer
Pittsburgh Catholic
Springfield Sunday Union and Republican (Mass.)
The Tablet (London)
Trenton Times (New Jersey)
Tribune Star (Terre Haute, Ind.)
Wall Street Journal
Washington Post
Wilkes-Barre Times (Pa.)

ONLINE SOURCES

"About Us." The Martyrs of La Florida Missions, http://www.martyrsoflaflorida missions.org/about. 22 September 2017.

Amato, Cardinal Angelo. "Prolusione al corso dello Studium della CCS (9 gennaio 2012)." Translated by Catherine Godfrey. Vatican website, http://www.vatican.va /roman_curia/congregations/csaints/documents/rc_con_csaints_doc_20120109 _prolusione-amato_it.html. 21 November 2017.

"American Saints and Blesseds." United States Conference of Catholic Bishops, http:// www.usccb.org/prayer-and-worship/prayers-and-devotions/saints/american- saints -and-blesseds.cfm. 6 November 2017.

"Angela Bolster rsm RIP." Mercy International Association News Centre, 10 February 2005, http://www.mercyworld.org/news_centre/view_article.cfm?loadref=0&id =311. 21 September 2017.

"Archbishop Robert John Seton." Catholic Hierarchy, http://www.catholic-hierarchy .org/bishop/bseton.html. 29 August 2017.

"Beginnings of Congregations." Sisters of Charity Federation, http://sisters-of-charity -federation.org/congregations/beginnings-of-congregations/. 7 September 2017.

Brockhaus, Hannah. "Mother Cabrini's Care for Immigrants Remains Relevant, Pope Francis Says." Catholic News Agency, 19 September 2017, http://www.catholic newsagency.com/news/mother-cabrinis-care-for-immigrants-remains-relevant -pope-francis-says-59416/. 22 September 2017.

Cadorin, Ettore. "Father Junipero Serra." Architect of the Capitol, https://www.aoc .gov/art/national-statuary-hall-collection/father-junipero-serra. 21 November 2017.

DeBernardo, Francis. "It's Time to Canonize Fr. Mychal Judge: Seeking Personal Testimony." New Ways Ministry, 17 July 2017, https://newwaysministryblog .wordpress.com/2017/07/17/its-time-to-canonize-fr-mychal-judge-seeking-personal -testimony/. 22 September 2017.

"Elizabeth Named Patron Saint of Maryland." Famvin, 1 May 2006, http://famvin .org/en/2006/05/01/elizabeth-named-patron-saint-of-maryland/. 15 May 2017.

Francis, Pope. "Angelus." Vatican website, 15 January 2017, http://w2.vatican.va /content/francesco/it/angelus/2017/documents/papa-francesco_angelus_20170115 .html. 22 September 2017.

———. "Homily of His Holiness Pope Francis." Vatican website, 24 September 2015, https://w2.vatican.va/content/francesco/en/homilies/2015/documents/papa -francesco_20150924_usa-omelia-vespri-nyc.html. 26 September 2016.

Gallo, Dee. "Unlocking the Archival Legalities of Donating the Seton Key." Daughters of Charity Archives, 28 September 2015, https://dcarchives.wordpress.com /2015/09/28/unlocking-the-archival-legalities-of-donating-the-seton-key/. 8 September 2017.

Gilgoff, Dan. "Obama Weighs In on New Saint." *U.S. News and World Report*, 9 October 2009, https://www.usnews.com/news/blogs/god-and-country/2009/10/09 /obama-weighs-in-on-new-saint. 15 March 2017.

Hagerty, Barbara Bradley. "Vatican Declares Boy's Recovery a 'Miracle.'" Morning Edition, 20 December 2011, http://www.npr.org/2011/12/20/143981760/vatican -declares-boys-recovery-a-miracle. 22 September 2017.

Hendriks, T. W. "Theodore Maynard: A Historian of American Catholicism." Catholic Culture, https://www.catholicculture.org/culture/library/view.cfm?recnum =8399. 2 February 2017.

"History of the Sisters of Charity of Seton Hill." Sisters of Charity of Seton Hill, http://www.scsh.org/who-we-are/history/. 22 November 2017.

"'If God Wills It': St. Therese's Audience with the Pope." Society of the Little Flower, 20 November 2016, http://blog.littleflower.org/therese-facts/audience-with-the -pope/. 15 October 2017.

John Paul II, Pope. "Address to the Extraordinary Consistory in Preparation for Jubilee Year 2000." Vatican website, 13–14 June, 1994, http://w2.vatican.va/content /john-paul-ii/it/speeches/1994/june/documents/hf-jp-ii_spe_19940613_concistoro -straordinario.html. 9 July 2018.

———. "Address of John Paul II to the Indians of North America." Vatican website, 24 June 1980, https://w2.vatican.va/content/john-paul-ii/en/speeches/1980/june /documents/hf_jp-ii_spe_19800624_pellerossa.html. 21 September 2017.

———. "Apostolic Journey to Pakistan, Philippines I , Guam (United States of America II), Japan, Anchorage (United States of America II) (February 16–27, 1981): Holy Mass for the Beatification of Lorenzo Ruiz: Homily of the Holy Father John Paul II." Vatican website, 18 February 1981, https://w2.vatican.va/content /john-paul-ii/en/homilies/1981/documents/hf_jp-ii_hom_19810218_beatificazione -ruiz.html. 20 September 2017.

———. "Apostolic Journey to the United States of America and Canada: Meeting with the Representatives of Catholic Universities: Address of His Holiness John Paul II." Vatican website, 12 September 1987, http://w2.vatican.va/content/john -paul-ii/en/speeches/1987/september/documents/hf_jp-ii_spe_19870912_xavier -university.html. 4 October 2017.

———. "Omelia, Canonizzazione di Simón de Rojas e Rose Philippine Duchesne." Vatican website, 3 July 1988, https://w2.vatican.va/content/john-paul-ii/it /homilies/1988/documents/hf_jp-ii_hom_19880703_santi-rojas-duchesne.html. 21 September 2017.

———. *Redemptoris missio* [On the permanent validity of the Church's missionary mandate]. Vatican website, 7 December 1990, http://w2.vatican.va/content/john -paul-ii/en/encyclicals/documents/hf_jp-ii_enc_07121990_redemptoris-missio .html. 22 September 2017.

"Kapaun's Men: Fellowship and Formation for Men." Father Kapaun Guild, https:// www.kapaunsmen.org/. 25 September 2017.

Kerr, David. "Pope Benedict Said to Have Declined Immediate Canonization for Pope John Paul II." Catholic News Agency, 27 April 2011, http://www.catholicnews agency.com/news/pope-benedict-said-to-have-declined-immediate-canonization -for-pope-john-paul-ii/. 10 May 2017.

Louisiana Works Progress Administration. "A Poem of Holiness (Mother Cabrini)." In *Description of Life and Beautification [sic] ceremony of Mother Francis Xavier Cabrini.* served by The Louisiana Digital Library, http://louisianadigitallibrary .org/islandora/object/state-lwp%3A7794. 2 February 2017.

Martins, José Saraiva. "New Procedures in the Rite of Beatification." Vatican website, 29 September 2005, http://www.vatican.va/roman_curia/congregations/csaints /documents/rc_con_csaints_doc_20050929_saraiva-martins-beatif_en.html. 12 May 2017.

"Mouton, Monsignor Charles Burton Canon." Obituary. Peterson-Shaw genealogical site, http://www.hpeterjr.us/getperson.php?personID=163917&tree=1. 15 June 2017.

"Our Beginnings." Sisters of Charity—Halifax, http://www.schalifax.ca/our-story/. 7 September 2017.

"Our El Salvador Connection." Holy Martyrs Catholic Church (Medina, Ohio), http://www.holymartyrs.net/el-salvador/. 22 September 2017.

"Our History." Damien Center, http://www.damien.org/history. 21 September 2017.

Paul VI, Pope. "Canonization of Elisabeth [sic] Ann Seton: Homily of the Holy Father Paul VI." Vatican website, 14 September 1975, https://w2.vatican.va/content /paul-vi/en/homilies/1975/documents/hf_p-vi_hom_19750914.html. 8 August 2017.

Pius X, Pope St. *Vacante Apostolica Sede.* Documenta Catholica Omnia, 25 December 1904, http://www.documentacatholicaomnia.eu/01p/1904–12–25,_SS_Pius_X, _Constitutio_'Vacante_Apostolica_Sede,'_LT.pdf. 7 August 2017.

Pius XI, Pope. *Cum Proxime.* Vatican website, 1 March 1922, http://w2.vatican.va /content/pius-xi/it/motu_proprio/documents/hf_p-xi_motu-proprio_19220301 _cum-proxime.html. 7 August 2017.

Sacred Congregation for the Doctrine of the Faith. "Declaration *Inter Insigniores*, on the Question of the Admission of Women to the Ministerial Priesthood." Vatican website, 15 October 1976, http://www.vatican.va/roman_curia/congregations /cfaith/documents/rc_con_cfaith_doc_19761015_inter-insigniores_en.html. 19 September 2017.

Second Vatican Council. *Gaudium et Spes.* Vatican website, 7 December 1965, http:// www.vatican.va/archive/hist_councils/ii_vatican_council/documents/vat-ii_const _19651207_gaudium-et-spes_en.html. 15 September 2017.

Second Vatican Council. *Lumen Gentium.* Vatican website, 21 November 1964, http://www.vatican.va/archive/hist_councils/ii_vatican_council/documents /vat-ii_const_19641121_lumen-gentium_en.html. 15 September 2017.

Second Vatican Council. *Perfectae Caritatis.* Vatican website, 28 October 1965, http://www.vatican.va/archive/hist_councils/ii_vatican_council/documents /vat-ii_decree_19651028_perfectae-caritatis_en.html. 13 July 2018.

"A Short History of the Sisters of Charity." Emmitsburg Area Historical Society, http://www.emmitsburg.net/archive_list/articles/history/stories/sisters_of _charity.htm. 22 November 2017.

"The Sinsinawa Dominican Sisters." Father Mazzuchelli Society, http://www.father
mazzuchellisociety.org/. 22 September 2017.

"Sisters of Charity—Halifax." Diocese of Antigonish, http://www.antigonishdiocese
.com/charities.html. 7 September 2017.

Skaggs, Michael. "Seton Schools." Google, https://www.google.com/maps/d/viewer
?mid=1C1IibRB9d_U_U7pPxJHAGzK65Oo&ll=46.34703180396454%2C-109
.44796604999999&z=4. 6 November 2017.

"St. Marianne Cope." Catholic News Agency, 23 January 2017, http://www.catholic
newsagency.com/saint.php?n=727. 25 September 2017.

Tertullian. *Angelicus.* Tertullian.org, http://www.tertullian.org/latin/apologeticum
_becker.htm. 22 September 2017.

"Timeline of Events." Sisters of Providence of Saint-Mary-of-the-Woods, https://
spsmw.org/saint-mother-theodore/steps-to-sainthood/saint-mother-theodores
-path-to-sainthood/timeline-of-events/. 27 November 2017.

Turner, Frederick Jackson. "The Significance of the Frontier in American History."
First delivered in 1894 at the annual meeting of the American History Association
in Chicago. American Historical Association, https://www.historians.org/about
-aha-and-membership/aha-history-and-archives/archives/the-significance-of-the
-frontier-in-american-history. 8 September 2017.

Ufficio delle Celebrazione Liturgiche del Sommo Pontefice. "Beatificazioni del Santo
Padre Giovanni Paolo II." Vatican website, http://www.vatican.va/news_services
/liturgy/saints/ELENCO_BEATI_GPII.htm. 20 September 2017.

———. "Canonizzazioni del Santo Padro Giovanni Paolo II." Vatican website, http://
www.vatican.va/news_services/liturgy/saints/ELENCO_SANTI_GPII.htm.
20 September 2017.

"Why John Paul II Proclaimed So Many Saints: Interview with Cardinal Saraiva Martins." Zenit, 4 April 2006, https://zenit.org/articles/why-john-paul-ii-proclaimed
-so-many-saints/. 19 September 2017.

"The Years of the Second Vatican Council." Dominican Sisters of Saint Cecilia,
https://www.nashvilledominican.org/community/congregation-history/the
-years-of-the-second-vatican-council/. 19 September 2017.

REFERENCE WORKS

Abbott, Walter, ed., and Joseph Gallagher, trans. *The Documents of Vatican II: With
Notes and Comments by Catholic, Protestant, and Orthodox Authorities.* Chicago:
Association Press, 1966.

Beccari, Camillo. "Beatification and Canonization." In *The Catholic Encyclopedia,*
edited by Charles George Herbermann, Edward A. Pace, Condé Pallen, Thomas J.
Shahan, and John J. Wynne. New York: Robert Appleton Company, 1907–1912.
http://www.newadvent.org/cathen/02364b.htm. 3 September 2015.

Becker, Thomas A. "American Bishops and Pastoral Care of Italians, 1884." In *Keeping
the Faith: European and Asian Catholic Immigrants,* edited by Jeffrey M. Burns,

Ellen Skerrett, and Joseph M. White, 163–64. Maryknoll, N.Y.: Orbis Books, 2000.

Boland, S. J. *A Dictionary of the Redemptorists*. Rome: Collegium S. Alfonsi de Urbe, 1987. http://www.santalfonsoedintorni.it/Libri/BolandDizio/Boland 00Dictionary.pdf. 11 July 2017.

Byron, Beverly. "Mother Seton School, Emmitsburg, MD." In *Congressional Record* 131, 20 February 1985, 2854. Washington, D.C.: United States Government Printing Office, 1985.

Day, E. "Christopher, St." In *New Catholic Encyclopedia*, vol. 3. Detroit: Thomson/ Gale, 2003.

Hilgers, Joseph. "Novena." In *The Catholic Encyclopedia*. New York: Robert Appleton Company, 1911. http://www.newadvent.org/cathen/11141b.htm. 7 November 2017.

Küng, Hans, Yves Congar, and Daniel O'Hanlon. *Council Speeches of Vatican II*. Glen Rock, N.J.: Paulist Press, 1964.

Lowth, Catherine. "Philippine-Rose Duchesne." In *The Catholic Encyclopedia*. New York: Robert Appleton Company, 1909. http://www.newadvent.org/cathen/05182a .htm. 22 November 2017.

Meehan, Andrew. "Papal Rescripts." In *The Catholic Encyclopedia*. New York: Robert Appleton Company, 1911. http://www.newadvent.org/cathen/12783b.htm. 25 November 2017.

"Military Services, USA, Archdiocese for." *New Catholic Encyclopedia Supplement 2009*. Detroit: Gale, 2009.

"Mundelein." *Britannica Academic*, http://academic.eb.com.proxy.library.nd.edu /levels/collegiate/article/Mundelein/54275. 20 July 2017.

"Neumann, St. John." In *Encyclopedia of American Catholic History*, edited by Thomas Shelley. Collegeville, Minn.: Liturgical Press, 1997.

Ott, Michael. "Pope Sixtus V." In *The Catholic Encyclopedia*. New York: Robert Appleton Company, 1912. http://www.newadvent.org/cathen/14033a.htm. 19 September 2017.

Peters, Edward. *The 1917 Pio-Benedictine Code of Canon Law: In English Translation with Extensive Scholarly Apparatus*. San Francisco: Ignatius Press, 2001.

The Roman Missal. Totowa, N.J.: Catholic Book Publishing, 2011.

Rynne, Xavier. *The Third Session: The Debates and Decrees of Vatican Council II*. New York: Farrar, Strauss, and Giroux, 1965.

Wynne, John. "Triduum." In *The Catholic Encyclopedia*. New York: Robert Appleton Company, 1912. http://www.newadvent.org/cathen/15041c.htm. 22 August 2017.

DISSERTATIONS

Flanagan, Mary Kathleen. "The Influence of John Henry Hobart on the Life of Elizabeth Ann Seton." Diss., Union Theological Seminary, 1978.

Lombardo, Michael. "Founding Father: John J. Wynne, S.J., and the Inculturation of American Catholicism in the Progressive Era." PhD diss., University of Dayton, 2014.

Sarno, Robert. "Diocesan Inquiries Required by the Legislator in the New Legislation for the Cause of Saints." Doctoral diss., Pontifical University Gregoriana, 1988.

MONOGRAPHS AND EDITED COLLECTIONS

Anderson, Emma. *The Death and Afterlife of the North American Martyrs*. Cambridge, Mass.: Harvard University Press, 2013.

Attwater, Donald. *Saints Westward: Some Colorful and Heroic Men and Women Who Planted and Watered the Seed of Faith in the Western Hemisphere*. New York: P. J. Kennedy and Sons, 1953.

Bancroft, George. *History of the United States, from the Discovery of the American Continent*. Vol. 3. Boston: Little, Brown, 1853.

[A Benedictine of Stanbrook Abbey]. *Frances Xavier Cabrini: The Saint of the Emigrants*. London: Catholic Books Club, 1946.

Blake, Ronald. *The Trial of Mother Cabrini: "The First American Saint."* Bloomington, Ind.: AuthorHouse, 2013.

Boehmer, M. Clare. *Echoes in Our Hearts*. Red Bud, Ill.: Adorers of the Blood of Christ, 1994.

Breckinridge, Robert. *Papism in the XIX Century: Being Select Contributions to the Papal Controversy during 1835–1840*. Baltimore: David Owen, 1841.

Briggs, Bill. *The Third Miracle: An Ordinary Man, a Medical Mystery, and a Trial of Faith*. New York: Broadway Books, 2010.

Bryan, Mary Lyn McCree, Barbara Bair, and Maree de Angury, eds. *The Selected Papers of Jane Addams*. Vol. 2, *Venturing into Usefuless, 1881–88*. Champaign: University of Illinois Press, 2009.

Burton, Katherine. *To the Golden Door: The Life of Katharine Drexel*. New York: P. J. Kennedy and Sons, 1957.

Byerley, Timothy E. *St. John Neumann, Wonder-Worker of Philadelphia: Recent Miracles*. Philadelphia: St. John Neumann Shrine, 1992.

Cabrini, Frances Xavier. *Journal of a Trusting Heart: Retreat Notes of St. Frances Cabrini*. Translated by Irene Connolly. Philadelphia: Missionary Sisters of the Sacred Heart, 1984.

———. *To the Ends of the Earth: The Missionary Travels of Frances X. Cabrini*. Translated by Philippa Provenzano. New York: Center for Migration Studies, 2001.

Calendarium Romanum Ex Decreto Sacrosancti Œcumenici Concilii Vaticani II Instauratum Auctoritate Pauli PP. VI Promulgatum. Vatican City: Typis Polyglottis Vaticanis, 1969.

Castagna, Luca. *A Bridge across the Ocean*. Washington, D.C.: Catholic University of America Press, 2014.

Catanoso, Justin. *My Cousin the Saint: A Story of Love, Miracles, and an Italian Family Reunited*. New York: Harper Perennial, 2009.

Chauchetière, Claude. *La vie de la B. Catherine Tegakoüita: Dite a Present: La Saincte*

Sauugesse par le R. P. Claude Chauchetière pretre missionnaire de la Compagnie de Iesus. Manate: La Presse Cramoisy de J. P. M. Shea, 1887.

Choate, Mark. *Emigrant Nation: The Making of Italy Abroad.* Cambridge, Mass.: Harvard University Press, 2008.

Cholenec, Pierre. *Catherine Tekakwitha: Her Life.* Edited by William Lonc. Hamilton, ON: Steve Catlin, 2002.

Ciciliot, Valentina. *Donne sugli altari: Le canonizzazioni femminili di Giovanni Paolo II.* Rome: Viella, 2018.

Cicognani, Amleto Giovanni. *Sanctity in America.* Paterson, N.J.: St. Anthony Guild Press, 1939.

Concilii Plenarii Baltimorensis II., in ecclesia metropolitana Baltimorensi, a die VII. ad diem XXI. octobris, a.d., MDCCCLXVI., habiti, et a Sede Apostolica recogniti, acta et decreta. Baltimore: John Murphy, 1877.

Cooney, John. *American Pope: The Life and Times of Francis Cardinal Spellman.* New York: Dell, 1984.

Cressler, Matthew J. *Authentically Black and Truly Catholic: The Rise of Black Catholicism in the Great Migration.* New York: New York University Press, 2017.

Cummings, Kathleen Sprows. *New Women of the Old Faith: Gender and American Catholicism in the Progressive Era.* Chapel Hill: University of North Carolina Press, 2009.

———. *Understanding US Catholic Sisters Today.* Washington, D.C.: Foundation and Donors Interested in Catholic Activities, 2015.

Cummings, Kathleen Sprows, Timothy Matovina, and Robert Orsi. *Catholics in the Era of Vatican II: Local Histories of a Global Event.* New York: Cambridge University Press, 2017.

Cunningham, Lawrence S. *A Brief History of Saints.* Hoboken, N.J.: Blackwell, 2005.

Curley, Michael. *Venerable John Neumann C.SS.R.: Fourth Bishop of Philadelphia.* Washington, D.C.: Catholic University of America, 1952.

Curtis, Sarah Ann. *Civilizing Habits: Women Missionaries and the Revival of French Empire.* New York: Oxford University Press, 2010.

Cussen, Celia. *Black Saint of the Americas: The Life and Afterlife of Martin de Porres.* New York: Cambridge University Press, 2014.

D'Agostino, Peter R. *Rome in America: Transnational Catholic Ideology from the Risorgimento to Fascism.* Chapel Hill: University of North Carolina Press, 2004.

Dailey, Edward V. *The Citizen Saint: The Life and Miracles of Saint Frances Xavier Cabrini.* Chicago: C. Elliot, 1947.

Day, Dorothy. *The Long Loneliness.* New York: Image Books, 1959.

de Maria, Saverio. *La Madre Francesca Saverio Cabrini.* Turin: Società Editrice Internazionale, 1928.

———. *Mother Frances Xavier Cabrini.* Translated by Rose Basile Green. Chicago: Missionary Sisters of the Sacred Heart, 1984.

Dolan, Jay P. *The American Catholic Experience: A History from Colonial Times to the*

Present. Notre Dame: University of Notre Dame Press, 1992. First edition 1985 by Doubleday (Garden City, N.Y.).

———. *Catholic Revivalism: The American Experience, 1830–1900*. Notre Dame: University of Notre Dame Press, 1978.

———. *The Immigrant Church: New York's Irish and German Catholics, 1815–1865*. Notre Dame: University of Notre Dame Press, 1975.

———. *In Search of an American Catholicism: A History of Religion and Culture in Tension*. New York: Oxford University Press, 2002.

Donato, Pietro. *Immigrant Saint: The Life of Mother Cabrini*. New York: McGraw-Hill, 1960.

Donnelly, Joseph P., ed. *Thwaites' Jesuit Relations*. Chicago: Loyola University Press, 1967.

Donohoe, Thomas. *The Iroquois and the Jesuits: The Story of the Labors of Catholic Missionaries among These Indians*. Buffalo: Buffalo Catholic Publication Co., 1895.

Duffy, Eamon. *The Stripping of the Altars: Traditional Religion in England, 1400–1580*. 2nd ed. New Haven, Conn.: Yale University Press, 1992.

Epistolario di Santa Francesca Saverio Cabrini (1868–1917). 5 vols. Rome: Istituto Missionarie del Sacro Cuore di Gesù, 2002.

Farley, Luke. *Saints for the Modern Woman: A United Nations of Holiness for the Woman of Today*. Boston: Daughters of St. Paul, 1961.

Feeney, Leonard. *Elizabeth Seton: An American Woman*. New York: America Press, 1938.

———. *Mother Seton: St. Elizabeth of New York*. Cambridge, Mass.: Ravengate Press, 1975.

Ferrara, Christopher, and Thomas Woods. *The Great Façade: Vatican II and the Regime of Novelty in the Roman Catholic Church*. Wyoming, Minn.: Remnant Press, 2002.

Fitzgerald, Maureen. *Habits of Compassion: Irish Catholic Nuns and the Origins of New York's Welfare System, 1830–1920*. Urbana: University of Illinois Press, 2006.

Foerster, Robert Franz. *The Italian Emigration of Our Times*. Vol. 20 of *The American Immigration Collection*. Cambridge, Mass.: Harvard University Press, 1919.

Fogarty, Gerald. *The Vatican and the American Hierarchy from 1870 to 1965*. Stuttgart, Ger.: Hiersemann, 1982.

G. E. M. *Venerable Philippine Duchesne: A Brief Sketch of the Life and Work of the Foundress of the Society of the Sacred Heart in America*. New York: America Press, 1914.

Gannon, John. *The Martyrs of the United States of America: Manuscript of Preliminary Studies Prepared by the Commission for the Cause of Canonization of the Martyrs of the United States*. Easton, Pa.: Mack Printing Co., 1957.

Gleason, Philip. *Contending with Modernity: Catholic Higher Education in the Twentieth Century*. New York: Oxford University Press, 1995.

Greer, Allan. *Mohawk Saint: Catherine Tekakwitha and the Jesuits*. New York: Oxford University Press, 2005.

Greer, Allan, and Jodi Bilinkoff, eds. *Colonial Saints: Discovering the Holy in the Americas*. New York: Routledge, 2003.

Griffith, R. Marie. *Moral Combat: How Sex Divided Christians and Fractured American Politics*. New York: Basic Books, 2017.

Grimes, Katie Walker. *Fugitive Saints: Catholicism and the Politics of Slavery*. Minneapolis: Fortress Press, 2017.

Guilday, Peter. *A History of the Councils of Baltimore, 1791–1884*. New York: Arno Press and The New York Times, 1969.

Habig, Marion. *Heroes of the Cross: The Franciscan Martyrs of North America*. New York: Fortuny's, 1939.

Halsey, William M. *The Survival of American Innocence: Catholicism in an Era of Disillusionment, 1920–1940*. Notre Dame: University of Notre Dame Press, 1980.

Hennesey, James J. *American Catholics: A History of the Roman Catholic Community in the United States*. New York: Oxford University Press, 1983.

Higgins, Michael. *Stalking the Holy: The Pursuit of Saint-Making*. Toronto, ON: House of Anansi, 2006.

Hoare, Mary Regis. *Virgin Soil: Mother Seton from a Different Point of View*. Boston: Christopher Publishing House, 1942.

Hoegerl Carl, and Alicia von Stamwitz. *The Life of Blessed Francis Xavier Seelos, Redemptorist, 1819–1867*. New Orleans: Seelos Center, 2000.

In Memoria della Rev.ma Madre Francesca Saverio Cabrini, Fondatrice e Superiora Generale delle Missionarie del S. Cuore di Gesù, volata al cielo in Chicago, il 22 Diciembre 1917. Rome: A. Bernasconi, 1918.

Koehlinger, Amy. *The New Nuns: Racial Justice and Religious Reform in the 1960s*. Cambridge, Mass.: Harvard University Press, 2007.

LaFarge, John. *The Manner Is Ordinary*. New York: Harcourt, Brace, 1954.

MacLeod, Xavier Donald. *Devotion to the Blessed Virgin Mary in North America*. New York: Virtue and Yorston, 1866.

Malak, Henry. *Theresa of Chicago*. Lemont, Ill: League of the Servant of God Mother Mary Theresa, 1975.

Markey, Eileen. *A Radical Faith: The Assassination of Sister Maura*. New York: Nation Books, 2016.

Maynard, Theodore. *The Catholic Church and the American Idea*. New York: Appleton-Century-Crofts, 1953.

———. *Too Small a World: The Life of Francesca Cabrini*. Milwaukee: Bruce, 1945.

McCann, Mary Agnes. *The History of Mother Seton's Daughters*. 2 vols. New York: Longmans, Green, 1917.

McCormack, Margaret, ed. *Saints and Their Cults in the Atlantic World*. Columbia: University of South Carolina Press, 2007.

McDannell, Colleen. *Material Christianity: Religion and Popular Culture in America*. New Haven, Conn.: Yale University Press, 1995. See especially chapter 5, "Lourdes Water and American Catholicism," 132–62.

McGinley, Phyllis. *Saint-Watching*. New York: Viking Press, 1969.

McGreal, Mary Nona. *Madisonen. Canonizationis servi Dei Caroli Samuelis Mazzuchelli, O.P., fundatoris Congregationis Sororum Dominicanarum a S. Rosario de Sinsinawa, 1806–1864.* Under the direction of Rev. Msgr. Fabijan Veraja. Rome: Congregation for the Causes of Saints, 1989.

McGreevy, John. *American Jesuits and the World: How an Embattled Religious Order Made Modern Catholicism Global.* Princeton: Princeton University Press, 2016.

McGuinness, Margaret M. *Called to Serve: A History of Nuns in America.* New York: New York University Press, 2013.

Melville, Annabelle M. *Elizabeth Bayley Seton, 1774–1821.* New York: Scribner, 1951.

A Member of the Congregation [Sister Mary Theodosia Mug]. *Life and Life-Work of Mother Theodore Guérin: Foundress of the Sisters of Providence at St.-Mary-of-the-Woods, Vigo County, Indiana.* New York: Benziger Brothers, 1904.

Metropolitan Catholic Alumnae and Laity's Directory for the United States, 1860. Baltimore: John Murphy, 1973.

Mooney, Catherine M. *Philippine Duchesne: A Woman with the Poor.* Mahwah, N.J.: Paulist Press, 1990.

Morris, Charles. *American Catholic: The Saints and Sinners Who Built America's Most Powerful Church.* New York: New York Times Books, 1997.

Muckenhirn, M[ary] Charles Borromeo. *The New Nuns.* New York: New American Library, 1967.Murphy, Francis X. *John Nepomucene Neumann, Saint.* Brooklyn: Custom Editorial Services, 2000. Originally published in 1977 by Erra Press of South Hackensack, N.J., as a book-length expansion of a *New Yorker* article from earlier in the year.

Murray, John O'Kane. *Lives of the Catholic Heroes and Heroines of America.* New York: J. Sheehy, 1879.

———. *A Popular History of the Catholic Church in the United States.* 5th ed. New York: D. and J. Sadlier, 1877.

O'Donnell, Catherine. *Elizabeth Ann Seton: A Life.* Ithaca: Cornell University Press, 2018.

The Official Catholic Directory. New Providence, N.J.: P. J. Kennedy and Sons, 2016.

O'Malley, John W. *What Happened at Vatican II.* Cambridge, Mass.: Harvard University Press, 2008.

Orsi, Robert A. *History and Presence.* Cambridge, Mass.: Harvard University Press, 2016. See especially chapter 2.

———. *Thank You, St. Jude: Women's Devotion to the Patron Saint of Hopeless Causes.* New Haven, Conn.: Yale University Press, 1996.

Osiek, Carolyn. *Kathryn Sullivan, RSCJ: Teacher of the Word.* St. Louis: Society of Sacred Heart, United States Province, 2011.

O'Toole, James. *The Faithful: A History of Catholics in America.* Cambridge, Mass.: Harvard University Press, 2008.

Parkman, Francis. *The Jesuits in North America in the Seventeenth Century.* Boston: Little, Brown, 1867.

Pearson, Timothy G. *Becoming Holy in Early Canada*. Montreal: McGill-Queen's University Press, 2014.

The Positio of the Historical Section of the Sacred Congregation of Rites on the Introduction of the Cause for Beatification and Canonization and on the Virtues of the Servant of God Katharine Tekakwitha, The Lily of the Mohawks. New York: Fordham University Press, 1940.

Quiñonez, Lora Ann, and Mary Daniel Turner. *The Transformation of American Catholic Sisters*. Philadelphia: Temple University Press, 1992.

Rousseau, Jean-Jacques. *Du contrat social, ou Principes de droit politique*. Paris: Didot jeune, 1795.

Rowe, Erin. *Saint and Nation: Santiago, Teresa of Avila, and Plural Identities in Early Modern Spain*. University Park: Pennsylvania State University Press, 2011.

Ruether, Rosemary, and Eleanor McLaughlin, eds. *Women of Spirit: Female Leadership in Jewish and Christian Traditions*. New York: Simon and Schuster, 1979.

Schneiders, Sandra. *Buying the Field: Catholic Religious Life in Mission to the World*. Mahwah, N.J.: Paulist Press, 2013.

Seton, Elizabeth Bayley. *Collected Writings: Elizabeth Ann Seton, Saint, 1774–1821*. 3 vols. Edited by Regina M. Bechtle and Judith Metz. Hyde Park, N.Y.: New City Press, 2000.

Shea, John Gilmary. *Our Faith and Its Defenders: Comprising the Trials and Triumphs of the Defenders of Our Faith in America*. 2 vols. New York: Office of Catholic Publications, 1894.

Storm, Marian. *The Life of Saint Rose: First American Saint and Only American Woman Saint*. Santa Fe: Writers' Editions, 1937.

Suenens, Léon-Joseph Cardinal. *The Nun in the World: New Dimensions in the Modern Apostolate*. Westminster, Md.: Newman Press, 1962.

Sullivan, Francis A. *Salvation outside the Church? Tracing the History of the Catholic Response*. Mahwah, N.J.: Paulist Press, 1992.

Sullivan, Mary Louise. *Mother Cabrini: Italian Immigrant of the Century*. New York: Center for Migration Studies of New York, 1998.

Tarry, Ellen. *Katharine Drexel: Friend of the Oppressed*. Nashville: Winston-Derek, 1990.

Taylor, Larissa Juliet. *Virgin Warrior: The Life and Death of Joan of Arc*. New Haven, Conn.: Yale University Press, 2009. See especially the epilogue.

Tusiani, Joseph. *Envoy from Heaven*. New York: I. Obolensky, 1965.

Tweed, Thomas. *America's Church: The National Shrine and Catholic Presence in the Nation's Capital*. New York: Oxford University Press, 2011.

Vauchez, André. *Sainthood in the Later Middle Ages*. New York: Cambridge University Press, 1997.

Walsh, James J. *Our American Cardinals: Life Stories of the Seven American Cardinals; McCloskey, Gibbons, Farley, O'Connell, Dougherty, Mundelein, Hayes*. New York: D. Appleton and Co., 1926.

Walworth, Ellen W. *The Life and Times of Kateri Tekakwitha: The Lily of the Mohawks, 1656–1680.* Buffalo: Peter Paul and Brother, 1891.

Ware, Ann Patrick, ed. *Midwives of the Future: American Sisters Tell Their Story.* Kansas City, Mo.: Leaven, 1985.

White, Charles I. *Life of Mrs. Eliza A. Seton, Foundress and First Superior of the Sisters of Daughters of Charity in the United States of America.* New York: Edward Dunigan and Bro., 1853.

———. *Mother Seton: Mother of Many Daughters.* Revised and edited by the Sisters of Charity of Mount St. Vincent-on-Hudson, New York. Garden City, N.Y.: Doubleday, 1949.

Williams, Shannen Dee. *Subversive Habits: Black Nuns and the Struggle to Desegregate Catholic America after World War II.* Forthcoming.

Woodward, Kenneth. *Making Saints: How the Catholic Church Determines Who Becomes a Saint, Who Doesn't, and Why.* New York: Touchstone, 1996.

Wynne, John J. *The Jesuit Martyrs of North America.* Auriesville, N.Y.: Ossernenon Press, 1925.

———. *Our North American Martyrs: The First Enrolled in the North American Calendar of Saints; Isaac Jogues, John Brebeuf, Anthony Daniel, Gabriel Lalemant, Charles Garnier, Noel Chabanel, Rene Goupil, John Lalande.* Societas Iesu: Home Press, n.d. [1930].

JOURNAL ARTICLES, CHAPTERS, AND ESSAYS

Alexander, Raymond Pace. "A Tribute to Mother Katharine Drexel." *Negro History Bulletin* 29 (Fall 1966): 181–82, 184, 189, 191–92.

Bechtle, Regina. "The 1846 Separation of the New York Sisters: Conflict over Mission or Clash of Wills?" *Vincentian Heritage Journal* 20, no. 1 (1999): 63–80.

Benedict XV, Pope. "Decretum approbationis virtutum in causa beatificationis et canonizationis Servi Dei Ioannis Nepomuceni Neumann." *AAS* 14 (1922): 23.

Boursiquot, Marie-Alberte, and Shirley E. Reddoch. "The Approved Miracle of Saint Elizabeth Ann Seton." *Linacre Quarterly* 79 (May 2012): 209–18.

Burke, Peter. "How to Be a Counter-Reformation Saint." In *The Reformation: Critical Concepts in Historical Studies*, edited by Andrew Pettegree, 4:153–64. London: Routledge, 2004.

Burns, Arthur J. "New Light on Mother Seton." *Historical Records and Studies* 22 (January 1932): 85–100.

Byrne, Patricia. "Catholic Education in the United States: Foundations." In *Creative Fidelity: American Catholic Intellectual Traditions*, edited by R. Scott Appleby, Patricia Byrne, and William L. Portier, 55–58. Maryknoll, N.Y.: Orbis Books, 2004.

Ciciliot, Valentina. "'Heritage Talks. Heritage Calls': Some Instances of the Canonization Policy of John Paul II in Italy." *Modern Italy* 18 (August 2013): 269–83.

Cicognani, Amleto Giovanni. Foreword to *Venerable John Neumann, CSsR: Fourth*

Bishop of Philadelphia, by Michael Curley, vii–x. Philadelphia: Bishop Neumann Center, 1952.

———. Foreword to *Mother of Many Daughters*, by Charles I. White, vii–xvii. New York: Doubleday, 1949.

Cipolla, Gaetano. "Francesca Cabrini: 'Figura Matris' in a Contemporary Novel." *Italiana Americana* 3 (Spring/Summer 1977): 162–73.

Code, Joseph B. "The Contribution of Europe to Holiness in America." In *Miscellanea Historica in honorem Alberti de Meyer, Universitatis catholicæ in oppido Iovaniensi iam annos 25 professoris*, 2:1217–36. Louvain, Belg.: Bibliothèque de l'Université, 1946.

Conway, Katherine E. "Individual Catholic Women." In *Catholic Builders of the Nation: A Symposium on the Catholic Contribution to the Civilization of the United States*, vol. 5, edited by William Shepherd Benson et al., 384–411. Boston: Continental Press, 1923.

Coston, Carol. "Open Windows, Open Doors." In *Midwives of the Future*, edited by Ann Patrick Ware, 146–60. Kansas City, Mo.: Leaven Press, 1985.

Cummings, Kathleen Sprows. "American Saints: Gender and the Re-imaging of U.S. Catholicism in the Early Twentieth Century." *Religion and American Culture* 22, no. 2 (2012): 203–31.

———. "Frances Cabrini, American Exceptionalism, and Returning to Rome." *Catholic Historical Review* 104 (Winter 2018): 1–22.

de Lourdes, Marie. "Travelogue to Beatitude." *Hospital Progress*, July 1963, 53–60.

Ditchfield, Simon. "Thinking with the Saints: Sanctity and Society in Early Modern Europe." *Critical Inquiry* 35 (Spring 2009): 552–84.

"Eucharistic Prayer III." In *The Roman Missal*, 3rd typical ed., translated by The International Commission on English in the Liturgy, no. 113. 4–5. Washington, D.C.: United States Catholic Conference of Catholic Bishops, 2011.

F. G. H. "S Rosa a S. Maria." *American Ecclesiastical Review* 16 (March 1897): 333–35.

———. "S. Rosa de Lima, Virgo." *American Ecclesiastical Review* 16 (January 1897): 91–92.

Feldberg, Michael. "[About the Cover]: American Heretic: The Rise and Fall of Father Leonard Feeney, S.J." *American Catholic Studies* 123 (Summer 2012): 109–15.

Fessenden, Tracy. "Worldly Madonna." In *Catholics in the Movies*, edited by Colleen McDannell, 251–76. New York: Oxford University Press, 2008.

Garneau, James. "Saint Katharine Drexel in the Light of the New Evangelization." *Josephinum Journal of Theology* 10 (Winter/Spring 2003): 122–31.

Garraghan, Gilbert J. "Holiness on the Frontier." *Thought* 15 (June 1940): 203–5.

Gibbons, James. Introduction to *Life and Life-Work of Mother Theodore Guérin: Foundress of the Sisters of Providence at St.-Mary-of-the-Woods, Vigo County, Indiana*, by a Member of the Congregation [Mary Theodosia Mug], xiii–xx. New York: Benziger Brothers, 1904.

———. "Pastoral Letter to the Archdiocese of Baltimore." In *The Memorial Volume:*

A History of the Third Plenary Council of Baltimore, November 9–December 7, 1884, 111–14. Baltimore: Baltimore Publishing Company, 1885.

Glennon, John J. Introduction to *Mother Philippine Duchesne*, by Marjory Erskine, v–x. New York: Longmans, Green, 1926.

Greer, Allan. "Colonial Saints: Gender, Race, and Hagiography in New France." *William and Mary Quarterly* 57 (April 2000): 323–48.

———. "Natives and Nationalism: The Americanization of Kateri Tekakwitha." *Catholic Historical Review* 90 (April 2004): 260–72.

H. A. F. "The Cause of the Ven. Bishop Neumann." *Fortnightly Review* 38, no. 1 (1931): 11.

Halley, Thomas. "How Saints Are Canonized." *American Ecclesiastical Review* 115 (July 1946): 337–50.

Hayes, Patrick. "'Bless Me Father, for I Have Rynned': The Vatican II Journalism of Francis X. Murphy, CSsR." *U.S. Catholic Historian* 30 (Spring 2012): 55–75.

Heiermann, Francis. "Sainthood: A Reply to Professor John M. Mecklin's 'The Passing of the Saint,' January, 1919." *American Journal of Sociology* 25 (July 1919): 24–40.

Holmes, Paula. "The Narrative Repatriation of Blessed Kateri Tekakwitha." *Anthropologica* 43 (January 2001): 87–103.

Holweck, F. G. "An American Martyrology." *Catholic Historical Review* 6 (January 1921): 495–516.

Hughes, James Ryan. "The Saints of To-morrow." *Homiletic and Pastoral Review* 35 (June 1935): 941–44.

Hutton, Leon. "The Future Pope Comes to America: Cardinal Eugenio Pacelli's Visit to the United States." *U.S. Catholic Historian* 24 (April 2006): 109–30.

Ireland, John. Introduction to *Memoirs Historical and Edifying of a Missionary Apostolic of the Order of Saint Dominic among Various Indian Tribes and among the Catholics and Protestants in the United States of America*, by Samuel Charles Mazzuchelli, iii–xviii. Chicago: W. F. Hall, 1915.

———. "Jeanne d'Arc: The Patron Saint of Patriotism." In *The Church and Modern Society: Lectures and Addresses by John Ireland*, 29–66. Chicago: D. H. McBride, 1897.

"Is the Church of Rome Idolatrous?" *Princeton Review* 26 (April 1854): 247–76.

Jameson, J. Franklin. "The American *Acta Sanctorum*." *American Historical Review* 13 (January 1908): 286–302.

Logan, John. "Recollection." In *Cycle for Mother Cabrini*, 6–9. New York: Grove Press, 1955.

McCormick, Patrick J. "Current Events." *Catholic Educational Review* 15 (1918): 357–67.

McGuinness, Margaret. "Let Us Go to the Altar: American Catholics and the Eucharist, 1926–1976." In *Habits of Devotion: Catholic Religious Practice in Twentieth-Century America*, edited by James M. O'Toole, 187–236. Ithaca: Cornell University Press, 2004.

McNeil, Betty Ann. "Sulpicians and Sisters of Charity: Concentric Circles of Mission." *Vincentian Heritage Journal* 20, no. 1 (1999): 13–38.

Mecklin, John M. "The Passing of the Saint." *American Journal of Sociology* 24 (January 1919): 353–72.

Melville, Annabelle. "Writing a Saint's Biography." *U.S. Catholic Historian* 10 (January 1991): 71–77.

Metz, Judith. "By What Authority? The Founding of the Sisters of Charity of Cincinnati." *Vincentian Heritage Journal* 20 (Spring 1999): 81–104.

———. "The Sisters of Charity in Cincinnati: 1829–1852." *Vincentian Heritage Journal* 17 (Fall 1996): 201–44.

Mize, Sandra Yocum. "'A Catholic Way of Doing Every Important Thing': U.S. Catholic Women and Theological Study in the Mid-Twentieth Century." *U.S. Catholic Historian* 13 (Spring 1995): 49–69.

Molinari, Paul. *Saints: Their Place in the Church,* New York: Sheed and Ward, 1965.

Moreau, Joseph. "Rise of the (Catholic) American Nation: United States History and Parochial Schools, 1878–1925." *American Studies* 38, no. 3 (Fall 1997): 67–90.

Novak, Michael. "The New Nuns." In *The New Nuns,* edited by M[ary] Charles Borromeo Muckenhirn, 13–30. New York: New American Library, 1967.

O'Gallagher, Marianna. "The Sisters of Charity of Halifax—The Early and Middle Years." *CCHA Study Sessions* 47 (1980): 57–68.

O'Sullivan, Donal. "St. Frances Xavier Cabrini: Canonised July 7, 1946." *Studies: An Irish Quarterly Review* 35 (September 1946): 351–56.

"Our American Beatified Martyr Priests." *American Ecclesiastical Review* 74 (1926): 72–78.

"Present Stage of the Inquiry Regarding the Beatification of the Ven. John Nepom. Neumann, C.SS.R., Bishop of Philadelphia." *American Ecclesiastical Review* 16 (1897): 393–403.

"Present Status of the Canonization Process of the Ven. John Nep. Neumann, Bishop of Philadelphia." *American Ecclesiastical Review* 23 (1900): 315–17.

Review of *The Life and Times of Kateri Tekakwitha,* by Ellen Walworth. *American Ecclesiastical Review* 5 (July 1891): 318–19.

Review of *Mother Philippine Duchesne,* by Marjory Erskine. *Ecclesiastical Review* 6 (March 1927): 332–34.

Rush, Alfred. "The Second Vatican Council, 1962–1965, and Bishop Neumann." In *He Spared Himself Nothing: Essays on the Life and Thought of St. John Nepomucene Neumann, C.Ss.R.,* edited by Joseph F. Chorpenning, 183–89. Philadelphia: Saint Joseph's University Press, 2003.

Sacra Congregatio Rituum. *Instructio: De calendariis particularibus et Officiorum ac Missarum propriis ad normam et mentem rubricarum revisendis,* 8 February 1961. In *Acta Apostolicae Sedis,* 33. Vatican City: Libreria Editrice Vaticana, 1961.

Salotti, Monsignor Carlo. Prefazione to *La Madre Francesca Saverio Cabrini,* by Mother Saverio de Maria, xi–xv. Turin: Società Editrice Internazionale, 1928.

Sandos, James A. "Junípero Serra, Canonization, and the California Indian Controversy." *Journal of Religious History* 15 (June 1989): 311–29.

Sarbanes, Paul. "Mother Seton School." In *Congressional Record* 131, 20 February 1985, 2761–62. Washington, D.C.: United States Government Printing Office, 1985.

Sarno, Robert. "Theological Reflection on Canonization." In *Canonization: Theology, History, Process*, edited by William H. Woestman. Ottawa: Saint Paul University, 2002.

Severance, Allen Dudley. "Beatification and Canonization with Special Reference to Historic Proof and the Proof of Miracles." *Papers of the American Society of Church History* 3 (March 1912): 41–62.

Shaw, Francis. "Some Heroines: Fact and Fiction." *Studies: An Irish Quarterly Review* 27 (December 1938): 623–36.

Shea, John Gilmary. "Catholic Church in American History." *American Catholic Quarterly Review* 1 (January 1876): 148–73.

Short, Edward. "Rose Hawthorne and the Communion of Saints." *Human Life Review* 36 (Winter 2010): 18–28.

Simoni, Aristeo V. Introduction to *Too Small a World: The Life of Francesca Cabrini*, by Theodore Maynard, ix–xii. Milwaukee: Bruce, 1945.

Souvay, Charles L. "Questions anent Mother Seton's Conversion." *Catholic Historical Review* 5 (July–October 1919): 223–38.

Spellman, Francis Cardinal. Foreword to *Mrs. Seton: Foundress of the American Sisters of Charity*, by Joseph I. Dirvin, ix–xi. New York: Farrar, Straus and Cudahy, 1962.

Stadick, Anna. "Saint Patrons: The Role of Archives in the Roman Catholic Process of Canonization." *Archival Issues* 24, no. 2 (1999): 123–43.

Suenens, Léon-Joseph Cardinal. "The Charismatic Dimension of the Church." In *Council Speeches of Vatican II*, edited by Hans Küng, Yves Congar, and Daniel O'Hanlon, 29–34. Glen Rock, N.J.: Paulist Press, 1964.

Thomas, Samuel J. "The American Press and the Church-State Pronouncements of Pope Leo XIII." *U.S. Catholic Historian* 1 (Fall 1980): 17–36.

Tweed, Thomas A. "After the Quotidian Turn: Interpretive Categories and Scholarly Trajectories in the Study of Religion since the 1960s." *Journal of Religion* 95, no. 3 (2015): 361–85.

———. "Catholic Studies after the Quotidian Turn: A Response." *American Catholic Studies* 122, no. 4 (2011): 82–87.

Vico, Cardinal Antonio. "Beatificationis et Canonizationis Ven. Servi Dei Ioannis Nepomuceni Neumann, Episcopi Philadelphiensis, e Congregatione Sanctiissimi Redemptoris." *Acta Apostlicae Sedis* 14 (1922): 23–26.

Waible, A. [Albert]. "Venerable John Neumann." *Records of the American Catholic Historical Society of Philadelphia* 52 (March 1941): 25–33.

Walsh, James Joseph. "Mother Cabrini: An Apostle of the Italians." In *These Splendid Sisters*, edited by James Joseph Walsh, 224–33. New York: Sears, 1927.

White, Joseph M. "Path to Sainthood and Episcopal Leadership: Mother Theodore

Guérin and Bishop Célestin de la Hailandière in History and Memory." *U.S. Catholic Historian* 29 (Winter 2011): 73–94.

Williams, Maria. "Mobilising Mother Cabrini's Educational Practice: The Transnational Context of the London School of the Missionary Sisters of the Sacred Heart of Jesus, 1898–1911." *Journal of the History of Education Society* 44 (September 2015): 631–50.

Williams, Shannen Dee. "Desegregating the Habit: Black Nuns and the Long Struggle to Integrate Female Religious Life in the U.S. Catholic Church." Under review.

MAGAZINES AND OTHER PERIODICALS (NONACADEMIC)

"American Indian Woman May Be Named a Saint." *New York Herald Tribune*, 9 August 1932, 5.

"An American Saint." *Commonweal*, 4 August 1931, 333–34.

"American Saints." *Ave Maria*, November 1873, 716–17.

Apple, Sam. "At the Vatican, Search for Cancer's Miracle Cure." *New Yorker*, 20 May 2015, http://www.newyorker.com/tech/elements/at-the-vatican-a-search-for-cancers-miracle-cure. 19 August 2017.

Barrett, Ellen. "A Word about the Old Saints." *Catholic World*, May 1894, 263–71.

Behrman, Arthur G. "A Valiant Woman: The Story of Blessed Philippine Duchesne." *Columbia*, 19 August 1940, 6, 20.

"The Billboard Music Popularity Charts: Record Reviews." *Billboard*, 16 December 1950, 35.

"Blessed Are Those Who Die in the Lord." *Mother Seton Guild Bulletin*, special ed., September 1959, 1, 4.

"Blessed Mother Seton's Remains Enshrined." *Mother Seton Guild Bulletin*, June 1963, 1, 4.

Burgio, Salvator. "A Case of Acute Leukemia." *Mother Seton Guild Bulletin*, May 1957, 1–2, 4.

Burton, Katherine. "Mother Katharine Drexel." *Sponsa Regis*, 30 June 1959, 254–60.

Cantwell, Daniel M. "The World Has Its Saints, Too." *Work*, November 1961, 1–2.

"Catherine Tegakwitha [*sic*]." *Catholic World*, April 1886, 78–87.

Chaput, Charles. "Homily at Mass of Thanksgiving for Sts. Kateri Tekakwitha and Marianne Cope." *Origins*, 7 February 2013, 565–66.

Clarke, R. H. "Beatification Asked for American Servants of God." *Catholic World*, March 1885, 808–20.

Clemens, M. E. "On the Hill of the Martyrs." *America*, 17 October 1925, 13–14.

Code, Joseph B. "Eulogy Preached at the Memorial Mass for Father Salvator Burgio, CM." Reprinted in *Mother Seton Guild Bulletin*, September 1959, 2–4.

"Communications: Solemnizing the Canonization of the American Martyrs," *Commonweal*, 8 January 1931, 354.

Congdon, Thomas. "The Making of a Saint." *Saturday Evening Post*, 23 March 1963, 74–78.

"Contributions Received for the Shrine of Our Lady of Martyrs, Auriesville, New York." *Pilgrim of Our Lady of Martyrs*, no. 4, 1888, 41.

Cummings, Kathleen Sprows. "The Doorway to Sainthood." *Notre Dame Magazine*, Winter 2010–11, https://magazine.nd.edu/news/the-doorway-to-sainthood/. 21 September 2017.

"Current Religious Comment—Items of Interest to Catholic Readers in the Magazines." *Sacred Heart Review*, 3 April 1897, 267.

Dirvin, Joseph. "Three Saints." *Seton Causeway* May 1977.

"Domestic Religious Intelligence." *Methodist Review*, May 1885, 449–50.

Donoghue, Thomas A. "How the Pope Makes Saints." *America*, 18 July 1925, 319–20.

Dorn, Rupert. "New Missioner Saint." *Catholic Mission Digest* 4, no. 8 (1946): 14–16.

Eckert, Robert P. "A Missionary in the Wilderness." *Catholic World*, February 1937, 590–95.

"An Editorial." *Mother Seton Guild Bulletin*, March 1963, 2–4.

"Editorial Notes." *The Vincentian*, January 1936, 2.

Elie, Paul. "The Patron Saint of Paradox." *New York Times Magazine*, 8 November 1998, http://www.nytimes.com/1998/11/08/magazine/the-patron-saint-of-paradox .html?mcubz=3. 25 September 2017.

Elliott, Walter. "Bishop Baraga, the Apostle of the Chippewas." *Catholic World*, April 1901, 78–87.

———. "St. Vincent de Paul and the Sisters of Charity." *Catholic World*, October 1899, 13–28.

Ellsberg, Robert. "Treating Saints Like Superheroes Is a Dangerous Game." *America*, 21 February 2017, https://www.americamagazine.org/faith/2017/02/21/treating -saints-superheroes-dangerous-game. 30 October 2017.

Emery, S. L. "Mother Duchesne, R.S.H., an Uncanonized American Saint." *Catholic World*, August 1897, 687–94.

"Father Burgio's Address." *Mother Seton Guild Bulletin*, November 1966, 1–4.

"Feeney Forgiven." *Time*, 14 October 1974, 107.

Ferrante, Nicola. "The Cause of the Beatification and Canonization of St. John Nepomucene Neumann, C.SS.R." *The Province Story: A Redemptorist Historical Review*, 4 October 1977, 39–66.

"First American Saint." *America*, 29 June 1946, 264.

Fremantle, Anne. "Sacred and Profane Success." *Commonweal*, 27 July 1945, 360–62.

Gerard, Lillian. "Mother Cabrini." *Catholic Mind*, October 1946, 587–92. Reprinted from *New York Times Magazine*, 7 July 1946, 12, 31–33.

Gilbert, Morris, and Russell Maloney. "A Reporter at Large: Blessed Mother Cabrini." *New Yorker*, November 1938, 34–43.

Gilmore, Florence. "Mother Duchesne's Progress to Sanctity." *Ave Maria*, 14 February 1942, 208–11.

Graham, Robert. "Are Canonizations an Unnecessary Expense?" *Columbia*, September 1975, 23.

Hanley, Boniface. "The Rose Hawthorne Story." *Catholic Digest*, July 1980, 73–79.

"In Memoriam: Mother Antonietta Della Casa." *Mother Cabrini Messenger*, no. 17, February 1955, 1–2.

"Interview with Benedict XVI." *Origins* 36, no. 14 (2006): 219–20.

Ireland, John. "Rt. Rev. Mathias Loras, First Bishop of Dubuque." *Catholic World*, September 1898, 721–31.

"Kateri Tekakwitha." *Catholic World*, August 1891, 776–77.

Kurth, Paula. "Holiness Chez Nous." *Ave Maria*, 18 January 1941, 83–85.

Labella, Vincent R. "A Day . . . in the Citadel of God." *Extension*, September 1946, 18–19, 54.

LaFarge, John. "Blessed Frances Cabrini, Citizen of the United States." *America*, 12 November 1938, 124–25.

———. "Blessed Martin: Patron of Social and Interracial Justice." *Catholic Mind*, December 1937, 481–88.

———. "Mother Cabrini's Requiem." *America*, 6 July 1946, 304.

LaRosa, Nicole. "Saint Kateri." *Fordham Magazine*, Spring 2012, 17–21.

Lind, Louise J. "Wanted: The Saint in a Business Suit." *Sign*, May 1956, 55.

"The Little Flower and the Nation." *America*, 4 July 1925, 281–82.

Lux, J. B. "Chicago's First Saint." *Extension Magazine* 33, no. 6 (1938): 4.

Lyons, Michael. "Saints of the United States." *St. Anthony Messenger*, September 1927, 188–89, 201.

MacKinnon, Donald. "Voices for Philadelphia." *The Lamp*, November 1956, 18–20.

Marie, Sister. "Three Nun Converts of the Last Century." *Ave Maria*, 9 October 1946, 451–60.

McGinley, Phyllis. "The Easiest to Love." *Time*, 19 July 1954, 52.

McSweeny, Edward. "Hidden Saints." *Catholic World*, July 1890, 533–39.

Meagher, Charlotte M. "A Sheaf of Letters (1901–1909): Rose Hawthorne Lathrop." *Magnificat*, April 1952, 306–12; May 1952, 8–14.

Meehan, Thomas. "Repaying Our Debt to Italy." *Columbia*, 9 August 1922, 4, 25.

Miccinelli, Charles, as told to John Killeen. "Postulators Are Offering More Candidates for Beatification Than Ever Before." *Queen's Work*, November 1937, 5, 11.

Miller, R. J. "A Miracle for the Bishop." *The Liguorian*, October 1960, 42–45.

Molloy, J. I. "Canonization of Mother Cabrini." *Catholic World*, August 1946, 466–67.

"Mother Seton Beatified." *Mother Seton Guild Bulletin*, March 1963, 1–2.

Nelson, Jack. "Apostle of the Midwest." *Visitor*, 20 November 1977, 23.

O'Connor, Cardinal John. "Dorothy Day's Sainthood Cause Begins." *Catholic New York*, 16 March 2000, reprinted by the Catholic Worker, http://www.catholic worker.org/pages/o'connor-cause-begins.html. 18 September 2017.

O'Reilly, Bryan M. "Saint over the Hudson." *Commonweal*, 12 May 1939, 66–67.

"Origin and Design of the Pilgrimage." *Pilgrim of Our Lady of Martyrs* no. 1, 1885, 5–6.

"Our Lady of Martyrs: Father Walworth's Poems." *Pilgrim of Our Lady of Martyrs* no. 4, 1888, 60–64.

Parton, James. "Our Roman Catholic Brethren." *Atlantic Monthly*, April 1868, 432–52.

Peters, Doris Revere. "What Does Seton Say to Modern Women?" *Columbia* 55, March 1975, 29–30.

"The Pope Urges Prayers for Miracles." *Mother Seton Guild Bulletin*, October 1947, 1–2.

"Religion: St. Knute, St. Joyce?" *Time*, 4 January 1937, 22.

"Reverend Mother M. Anselm's Invitation." *The Peacemaker*, April–June 1964, 1.

Ricci, Marina. "Discussioni: Troppi Santi? Davvero nella Chiesa cattolica si registra un'inflazione di aureole?" *30 Giorni*, May 1989, 16–20.

Rynne, Xavier. "Saint." *New Yorker*, 27 June 1977, 24–26.

"A Saint for America." *Time*, 22 September 1975, 59.

"Saint Frances Xavier Cabrini." *Commonweal*, 19 July 1946, 325.

Shea, John Gilmary. "Holy Personages of Canada and the United States Whose Canonization Is Begun." *Ave Maria* 30 (1890): 100–123, 129–32, 145–48, 179–83.

"The Shrine on the Mohawk." *New York Freeman's Journal*, 22 August 1885, 1.

Simoni, A. V. "Mother Cabrini's Secret." *Mother Cabrini Messenger*, February 1942, 2.

Slominski, George. "Mother Cabrini, Directress of the Spiritual Life." *Mother Cabrini Messenger*, June 1949, 1.

"Statue of St. Frances Cabrini to Stay on Public Ground Despite Protestant Suit." *Mother Cabrini Messenger*, June 1952, 4.

Stritch, Samuel A. "Christian Perfection." *Mother Cabrini Messenger*, February 1943, 1–2.

Taylor, Miss T. "Sisters of Charity." *Ladies Repository*, January 1869, 50–56.

"TJC." Review of *Memoirs of Father Mazzuchelli, OP. America*, July 1915, 378–79.

Tobin, Mary Luke. "Women and the Church since Vatican II." *America*, 1 November 1986, https://www.americamagazine.org/issue/100/women-church-vatican-ii. 8 September 2017.

Traxler, Mary Peter. "After Selma, Sister, You Can't Stay Home Again!" *Extension*, June 1965, 16–18.

Turner, Frederick Jackson. "The Problem of the West." *Atlantic*, September 1896, http://www.theatlantic.com/past/docs/issues/95sep/ets/turn.htm. 8 September 2017.

Vaccariello, Linda. "The Sister Who Leaned In." *Cincinnati Magazine*, April 2016, 70–72, 130–33.

"The Vatican's No. 2." *Time*, 25 August 1961, 52.

"The Venerable Mother Mary of the Incarnation," *Catholic World*, August 1878, 608.

Walworth, Clarence A. "René Goupil." *Pilgrim of Our Lady of Martyrs* 4, 1888, 63–64.

Wedge, F. "Saint from the Sidewalks of New York." *Crosier Missionary*, March 1960, 9–15.

Weigel, E. M. "The New Glory of the American Hierarchy." *America*, 25 February 1922, 439–41.

Weigel, George. "Why Hasn't Francis Ford Been Beatified?" *First Things*, 27 July 2011, https://www.firstthings.com/web-exclusives/2011/07/why-hasnt-francis-ford-been-beatified. 22 September 2017.

Wielanga, David. "Serra One Step from Drinking Holiday." *OC Weekly*, 30 March 2000, http://www.ocweekly.com/news/serra-one-step-from-drinking-holiday-6392880. 21 September 2017.

Wilbur, H. Clifford. "An American Lourdes." *Rosary Magazine*, January–June 1905, 278–83.

Windeatt, Mary Fabryan. "Gemma and Euphrasia, Rose Philippine and Joaquina: Four More Ladies Are to Be Called Saints and Blessed." *America*, 4 May 1940, 92–94.

Wüst [Wuest], Jos. "John N. Neumann, a Saintly Bishop." *Catholic World*, December 1892, 322–38.

INDEX